British Social Attitudes
the
8th report

Social and Community Planning Research (SCPR) is an independent, non-profit institute specialising in social surveys with its own research, interviewing, coding and computing resources. Some of SCPR's work - such as the survey reported in this book - is initiated by the institute itself and grant-funded by research councils or foundations. Other work is initiated by government departments, local authorities or quasi-government organisations to provide information on aspects of social or economic policy. SCPR also works frequently with other institutes and academics. Founded in 1969 and now one of the largest social research institutes in Britain, SCPR has a high reputation for the standard of its work in both qualitative and quantitative research. SCPR also houses the Joint Centre for Survey Methods and, with Nuffield College Oxford, the Joint Unit for the Study of Social Trends (JUSST), which is an ESRC Research Centre.

The contributors

Yoav Ben-Shlomo
Wellcome Research Fellow in Clinical Epidemiology at University College and Middlesex School of Medicine, London

Lindsay Brook
Research Director at SCPR and Co-director of the *British Social Attitudes* survey series

Ed Cape
Senior Lecturer in Department of Law, Bristol Polytechnic

John Curtice
Senior Lecturer in Politics, and Director of the Social Statistics Laboratory, at University of Strathclyde

Tony Gallagher
Research Officer in Centre for the Study of Conflict at University of Ulster

A.H. Halsey
Professor Emeritus at Nuffield College, Oxford

Anthony Heath
Official Fellow at Nuffield College, Oxford

Roger Jowell
Director of SCPR and Co-director of the *British Social Attitudes* survey series; Visiting Professor at the London School of Economics and Political Science

Dorren McMahon
Research Officer at Nuffield College, Oxford

Michael Marmot
Professor of Epidemiology and Public Health at University College and Middlesex School of Medicine, London, and Professor of Epidemiology at London School of Hygiene and Tropical Medicine

Gillian Prior
Researcher at SCPR and Co-director of the *British Social Attitudes* survey series

Aubrey Sheiham
Professor of Dental Public Health at University College and Middlesex School of Medicine, London

Bridget Taylor
Researcher at SCPR and Co-director of the *British Social Attitudes* survey series

Peter Taylor-Gooby
Professor of Social Policy at University of Kent

Sharon Witherspoon
Formerly Research Director at SCPR and Co-director of the *British Social Attitudes* survey series; now a graduate student at State University of New York at Stony Brook

Ken Young
Professor of Politics at Queen Mary and Westfield College, University of London

British Social Attitudes

the
8th report

Edited by
Roger Jowell
Lindsay Brook
& Bridget Taylor
with Gillian Prior

Dartmouth

SOCIAL & COMMUNITY
SCPR
PLANNING RESEARCH

Published by
Dartmouth Publishing Company Limited
Gower House
Croft Road
Aldershot
Hants GU11 3HR
England

Dartmouth Publishing Company Limited
Distributed in the United States by
Ashgate Publishing Company
Old Post Road
Brookfield
Vermont 05036
USA

A CIP catalogue record for this book is available from the British Library and the US Library of Congress

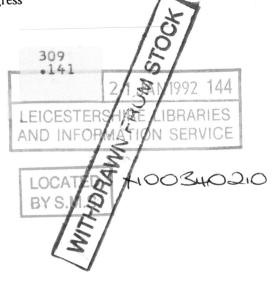

ISSN 0267 6869
ISBN 185521 258 7

Printed in Great Britain at the University Press, Cambridge

Contents

CHAPTER 3. FAILING EDUCATION?
by A. H. Halsey 43

CHAPTER 4. JUSTICE AND THE LAW IN NORTHERN IRELAND
by Tony Gallagher 59

Introduction

SCPR's first *British Social Attitudes* survey took place in 1983 with seed-funding from the Nuffield Foundation and from the Economic and Social Research Council (ESRC). Both of these organisations have continued to support aspects of the series over the years, and we are grateful indeed to them. But the sustenance of the series owes most to the steadfast support it has received from the Sainsbury Family Charitable Trusts. They became core-funders in 1984 and still provide about 40 per cent of the funds we need each year to carry out the survey and related activities.

Further funding from the Trusts until 1996 has been secured, enabling us to plan ahead productively. Their support not only ensures the continuation of the series but is also a critical factor in maintaining its independence: core-funding from a disinterested source enables the investigators, not the funders, to determine the coverage and content of the survey questionnaires and the interpretation of the results. So we reiterate our gratitude to the trustees and the directorate for their continuing confidence.

The aim of this volume, like its seven predecessors, is to take a first look at the findings from the latest survey on selected topics and, where we have trend data, to report on changes over time; as in *The 7th Report*, we also have a chapter on selected findings from the latest *Northern Ireland Social Attitudes* survey. We do not attempt here to undertake comprehensive analyses or arrive at definitive interpretations. Each year we deposit a fully-documented dataset - for both the British and Northern Ireland surveys - at the ESRC Data Archive at the University of Essex for others in the wider social science community to quarry at leisure.

The majority of questions on each year's questionnaires are replications from earlier years - some inserted annually, others less frequently - but there are new questions too, and new modules, which attempt to cover fresh concerns and to fill gaps.

This book reflects the blend of continuity and change which is the hallmark of any time-series. We report for the first time on assessments of different types of childcare arrangements for working mothers (Chapter 7), on attitudes to smoking and health (Chapter 8), and on libertarian values (Chapter 9). We also include an analysis of consensus and dissensus in British society (Chapter 1) which searches for clusters of issues or values that make up Britain's attitudinal culture. Chapter 6 brings us up to date on environmental issues and also reports on new questions about 'green' consumerism and environmental activism. Three other chapters review recent trends in public attitudes: to the welfare state (Chapter 2), education (Chapter 3) and housing (Chapter 5). We bring together in Chapter 10 trends on expectations about and attitudes towards the economy. And, finally, we include once again a chapter based on the *Northern Ireland Social Attitudes* survey (Chapter 4) about attitudes to law and order, comparing public opinion in the Province with that on the mainland.[*]

We are indebted as editors to all the authors for their contributions, and also for their tolerance and co-operation both in meeting our demanding deadlines and in submitting their drafts to such fierce editing. As always, final responsibility for the findings reported in this book and their interpretation is that of SCPR and the authors, just as final responsibility for the questionnaire content and question wording rests with SCPR.

Published (by Gower) at the same time as this *Report* is the first *British Social Attitudes Cumulative Sourcebook*. The *Sourcebook* brings together all the questions asked in the series from 1983 to 1989 (with all variations noted), together with year-by-year distributions of answers (numbers and percentages), and each variable's SPSS label. Fully cross-referenced with three indexes for ease of reference, the *Sourcebook* is intended both as a complement to the commentaries contained in these annual volumes and as a comprehensive codebook for users of the datasets.

Our source material will be supplemented further in early 1992 by the publication of a combined dataset, providing in one computer file the data (organised by variable) for all eight surveys carried out between 1983 and 1991. It will be complemented by a parallel dataset for Northern Ireland containing the data from the 1989, 1990 and 1991 surveys. The ESRC has generously provided funding for this project and the datasets will, like the annual datasets, be deposited at the ESRC Data Archive at the University of Essex with full documentation. These additional sources should make life much easier for those users who wish to study time-

---

[*] A fuller treatment of the 1990 survey data will appear in Stringer, P. and Robinson, G., (eds), *Social Attitudes in Northern Ireland: the 2nd report,* Blackstaff Press, Belfast (1992).

trends or to combine data from more than one year, for example to study small subgroups of the population. In addition, the Archive has recently brought out its first CD-Rom disk - containing the *British Social Attitudes* datasets (organised by year) from 1983 to 1990.

In 1990 the Department of Employment, the Department of the Environment, the Health Education Authority, the Countryside Commission and the Central Community Relations Unit in Belfast were joined as public sector co-funders of the series by the Home Office and the Department of Health. More recently, we have secured funding - for three years in each case - from the Department of Social Security and the Department of Education and Science. We are extremely grateful for this governmental support, not only because it helps to fund and develop the series but also because it helps us to focus at least part of the questionnaire on policy concerns, and because it enables us to get valuable advice and guidance from our expert colleagues in government. In case it still needs reiterating, however, all government funding for the surveys is effectively by way of grants and *not* on a customer-contractor basis.

Thanks to two recent foundation grants, we have been able to introduce a new module in each of the last two rounds. A new grant from The Nuffield Foundation supports the module on civil liberties reported in Chapter 9 and to be repeated in 1993. And a grant from the Charities Aid Foundation supports a module on attitudes to charitable giving, the findings of which will be in next year's book.

The next book in the series - based on the 1991 survey already completed - will come out in the autumn of 1992. But the next fieldwork round will not now be carried out until 1993. Instead, our core-funds next year will, as in 1987, be devoted to the latest in the series of *British General Election* studies, supplemented by a grant from the ESRC. To fill the gap in this series of reports we may produce a second *special* report in 1993 on the accumulating data from the *International Social Survey Programme.*

The ISSP continues to grow and to flourish. The initial membership of four countries has now expanded to eighteen (Australia, Austria, Bulgaria, Canada, Czechoslovakia, Germany, Great Britain, Hungary, Israel, Italy, Japan, the Netherlands, New Zealand, Norway, the Philippines, the Republic of Ireland, Russia, and the USA). Research teams in each of these nations undertake an annual, jointly-designed self-completion survey on a rotating set of topics. The participation of Britain in the ISSP is made possible through the support of the ESRC.

Closer to home, the Joint Unit for the Study of Social Trends (JUSST), an ESRC *Research Centre* linking SCPR and Nuffield College Oxford, continues to undertake methodological research *via* the *British Social Attitudes* and the *British General Election* series. It is now producing results which promise to contribute to the improvement of attitude measurement not only in these two series but also, we hope, in others.

As always we owe a debt to our colleagues at SCPR who each year have to absorb the pressure placed on them by this survey and the production of the annual book. We are particularly grateful to the field controllers, interviewers, coding supervisors, coders and programmers who have once again worked so skilfully in bringing the survey to fruition. And as we send the final copy to the publishers we have reason to be especially appreciative of SCPR's excellent secretarial team for their skill and patience in converting successive messy drafts into final text and - for the first time this year - camera-ready copy.

A special tribute also goes from all of us to our former colleague, Sharon Witherspoon, who has contributed a chapter this year but who now lives in the USA. As a Co-director of the series from 1984-1990 and as co-editor of each of the last six books, her contribution to the series has been incalculable, and we are still benefiting from it.

Our heartfelt thanks are due to the thousands of anonymous respondents in Britain and Northern Ireland who agreed to provide the raw material for this volume.

RMJ
LLB
BJT
GMP

1 Consensus and dissensus

Anthony Heath and Dorren McMahon [*]

Our central aim in this chapter is to explore the extent of agreement and disagreement in Britain on various core elements of our beliefs and values. What are the beliefs and values on which British people are united, and what are the ones that divide them? There is a long tradition of sociological theory which holds that value consensus is an important ingredient for a stable society, and it is a plausible hypothesis that disagreement over basic values will have the potential to become the focus of social and political conflict. (Two of the classic texts on this theme are Durkheim, 1893, and Parsons, 1935.)

Britain has often been held to be an example of a society divided by class rather than by, for instance, religion, language or ethnicity which polarises other societies (Marshall *et al*, 1988). So we might expect to find greatest disagreement on values likely to be associated with class - those concerned with equality for example. We can compare these with other divisions, such as on 'traditional' moral issues relating to gender roles and sexual morality. While these sorts of issues do not figure as prominently as, say, economic ones in current political debates, we shall see later that they rival (and in certain respects vanquish) class issues in their potential for dividing British society.

Alongside these divisions, and perhaps mitigating them, there are also traditions of political and civil tolerance in Britain. We would expect to find a high level of agreement in the society at large, and broad

---

[*] Anthony Heath is Official Fellow at Nuffield College, Oxford; Dorren McMahon is a Research Officer at Nuffield College.

agreement between different social groups, on such things as freedom of speech, freedom to protest against the government, and so on. Our initial hypothesis, then, is that while the British may disagree on many *substantive* questions, they would tend to agree on *procedural* matters. For example, they may differ in their attitudes towards equality or sexual morality but would unite in the view that their opponents should be allowed to state their case freely. Agreement on how to resolve disputes may matter more for the health of a society than agreement on the substantive matters themselves.

This chapter takes an exploratory look at some focal points of consensus and dissensus, using responses to questions asked in the 1990 *British Social Attitudes* survey.   Our conclusions will necessarily be provisional, but we hope to expand our focus in future to include a wider range of questions on both substantive and procedural matters.

The approach

We will start by looking at the extent of consensus in Britain as a whole on a range of economic, moral and procedural matters. Our concern is with the *spread* of answers to the survey questions. So we are not primarily interested in whether people in Britain are 'traditional' or 'progressive' on, say, sexual morality, but in whether they are united in their views, whatever those views happen to be. Do the British tend to share values on sexual morality and other subjects, or are they at odds with one another?

We will then consider whether the issues on which people *do* disagree are isolated or form a cluster. A single issue on which people disagree may not have the same implications for potential social conflict as disagreement on a cluster of issues which may serve to reinforce each other. This may be the reason that economic issues are considered to be the main basis for social and political conflict in Britain: attitudes towards a cluster of economic issues - equality of income, public ownership of industry, full employment and the free market - tend to cohere within a single general system of values (see Heath *et al*, 1991).

Where we find dissensus on an issue, or cluster of issues, we will try to find its roots. Some differences of opinion may have clear social roots, such as in class or religious affiliation. These may have rather more significant social and political implications than those where the disagreement is of a more amorphous character, with no distinctive social roots. In fact some differences of opinion may appear to have no clear structure or pattern at all, and then we may suspect the existence of a 'non-attitude' - that is, an issue on which people have no clear or coherent views, and hence answer at random (see Converse, 1964, and the subsequent debate).

We distinguish, then, between issues on which there is (relatively speaking) agreement, those on which there is structured disagreement, and those on which there appears to be only amorphous disagreement.

Before beginning the analysis we must mention one methodological caveat. The spread of answers to a particular question will, of course, depend on the number and nature of the response categories offered to respondents, as well as on the issue that the question addresses. If we offer people five possible answer categories (for example, 'strongly agree', 'agree', 'neither agree nor disagree' 'disagree' and 'strongly disagree') we should expect a greater spread of answers than if they are offered only three or four options. We have to take this into account in our analyses.[1]

Issues which unite and issues which divide

Economic issues and the welfare state

The series includes a number of questions on key economic issues, in particular on income redistribution and unemployment. We have chosen to look at a group of questions about the responsibility of government in various fields, which enables us to compare attitudes towards distributive policies in general with those towards aspects of the welfare state in particular. Respondents were asked:

> *On the whole, do you think it should or should not be the government's responsibility to:*
>
> *... provide a job for everyone who wants one?*
> *... reduce income differences between the rich and poor?*
> *... provide health care for the sick?*
> *... provide a decent standard of living for the old?*
> *... provide a decent standard of living for the unemployed?*

These items have four answer categories - 'definitely should be', 'probably should be', 'probably should not be', and 'definitely should not be' the government's responsibility. By our definition, then, there would be maximum *consensus* if 100 per cent of the sample fall into a single response category, for example that providing health care should definitely be the government's responsibility, while there would be maximum *dissensus* if people divide evenly, with 25 per cent endorsing each of the four response categories. At this point, it is important to distinguish between dissensus and polarisation. Perfect polarisation would occur if 50 per cent of respondents were at each of the two extreme points of the range of categories, one half saying that something should definitely be the government's responsibility and the other half saying it definitely should not. As we shall see, polarisation is much rarer than dissensus.

It is apparent from the table below, that there is almost complete consensus over state responsibility for health care for the sick: 85 per cent agree that health care definitely should be the government's responsibility, while the remaining 15 per cent feel that it probably should be. Not one respondent takes the opposite view. A very similar level of consensus exists over state responsibility to provide a decent standard of living for the elderly. These are among the highest levels of consensus that we shall find.

The economy, redistribution and the welfare state

Should it be the government's responsibility to:		Definitely should be	Probably should be	Probably should not be	Definitely should not be
Provide a job for everyone who wants one	%	24	40	22	15
Provide health care	%	85	15	-	-
Provide a decent standard of living for the old	%	79	20	1	-
Provide a decent standard of living for the unemployed	%	32	48	15	5
Reduce income differences	%	42	32	16	10

The very small number of respondents who said 'don't know' or failed to answer the questions have been omitted from the percentage base on this table and on all others in this chapter.

In contrast, there is substantial dissensus over whether or not it is the government's responsibility to provide a job for everyone who wants one, with the spread of answers almost as close to perfect dissensus as the answers on health care are to perfect consensus; in any event, the answers are fairly equally spread across the four answer categories on this issue. On the other two issues - government's responsibility to reduce income differences and to provide a decent standard of living for the unemployed - the answers are not quite so spread out as over the issue of full employment but are closer to dissensus than to consensus on our definition, even though three-quarters or more of the sample in each case endorse the general view that these responsibilities ought (probably or definitely) to be taken by government.

As we had anticipated then, these economic issues of full employment and redistribution are not ones on which there is any great measure of agreement. In contrast, the government's responsibilities to provide health care and pensions are consensual matters; in this respect Britain is not all that different from most other European social democracies (see Haller, Hoellinger and Raubal, 1990).

However, as Taylor-Gooby (1990) has pointed out in *The 7th Report,* the public is not as equally united in its enthusiasm for other areas of welfare provision. As we have noted, providing a decent standard of living for the unemployed does not attract anything like the same measure of endorsement as health care or pensions. So support for the welfare state is of a somewhat conditional kind. We suspect that the public still distinguishes between the 'deserving' and the 'undeserving' poor (see Matza, 1966), and that people's attitudes towards different welfare state programmes are shaped by their perceptions of how 'deserving' recipients are.

We should also note that there is not quite so much consensus when the *costs* to the taxpayer of extra government spending - even on mass services - are mentioned. Another question ran:

> *Listed below are various areas of government spending. Please show whether you would like to see more or less government spending in each area. Remember that if you say 'much more', it might require a tax increase to pay for it.*

On the list were eight spending areas (shown in the table below). As can be seen, there is no longer quite the consensus on health spending as was evident in response to the previous question. Nonetheless, it is still fairly impressive: the main disagreement occurs over *how much* more to spend on health care; nine in ten people still take the view that more should be spent, even though "it might require a tax increase to pay for it".

Areas of government spending

		Spend much more	Spend more	Spend the same as as now	Spend less	Spend much less
The environment	%	15	49	33	2	1
Health	%	39	51	9	*	*
The police and law enforcement	%	13	40	44	3	1
Education	%	29	51	19	1	*
The military and defence	%	2	7	42	33	17
Old age pensions	%	30	52	17	1	*
Unemployment benefits	%	8	29	45	14	4
Culture and the arts	%	2	11	44	28	15

Once again, health care attracts the greatest level of consensus, followed by pensions and education. The environment and the law enforcement are not far behind. The spending area that provokes the greatest measure of dissensus is unemployment benefits, followed by the arts and defence. In these three cases, keeping to the *status quo* is the most popular single option (as it is on law enforcement), but there is also a fair degree of spread, in both directions, among the other answer categories.[2]

Moral traditionalism

The next set of questions we examine are those dealing with what we have called moral traditionalism (Heath and Topf, 1987). They cover sexual relations, the death penalty, censorship, and women's roles.

The three questions on sexual relations were as follows:

If a man and a woman have sexual relations before marriage, what would your general opinion be?

What about a married person having sexual relations with someone other than his or her partner?

What about sexual relations between two adults of the same sex?

Five answer categories were offered: 'always wrong', 'mostly wrong', 'sometimes wrong', 'rarely wrong', and 'not wrong at all'.

For the other questions on moral traditionalism, respondents were asked to say, for each of a series of statements, how much they agreed or disagreed with it. The statements were:

For some crimes, the death penalty is the most appropriate sentence

Censorship of films and magazines is necessary to uphold moral standards

A husband's job is to earn money; a wife's job is to look after the home and family

All in all, family life suffers when the woman has a full-time job.

Again five answer categories were offered: 'agree strongly', 'agree', 'neither agree nor disagree', 'disagree', and 'disagree strongly'.

These questions cannot be compared directly with the previous ones on government responsibility, since they are asked in a different format and with five rather than four answer categories. Here, for instance, perfect dissensus would be reached when 20 rather than 25 per cent of respondents are in each category. Fortunately, however, we are able to use as our yardstick responses to another question on redistribution which *was* asked in the same format as were the moral traditionalism questions. Respondents were asked about their extent of agreement or disagreement with the statement: "government should redistribute income from the better-off to those who are less well off". The table below groups the answers to the three questions on sexual relations and the four questions on other aspects of moral traditionalism, and in the last row it shows the answers to the 'yardstick' question on redistribution.

Moral traditionalism

		Always wrong	Mostly wrong	Sometimes wrong	Rarely wrong	Not wrong at all
Pre-marital sexual relations	%	13	10	24	9	45
Extra-marital sexual relations	%	56	29	12	1	2
Homosexual relations	%	59	11	12	4	15

		Strongly agree	Agree	Neither	Disagree	Strongly disagree
Death penalty appropriate	%	33	37	8	13	10
Censorship necessary	%	19	48	15	14	4
Wife's job is to look after the home	%	7	20	19	35	20
Family life suffers if the woman works	%	10	37	17	28	8
Government should redistribute income	%	17	33	20	25	6

Considering first our 'yardstick' question on income redistribution, we find as before (with the four-point scale question) that people tend towards the political left rather than the right. But, as before, there is substantial spread in the answers and the distribution is thus much closer to dissensus than to consensus.

Notably, there is almost as much dissensus on the two gender role questions about women and work as there is on income redistribution. The shape and spread of the distribution of answers are very similar. We must, of course, be wary about putting too much weight on the responses to just two questions, but it does seem that gender roles are as much a source of disagreement in Britain as is economic inequality.

Turning to the other questions on moral traditionalism, we find slightly less dissensus on the issues of the death penalty and censorship and move even closer to consensus about extra-marital sexual relations: 56 per cent say that extra-marital relations are always wrong, while a further 29 per cent say they are mostly wrong. Hardly anyone takes the opposite moral viewpoint.

However, our most striking results are those on pre-marital and homosexual relations. Here we see a phenomenon we have not come across previously - polarisation. In general, the distributions that we have so far reported have had a single peak. The position of the peak has varied - sometimes at one end of the scale, sometimes at the other, sometimes in the middle - but there have been relatively smooth downward slopes as one moves away from the peak.[3]

The distribution of answer on homosexual relations, however, shows a very different pattern, with two distinct peaks at the extremes. There is a relatively high peak of 59 per cent (those who believe that homosexual relations are always wrong) which at first sight looks like something approaching consensus. But we find at the other extreme a second - albeit much lower - peak of 15 per cent (those who say that homosexual relations are not at all wrong). Since this broad pattern appears in previous *British Social Attitudes* surveys we can be sure that it is not a chance product of sampling variation in one year. The same pattern (though in the opposite direction) occurs in response to the answers on pre-marital sex.

Whereas on inequality, unemployment and gender roles we found widespread disagreement, we find here in response to two questions about sexual *mores* not only disagreement but polarisation: these questions divide society into two opposing groups (admittedly of very different sizes), facing each other from opposite ends of the spectrum.

The exceptional nature of these responses, particularly to the homosexuality question, also highlights the lack of polarisation elsewhere. The British public disagrees on many matters, but in most cases the disagreements are not all that extreme, one viewpoint shading into another across the spectrum.

Freedom of speech

One of the key questions we need to address is whether there is greater agreement on what we have called procedural matters - how to settle differences - than on moral or distributional ones. The following questions covering rights to free expression and association are useful starting points. We asked respondents:

> *There are many ways in which people or organisations can protest against a government action they strongly oppose. Please show which you think should be allowed and which should not be allowed:*
>
> *Organising public meetings to protest against the government*
> *Publishing pamphlets to protest against the government*
> *Organising protest marches and demonstrations*
> *Occupying a government office and stopping work there for several days*
> *Seriously damaging government buildings*

These questions offered four answer categories - 'definitely', 'probably', 'probably not' and 'definitely not' be allowed. The table below shows the distribution of results.

Tolerance of protest

Should it be allowed:		Definitely	Probably	Probably not	Definitely not
Organising public protest meetings	%	64	27	5	4
Publishing protest pamphlets	%	55	33	8	5
Organising protest marches	%	41	32	14	13
Occupying a government office	%	4	8	28	61
Seriously damaging government buildings	%	1	1	4	94

We find considerable consensus on all bar one of these forms of protest. While there is widespread agreement that public meetings and pamphlets definitely should be allowed, and that occupying government offices or damaging government buildings definitely *should not* be allowed, there is disagreement over organising protest marches. The spread of viewpoints on this particular form of protest is much greater than on the others.

Yet on these procedural matters (apart from the not unexpected intolerance towards allowing protesters to damage government buildings) there is not quite so much consensus as there is on the government's responsibility to provide health care for the sick or a decent standard of living for the old. This of course refutes our hypothesis that Britain displays consensus on procedural matters but not so much on distributional ones. But it also perhaps highlights the special place in Britain reserved for the welfare state (or at least those aspects of it that involve mass provision).

Moreover, as with the welfare state, consensus on procedural matters is somewhat conditional. Agreement drops steeply in respect of the rights of 'extreme' groups such as revolutionaries or racists (rather than abstract political protesters). The question ran:

There are some people whose views are considered extreme by the majority. First, consider people who want to overthrow the government by revolution. Do you think such people should be allowed to

... hold public meetings to express their views?
... publish books expressing their views? [*]

---

[*] A parallel question was asked about "people who believe that whites are racially superior to people of all other races"; responses to which are shown and discussed in Chapter 9.

Respondents were offered the same four options - from 'definitely' to 'definitely not' - as in the earlier question on political protest. As we see, however, the public is not nearly so steadfast in its support for freedom of expression for people who wish to overthrow the government as it is about free speech for (unnamed) protesters. Indeed, the distribution of answers below is the closest we shall come to complete dissensus.[4]

Tolerance of 'revolutionaries'

		Definitely	Probably	Probably not	Definitely not
Should people who want to overthrow the government by revolution be allowed to:					
Hold public meetings to express their views	%	23	28	18	31
Publish books expressing their views	%	23	39	17	21

Although at first sight, then, we seemed to have found consensus on the welfare state and on procedural matters, now we are not so sure. Rather, there is a limited core of topics on which we find substantial agreement and, as soon as one moves away from this core - for instance, to related issues like benefits for the unemployed or free speech for revolutionaries - the consensus seems to disappear. The explanation for this may be that many people have rather strong views about the unemployed and about revolutionaries, which interfere with their endorsement of the welfare state or of the principle of free speech. The *principle* of, say, freedom of speech is perhaps not always strongly-enough held to override their strong disapproval of certain minorities.

The structure of dissensus

As we noted earlier, the implications of dissensus for any society may vary according to how it is structured. We look now at whether the disagreements on redistribution, public spending, moral traditionalism and free speech are amorphous, or whether people's attitudes to these issues line up alongside their attitudes towards other similar issues, thus forming strong and coherent normative patterns.

One way to look at the structure of values is through factor analysis, which shows the interrelationship between attitudes. The table below gives the results of a factor analysis[*] of some of the key items we have

---

[*] The results given are those after oblique rotation, since the factors are correlated. For ease of presentation, the factors were constrained to three.

discussed above, and the pattern is not unexpected. One factor consists of attitudes towards the standard economic issues that form the basis of what is often called the 'left-right' dimension of British politics - income redistribution, the government's responsibility to provide jobs, and spending on unemployment benefits. Another factor comprises the questions which we have described as tapping moral traditionalism - the death penalty, homosexuality, and gender roles.

The structure of attitudes

In favour of:	Factor 1	Factor 2	Factor 3
Income redistribution	.73		
Jobs for all who want them		.72	
Spending on unemployment benefits	.64		
Spending on pensions	.61		
Spending on health		.57	
Death penalty		.64	
Spending on defence		.61	
Homosexual relations		.59	
Wife's job to look after home		.53	
Allowing 'revolutionaries' to publish pamphlets		-.47	
Allowing 'revolutionaries' to hold public meetings		-.47	
Spending on environment			.65
Spending on police		.50	.58
Spending on culture and the arts			.57
Spending on education	.41		.51
Eigen value	2.97	2.02	1.38
% of variance explained	19.8%	13.4%	9.2%

This factor analysis by no means explains all or even most of the variance (42 per cent in all). It does, however, produce some interesting and unexpected relationships. First, we see that the consensual welfare state issues - spending on pensions and health - line up alongside the dissensual economic issues of redistribution and unemployment (in Factor 1). Thus, although the overall level of disagreement about extra health spending is small, people who favour 'much more' spending tend also to take more left-wing attitudes towards redistribution as well.

Secondly, we find that attitudes towards free speech and free association line up with moral traditionalism (in Factor 2). People who are in favour of preserving traditional gender roles or who believe homosexual relations to be wrong also tend to be in favour of limiting freedom of speech for revolutionaries. They seem to conform to a degree to a personality type which has been described as 'authoritarian' (see Adorno et al, 1950).

We had expected that consensual issues, particularly those of a more procedural kind, might mitigate conflicts on substantive issues such as redistribution or morality. But this now looks less plausible. Attitudes towards procedural matters (and, for that matter, attitudes towards the welfare state) are in fact part and parcel of the mainstream of value dissensus in British society.

It is also interesting to note which topics are largely unrelated to the two main economic and moral dimensions that we have been discussing. The environment and culture and the arts belong to the a third factor, with no noticeable links elsewhere. Indeed this third factor is a rather weak one, explaining little of the overall variance in the dataset, which suggests that it contains variables which produce a more amorphous lack of agreement. As we saw from the table on page 5, the environment and culture and the arts fall in the middle, being the spending areas on which there is neither the greatest nor the least consensus. Now we see the rather 'nondescript' nature of these issues. They do not link with the major lines of value conflict in Britain and they do not themselves go together all that strongly. They seem to fit our earlier designation of 'isolated' issues, and as such have no great potential (as yet anyway) to be divisive. The only linking theme seems to be that they are all spending issues. So perhaps some people are simply in favour of or against all increases in public spending (or, as it turns out, nearly all).

The social bases of disagreement

These patterns are to a large extent repeated when we consider the social bases of disagreement. We examine first the relationship between class and attitudes to redistribution and the welfare state; then we look at the relationship of age and education with moral traditionalism.

Social class, redistribution and the welfare state

When we examine the spread of responses to the statement: "government should redistribute income from the better-off to those who are less well-off", we find, not unexpectedly, that attitudes are more strongly linked to class than they are to other social or cultural factors such as religion, gender or education. Also, as we know from previous research, the working class is the most in favour of redistribution, while the petty bourgeoisie and the salariat are the least in favour.

Social class and attitudes towards redistribution

Social class:		Strongly agree	Agree	Neither agree nor disagree	Disagree	Strongly disagree
Salariat	%	13	29	16	34	8
Routine non-manual	%	13	33	22	25	7
Petty bourgeoisie	%	13	28	17	36	7
Manual foremen and supervisors	%	18	39	18	20	4
Working class	%	25	35	22	16	2
All	%	17	33	20	25	6

For a description of the Goldthorpe class schema (compressed) used here, see Appendix I.

Even in respect of class, however, the differences in attitudes towards redistribution are relatively modest, and in no class is there anything approaching a consensus. Working-class people are the least divided, but even here we are a lot closer to dissensus than consensus. Indeed there is almost as much spread *within* classes as there is within the population as a whole. So Britain may be divided by class in its attitudes towards redistribution, but it is certainly not polarised.

A useful summary index for measuring differences such as these is the index of dissimilarity.[*] The higher the figure on the index the greater is the between-group difference. And class does come out high: the working class:petty bourgeoisie difference is 24 points, compared with 10 points for age (youngest *versus* oldest age groups) and 7 points or under for gender, religion (Anglicans *versus* no religion) and education (graduates *versus* unqualified). But there is an even larger index of dissimilarity between income groups than between social classes: if we compare attitudes to redistribution among people with annual household incomes below £3,000 and those with incomes above £32,000, the index reaches 35 points.

The picture is similar when we consider attitudes to state responsibility for full employment and for providing a decent standard of living for the unemployed. Once again, the classes disagree, but are not polarised; and, once again, the differences between income groups are larger (the index reaching 33 points). Social class and income are the principal sources of dissimilarity; none of the other social divisions come into the reckoning on these issues of redistribution and unemployment.

Our factor analysis suggested that the welfarist issues of health care and old age pensions lined up with the more divisive issues of redistribution and unemployment. Analysis of the social bases of

---

[*] The index of dissimilarity measures the proportion of respondents who would need to change their responses to make the two distributions in question identical. The index is obtained by summing the differences between the two distributions and dividing by two.

disagreement confirms this. Class and income once again lead the way, although, as we might have anticipated considering that these were consensual issues, the differences tend to be much smaller.

Age, education and moral traditionalism

When we turn to moral traditionalism and consider first gender roles, and in particular responses to the statement: "a husband's job is to earn money, a wife's to look after the home and family", we find that gender itself does not divide opinion to any very marked degree. True, women are somewhat less 'traditional' than men, but the index of dissimilarity reaches only a modest 12 points.

There are, however, much larger divisions between different groups of women. Not surprisingly, women who are looking after the home are much more traditional in their attitudes: using the index of dissimilarity, the difference between women who are currently looking after the home and those in full-time paid work is 36 points. But more surprisingly it increases even further (to 48 points) when we compare women graduates with those who have no formal qualifications. And it reaches a striking 56 points when we compare the youngest group of women (aged 18-24) with the oldest (aged 65 and over). The age differences are spelled out below.

Women's attitudes to gender roles

"A husband's job is to earn money, a wife's to look after the home and family"

Age of woman:		Strongly agree	Agree	Neither agree nor disagree	Disagree	Strongly disagree
18 - 24	%	4	5	11	31	49
25 - 34	%	2	10	10	40	37
35 - 44	%	3	10	16	45	26
45 - 54	%	6	16	16	46	17
55 - 59	%	2	28	21	37	13
60 - 64	%	9	33	21	31	7
65+	%	17	37	23	20	4
All women	%	6	18	16	37	24

So here we do see something like polarisation. Four in five 18-24 year-old women feel that it is *not* the wife's job to look after home and family, while more than half of women aged 65 and over take the *opposing* view.

Young and older men, graduate and unqualified men also differ in their attitudes towards gender roles, but the differences here are not nearly as marked as the ones between the women themselves. (The difference between the youngest and oldest group of men, for example, is 38 points rather than the 56 points for women, while the difference between men with degrees and men who are unqualified is 35 points, rather than the women's 48 points.)

It is a remarkable finding that men differ much less from women in their attitudes towards gender roles than different groups of women differ. In some respects the divisions among women represent the sharpest attitudinal divide in British society. This would not perhaps come as much of a surprise to students of American politics, where it was one group of women - the Concerned Women of America - who were in large part responsible for defeating the Equal Rights Amendment backed by the 'feminist' National Organisation of Women (Bernotsky, 1991). The American experience thus suggests that differences between women have the potential to stimulate group organisation and conflict. Our attitudinal data suggest that the same may be true for Britain.

Another major social difference in attitudes towards moral issues is that between graduates and others in attitudes to the death penalty. Graduates are much less likely to be in favour, with a difference on our index of 46 points between them and the unqualified. We find similar differences in attitudes to homosexuality: not only are graduates less intolerant (51 points), but so are the youngest age group compared with the oldest (27 points).

Despite the very large differences between graduates and the unqualified, however, education does not polarise them on the issue of homosexual relations in the way that perceptions of gender roles polarise younger women from older women. Unlike either the younger women or the older women in our sample, graduates *themselves* are divided in their stance towards homosexuality, with a remarkably even spread across the five response categories from 'always wrong' to 'not at all wrong'.

Finally on this subject, our analysis of inter-group differences in relation to free speech reinforces the story already told by our factor analysis. Attitudes towards free speech are associated with attitudes towards the moral questions, and the same social divisions that are associated with moral traditionalism - those by age and education - reappear here.

Life-cycle or generational effects?

The long-run implications of the age-related differences we have found in attitudes, and in particular their potential for social division, will depend on whether they represent life-cycle changes or generational changes. In other words, do people become more in favour of 'traditional' gender roles as they grow older, or has there been a fundamental change over time, with the older generations still holding on to the attitudes they learned when they were young and the younger generations representing the more progressive attitudes of recent years? If there is a *life-cycle* effect, we may expect the age differences to persist and to provide a lasting potential for division. If the explanation is *generational,* we may expect the differences to fade as younger, more liberal generations replace older, more traditional ones.

Since some of these questions on moral traditionalism have been asked through the life of the *British Social Attitudes* series, we can *begin* to explore the life cycle and generational hypotheses. (For a detailed exposition of the nature and limitations of this kind of analysis see Glenn, 1977.) As examples, we shall take two questions. The first asks about homosexual relations and the second about gender roles.

The following table shows the pattern over time in attitudes to homosexuality. We have divided the sample in each survey year into the *same* birth band (or cohort), so that we can see what happens to each cohort's attitudes as it ages.

% saying that sexual relations between two adults of the same sex are always or sometimes wrong

	1983	1984	1985	1987	1989	1990	Difference in % 1983-90
Birth cohort:							
1896-05	85	88	94	94	95	-	-
1906-15	86	92	88	95	91	87	+ 1
1916-25	76	78	86	92	86	86	+ 10
1926-35	64	73	82	89	85	77	+ 13
1936-45	54	63	68	77	73	72	+ 18
1946-55	47	54	55	63	58	63	+ 16
1956-65	57	61	62	64	53	55	- 2
1966-72*	-	58	62	59	55	60	-
All	63	68	70	75	69	70	+ 7

* Those under eighteen years old were ineligible for interview.

Consider, for example, the fifth row of the table. This shows the proportion of the 1936-45 birth cohort who thought in each year that homosexuality was wrong. In the 1983 survey, when this question was first asked, 54 per cent of these (then) 38 to 47 year-olds said it was wrong. By 1987 (when they were aged 42 to 51), 77 per cent of this cohort held this view. But by 1990 (when they were aged 45-54) the figure had fallen back to 72 per cent. Note that we are not reporting here the attitudes of the *same individuals* as they age, but of samples drawn from the *same birth cohort.*[5]

At first sight this seems to be a rather strange life-cycle pattern. However, as we can see from the overall figures (the bottom row of the table), there has also been what is technically called a 'period' effect (influencing attitudes in the short term). Thus attitudes towards homosexual relations became in general rather more disapproving during the first four years of the survey series, largely (we suspect) because of the fear of AIDS (Brook, 1988). After 1987 the trend reverses (Wellings and Wadsworth, 1990).

What we need to do therefore is to compare the changes in each birth cohort with those in the sample as a whole. The last column on the table above shows the net changes between 1983 and 1990. We can see that for the 1936-45 cohort (people now aged between 45 and 54) the net change was 18 percentage points, compared with an overall 7 point change between 1983 and 1990. So this particular cohort does seem to have become much more disapproving as it has aged in its attitudes towards homosexuality, compared with the sample as a whole.

Changes in attitude over the life cycle do not however appear to proceed at a uniform pace. In the early years of adulthood they seem to be slow, or even nonexistent, becoming more rapid during middle age and reaching a plateau after retirement. Thus the *net* changes between 1983 and 1990 were not of equal size in all the birth cohorts. There is a clear pattern, with the 1906-15 and 1956-65 birth cohorts showing rather small net changes, and the birth cohorts in between showing much larger changes. A very similar pattern is found if we look down any of the columns. Thus people in the youngest cohorts (towards the bottom of the table) tend to be rather similar to one another in their attitudes; there are then big differences in the level of disapproval as we move up the column through the middle age groups, and finally the older age groups (at the top end of the table) are again rather similar to one another.

On attitudes to homosexuality, then, we conclude that there have not been any marked generational changes. Age differences seem largely to represent life-cycle phenomena, and as such are likely to persist.

Attitudes towards gender roles are more interesting. Unfortunately, however, the relevant question has not been asked as often as the one on homosexual relations. Moreover, there have been minor changes in the wording of the response categories, making strict comparison over time (and the assessment of period effects) much more difficult. However, by using the technique known as 'Mostellerization' to adjust the 1990 results, we can take account of the changes in the response categories.[6]

% agreeing strongly or just agreeing that
"a husband's job is to earn money; a wife's job is
to look after the home and family"

Birth cohort:	1984	1990	Difference in % 1984-90
1896-05	80	85	+ 5
1906-15	74	79	+ 5
1916-25	63	68	+ 5
1926-35	48	60	+12
1936-45	33	46	+13
1946-55	28	31	+ 3
1956-65	28	25	- 3
1966-72	24	25	+ 1
All	43	43	-

As on the issue of homosexual relations, a glance up the columns of the table suggests that there is a curvilinear relationship between age and attitudes. The younger birth cohorts are rather similar, and progressive, in their attitudes towards gender roles; there is then a steep rise through middle age to a more traditional stance, and subsequently a levelling off among the older people.

If we now look along the rows, that is at the same birth cohorts as they age, the same pattern emerges. The younger birth cohorts (the bottom three rows) show very little change in their attitudes over the six years spanned by the two surveys. We then find extraordinary changes in the attitudes of the people born between 1926 and 1945 (the middle two rows), rising in 'traditionalist' views by over 12 percentage points in 6 years.

This increase over six years is quite close to the gap of 15 points which exists in 1984 *between* the 1926-35 and the 1936-45 birth cohorts. Given that we are comparing ten-year birth cohorts with a six year gap between surveys, it seems very plausible that the age differences revealed in the cross-sectional surveys can be entirely explained by life-cycle changes. And this in turn suggests that age differences in attitudes towards gender roles too will persist.

It is wise to be tentative in drawing conclusions from cohort analysis, particularly when (as in the present case) we have had to adjust the data. But the limited evidence we have does suggest that people's attitudes towards both homosexual relations and gender roles become more traditional as they age. If, in contrast, older people had retained the attitudes they had learned in the more traditional 1920s and 1930s, then the middle-aged cohorts would not have changed so much in the brief period spanned by our surveys.

We cannot of course be sure that the same pattern will be displayed by the younger birth cohorts as they age. Many more women with families now go out to work; and many more have smaller families. The way they see the world may therefore be different from that of their older counterparts. But it is probably safest to assume that wide age differences in attitudes towards gender roles will be with us for the foreseeable future, providing a continual potential for social conflict.

Conclusions

Taking into account our methodological caveats, we have discovered a picture of a society which is divided to a greater or lesser extent on almost every issue we have considered. As expected we have found dissensus on the economic issues of redistribution of wealth and unemployment, and while there is consensus on specific aspects of welfare provision - notably health care and pensions - it does not extend to others (such as provision for the unemployed) which are more closely related to economic issues. There is similar dissensus on moral issues such as gender roles. Moreover, the consensus we anticipated on procedural matters has been somewhat elusive. The more we probed, the greater the extent of disagreement proved to be.

However, on most issues, attitudes are divided, not polarised. This is particularly clear for economic issues. Class provides the social roots of economic dissensus, but there is almost as much dissensus within each class as there is between classes. Where polarisation does emerge, it is in respect of moral rather than economic questions - in attitudes towards such issues as gender roles and homosexuality. Yet these are not issues which are usually thought of as providing the major lines of division in British society. They are much less visible than the economic ones, partly because the political parties do not represent distinct positions in relation to them, leaving them for pressure groups to promote, and partly because they do not get regular media coverage as do those issues that have a class basis.

Nonetheless, while at present these sorts of moral issues do not constitute a major threat to social and political stability in Britain, they clearly seem to have the potential to grow in political significance alongside the more familiar class-based issues on which British politics continues to thrive.

Notes

1. Three options is really the minimum required for any analysis of spread, and we therefore exclude from consideration questions which offered people only two options. For example, there are some valuable questions in the survey which asked people whether they thought abortion should be allowed by law in a range of different circumstances. But respondents were simply asked to reply 'yes' or 'no', and so these questions cannot therefore be compared with ones which allowed for a spread of answers.

2. Our judgements of the level of consensus displayed in this table are based on the standard deviation of the responses to each question. This assumes that the scale is an equal interval one, which is a rather stronger assumption than is perhaps warranted. The standard deviations are:

Health 0.65	Police 0.78
Pensions 0.71	Defence 0.92
Education 0.74	Culture 0.94
Environment 0.75	Unemployment 0.94

3. As we can see, the slopes are generally more uneven on the five point 'agree/disagree' questions than on the four-point scale questions which we looked at earlier. This may be due to respondents' reluctance to use the 'neither agree nor disagree' response.

4. We should note the possibility that the difference between the level of agreement on these two sets of questions may be partly a methodological artefact. What we may have here is a 'contrast' effect. For further discussion of this concept, see Schwarz and Bless (1991).

5. Only panel studies (that is, ones that track the attitudes, characteristics or behaviour of the same people over time) can study *individual* changes (see Lievesley and Waterton, 1985). A further problem to bear in mind with any birth cohort analysis is that there will be selective attrition over time as its members die; so we are not strictly comparing like with like. Our retrospective annual samples are necessarily samples of survivors. This, of course, happens with panel data too.

6. The question was first asked in the Women in Employment Survey (Martin and Roberts, 1984). There the answer categories were 'agree strongly', 'agree slightly', 'neither agree nor disagree', 'disagree slightly' and 'disagree strongly'. In the 1984

British Social Attitudes (BSA) survey the second and fourth answer categories were 'just agree' and 'just disagree'. And in the 1990 BSA survey, the second and fourth answer categories were simply 'agree' and 'disagree'. These changes may well have affected the overall distribution of answers. We have used the technique of Mostellerization (named after its inventor) to preserve the internal structure of the table. See Mosteller (1968) for further details. The 1990 results have been adjusted so that they have the same column totals as in 1984 but retain the row totals that the 1990 data exhibited.

7. The 'All' figures are 43 per cent for both the 1984 and 1990 columns as a result of the Mostellerization. (We have adjusted the figures to yield the same overall totals because of the problem of the changed response categories. In effect we have assumed that there is no period effect but only cohort and generation effects.) It may seem puzzling that no overall change accompanies positive increases for seven of the eight birth cohorts, but this is because the size of the birth cohorts has changed: the older and most illiberal birth cohorts have declined in size (through mortality), whereas the youngest and most liberal cohort has increased in size (as more of them have reached the age of 18). We have left these changes in the size of the cohorts unadjusted.

References

ADORNO, T.W., FRENKEL-BRUNSWIK, E., LEVINSON D.J., and SANFORD, R.N., *The Authoritarian Personality*, Harper, New York (1950).

BERNOTSKY, L., *A Step into Politics: Concerned Women for America and the Political Mobilisation of Traditional Women*, (unpublished) M Phil (Politics) thesis, University of Oxford (1991).

BROOK, L., 'The public's response to AIDS', in Jowell, R., Witherspoon, S. and Brook, L. (eds), *British Social Attitudes: the 5th Report*, Gower, Aldershot (1988).

CONVERSE, P., 'The nature of belief systems in mass publics', in Apter, D. (ed), *Ideology and Discontent*, Free Press, New York (1964).

DURKHEIM, E., *De la Division du Travail Social: Etude sur l'Organisation des Sociétés Superieures*, Alcan, Paris (1893).

GLENN, N.D., *Cohort Analysis*, Sage, Beverly Hills (1977).

HALLER, M., HOELLINGER, F. and RAUBAL, O., 'Leviathan or welfare state? The role of government in six advanced western nations', in Alwin, D.F. *et al.*, *Attitudes to Inequality and the Role of Government*, Social and Cultural Planning Office, Rijswijk, The Netherlands (1990).

HEATH, A.F. and TOPF, R.G., 'Political culture', in Jowell, R., Witherspoon, S., and Brook, L. (eds), *British Social Attitudes: the 1987 Report*, Gower, Aldershot (1987).

HEATH, A.F., EVANS, G., LALLJEE, M., MARTIN, J. and WITHERSPOON, S., 'The measurement of core beliefs and values', *JUSST Working Paper No. 2*, SCPR and Nuffield College, Oxford (1991).

LIEVESLEY, D. and WATERTON, J., 'Measuring individual attitude change', in Jowell, R. and Witherspoon, S. (eds), *British Social Attitudes: the 1985 Report*, Gower, Aldershot (1985).

MARSHALL, G., NEWBY, H., ROSE, D. and VOGLER, C., *Social Class in Modern Britain,* Hutchinson, London (1988).

MARTIN, J. and ROBERTS, C., *Women and Employment: A Lifetime Perspective,* HMSO, London (1984).

MATZA, D., 'The disreputable poor', in Smelser. N.J. and Lipset, S.M. (eds), *Social Structure and Mobility in Economic Development,* Routledge, London (1966).

MOSTELLER, F., 'Association and estimation in contingency tables', *Journal of the American Statistical Association,* vol.63 (1968), pp.1-28.

PARSONS, T., 'The place of ultimate values in sociological theory', *International Journal of Ethics,* vol.45 (1935), pp.282-316.

SCHWARTZ, N. and BLESS, H., 'Assimilation and contrast effects in social judgement', *Survey Methods Newsletter, Spring 1991,* SCPR, London (1991).

TAYLOR-GOOBY, P., 'Social welfare: the unkindest cuts', in Jowell, R., Witherspoon, S. and Brook, L. (eds), *British Social Attitudes: the 7th Report,* Gower, Aldershot (1990).

WELLINGS, K. and WADSWORTH, J., 'AIDS and the moral climate', in Jowell, R., Witherspoon, S. and Brook, L. (eds), *British Social Attitudes: the 7th Report,* Gower, Aldershot (1990).

Acknowledgements

The authors would like to thank Clive Payne for his help with 'Mostellerisation', and Geoff Evans for his comments on the chapter.

2 Attachment to the welfare state

Peter Taylor-Gooby [*]

The foundations of the British welfare state were laid at the close of the second World War and remained substantially in place until the late 1970s. Government agencies were set up to administer mass services, financed by a progressive tax system and free at the point of demand, to meet a defined range of social needs. Though these needs were periodically redefined as demand increased, new social problems emerged or priorities shifted, changes were mainly at the margins. The core of state welfare provision went largely unchallenged, either from left or right. During the 1980s, however, successive Conservative governments set themselves the task of challenging this consensus and of reducing state welfare spending, especially by encouraging the expansion of private services - an attempt to restructure welfare provision which provoked intense debate. Ideology was no doubt the driving force behind some of the welfare reforms but social change had also resulted in changing patterns of popular demand for welfare services, and these factors would have been influential whatever party was in power during the 1980s.

In this chapter we review evidence from the *British Social Attitudes* survey series to show what effect, if any, the policies of the last decade have had on public attitudes toward the 'core' state services. In particular we examine priorities for state welfare spending among different social classes and different income groups. We take up a theme introduced in *The 7th Report* and ask what effect the widening gap between rich and poor may have on support for common provision financed through progressive taxation. We also re-examine the evidence of dissatisfaction

[*] Professor of Social Policy, University of Kent

with the performance of the National Health Service over recent years, and consider whether or not this has resulted in gaining converts to the private sector.

State intervention and spending priorities

The *British Social Attitudes* survey series asks a number of questions about people's priorities for welfare spending, about their attitudes to the taxation necessary to finance it, and what they think the relationship between the private and state sector should be.

Evidence from the latest survey points to two main conclusions. First, the pattern (revealed by previous surveys) of increased public support among all social groups for more state spending, and of growing concern about quality of provision, especially in the NHS and state education, continues into the 1990s. Secondly, the differing attitudes among people with different political affiliations will ensure that welfare policy will remain at the centre of the political debate well into the 1990s and beyond.

The responsibilities of government

We begin by examining responses to a series of general questions which ask people whether or not "it should be the government's responsibility" to intervene in a number of social and economic policy domains, mainly to do with welfare provision. The 1990 results show that there has been no shift away from public support for a high level of state involvement in the core services.

% saying it should definitely or probably be the government's responsibility to...	1985	1990
... provide health care for the sick	98	98
... provide a decent standard of living for the old	97	97
... provide industry with the help it needs to grow	92	91
... give financial help to university students from low-income families	n/a	90
... provide decent housing for those who can't afford it	n/a	90
... keep prices under control	91	87
... provide a decent standard of living for the unemployed	81	77
... reduce income differences between the rich and poor	69	71
... provide a job for everyone who wants one	68	60

The striking thing about these findings is the lack of differentiation not only between years but also between different forms of social and economic intervention. The British public can hardly be accused of being *laissez faire* in their demands of government. The small fall between 1985 and 1990 in support for meeting the needs of unemployed people probably reflects the fall in the level of unemployment in Britain[*] in the latter part of the 1980s. If so, the subsequent rise in unemployment in the recession of the early 1990s will lead to a rise in support for this group at the time of the next survey. In other respects, there is still no evidence that a rolling back of the welfare state would be in accord with popular opinion.

Spending priorities and taxation

Moreover, public endorsement of a strong role for government in welfare provision is reinforced by responses to questions on public spending and taxation. Enthusiasm for more state spending (and willingness, in *principle* at least, to pay the taxes necessary to sustain it) has risen steeply over the 1980s. The proportion demanding increased spending has risen from around a third to more than one half:

If the government had to choose, it should ...	1983 %	1986 %	1990 %
... reduce taxes and spend less[*]	9	5	3
... keep taxes and spending at the same level as now	54	44	37
... increase taxes and spend more	32	46	54

[*] The spending areas asked about were 'health, education and social benefits'

Enthusiasm for increased state spending is common to all social groups. The main spending priorities are, as always, the mass services - the NHS and state education - and, among social benefits, retirement pensions. The erosion of child benefit levels since 1979, followed by a freeze in 1987 (partially lifted in the 1991 budget), is clearly of concern: the proportion naming child benefit as first or second priority has risen from one in five in 1983 to nearly one in three in 1990. This may, however, partly be caused by the reduction in priority accorded to benefits for unemployed people - from 33 to 21 per cent over the same period - linked with the reduction in concern over unemployment *per se.* Nonetheless, provision for those without jobs is still seen by many as inadequate: the proportion endorsing the view that "benefits for the

---

[*] From 11.2 per cent in 1985 to a low of 6.9 per cent in 1990, according to the OECD definition (National Institute for Economic and Social Research, 1991, p.115).

unemployed are too low and cause hardship" has risen slightly (from 46 to 50 per cent) between 1983 and 1990, and the proportion believing they are "too high and discourage people from finding jobs" has fallen from 35 to 29 per cent over the same period.

The impression of concern about the level of state spending on welfare is bolstered by responses to a further question which did not require respondents to name spending priorities. Instead we asked separately, for eight areas, whether respondents would like to see more or less government spending on each. However this time respondents were specifically informed in the question wording that, if they said 'much more', a tax increase might be needed to pay for it. Even in response to this somewhat argumentative question, the mass welfare areas - health, education and pensions - still command high and growing priority for 'much more' government spending. As might have been expected from responses to previous questions, priority for spending on benefits for unemployed people is, by comparison, low and in decline. (Note also the strong rise in priority for spending on the environment (see Chapter 6) and the reduction in priority for defence: fieldwork was carried out well before the Gulf War.) What remains striking, however, is the extent by which welfare spending areas lead the list of priorities.

% saying they would like much more government spending on:	1985	1990
Health	35	38
Old age pensions	25	30
Education	22	28
Unemployment benefits	12	8
The environment	6	14
Police and law enforcement	8	12
Military and defence	5	2
Culture and the arts	1	2

Private provision and public resources

The 1990 survey did not include many questions about private welfare provision. But we did repeat one first asked in 1983 designed to gauge attitudes to the hypothetical restriction of state medicine "to those with lower incomes", so that "most people would then take out medical insurance or pay for health care". Support for such a two-tier system, never strong anyway, has fallen since 1983 (from 29 to 22 per cent), and opposition to it has risen accordingly (from 64 to 73 per cent).

The recent reforms of state education and the NHS have sought to introduce market principles into both services. In education (see also Chapter 3) the move towards local management of schools, financed in relation to pupil numbers and combined with enhanced parental choice, is designed to bring some of the benefits of private schools to 'consumers' of state education. The introduction of internal markets into the NHS is designed to bring about decentralisation, also for the benefit of the 'consumer'. The intention is to make more efficient use of increasingly stretched health resources, as government strives to limit spending in the face of growing public expectations and an ageing population with a longer life-expectancy.*

None of these reforms was yet in place in the spring of 1990 when our fieldwork was carried out, so it was too early to try to gauge public response to their introduction. In any case, we suspect it will be difficult in a general population survey such as the *British Social Attitudes* survey, to investigate the perceived effectiveness or otherwise of any of the specific measures. But our standard questions designed to tap general levels of satisfaction and concern and new ones introduced in 1991 about perceptions of in-patient services and care will eventually enable us to gauge whether the radical restructuring of the NHS has led to an improvement in its public image.

Since the party political debate over both health and education focuses on resource levels *versus* cost-effectiveness and 'consumer choice', useful proxies for questions on detailed aspects of the reforms are those on service performance in the NHS and state education. A series of questions asks which aspects of each service are most in need of improvement.** By a wide margin the aspects that attract most attention are ones that require most resources to improve, such as the need for improvements in staffing levels and waiting times in hospitals, smaller classes and more books and equipment in primary schools, more job training, discipline, and books and equipment in secondary schools. These priorities do not, of course, rule out the wish for wider choice (and admittedly few of our questions covered this area), but there is little doubt that there is still widespread criticism of the basic level of resources devoted to both health and education (see also Chapter 3).

Political consensus and dissensus

So far then, the evidence is of widespread public support for the welfare state and of concern about its future. But this overall endorsement of state welfare provision conceals substantial differences in the priorities that identifiers with the three main political parties choose. As the table

---

* The UK already spends a smaller proportion of GNP on these services than almost any other country at a comparable stage of economic development (OECD, 1988, Table 3).

** For education, respondents are asked which of a number of aspects is the most important factor in improving primary and which the most important for secondary schools. For health, respondents are asked, for a number of aspects of health service provision, "whether the National Health service in your area is, on the whole, satisfactory or in need of improvement".

below shows, there is majority support for increased spending and higher taxes among Labour and Liberal Democrat identifiers, but not among supporters of the party of government, and while no party divisions are apparent when it comes to according the NHS the top priority for extra expenditure, there are clear differences between parties in the level of support they give to lower order priorities.

	Conservative	Liberal Democrats	Labour
% saying the government should increase taxes to pay for extra spending*	42	66	65
% nominating as first or second priority for extra spending			
Health	78	82	83
Education	62	69	57
Housing	17	15	21
Social security benefits	7	11	17
% nominating as first or second priority for extra spending on social benefits			
Old age pensions	71	70	61
Disablement benefits	68	63	49
Child benefit	26	30	37
Single parents' benefits	17	17	19
Unemployment benefits	15	17	28

* The spending areas asked about were 'health, education and social benefits'.

Labour identifiers give more priority to housing, social security, child benefit and unemployment benefits (conspicuously *not* to pensions which is one of the Party's main priorities). Liberal Democrat identifiers give more priority to education, while Conservative identifiers give more priority to old age pensions and disablement benefits.

But the next table shows even more marked party political differences, particularly in relation to the needs of unemployed people, the belief that government should reduce income inequalities, and the provision of social housing. All these issues are taken up more by Labour identifiers than by those of other parties, but Conservative:Liberal differences on the issue of state involvement (measured by commitment to the view that it is definitely the state's responsibility to provide for a range of needs) also emerge clearly.

	Conservative	Liberal Democrats	Labour
% saying unemployment benefits are too low and cause hardship	30	51	68

% saying it should definitely be the government's responsibility to ...

	Conservative	Liberal Democrats	Labour
... provide health care for the sick	78	88	89
... provide a decent standard of living for the old	67	83	85
... provide industry with the help it needs to grow	36	34	50
... give financial help to university students from low-income families	36	59	59
... provide decent housing for those who can't afford it	26	43	62
... keep prices under control	39	43	57
... provide a decent standard of living for the unemployed	15	23	46
... reduce income differences between rich and poor	17	43	60
... provide a job for everyone who wants one	9	17	35

The small group of Green party supporters in the 1990 sample resemble the Liberal Democrats in their welfare politics; they are strongly committed on some issues and less so on others, but their distrust of too large a sphere of state responsibility, in comparison with Labour identifiers, is also apparent.

This review of attitudes to social provision suggests that any sustained challenge to the state-centred welfare tradition in Britain would be decidedly unpopular. There are certainly differences between supporters of the main political parties in the degree of sympathy they express for the needs of various social groups (for instance Labour identifiers' strong commitment to unemployed people), but there is also firm evidence that even Conservative identifiers cherish the mass state services, such as the NHS, education and pensions.

Self-interest and state provision

People's beliefs about the future of the welfare state are likely to be strongly influenced by their beliefs about their own interests. Social class is a crucial dimension along which such interests operate, partly because middle-class people tend to be better off, but also because they tend to be better able than working-class people are to articulate their demands and to exert pressure to get the sorts of services that suit them and their families.

'Middle-class benefits' and 'working-class benefits'

Research carried out in the 1980s has enabled us to identify with greater precision than in the past those services which tend to benefit working-class people almost exclusively, and those which benefit the whole population and so confer substantial advantage on the middle classes (such as the NHS, state education, child benefit and pensions). Since 1975, spending cuts have fallen more heavily on 'working-class benefits' such as council housing, benefits for unemployed people and other means-tested benefits than on universal benefits (Le Grand, 1990, pp. 345-46). Middle-class people tend to derive greater benefit than working-class people from universal services: for instance, they are more likely to by-pass the mechanisms that restrict referral to the most expensive parts of the NHS, they tend to have more children, their children tend to be more successful in gaining admission to sixth forms and universities, and they live longer to enjoy pension benefits.

In addition, changes in the organisation of the NHS and the state education service (both of which employ large numbers of people, both professionals and ancillary workers)[1] have affected working-class jobs much more severely than middle-class jobs. The sub-contracting of ancillary services has had a serious effect on cleaners, cooks, hospital porters and school caretakers. Many have also lost their jobs. Until recently anyway, middle-class professional employees have largely escaped these problems (although many would argue that spending constraints have made their jobs more difficult).

State services are, of course, financed by taxation raised from the whole population, and most groups do not want taxes to be too high. But the 1980s have seen sharp increases in indirect taxation (notably VAT), local government taxes and National Insurance contributions, alongside more substantial reductions in the direct taxation of high earners than in any other western country (Heidenheimer *et al*, 1990, Table 6.7). The resulting transfer of the tax burden downwards means that working-class people have a stronger financial interest now in the restoration of a redistributive welfare regime than at any time in the post-war period, an interest not shared by most middle-class people, who have gained from the changes.

Our survey evidence allows us to examine first how far attitudes to welfare relate to 'class' interests. Then we see how far they relate to 'employment' interests, that is the extent to which public sector employees in our sample differ from those in the private sector.

Class interest

As the table below shows, the salaried middle class professes to be more willing than others to pay increased taxes to finance an expansion of government spending on health and education.

General support for state welfare provision[*]

If the government had to choose, it should ...	Salariat %	Routine non-manual %	Petty bourgeoisie %	Manual foremen %	Working class %
... reduce taxes and spend less on health, education and social benefits	2	3	3	3	4
... keep taxes and spending at the same level as now	35	38	42	40	37
... increase taxes and spend more on health, education and social benefits	61	55	51	53	52

This greater willingness on the part of those who are already more highly taxed under a progressive system of taxation is not all that surprising if we take into account the point made earlier that public expenditure is not necessarily designed to serve the interests of the most obviously needy. Moreover, there are clear class differences in support for different services, which underline this point. We look first at support for 'working-class benefits' and see that middle-class support is comparatively low.

---

[*] We use the Goldthorpe class schema (compressed) here which takes account of a job's employment conditions and pay, security, status, autonomy and authority. It also identifies the important separate category of the petty bourgeoisie which comprises the self-employed, who have distinct political values (see Heath *et al*, 1985, and Appendix 1).

Support for 'working-class benefits'

% saying it should definitely be the government's responsibility to ...	Salariat	Routine non-manual	Petty bourgeoisie	Manual foremen	Working class
... provide decent housing for those who can't afford it	38	39	36	52	56
... provide a decent standard of living for the unemployed	25	26	23	31	38
... provide a job for everyone who wants one	16	14	17	39	31
% nominating as first or second priority for extra spending					
Housing	15	20	23	23	22
Social security benefits	8	9	11	9	19
% nominating as first or second priority for extra spending on social benefits					
Benefits for the unemployed	22	20	16	21	24
% saying unemployment benefit is too low and causes hardship	49	45	39	49	57

Working-class people, particularly the core of the working class in routine manual jobs, are especially likely to regard the provision of jobs, unemployment benefits and housing for poorer groups as essential government responsibilities, to name social security as a priority for extra spending, and to criticise unemployment benefit as being too low. However, enthusiasm for extra expenditure on social security, housing and unemployment benefits is perhaps not as high as might have been expected. This may be because the proportion living in council housing is declining as the sector contracts (see Chapter 5), and because (in early 1990 anyway) only a relatively small and geographically concentrated part of the population was either unemployed or heavily dependent on social security benefits. Even so, working-class support for all these benefits is consistently and often substantially higher than salariat support, and there is in general a clear class gradient in attitudes.

In contrast, support for services that are available to the mass of the population, but (as we have noted) confer greater benefits on middle-class people, is much more widespread, and the class gradient is much less apparent.

Support for 'middle-class benefits'

	Salariat	Routine non-manual	Petty bourgeoisie	Manual foremen	Working class
% saying it should definitely be the government's responsibility to...					
... provide health care for the sick	85	80	78	91	87
... provide a decent standard of living for the old	71	77	68	87	83
% nominating as first or second priority for extra spending					
Health	78	83	74	81	82
Education	68	62	58	64	53
% nominating as first or second priority for extra spending on social benefits					
Retirement pensions	63	66	67	70	66
Child benefits	28	35	30	27	34
% opposing a 'two-tier' health service	77	72	79	75	70

Interestingly, working-class people are noticeably keen on pension provision, with well over 80 per cent regarding it as an essential state responsibility. This enthusiasm may be the result of real cuts in the value of the basic state pension during the 1980s and, since the passing of the 1986 Social Security Act, the expansion of the subsidised private earnings-related pension industry with its particular benefits for middle-class people.

So the different interests of the different social classes are reflected in support for welfare state services. But the middle classes are fortunate in having support across *all* social classes for those services which in practice confer the greatest benefit on its members. In contrast, the 'working-class benefits' do not attract such widespread support from the middle classes.

Next we consider how class interests operate on attitudes to redistributive policies, from which the working class will gain and the middle class lose. As the table below shows, there are clear differences in attitudes to inequality and to redistribution.

Support for redistributive policies

% saying that ...	Salariat	Routine non-manual	Petty bourgeoisie	Manual foremen	Working class
... the gap between those with high incomes and those with low incomes is too large	79	80	73	86	85
% agreeing strongly that ...					
... it is the responsibility of the government to reduce the differences in income between people with high incomes and those with low incomes	13	16	19	27	23

Generalised statements that refer to abstract inequalities and the desirability of redressing them do not seem to reveal such sharp inter-class differences as do those which refer to specific benefits. It appears then that many people are at least implicitly aware of their class interests in relation to particular options for expenditure.

Employment interests

Earlier we speculated that people employed in the state sector might also be particularly strong defenders of the welfare state. But, as the table below shows, their views did not differ greatly from those of private sector employees as a whole.

	Public sector employees	Other employees
% saying the government should increase taxes to pay for extra spending	61	53
% opposing a 'two-tier' health service	77	71
% nominating as first or second priority for extra spending		
Health	86	80
Education	62	60
Social security benefits	12	13
Housing	18	20

True, public sector workers are rather keener on welfare spending than other employees, more supportive of the NHS as a spending priority, and rather more firmly opposed to the contraction of the NHS so that it

covers only poorer people. Significantly, however, their enthusiasm for
the areas that do not employ welfare state *professionals* in any numbers -
housing and social security - is slightly lower than that of other
employees. Even so, it would be very difficult to argue from these figures
that interests derived from employment are a strong influence on
attitudes to the welfare state.

These findings indicate that whichever way the debate about the future
of the welfare state goes, it is those services which confer the strongest
benefits on the middle class that will continue to have the strongest and
most widespread public support.

Inequality and state welfare

Living standards in Britain during the 1980s were characterised by two
main trends. First, there was real growth in the economy. Average living
standards rose sharply, so that for most people the period was one of real
increases in prosperity, despite two recessions and recurring economic
problems. The second trend was a growing income inequality between
the most prosperous and the poorest in society. Published data shows
that the share of total income (taking the impact of taxation, cash benefits
and housing costs, and the different needs of larger and smaller
households into account) received by the lowest 20 per cent fell by a fifth
from 9.5 to 7.6 per cent between 1979 and 1987, whereas that of the top
20 per cent rose by a sixth, from 35 to 41 per cent (Central Statistical
Office, 1990).[*]

As people grow richer, they demand and are prepared to pay for a
wider range of goods and services, including perhaps services which are
traditionally provided by the state. So we might expect the rise in
average living standards to lead to a decline in support for the uniform
provision of the welfare state, and a greater demand for the individualised
services of the private sector. The evidence from this series indicates that
this has not been the case so far. The 1980s were in fact a decade of
sharply rising public support for state welfare services, conspicuously so
for cherished institutions such as the NHS.

The trend towards greater inequality may go some way in explaining
this. In the table below we contrast the highest income groups, those for
whom the decade of the 1980s was, on average, a bonanza, with the
lowest income groups.

---

[*] Official statistics are not currently available for the period beyond 1987.

Changes in attitude to state welfare by income

	Poorest 35 per cent		Wealthiest 20 per cent	
	1983	1990	1983	1990
% saying the government should increase taxes to pay for extra spending	35	54	32	59
% nominating as first priority for extra spending				
Health	62	78	62	78
Education	41	47	60	72
Housing	23	35	16	13
Social security benefits	22	24	4	6
% nominating as first priority for extra spending on social benefits				
Old age pensions	68	70	62	60
Disablement benefits	59	58	60	63
Unemployment benefits	32	22	30	19
Child benefits	20	30	19	28
Single parents' benefits	18	15	26	24
% saying unemployment benefits ...				
... are too low and cause hardship	49	53	44	44
... are too high and discourage people from finding jobs	34	27	37	37

The pattern of answers shows clearly that the sharp increase in support for state welfare is by no means confined to a particular income group. The *growth* in support since 1983 for more spending is remarkably similar across the richest and poorest sections of the population. Yet, the gap between the better-off and the worst-off in support for education as a spending priority is striking, as is the greater enthusiasm of the lower income group for spending on housing, social security and pensions, and their awareness of the hardship caused by the level of unemployment benefits.

While there are clear differences in interests in relation to state welfare provision between the different income groups, it is equally clear that support for the welfare state is not confined to those on low incomes. Nor has rising inequality appeared to undermine support for state welfare in predictable directions. On the contrary, among those on the highest incomes enthusiasm for the strengthening of core welfare provision is greater in 1990 than it was in 1983.

The state of the National Health Service

During the late 1980s the NHS has served as a focus for the debate between those who favour the introduction of market forces into the welfare system and those who favour the traditional model, substantially unchanged since 1948. The repeated warnings of the British Medical Association and of the Royal Medical Colleges that the health service is severely underfunded have served to intensify public debate about its future direction. Of course, the NHS reforms were not yet in place in the spring of 1990 when fieldwork took place. Although the main provisions of the 1990 Act[2] were being hotly contested at that time, the arguments at that stage were mainly confined to ministers and health service professionals.

The public mood

Our findings indicate that the NHS - the centre-piece of the welfare state in Britain - is widely seen to be in need of improvement. Public dissatisfaction with "the way the NHS runs these days" has grown rapidly during the past decade. In 1983, only 26 per cent were 'quite' or 'very' dissatisfied; by 1986 this proportion had risen to 39 per cent, and by 1990 to 47 per cent. As the table below shows, concern about the service has increased equally among all social groups - although it remains less prevalent among Conservative identifiers than among others. Yet the better-off are in general more critical, while elderly and working-class people are less so, perhaps because their expectations are lower.

	% saying they are quite or very dissatisfied with the NHS	
	1983	1990
All	26	47
Party identification:		
Conservative	23	36
Liberal Democrat	34	52
Labour	26	59
Social class:		
I/II	30	51
III non-manual	24	43
III manual	28	51
IV/V	23	41
Age:		
18 - 34	27	53
65+	14	37
Household income:		
Poorest 35 per cent	21	45
Wealthiest 20 per cent	24	51

Areas of concern

Further questions explore which aspects of the NHS are causing most concern and which are seen to be in most need of improvement. Again, a familiar pattern emerges, with concern most marked in the areas where money has been tightest.

	% saying they are quite or very dissatisfied with each service*	
	1983	1990
Attending hospital as an out-patient	21	28
Local doctors/GPs	13	11
NHS dentists	10	11
Being in hospital as an in-patient	7	15

* We also asked about health visitors and district nurses, figures for whom are shown in Appendix III.

Public dissatisfaction, always fairly high, has risen most sharply in relation to hospital services - the sector of the NHS which has born the most severe cuts during the 1980s. Clinics were closed, and 3,000 beds were cut in the winter of 1987, and a further 3,500 beds were cut in the run-up to the internal market in 1989/90. Cash limits had not yet been applied to the GP sector.

We have asked detailed questions since 1987 about whether particular aspects of the NHS "in your area are, on the whole, satisfactory or in need of improvement". The answers show a high level of concern about waiting lists, staffing levels, casualty departments and hospital buildings, and again indicate that public anxiety is focused on the hospital sector, although there is evidence of some unease about certain aspects of the service provided by family doctors. However, as the table below shows, public dissatisfaction with some services appears to have eased slightly since the cash crisis in the run-up to the 1987 general election. In any event there has certainly been no perceptible increase in the proportions expressing concern about any of the aspects of the NHS that we nominated, despite the overall increases in concern we have noted.

Aspects of the NHS in need of improvement

	1987	1989	1990
% saying in need of a lot or some improvement			
Hospital service:			
Hospital waiting-lists for non-emergency operations	87	85	83
Waiting-time before getting appointments with hospital consultants	83	86	82
Staffing level of nurses in hospitals	75	75	72
Staffing level of doctors in hospitals	70	75	68
Hospital casualty departments	54	59	52
Condition of hospital buildings	53	61	54
Quality of medical treatment in hospitals	21	36	31
GP service:			
GPs' appointments systems	47	45	41
Amount of time GP gives to each patient	33	34	31
Being able to choose which GP to see	29	30	27
Quality of medical treatment by GPs	26	27	24

Allegiance to the service

The main obstacle for anyone who wishes to restrict access to the NHS to those who cannot afford to pay for private treatment is the enormous (and growing) popularity of state medical care in Britain, charted throughout the *British Social Attitudes* series. Yet might not growing dissatisfaction with the current state of the NHS in the end reduce public allegiance to the service and thus diminish resistance to future 'privatisation' policies? We might get a clue from examining the responses of the most dissatisfied sections of the middle classes who have most access to alternatives and who might therefore be more likely than others to abandon the health service. Are they less likely to support spending on the NHS, more likely to favour a two-tier health service, and less likely in general to place priority on the NHS as a mass resource? The table below shows the differences between the most satisfied and the most dissatisfied people (in relation to the NHS in general) within the middle classes and the working classes respectively.

% saying:	Salariat/routine non-manual		Working class	
	Very or quite satisfied with the NHS	Very dissatisfied with the NHS	Very or quite satisfied with the NHS	Very dissatisfied with the NHS
The government should increase taxes to pay for extra spending	45	75	44	70
NHS should be first priority for extra state spending	47	65	52	65
Definitely the government's responsibility to provide health care for the sick	77	93	83	91
Oppose a 'two-tier' health service	73	81	70	74

In this table we have combined response categories 'very' and 'quite' satisfied because of the small number of respondents saying they are 'very satisfied'.

Far from reducing allegiance to the NHS, dissatisfaction appears to fuel demands for extra expenditure and attention. Moreover, when we focus specifically on those with and without private medical insurance, we find that their answers are broadly similar, as the table below shows.

% saying:	Has private health insurance		Does not have private health insurance	
	Very or quite satisfied with the NHS	Very dissatisfied with the NHS	Very or quite satisfied with the NHS	Very dissatisfied with the NHS
The government should increase taxes to pay for extra spending	43	69	42	73
NHS should be first priority for extra state spending	44	71	50	64
Definitely the government's responsibility to provide health care for the sick	77	94	79	92
Oppose a 'two-tier' health service	66	71	73	80

In this table we have combined response categories 'very' and 'quite' satisfied because of the small number of respondents saying they are 'very satisfied'.

So even secure access to private medicine does not appear to lead people to abandon their allegiance to the NHS, regardless of their level of satisfaction with state medicine.

These answers suggest a strong public belief that the problems of the NHS could be alleviated by more expenditure on it (and perhaps by more public expenditure in general). In any case, most people want the longstanding pattern of state health care in Britain to be continued and improved.

We have also seen that the groups with the easiest access to private health care provision (those in the 'higher' social classes and those with private insurance) are in general as likely to want more state provision as those who would not have easy access to private medicine. In a celebrated monograph, Hirschman (1970) argued that those who are dissatisfied with centralised state provision have in principle three options: exit to the private sector (if they can afford it); voice in protesting through the political system about their concerns; and loyalty which may be the sullen refuge of those for whom there is no escape. Our findings suggest very little demand for exit from the NHS, even from those for whom departure to the private sector is a realistic option.

Conclusion

The 1980s have been a decade of rapid and profound welfare reform. The forty-year tradition of the state as the dominant agency in welfare provision has been challenged by cuts, by the privatisation of ancillary services, and by new policies which emphasise the importance of market forces in creating greater efficiency, flexibility and responsiveness to 'consumer' demands. The 1980s have also seen a widening gap emerge between the rich and poor which many people felt would erode support for the traditional pattern of state welfare provision. Yet the evidence from this series, and from the latest survey in particular, is that, far from a reduction in support for health and welfare expenditure, the 1980s have seen a strengthening of public endorsement of centralised, tax-financed state welfare.

Notes

1. The number of professional and technical staff employed in the NHS increased by 24 per cent from 65 to 81 thousand between 1981 and 1989, whereas the number of ancillary staff fell by 41 per cent from 172 to 102 thousand (The Government's Expenditure Plans: Department of Health, 1991-2 to 1993-4. Cm 1513, 1991, Table 9).
2. The three provisions of the 1990 National Health Service and Community Care Act which attracted most attention were those to allow some hospitals to 'opt out' of health authority management and become self-governing trusts; to allocate resources within the NHS through an internal market rather than by bureaucratic decision; and

to allow GPs to become budget-holders, so that they would have discretion to purchase care for their patients from the most appropriate supplier in the state or private sector.

References

CENTRAL STATISTICAL OFFICE, *Social Trends*, HMSO (1991).

HEATH, A., JOWELL, R. AND CURTICE, J., *How Britain Votes*, Pergamon Press, Oxford (1985).

HEIDENHEIMER, A., HECLO, H. and ADAMS, C., *Comparative Public Policy*, St. Martin's Press, New York (1990).

HIRSCHMAN, A., *Exit, Voice and Loyalty*, Harvard University Press, Cambridge, Mass. (1970).

LE GRAND, J., 'The state of welfare' in Hills, J. *et al* (eds), *The State of Welfare: the Welfare State in Britain since 1974*, Clarendon Press, Oxford (1990).

NATIONAL INSTITUTE FOR ECONOMIC AND SOCIAL RESEARCH, *Economic Review,* no 136, (1991).

ORGANISATION OF ECONOMIC CO-OPERATION AND DEVELOPMENT, *The Future of Social Protection*, OECD, Paris (1988).

Acknowledgement

SCPR is grateful to the Department of Health for its financial support which helps to ensure that we can continue to field questions on health care, and in particular to Anne Kauder for her help and advice.

3 Failing education?

A. H. Halsey [*]

The Education Reform Act of 1988 was, of course, in place when our 1990 fieldwork was carried out, but many of its measures had yet either to be implemented or to begin to show results. Nevertheless changes were certainly on the way. As a result, stories about educational problems in schools featured regularly on television and radio and in the newspapers, against a background of political battles between the main parties about the state of British schools and what was needed to improve them. Teachers were said to be leaving the profession in droves; there were reports that some local authorities were scouring European and Commonwealth countries to make up the shortfall. Unflattering comparisons with other countries featured prominently in the press; South Korea was held up as a reproach to British educational standards. Parents' worries about the availability of textbooks and the state of school buildings surfaced regularly. Reform of some kind, it was generally agreed, was long overdue.

The debates at that time centred around four main questions. First, there were resource problems - the budget allocated to education generally, the supply of teachers and their pay, the delegation of responsibility for finance and staffing to individual schools. Second, there were wider controversies over control - schools being allowed to opt out of Local Education Authority control and the introduction of City Technology Colleges. Third, there were quarrels about assessment - the reliability of tests and examinations, the feasibility and purpose of testing

---

[*] Professor Emeritus, Nuffield College, Oxford

young children, and the perennial problems of children's reading standards and school discipline. Fourth, there was a continuing debate about access to higher education, including methods of financing students.

Education was, in short, in turmoil. The Labour Party had pinned its flag firmly to the mast of education and training, as the ship to carry the UK into a new era as a 'world-class economy'; Neil Kinnock confirmed priority for education as the core of their political and economic 'big idea' for the 1990s. Mrs Thatcher, still Prime Minister, took up the challenge thus securing education a place at the centre of the forthcoming electoral battleground, hinting that a school's voucher scheme might be in the Conservative manifesto. This was repudiated by the incoming Secretary of State for Education and Science in November 1990. Subsequently, Mrs Thatcher's replacement by John Major, with his much-publicised six O'levels and his declared aspiration towards a classless society, brought a decidedly more conciliatory tone towards the educational establishment, although the new Secretary of State for Education was expected to be an aggressive reformer, following his record in the Department of Health. These events took place after our fieldwork period. Nonetheless, policy initiatives on education and the media response to them must have been much in the public mind during the fieldwork period in the spring and early summer of 1990.

Against this background, the 1990 *British Social Attitudes* survey might have been expected to show movements in public attitudes on those educational issues which we had covered in previous surveys in the series. In a chapter in *The 5th Report*, on the 1987 survey, Paul Flather interpreted the trends as generally favourable to the policy aims of the Conservative government. He anticipated support for many of the measures which were to be included in the 1988 Education Reform Act and he looked forward to the results of the present survey as an indicator of public approval or disapproval of the new measures.

Resource allocation

Over half the respondents name education as first or second priority for extra government spending, with an increase of 10 percentage points since the first survey in 1983, bringing it close behind health and far ahead of any other areas of expenditure. This provides evidence of an increase in concern in recent years about education. Nonetheless, as the table below shows, education scores no higher in 1990 as the top priority than it did in 1983. Health still dominates as an issue of public concern, partly reflecting its universal relevance.

Priorities for extra government spending

	First priority 1983 %	First priority 1990 %	First or second priority 1983 %	First or second priority 1990 %
Health	37	56	63	81
Education	24	24	50	60
Housing	7	6	20	20
Social security benefits	6	5	12	12
Help for industry	16	3	29	6

In 1990 as in 1983, all the main population sub-groups still put health first. Although better qualified respondents are more likely than others to give first priority to education - 31 per cent of those with A'levels or higher qualifications compared with 21 per cent of the less well qualified - even graduates favour health (48 per cent) over education (32 per cent), a marked shift in priorities among this group since 1987. Labour Party identifiers are still less likely to give education absolute priority because health is such a dominant issue among Labour identifiers. Thus, Liberal Democrats are the most likely to choose education as first or second priority (69 per cent) compared with 62 per cent among Conservative identifiers and 57 per cent among Labour identifiers. Social class is positively correlated with support for education spending. The middle classes have more to gain from it for their children. Thus more than a quarter (27 per cent) of those in the non-manual classes compared with less than a quarter (21 per cent) of those in the manual classes give education the first priority for extra government spending.

We also asked, in previous years, about priorities for extra spending *within* education. As we see from the table below, the order of priority has changed little since 1983. First priority still goes to less able children with special needs and to secondary school children respectively. Nursery and pre-school children are seen as a lower but fast growing priority while the priority accorded to primary school spending has remained stable at around 15 per cent. Less than one in ten respondents saw, or see, higher education as the first priority for extra spending.

First priority for extra spending on education

	1983 %	1985 %	1987 %	1990 %
Less able children with special needs	32	34	28	29
Secondary school children	29	31	37	27
Primary school children	16	13	15	15
Nursery or pre-school children	10	10	8	16
Students at colleges, universities or polytechnics	9	9	9	9

While the priority attached to additional spending on secondary schools rose between 1983 and 1987 mainly at the expense, it seemed, of expenditure on less able children with special needs, it now seems to have fallen victim to the sharp increase in the priority given to expenditure on nursery and pre-school children: thus the proportion according first priority to expenditure on secondary school children has fallen back to around the level it was at in 1983. (As we shall see, this hardly seems to reflect the high level of concern felt about the performance of secondary schools.)

Why this new pattern? The increase in the priority accorded to nursery and pre-school provision may be partly attributable to the growth in public awareness of the low level of provision for childcare in Britain compared with many of our competitors. There is also concern among employers about the increasing urgency of recruiting a higher proportion of women into the workforce in view of the forecast reduction in the number of school leavers for the rest of the decade (NEDO 1989). Supporters of the Conservative Party are the least enthusiastic about nursery and pre-school provision (12 per cent nominated it their first priority) while Liberal Democrat identifiers are the keenest (22 per cent) (see also Chapter 7). Graduates are also especially enthusiastic (28 per cent), reflecting, it may be guessed, the greater involvement of their families in a labour market which offers relatively high rewards, thus providing more incentive to return to work early after childbirth, which would be facilitated by improved pre-school provision.

Age and sex differences in attitudes on this issue are also marked. Respondents in the main child-rearing age group (25-34) are more strongly supportive of pre-school provision than those either younger or older: 22 per cent name this their first priority compared with 16 per cent overall. And while women are only marginally keener than men on nursery provision (18 per cent against 14 per cent), it is when we look at age and sex together that the largest differences emerge. Almost two in five (38 per cent) of younger women (aged 18-34) name pre-school provision as their first or second priority compared with just 23 per cent of their male peers, and with 29 per cent of older women (aged 35 or over).

First or second priority for extra spending on education

	Men			Women		
	18-34	35-54	55+	18-34	35-54	55+
	%	%	%	%	%	%
Less able children with special needs	47	50	57	59	58	65
Secondary school children	61	58	43	46	49	39
Primary school children	32	35	39	30	33	30
Nursery or pre-school children	23	25	24	38	30	28
Students at colleges, universities or polytechnics	29	26	24	22	24	22

Thus even among those men in the main child-rearing age group support for pre-school provision is much weaker than among their female counterparts, presumably because responsibility for childcare continues to devolve mostly on women.

Reassuringly, perhaps, particularly high first priority support (29 per cent) for nursery school provision comes from parents of children under five years old, just as the highest priority support (20 per cent) for primary schools comes from parents of children aged 5-11, and the highest priority (38 per cent) for secondary schools comes from parents of children aged 12-16. Households with no children accord especially high first priority (31 per cent) to children with special needs.

Improving schools

Since 1983 we have regularly asked respondents which of a number of factors was most important for improving education in state primary schools and secondary schools. Priorities have not changed much over the years. As the table below shows, the major priority for primary schools continues to be for smaller classes, followed by more books and equipment, and more emphasis on developing the child's skills and interests - all of which require large additional resources. In contrast, government preoccupations have been with teaching basic skills such as English and mathematics, with parental involvement in governing bodies, with testing, and especially with discussion between parents and teachers, none of which finds an echo in public priorities.

Most important factors* for improving education in ...

	Primary schools		Secondary schools	
	1983	1990	1983	1990
	%	%	%	%
Smaller classes	31	28	10	10
More resources for books and equipment	15	19	10	13
Developing skills and interests	19	18	13	10
Stricter discipline	11	9	19	18
Better pay for teachers	1	7	1	7
More discussion between parents and teachers	9	5	5	3
More training and preparation for jobs	1	1	27	21
Preparation for exams	1	1	7	8

* We also asked about better buildings, more involvement of parents in governing bodies, more emphasis on arts subjects, more emphasis on mathematics and more emphasis on English, but since none of these was chosen as most important by more than three per cent for either type of school, percentages are not shown here.

The only notable reflection of policy debate in public concern is with better pay for teachers. In 1983 it was not an issue at all; now it appears to be an emergent one, though, at seven per cent, still small. Nevertheless, the shift is made more remarkable by the evidence below that people generally overestimate the progress - or rather underestimate the regress - of teachers' pay.

Support for smaller classes in primary schools is common across all groups, but is particularly strong among Conservative identifiers (31 per cent), parents of children under 12 (34 per cent), and those with a professional qualification or degree (34 per cent). Emphasis on provision of more books and equipment is more characteristic of younger respondents, aged 18-24 (27 per cent), who are perhaps remembering their own experience, and of Labour identifiers (22 per cent). Older people, especially those aged 65 or over, tend to favour stricter discipline (17 per cent), while younger respondents stress the development of children's skills and interests (29 per cent of 18-24 year olds). Raising teachers' pay is encouraged a little more by opposition party identifiers (8 per cent) than by Conservatives (5 per cent).

The pattern of preferences with respect to improving secondary schooling is markedly different. Here two main concerns emerge: training for the labour market and discipline within schools, with the greatest emphasis on training and preparation for jobs (named by one in five respondents). However the strength of that priority has declined in 1990 compared with 1983, perhaps because the labour market for young people was improving somewhat at that time.

Nearly as high a proportion (18 per cent) give priority to discipline in secondary schools. This probably reflects anxiety arising from stories of truancy, of aggression against teachers, of bullying, and of a general failure to maintain order and authority among adolescents. This emphasis on discipline in secondary schools is much higher among less well-qualified respondents (19 per cent) than among those with a degree (4 per cent), among Conservative than Labour identifiers (22 per cent against 14 per cent), and among those aged 35 or over than among those under 35 (21 per cent against 11 per cent).

The general trend since the survey series began in 1983 has been towards an increasing scatter of concern over all the factors we have tacitly defined in our list of questions as the determinants of the quality of educational life in state secondary schools. Even so, the pattern of preferences for improvement does not, once more, seem to match the priorities of the government's reform programme. Neither parental involvement in decision-making in schools nor the necessity of testing standards of literacy and numeracy are dominant in public concerns about education. On the contrary, the most conspicuously rising popular preference is for better pay for teachers (though admittedly this is still only a lower order priority). Still, the unpopularity of the teaching unions, arising from the chronic battles in the 1980s over pay negotiation, may now be receding. Though there was a one day strike by NAS/UWT in April 1990 and the union warned of the possibility of selective strikes if redundancies followed from implementing the programme for Local Management of Schools; in the same month the NUT voted for possible industrial action at its annual conference. But also in April 1990, the government offered to reinstate national collective pay bargaining and union leaders welcomed the offer while complaining about the strings attached. In July 1990, the then Secretary of State for Education announced that local authorities would offer local pay deals to counteract teacher shortages. (In November a School Teachers' Pay and Conditions Bill, to restore to teachers limited rights to negotiate pay and give local authorities freedom to negotiate locally, was introduced in Parliament.)

The declarations from all quarters, including government, that teaching should be a more valued profession may be bearing fruit. Unsurprisingly, it is graduate respondents who most frequently mention increased teacher salaries as first priority (20 per cent for secondary schools) but the important point is that concern about remuneration of teachers, while not widespread, has risen and continues to rise since these surveys began in 1983.

Selectivity and control of the curriculum

Questions about private schooling asked in previous rounds were not repeated in 1990. Meanwhile the purchase of private education has continued to grow, albeit slowly, from its numerically small if socially important base of six per cent of school children in 1980 to over seven per cent in 1990. Trends in attitudes to private education will be discussed in future reports in this series.

Against the background of government encouragement to schools to 'opt out' of the control of Local Educational Authorities (LEAs) we continued to monitor attitudes to the organisation of secondary education. Schools which 'opt out' will be able to change their status (sooner than envisaged), a provision which is seen by some as a return to selectivity by the back door. A trickle of schools decided to apply for grant-maintained status during 1990, the number rising to fifty by October of that year. Removal of the restriction of opting out for primary schools with less than 300 pupils made a further 15,000 schools eligible. With incentives increased towards the end of 1990, including doubling of the transition grant to a maximum of £60,000 per school, a rise in opting out was anticipated for 1991. In April 1990, during our fieldwork, the then Secretary of State for Education was presiding over the transfer of financial and managerial control from LEAs to school governing bodies and complaining that LEAs, Conservative-controlled as well as others, were in some cases delegating as little as 60 per cent of their education budgets to the schools. At the end of 1990 education ministers were planning new regulations design to force LEAs to hand over more money to the direct control of schools and to give schools the right to use the private sector to provide services previously monopolised by the local authorities.

In 1990, we repeated two of our relevant standard questions; about selective *versus* comprehensive education and about control over decision-making. Respondents were asked, after a short explanation of the two systems:

> *... on balance, which system do you think provides the best all round education for secondary school children ... a system of grammar and secondary modern schools or a system of comprehensive schools?*

Since 1984, when the question was first asked, the proportions favouring either system have oscillated, but with a slight trend upwards in favour of the comprehensive system. However, comprehensive education still fails to capture the allegiance of even one half of the population. In 1990, preference for a binary system of grammar and secondary modern schools (48 per cent) is more or less the same as that for comprehensives, (45 per cent), compared with 50 per cent and 40 per cent respectively in 1984. This more or less even division in public opinion is perhaps surprising given the transformation of policy during the 1960s and 1970s which had placed the vast majority of state secondary school children in comprehensives. By 1976, three-quarters of pupils in state secondary schools were in comprehensives; in 1984 the percentage was 82 (and in Scotland and Wales 96 per cent). The division in public opinion may reflect more a general sense of dissatisfaction with state secondary schools, most of which are comprehensive, than a real enthusiasm for selection and the eleven-plus, but maybe not. It also may reflect people's knowledge and experience. Thus, there is majority support for comprehensives among people aged under 35; older people who did not go to comprehensive schools are less likely to support the comprehensive system.

Not surprisingly, Labour Party identifiers are much more in favour of the comprehensive system than are Conservatives (58 per cent against 28 per cent), with opinion among Liberal Democrats much closer to that of Labour supporters on this issue (54 per cent). It is notable, however, that as many as 35 per cent of Labour identifiers prefer a selective system. Similarly, as might be expected, selective education is preferred heavily by those who had themselves been to independent schools (64 per cent compared with 44 per cent of those who had not).

Since our 1990 survey, the rules for 'opting out' of LEA control have now been relaxed, and those schools choosing to do this can now apply adopt selective admission criteria much sooner than was stipulated when the Education Reform Act was passed. The re-introduction of selectivity of admission to many schools, which will inevitably create losers as well as winners, may begin to influence attitudes to the relative merits of selectivity, and we shall, of course, continue to monitor trends on this question.

Controversies over the national curriculum continued during our 1990 survey. That these should be such a standardisation was agreed by all political parties. But exactly what the curriculum should be, how it should be tested and by whom validated was more controversial. One focus of division was over the testing of seven year olds (Stage 1). Critics felt this would disrupt classroom teaching and that it was in any case underfunded. Another focus was on Stage 4 (14-16 year olds) where the demand for a broad curriculum of ten subjects threatened to overload the timetable and to clash with the needs of pupils preparing for GCSE. And a third debate centred similarly on the renewed demand for a wider syllabus for sixth formers.

On the issue of central and local decision-making about curricula the question we put was:

> *Do you think that what is taught in schools should be up to the **local** education authority to decide or should **central** government have the final say?*

In 1984 we found a small majority in favour of the LEAs on this issue (53 per cent), but it has disappeared by 1990 (46 per cent), while support for central control has risen sharply from 39 per cent in 1984 to 48 per cent in 1990. Devolving and centralising sentiments are thus fairly evenly balanced nowadays. But it is difficult to interpret attitudes on this issue against the backdrop of the abolition of the Inner London Education Authority (and transfer of its schools to the inner London boroughs) in April 1990, and of the more general attacks by the government on local government powers during the 1980s, which were far from over by the time of the 1990 survey. Indeed the poll tax controversy was still at its height.

Not surprisingly, therefore, those who identify with the Conservative Party are the main contributors to the centralising impulse in education - 60 per cent compared with 38 per cent of Labour supporters and 49 per cent of Liberal Democrats. However, Conservative identifiers have tended to favour central control since we first began asking this question in 1983, and their views have since remained unchanged. Among Liberal Democrats and Labour identifiers, however, there has been a shift away from the LEAs in favour of central control, that is towards the government's position, as shown below.

Control of the curriculum

	Party identification					
	Conservative		Liberal Democrat		Labour	
	1987	1990	1987	1990	1987	1990
	%	%	%	%	%	%
Should be decided by:						
Local education authority	34	35	51	47	62	57
Central government	62	60	44	49	31	38

Respondents without formal educational qualifications are more in favour of local control (57 per cent) than those with some qualifications (39 per cent), as are women, (50 per cent against 41 per cent of men). In contrast, those who attended private schools are more centralist (59 per cent against 46 per cent of those who attended state schools). The national curriculum is, of course, imposed only on state schools and not on the independent sector, but this group may in effect simply be more distanced from local education authorities anyway. Parents of children aged under 16 are more in favour of central government control (53 per cent), than are other respondents (46 per cent). Interestingly, respondents who are themselves school teachers also favour central control somewhat more than other respondents (54 per cent compared with 48 per cent).

Examinations and testing

The Education Reform Act of 1988 was designed in part to improve national standards by the systematic testing of children at each of the key stages of their education. The arrangements had not been completed at the time of the 1990 fieldwork, but controversy, especially over the testing of seven year-olds, was heated. The new GCSE examinations had been put in place in 1987 so that there had been some time for both parents and teachers to assess them. Their purpose was to draw more secondary pupils into a certification net and out of the 'bottom 40 per cent' who had hitherto left school with no paper qualifications to present to prospective employers. Accordingly, as in 1987, we included two pertinent questions on examinations.

First we asked how far respondents agreed or disagreed that "formal exams are the best way of judging the ability of pupils". Opinion about the validity or legitimacy of formal examinations in secondary schools as a way of judging the ability of pupils remains somewhat divided, as it was in 1987, but there is a decided and growing leaning towards approval (48 per cent approve, 33 per cent disapprove). It might have been expected that approval would have been stronger among the more highly educated, that is those who had themselves been more successful in passing academic examinations. But this is not so; indeed in 1990, support for exams is lower among respondents with degrees (42 per cent) than among those without formal qualifications (51 per cent). Perhaps it is not so surprising that paper qualifications are valued most by those who lack them. What did emerge again, in 1990 as in 1987, is that older respondents have more faith than younger respondents do in formal examinations: approval increases with distance from the ordeal, but it is also a function of fewer qualifications and, perhaps, experience of the effects of their lack.

We also asked for opinions on the view that "so much attention is given to examination results that a pupil's everyday classroom work counts for too little". Here, the weight of opinion is still heavily though decreasingly towards agreement. So criticism of formal examinations is also less strong than it was in 1987, suggesting again that the government's efforts to reassert the legitimacy of formal examinations may have found some converts. Nonetheless, greater support for classwork than for exams is common to all age groups, even (barely) among the oldest respondents. In contrast, however, graduates and those with professional qualifications are more supportive of formal examinations as opposed to classwork than are the less qualified (55 per cent of them agree with the critical statement, as against 65 per cent of the unqualified).

A more strongly held criticism of secondary schools (and one which is also relevant to the issues of examinations and testing) is that "on the whole, pupils are too young when they have to decide which subjects to specialise in". A clear majority (two-thirds of the population) take this critical view of secondary school organisation. But the thrust of the national curriculum reforms was to ensure that both those who went on to higher examination and those who entered directly into the labour market were sufficiently widely educated to form a workforce capable of adapting to modern needs, including transfer from one occupation to another.

We cannot know from the survey findings (but could reasonably suspect) that enforced early specialisation, being debated in 1990 in the context of renewed attempts to broaden the sixth-form curriculum, may be at least one of the factors accounting for the majority opposition (also shown below) to raising the school leaving age. In addition, many teachers as well as parents were reacting to the discontent of adolescents who saw the last years of compulsory schooling as custodial rather than as preparation for adult work. Meanwhile, others were keen to see scarce resources spent on new provisions for 16-19 year olds which would induce partnership between schools and workplaces - a mix of learning and work experience. Although, this opposition declined somewhat between 1987 and 1990, still only one-quarter of respondents believe that "the present law allows pupils to leave school when they are too young".

			% agreeing	% disagreeing
Formal exams are the best **way of judging the ability** **of pupils**	1987	%	44	38
	1990	%	47	33
A pupil's everyday classroom **work counts for too little**	1987	%	70	17
	1990	%	62	19
Pupils are too young when they **have to decide which subjects** **to specialise in**	1987	%	63	20
	1990	%	66	16
The present law allows pupils **to leave school when they are** **too young**	1987	%	25	53
	1990	%	26	47

How then can we summarise current attitudes towards the performance of state secondary schools? The picture in 1990 was on the whole a discouraging one and little changed since 1987, despite the 1988 Education Reform Act. It is true that state secondary schools were thought (by a bare majority) to be doing very well, or quite well, in teaching young people basic skills such as reading, writing and mathematics, a view held most strongly among recent pupils, 18-24 year olds. But we should perhaps remember that this limited cheerfulness was expressed before a spate of reports in the mass media of poor standards in many schools, and dissatisfaction among employers about the standard of applicants.

What is most dispiriting in the light of the consensus on Britain's need for a 'world-class' labour force, so vigorously demanded by both the Confederation of British Industry (CBI) and the Labour Party, is that a sizeable majority (61 per cent) of the population still sees schools as ineffective in preparing young people for work. Although this proportion has declined slightly since 1987, an almost identical majority believes that state secondary schools "fail to bring out young people's natural abilities". In partial mitigation, perhaps, a small majority (57 per cent, much the same as in 1987) does believe that schools nowadays teach the 'three Rs' well; yet, alarmingly, 41 per cent still disagree.

How well do state secondary schools nowadays ...			Very well	Quite well	Not very well	Not at all well
... prepare young people for work?	1987	%	2	27	54	15
	1990	%	2	35	50	11
... teach young people basic skills such as reading, writing and maths?	1987	%	10	46	31	11
	1990	%	9	48	33	8
... bring out young people's natural abilities?	1987	%	3	32	49	15
	1990	%	4	32	50	12

The status of teachers

Nor is this the whole of a gloomy story. The belief that classroom behaviour has deteriorated over the last ten years is held by over four in five respondents. Respect for school-teachers, by both parents and pupils, is thought by overwhelming majorities to have declined over the last ten years. Graduates are especially likely to believe this. Teachers are thought to be less dedicated to their jobs and, in the state schools, to be faced by more difficult problems of classroom behaviour. Furthermore, one of the largest changes since these questions were first asked in 1987, is a *rise* in the proportion who believe that the job of secondary school-teachers has in general become more difficult, from 62 per cent in 1987 to 70 per cent in 1990 (see DES, November 1990).

State secondary schools:

	% saying *better* than 10 years ago		% saying *worse* than 10 years ago	
	1987	1990	1987	1990
Teachers' pay	55	43	24	34
Classroom behaviour	2	3	86	83

	% saying *more* than 10 years ago		% saying *less* than 10 years ago	
	1987	1990	1987	1990
Parents' respect for teachers	5	7	71	65
Pupils' respect for teachers	2	3	88	83
Dedication of teachers	6	9	60	53
Difficulty of teachers' job	62	70	22	15

Moreover, a much higher proportion now than in 1987 (34 per cent as opposed to 24 per cent) believe that teachers' pay has deteriorated in the last decade (though a majority still thinks that it has improved), which accords with the unions' position. They claim that in real terms as well as relative to other professions, teachers have not kept up. The graduates in our sample are much more likely than those who are less well-qualified to believe that teachers' pay has declined (67 per cent compared with 32 per cent), but this is influenced by the fact that more than one in five (22 per cent) are themselves school teachers.

Higher education

Great prominence was being given in 1990 to plans to expand higher education, partly in response to vigorously expressed demands by the CBI and the educational establishment for a widening of opportunities. It is therefore no surprise to find increasing support for the view that opportunities to go on to a university, polytechnic or college should be improved. Moreover, as many as one-third of respondents now believe that opportunities should be increased a lot. Graduates (52 per cent) and Labour Party identifiers (41 per cent) are particularly enthusiastic about expansion. Younger respondents (aged under 45, particularly women) are more in favour than their elders (36 per cent against 27 per cent). Rise in support for expansion of higher education has been apparent among the supporters of all three main political parties, though among Conservatives the movement since 1983 has been smaller and more volatile.

Opportunities for higher education should be:

	1983 %	1985 %	1987 %	1990 %
Increased a lot	22	25	29	32
Increased a little	22	24	23	19
About right level now	49	42	42	43
Reduced a lot or a little	5	5	3	2

The government has recently set a target of 30 per cent participation by young people in higher education by the end of the century. On our evidence, there is widespread public support for expanded opportunities so that such a target by no means over-reaches popular aspiration. There remains, however, the closely related question of how this expansion is to be funded. The government in 1990 was offering no guarantee of state support along traditional lines (DES, May 1991). There are still questions about all aspects of financing higher education amid rumours of budgetary crises and even bankruptcy in some universities, polytechnics and colleges.

Meanwhile, the government's drive is towards self-funding by students themselves in the form of loans rather than grants. On this issue we have trend figures since 1983, which show clearly that this policy runs strongly counter to public opinion. Indeed, support for loans has declined steadily since 1983 and appears still to be falling, as the table below shows.

% in favour of:	1983	1984	1987	1990
	%	%	%	%
Grants	57	60	65	71
Loans	38	34	31	24

In 1989 the grants to students in universities, polytechnics and colleges was £2,155 and students had the right to apply for having housing benefit and unemployment benefit in the summer vacation. In 1990 they lost the right to claim any benefit, had to start paying the poll tax and saw grants frozen at £2,265 indefinitely. The loans scheme which started in October 1990 gave students the opportunity to borrowing up to £420 a year at a rate of interest equal to inflation, (they would begin repayment of a total debt of over £1,000 in the April following graduation). After rejection from the 'high street' banks, the loans scheme was taken up by a Glasgow-based student loans company. By the end of 1990 it was unclear how successful the scheme would be, though unlikely that it would come up to government expectations. A recent survey found that more than a fifth of students in polytechnics and colleges were doing paid work during term-time (Independent, August 1991).

Even Conservative Party identifiers, the least enthusiastic about grants in 1983 (51 per cent in favour of a grants-only system), have increased in their support (to 58 per cent), though more cautiously than have Labour identifiers (from 66 per cent to 83 per cent) or Liberal Democrats (from 58 per cent to 75 per cent).

Conclusion

In the 1980s the Conservatives increasingly defined the terms of the educational debate, and this served to polarise opinion along party lines. Our survey data show that the views of Labour Party identifiers on most of the educational issues we addressed have continued to diverge from those of Conservatives and to converge with those of Liberal Democrats. At the same time, there are increasingly widespread public worries about a number of aspects of education. Large class sizes in state primary and secondary schools, shortages of books and equipment, early specialisation, lack of discipline in the classroom, perceived disrespect for teachers and their declining real pay are all focal points of concern. Public perceptions of the performance of secondary schools in particular are decidedly gloomy.

Meanwhile, the purchase of private education is still on the increase, despite its rising real cost, no doubt in part explained by the malaise seen to be overtaking state schooling. In our 1987 report we anticipated that the then forthcoming Education Reform Act would help (to an extent at least) to alleviate public anxieties. But our 1990 findings do not, on the whole, confirm this prediction, even though the Act's emphasis on both the importance of exams and on the national curriculum seem to have struck a chord in public opinion. In general, however, the education system is seen to be in crisis, and its problems unaffected so far by educational reform. In fairness, however, the most recent reforms have yet to feed through into the system if they are to produce results. Education has meanwhile become a major party political issue in a way that it has not been for at least four decades.

References

CONFEDERATION OF BRITISH INDUSTRY (CBI), *Towards a Skills Revolution,* CBI, London (1989).

DEPARTMENT OF EDUCATION AND SCIENCE (DES), *Violence to Staff in the Education Sector,* HMSO (November 1990).

DES, *Higher Education: a New Framework,* HMSO, Cm 1541, London (May 1991).

DES, EMPLOYMENT DEPARTMENT AND WELSH OFFICE *Education and Training for the 21st Century,* HMSO, Cm 1536, 2 vols, London (May 1991).

HM SENIOR CHIEF INSPECTOR OF SCHOOLS, *Standards in Education 1989/90,* DES, London (1990).

NATIONAL ECONOMIC DEVELOPMENT OFFICE (NEDO), *Defusing the Demographic Time Bomb,* NEDO, London (October 1989).

SMITHERS, A. and ROBINSON, P., *Increasing Participation in Higher Education,* BT Educational Services and School of Education, University of Manchester (1989).

4 Justice and the law in Northern Ireland

Tony Gallagher *

The need for emergency legislation arises when a state is under threat. Under such conditions, two priorities of a democratic government - safeguarding the civil liberties of its citizens and maintaining the integrity of the state - almost inevitably come into conflict (O'Boyle, 1977). This creates a dilemma: if emergency measures are not put in place quickly enough or are not effective enough, then government may begin to lose control; alternatively, if the measures used are too severe, then the problem may be exacerbated and sections of the population may become alienated.

O'Boyle suggests that emergency legislation has three main characteristics. First, there is a concentration of power at the centre. Secondly, executive power increases through for example enhanced powers of arrest and detention. Thirdly, there is a curtailment of constitutional and legal constraints, such as the establishment of special courts, derogation from established human rights conventions or a weakening of legal protection, say for suspects.

Another danger is the possibility of the abuse of emergency powers, for instance to suppress 'legitimate' opposition. As important, perhaps, there is also a danger of habituation - on the part of both government and the public. Thus government may come to use emergency powers simply because they seem to work, while public opinion may become desensitised to human rights abuses. Moreover, an over-zealous use of emergency

---

* Research Officer in the Centre for the Study of Conflict, University of Ulster.

powers or an over-long period in which they operate may in the end jeopardise public confidence in the security forces.

Ample evidence has been accumulated over the years to suggest that many Catholics lack confidence in the administration of justice in Northern Ireland. For example, as Smith (1987) argued, confidence decreased as the security forces dealt with the rising tide of protests in the 1970s. A 1974 survey found 88 per cent of Belfast Catholics who believed people did not get a fair trial in Northern Ireland, compared with 27 per cent of Belfast Protestants (Boyle, Hadden and Hillyard, 1975, p.148). In 1971, Catholics opposed to the introduction of internment without trial withdrew from public bodies and widely supported a rent and rates strike. In response, among the package of reforms initiated in the early years of the troubles was a restructuring and reorganisation of policing and security police (Brewer, 1991; Ryder, 1989). More recently, Article 8 of the 1985 Anglo-Irish Agreement explicitly recognised the importance of measures designed to ensure public confidence in the administration of justice.[1]

The 1990 *British Social Attitudes* survey included questions on fear of crime, attitudes to the police, the legal system and a range of civil libertarian issues. The *Northern Ireland Social Attitudes* (*NISA*) survey fielded all these questions, together with additional ones relevant to the troubles. The two surveys thus provide an opportunity to assess public confidence in the administration of justice on both sides of the Irish Sea. This is the main focus of this chapter. But first we will look briefly at some of the main conclusions drawn from the 1989 surveys (Curtice and Gallagher, 1990) in the light of the latest data.

The religious and constitutional background

Religion

The 1989 surveys pointed to the much greater significance of religion (affiliation and practice) in Northern Ireland than in Britain. This is confirmed in the 1990 survey. We also suggested there had been a decline in the importance of religion in Northern Ireland over the two previous decades. For instance, in 1968 and again in 1978 three per cent or less of respondents professed *no* religious affiliation (Rose, 1971; Moxon-Browne, 1983). By 1989 and 1990 these proportions had risen to 12 and 13 per cent respectively (see, however, Note 2). So this pattern of decline is also confirmed. However, nearly all of the 13 per cent in *NISA* claiming no religious affiliation themselves say that they were *brought up* in one religion or another.

We also noted that among Catholics there had been a long-term decline in *regular* church attendance, and that more Protestants than before had ceased attending religious services *at all*. Again, this pattern is confirmed in 1990. Nonetheless, regular church attendance among both Protestants and Catholics remains much higher than in Britain.

Finally, the higher levels of non-attendance among young people in 1989 is found also in 1990. Around one in five aged under 35 in both years profess never to attend church, and only 47 per cent of the under-35s (in 1990) claim to be regular attenders (attending church once a week or more often) compared with 58 per cent of the those aged 55 and over.

So our conclusion based on the 1989 results that religion was in decline in Northern Ireland is confirmed by the 1990 survey. Further *NISA* surveys will show whether this trend will have wider social and political impacts.

The state of the Union

In 1989 we suggested that the Union between Northern Ireland and Britain rested on "somewhat shaky foundations" (Curtice and Gallagher, 1990, p.204). Although a majority in Northern Ireland wishes the province to remain a part of the United Kingdom, this view was not shared by most people in Britain. Furthermore, many more people in Britain favoured the withdrawal of British troops from the province than did those living in Northern Ireland. In 1990, there is little sign of change on either count:

	In favour of ...	
	...reunification of Ireland	...withdrawal of British troops
Britain	%	%
1989	55	59
1990	56	60
Northern Ireland	%	%
1989	24	33
1990	25	30

Moreover, within Northern Ireland the religious divide remains as wide as ever: in 1990, 55 per cent of Catholics favour reunification with the rest of Ireland, as against 93 per cent of Protestants who do not, and wish to maintain the Union. So Catholic opinion is not as unanimous as is Protestant opinion on this issue: one-third of Northern Irish Catholics wish to maintain the Union. Similarly, while 56 per cent of Northern Irish Catholics support the withdrawal of British troops, only 14 per cent of Protestants would endorse such a move. So the differences within Northern Ireland on its constitutional future remain at least as wide as the differences in public opinion between Northern Ireland and Britain.

In 1990 we asked two further questions on the consequences of withdrawing British troops from Northern Ireland:

> *If British troops were withdrawn from Northern Ireland, do you think there would be **more** or **less** bloodshed in **the short-term**, or would it make no difference? IF MORE/LESS: A lot (more/less) bloodshed or a little (more/less)?*
>
> *And in the **long-term**, if British troops were withdrawn, do you think there would be **more** or **less** bloodshed or would it make no difference? IF MORE/LESS: A lot (more/less) bloodshed or a little (more/less)?*

Most people believe that withdrawal would lead to an increase in bloodshed *in the short-term.*

% saying (in 1990) withdrawal of British troops would lead to ...

	... a lot/ a little more bloodshed ...	... no difference ...	... a lot/ a little less bloodshed ...
... in the short-term:			
Britain	% 57	23	16
Northern Ireland	% 70	19	8
... in the long-term:			
Britain	% 25	27	39
Northern Ireland	% 44	24	28

Views on the *long-term* consequences of withdrawing the troops are more mixed. In Northern Ireland the predominant view is that it would make the situation no better, with 44 per cent saying it would lead to more bloodshed. In Britain, although a quarter believe that withdrawing the troops would lead to more bloodshed, the largest group, nearly two in five, believe it would lead to *less* bloodshed in the long-term. Within Northern Ireland a majority of Protestants (58 per cent) believe that withdrawal of the troops would lead to an increase in bloodshed in the long-term, a view held by only 22 per cent of Catholics.

Just as there are striking differences in views about the constitutional future of the province, so there are important differences both within Northern Ireland and between Britain and Northern Ireland on the perceived consequences of British troop withdrawal.

Crime and the administration of justice

Among the issues covered by the 1990 surveys are law and order and the operation of the legal system. In both surveys (British and Northern

Irish) we asked respondents about their fear of crime, their perception of its extent and their attitudes towards, and contact with, the police. In Northern Ireland we extended the range of questions to cover issues relating to security, and where necessary we made a distinction between 'sectarian' and 'non-sectarian' crime.

Perceptions and experience of crime

Northern Ireland has an image abroad as a dangerous place; in the media Belfast and Beirut have been alliteratively coupled, although the scale of violence in the two cities is hardly comparable.[3] Given this popular image, it may come as a surprise that, in comparison with people in Britain, somewhat fewer people in Northern Ireland think that certain sorts of crime are common in their area.

% saying that in their area, it is very or fairly common ...	Northern Ireland[*]	Britain
... for people's homes to be burgled	31	45
... to have deliberate damage done by vandals	29	41
... for people to be attacked and have things stolen from them in the street	5	12

* In Northern Ireland, these questions were described as relating to 'non-sectarian' crime, that is, crime not directly related to the troubles.

Not only is the perception of the level of these sorts of crime markedly lower in Northern Ireland than in Britain, but so also is people's expressed fear of crime. While 63 per cent in Northern Ireland say they worry about the possibility that they, or people they live with, might be victims of (non-sectarian) crime, 76 per cent of British respondents express concern. Moreover, for those who do express fear of crime, rather more British respondents say that it is a 'big worry' (23 per cent in Britain compared with 18 per cent in Northern Ireland). Similarly, while three-quarters of Northern Irish citizens feel 'very' or 'fairly' safe walking alone in their area at night, this is true for fewer than 60 per cent of British citizens.

Public perceptions of crime rates in Northern Ireland are not belied by official statistics. These suggest that Northern Ireland's overall reported crime rate is lower than that in 40 of the 42 police authority areas of England and Wales (Northern Ireland Office, 1988). A survey in 1988 indicated that Northern Ireland had the lowest proportion of victims of crime of the fourteen jurisdictions[*] examined (Barclay, 1991).

Of course, Northern Ireland's image abroad is based largely on the religious and social conflicts that have continued unabated for over twenty years. Between mid-July 1969 and mid-1989, 2,763 people were killed as a consequence of the troubles (McKeown, 1989), a rate equivalent to approximately 100,000 deaths in Britain. However, this bald statistic disguises a very uneven distribution of killings within the province: thus, over this period 39 per cent of deaths occurred within the two Westminster parliamentary constituencies of West and North Belfast, which together account for only 11 per cent of the electorate of Northern Ireland. So, despite the overall high level of violence in Northern Ireland, there are many areas of the province that remain largely untouched by it. In support, a survey in 1986 found that fewer than 5 per cent of Protestants and fewer than 10 per cent of Catholics had witnessed a shooting, an explosion or a hijacking. In contrast, among *Belfast* Catholics the proportion who had witnessed a shooting was 16 per cent, an explosion 20 per cent and a hijacking 25 per cent (Smith, 1987).

Another, even more chilling side to these experiences, reported in the same survey, is that 47 per cent of people in Northern Ireland had known personally a fatal victim of political violence, and in nearly a quarter of these cases it was a relative. Again there are marked geographical differences, and it remains the case that relatively few people in Northern Ireland have directly witnessed violent incidents. Nonetheless, a much larger proportion in both religious communities have been touched by the consequences of violence.

Reporting crime and giving evidence

Our survey provides one illustration of the effects of living in a society where the level of political violence is so high. We asked respondents to say, from a list of options, what they would be most likely to do, firstly if they happened to see a house being burgled, and secondly if they saw a car being hijacked. We then asked how likely they would be to come forward to give evidence in court for each.

While most people would report both sorts of crime to the police, there are noteworthy differences in *how* they would go about it. When the crime appears unrelated to the troubles, the great majority of people would go directly to the police; but when the crime may be related to the conflict, a higher proportion (although still a minority) prefers the anonymity of the confidential telephone. As many as one in five

---

[*] The jurisdictions examined were Australia, Belgium, Canada, England and Wales, Finland, France, the Netherlands, Northern Ireland, Norway, Scotland, Spain, Switzerland, the USA and West Germany.

Catholics say they would not report a car hijacking at all, and there is even greater reluctance to give evidence in court: two-thirds or more overall say they would give evidence if the crime were a burglary, but only just over half say they would for a car hijacking. Indeed, in the latter case, a majority of Catholics (51 per cent) say they would probably or definitely *not* come forward to give evidence in court.

	Northern Ireland		
		Religious affiliation	
	All[*]	Protestant	Catholic
What people would do if they happened to see ...[**]			
... a house being burgled:	%	%	%
Use the confidential telephone[***]	10	9	11
Phone the police directly	77	82	71
Not report it at all	3	2	5
... a car being hijacked:	%	%	%
Use the confidential telephone	19	17	20
Phone the police directly	62	71	47
Not report it at all	8	3	17

[*] Includes those with no religion.
[**] Two other ways of reporting the crime were offered to respondents, but both were chosen by only a handful: 'ask someone else to report it' was chosen by 4 per cent (for both burglary and hijack); 'go to the police myself' by 3 per cent (for both burglary and hijack).
[***] The confidential telephone was established in 1972 to allow people to pass information anonymously to the security forces.[4]

In Northern Ireland then, 'ordinary' crime may not be as much a problem as it is in Britain, but significant numbers (particularly among the Catholic community) are unwilling to report crimes or give evidence, especially where those crimes may be linked to the troubles.

Emergency legislation

The remainder of this chapter deals directly with the impact of emergency legislation in Northern Ireland upon public attitudes. In particular, have Catholics become alienated from the administration of justice through a reduction in their confidence in its evenhandedness or effectiveness? And is public opinion in general, among both Catholics and Protestants, becoming desensitised to the increased powers of the state and the diminished civil liberties? We examine below differences in attitudes to these issues, between Northern Ireland and Britain and, within Northern Ireland, between the Protestant and Catholic communities.

The security forces

Northern Ireland has long been a heavily policed society.   At the outbreak of the present troubles in 1967 the security forces comprised 3,183 officers of the Royal Ulster Constabulary (RUC) and 10,342 members of the (part-time) B Special Constabulary.[5] Unlike police forces elsewhere in the United Kingdom, the RUC had a dual role involving activities associated with normal policing and security duties of a military or paramilitary character. Both the RUC and the B Specials routinely carried firearms. Following the outbreak of violence three tribunals (chaired by Lord Cameron, Mr Justice (now Lord) Scarman and Lord Hunt) were established in quick succession to report on its causes. The third commission was asked specifically to examine the role of the RUC and the B Specials, and it recommended major reforms.   As a consequence, the B Specials were disbanded and replaced by a new RUC Reserve force - soon augmented by a locally recruited and deployed regiment of the British Army, the Ulster Defence Regiment (UDR). The RUC was disarmed, although only temporarily because of the rise in paramilitary violence.

As the reforms to the RUC were being implemented, the British Army took over the main responsibility for security in Northern Ireland. In the mid-1970s 'police primacy' was re-established, with the objective of trying to 'normalise' the conflict by presenting it as a 'law and order' problem, rather than as a 'war'.   Commentators remain divided on the extent to which the reforms of the RUC were successful (Walsh, 1983, 1988; Ryder, 1989; Brewer, 1991).

Contact with the police

Despite the high level of policing in Northern Ireland, our results suggest that people in Northern Ireland have a little less (voluntary and involuntary) contact with the police than do the British. We asked the same three questions on both surveys. Following are the responses to the first two.

	Britain	Northern Ireland
% who, during the past two years, have:		
Reported a crime or accident to the police or gone to them for help or advice	35	29
Been stopped or asked questions by the police about an offence which they thought had been committed[*]	16	11

[*]   This question specifically excluded random checks by the police, which are permitted in Northern Ireland.

Moreover, when contacted voluntarily, the police in Northern Ireland were seen as rather more obliging than their British counterparts. Of those who have gone to the police, one in four British respondents describe them as unhelpful, in comparison with one in eight in Northern Ireland. On the other hand among those who have actually been stopped or questioned, a higher proportion in Northern Ireland than in Britain say the police were 'very' or 'fairly' impolite.

Experience of the police

Just over half of both Northern Irish and British respondents say that they, or someone they knew, have had "any form of direct or indirect contact with the police in the past two years". These experiences are evaluated in broadly similar terms on either side of the Irish Sea. Around one in five respondents in either place have been 'really annoyed' about the way the police behaved towards them or someone they knew, while a little under a third have been 'really pleased'. Within Northern Ireland, however, twice as many Catholics as Protestants have been 'really annoyed' (27 per cent compared with 14 per cent), and a smaller proportion of Catholics have been 'really pleased' (23 per cent as opposed to 32 per cent).

We then asked respondents (again on both surveys) whether, in general, they were satisfied or dissatisfied with the way the police do their job. The overall pattern of responses is almost identical in Northern Ireland and Britain, with over two-thirds expressing satisfaction with the police and only one in seven expressing dissatisfaction. Once again, however, Catholics and Protestants in Northern Ireland express sharply differing views:

Satisfaction in Northern Ireland with the way the police do their job

	All	Religious affiliation	
		Protestant	Catholic
	%	%	%
% saying:			
Very or fairly satisfied	70	85	50
Neither satisfied nor dissatisfied	15	9	23
Fairly or very dissatisfied	14	6	27

While Protestants in Northern Ireland show a very high level of satisfaction with the police, only a half of Catholics are satisfied. More than one in four Catholics are generally *dis*satisfied.

We asked two additional questions in Northern Ireland about the RUC: does it do a good or bad job in controlling, first, *non-sectarian* crime and secondly, *sectarian* crime? While 92 per cent of Protestants and 76 per cent of Catholics are satisfied with the RUC in respect of non-sectarian crime, this relatively high degree of consensus disappears in respect of sectarian crime: 84 per cent of Protestants think the RUC does a good job in controlling sectarian crime, but only 53 per cent of Catholics hold this view. Already then we begin to see the extent of differences between Northern Irish Protestants and Catholics in their perception of the police.

Evenhandedness of the security forces

Moving on from perceptions of the police to those of the security forces more generally, respondents in Northern Ireland were asked in effect whether they thought the different branches of the security forces operated evenhandedly.

| | | All* | Religious affiliation | |
			Protestant	Catholic
% saying that Protestant and Catholic members of the public are treated equally by:				
The RUC	1986	63	75	42
	1989	56	71	38
	1990	59	75	38
The British Army	1986	78	85	68
	1989	61	74	43
	1990	60	71	46
The UDR	1986	53	68	27
	1989	44	62	22
	1990	45	66	20

* Includes those with no religious affiliation.
Sources: 1986, Smith (1987), 1989, *NISA* (Curtice and Gallagher, 1990).

The differences in this table between years, and between Protestant and Catholic responses, are striking. While the differences between the two communities are marked for all three organisations, they are particularly wide in respect of the UDR: indeed, in 1990 as many as one in five *Protestants* believe that the UDR treats Protestants better. The findings here and elsewhere underline the widespread feeling of mistrust among the minority community and the extent of polarisation. For instance, some three-quarters of Catholics believe that the UDR should (probably or definitely) be disbanded,* while 86 per cent of Protestants take the opposite view.[6]

It appears that confidence in the evenhandedness of all three branches has diminished in recent years, especially among Catholics. While the

---

* We should note here that in the latest defence review it was decided to merge the UDR with the Royal Irish Rangers to form the Royal Irish Regiment, in 1992. About 15 per cent of the Royal Irish Rangers come from the Republic of Ireland, and it has a significant proportion of Catholics in its ranks.

British Army is still (just) seen as the most evenhanded of the three forces, confidence in it (at least on this measure) appears to have declined quite sharply in recent years among people in *both* communities (though this could be a function of a different measurement context).

The 1985 Anglo-Irish Agreement sought to increase confidence in the administration of justice. These data seem to suggest that, in respect of evenhandedness at any rate, the Agreement has had little success.

Security measures

We turn now to consider people's views on a number of specific security measures that have been, and continue to be, used in Northern Ireland. We presented respondents with a list and asked for each item if it was used 'too much', 'about the right amount' or 'too little'. Responses were scored +1 for 'too much', 0 for 'about right' and -1 for 'too little'. Once again we found wide differences in the perceptions of Protestants and Catholics among those who offered an opinion in respect of all the security measures we asked about.

Attitudes to the use of security measures

	All[*]	Religious affiliation	
		Protestant	Catholic
Vehicle checkpoints	-0.04	-0.27	0.33
Random searches of pedestrians	-0.05	-0.38	0.46
House searches	-0.03	-0.33	0.49
Controls on Catholic demonstrations	0.03	-0.21	0.45
Controls on Protestant demonstrations	-0.14	0.00	-0.33

[*] Includes those with no religious affiliation. Scores run from -1 (too little use) to 1 (too much use); those not answering or saying 'don't know' are excluded from the calculation.

When we examined the proportions in more detail, we found that, on four of the five measures, Catholics are at least five times more likely than Protestants to say they are used too much. The exception is controls on Protestant demonstrations. This may suggest that Catholics feel themselves to be disproportionately targeted.

Surprisingly, however, quite large proportions among both communities offer no opinion on some of these security measures. For instance, over a fifth of respondents have no view about random searches of pedestrians; and as many as a third voice no opinion about house searches. While these data undoubtedly reflect the more selective use of these last two measures, they are not all that rare: between 1973 and 1987 the security forces carried out more than 80,000 house searches[*] in Northern Ireland including, of course, many multiple searches (Hillyard, 1988).[7]

The courts

As with the security forces, we asked people in Northern Ireland whether they felt the courts treated Protestants and Catholics equally. As in 1989, there is a wide consensus that equal treatment is provided when the courts deal with non-sectarian offences: thus for "non-terrorist" offences, 86 per cent of Protestants and 80 per cent of Catholics feel that the courts give equal treatment. In contrast, when we asked about sectarian offences, 73 per cent of Protestants and only 56 per cent of Catholics believe this to be so. This gap widened still further when we asked people to agree or disagree with the view that "when the police or the army commit an offence in Northern Ireland, they usually get away with it": 70 per cent of Catholics agree while 64 per cent of Protestants *disagree.*

A particular area of controversy in Northern Ireland has been the use of non-jury courts for conflict-related, or 'scheduled', offences (Hadden and Boyle, 1989; Greer and White, 1986). We asked respondents whether people charged with serious crimes should always have the right to a jury trial (this time we did not distinguish between sectarian and non-sectarian offences). Around two-thirds of Catholics believe that people should always have this right, while 58 per cent of Protestants believe that jury trials should *not* be automatic.

There are also wide differences along the religious divide on the question of the severity of sentences. An overwhelming 83 per cent of Protestants and only 30 per cent of Catholics feel that conflict-related sentences are too lenient. These differing perceptions on the severity of punishments meted out by the courts are most marked on the issue of capital punishment: between two-thirds and three-quarters of Protestants, and only around one in five Catholics, tend to be in favour.

	All[*]	Religious affiliation	
		Protestant	Catholic
% favouring the death penalty for:			
Murder in the course of a terrorist act	54	74	21
Murder of a police officer	54	76	19
Other murders	47	64	21

[*] Includes those with no religious affiliation

---

[*] Between 1973 and 1987 the Army carried out 80,720 searches of occupied premises and 192,054 searches of unoccupied or derelict premises. Over the same period the RUC carried out 16,114 searches of premises (including occupied and unoccupied premises).

So, on a wide range of issues to do with the legal system and especially those touching (explicitly or implicitly) upon the troubles, we find marked differences in perceptions and prescriptions between Protestants and Catholics. While Protestants tend to express the view that the security forces and the courts operate in a fair and equal manner, Catholics are much more likely to question the impartiality of the legal and security system. Catholics are also more likely to feel that security measures are applied too rigorously.

Civil liberties and the state

Both the *BSA* and *NISA* surveys in 1990 addressed broad questions of civil liberties and state power. So we can compare and contrast 'libertarian responses' in Britain and Northern Ireland; and, within Northern Ireland, we can note similarities (but more often divergences) between Protestant and Catholic opinion.[*]

The method we use is similar to that of Davis (1986), in that we have identified two 'banks' of items, the first relating to the powers of the state and the second to the right to dissent. Responses to these twenty-five items are dichotomised into 'libertarian' *versus* 'all other' responses.[8] Patterns of libertarian responses can then be compared by plotting a regression line, with British responses on the vertical (or *y*) axis and Northern Irish responses on the horizontal (or *x*) axis. (A regression equation is simply the line of best fit between the plotted points.) If there were perfect agreement between the two sets of responses (in other words, if Northern Irish and British attitudes were the same) then the plotted points would lie exactly along the main diagonal of the graph (and the regression equation would take the form $y = x$, or Britain = Northern Ireland or Catholics = Protestants). To interpret the figures that follow, it is important to note that if the plotted line lies *above* the main diagonal, the group on the vertical axis displays a more libertarian pattern of responses: conversely, if the plotted line lies *below* the main diagonal the group on the horizontal axis displays a more libertarian pattern of responses.[9]

State power

We used fifteen items[**] to compare attitudes to state power. Four of these dealt with the sort of action the police might take when they received anonymous information about a possible crime; the remaining

---

[*] In Chapter 9, this subject is discussed again, but almost entirely in the British context.

[**] The items used, and percentages giving a libertarian response, are shown in **Table 4.1**.

eleven were concerned more generally with state and legal powers. The figure below compares overall attitudes in Northern Ireland with those in Britain.

'Libertarianism' in relation to state power in Britain and Northern Ireland

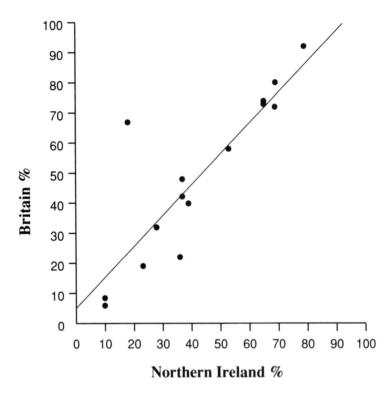

The regression line shows that, on most items, British attitudes are generally more libertarian than those in Northern Ireland - that is, British respondents *overall* are somewhat less willing to entrust greater power to the state. Note that the 'goodness-of-fit' of the regression line (see Note 9) is quite low (r^2 = 0.748), which reflects very wide differences in attitudes to one item in particular. While 67 per cent in Britain disagree that on-duty police officers should always carry guns, this is so for only 18 per cent in Northern Ireland.

This difference is understandable: unlike the rest of the UK, the police in Northern Ireland routinely carry arms both on-duty and, for reasons of personal security, off-duty. The Northern Irish public, particularly the Protestants (see the figure below), take the view that this is acceptable.

When this item is excluded from the analysis, the regression equation changes and the goodness-of-fit increases (r^2 = 0.960). In other words, there is a greater similarity in attitudes to state power in Northern Ireland and Britain on the other items, especially those on which there is a relatively low level of support for a libertarian position on both sides of the Irish Sea. Even so, attitudes in Britain are somewhat more libertarian than those in Northern Ireland.

The figure below shows the comparison on these same items between Northern Irish Protestants and Catholics.

'Libertarianism' in relation to state power within Northern Ireland

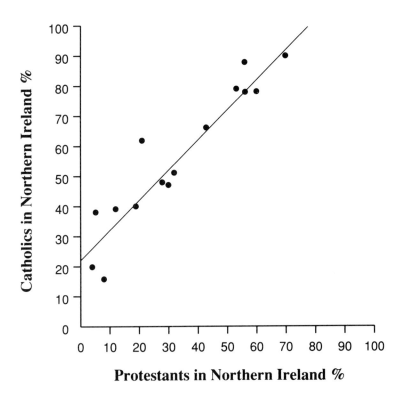

The pattern of responses here is even less ambiguous, with Catholics adopting a markedly more libertarian stance than Protestants on every item.

The right of dissent

The second bank of items deals with the right of dissent.* Six of these items concerned forms of protest that could be used against a government action; the remaining four deal with the rights of revolutionary or racist groups to hold meetings or publish books to publicise their views.

---

* The items used, and percentages giving a libertarian response, are shown in **Table 4.2**.

The figure below shows the overall pattern of responses in Britain and Northern Ireland.

'Libertarianism' in relation to dissent in Britain and Northern Ireland

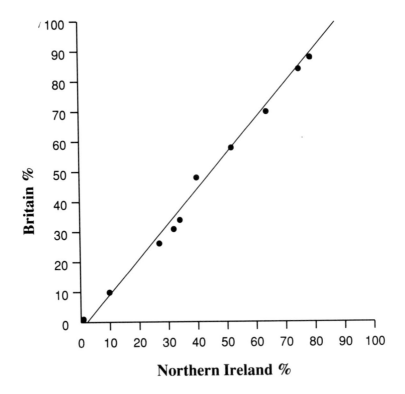

The graph suggests a general pattern of agreement across all the items (a good fit); but on those items for which there is generally a high level of endorsement for the libertarian position, attitudes in Britain are again somewhat more libertarian.

The figure below shows the pattern of responses on the same items for Northern Irish Protestants and Catholics. Again in general, Catholics adopt a more libertarian position. But the pattern is not so clear-cut, for Protestants reveal a more libertarian attitude than Catholics on two items, both of which refer to freedom of expression for racist groups.

'Libertarianism' in relation to dissent within Northern Ireland

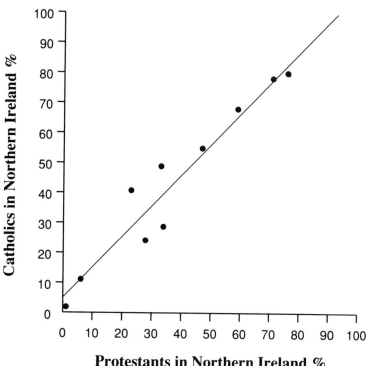

The general pattern that emerges from these analyses is that Catholics in Northern Ireland are, not unexpectedly, decidedly more tolerant of the expression of dissident views, and less likely than Protestants to trust the state.

Responses to questions dealing with aspects of political and religious censorship are also illuminating. A number of questions dealt (though not explicitly) with the ban imposed in 1988 on media broadcasts by representatives of a number of groups linked to terrorist activity in the UK, including two otherwise legal organisations, Sinn Fein and the Ulster Defence Association (Article 19, 1989). These questions asked whether the law should permit television or newspapers to publish interviews with "people who support acts of terrorism in the UK" and whether the law should allow such people to publish books expressing their views. Overall only about three in ten feel that the law *should* permit the public expression of the views of such people; levels of endorsement were broadly similar among both British and Northern Irish respondents. However, within the Northern Irish sample there is a wide difference in the attitudes of Protestants and Catholics. Only around one in six Protestants would allow those supporting terrorism to publish books expressing their views or propagate them in newspaper interviews, and only around one in eight support the legal right of television to broadcast interviews with them. In contrast, around one-half of Catholics support the legal expression of these views through books, newspapers and television.

This markedly less censorious attitude of Northern Irish Catholics towards political censorship on this subject does not, however, seem to extend to other areas. A further series of questions about religious censorship revealed a conservatism common to both religious communities in Northern Ireland - in sharp contrast to the views expressed by British respondents. While in Britain one in three would support a ban on "books or films that offend religious beliefs", around one-half of Northern Irish respondents would support such a ban. In addition, we offered three options for the future of the current blasphemy law in the United Kingdom: should it apply just to Christianity, to other religions as well, or should it be abolished altogether? In both Britain and Northern Ireland only small minorities, about one in ten, feel that the blasphemy law should apply only to Christianity, while the British overall favour abolition. (On the other hand, Christians in Britain - both Protestants and Catholics - are evenly divided between abolition and the extension of the law to other religions.) In Northern Ireland, the overall preference is for the law to be extended to other religions: only around a third of both Protestants and Catholics favour its abolition. So the greater libertarianism among Catholics appears to be limited to the political domain, rather than indicating a deeper commitment to civil liberties *per se*, particularly on religious matters.

One possible interpretation of these results is that, as we have seen, a significant proportion of Catholics question the impartiality of the security apparatus in Northern Ireland, and so their libertarian responses to these items may simply be another reflection of their suspicion of the state. A second interpretation is that Protestants in Northern Ireland appear to attach less importance to civil liberties only because they place a higher priority on the maintenance of the *status quo*. A combination of both interpretations seems likely. When we examine responses to the fifteen items on state power, we find that Northern Irish Catholics are more libertarian on most of them than are people in Britain, while Northern Irish Protestants are less libertarian on all the items.

Increasing confidence in the administration of justice

Finally, we look at attitudes to a number of measures which might increase confidence in the administration of justice in Northern Ireland. We asked respondents to consider three possible measures: the establishment of a Bill of Rights in the UK, increasing the number of Catholic recruits to the RUC, and procedures for dealing with complaints against the police in Northern Ireland.

A Bill of Rights

In recent years there have been increasing calls for the introduction of a Bill of Rights in the United Kingdom (see, for example, Dworkin, 1990). There is, of course, a range of views on the effectiveness of such a step: Thornton (1989) has questioned whether a strong enough Bill could be drafted in the short-term, while Ewing and Gearty (1990) have argued that such a Bill would be hopelessly inadequate to deal with the danger to civil liberties in Britain. The call for a Bill of Rights has been supported by civil libertarian groups in Northern Ireland, the most recent detailed proposal having been put forward by the Committee on the Administration of Justice (CAJ, 1990). This proposal lays out a number of options including a Bill of Rights for Northern Ireland alone, for the UK, or for the UK and the Republic of Ireland combined.

We asked respondents whether they favoured "a Bill of Rights for the UK which would give the courts rather than parliament the final say on any laws or government actions which threaten basic freedoms". About three in five in Britain *and* Northern Ireland would support such a Bill of Rights. Support is somewhat higher among Northern Irish Catholics than among Protestants: about two-thirds of the former, as opposed to a little over a half of the latter, endorse the proposal. Not unexpectedly, however, a relatively high proportion (about a quarter) of respondents fails to express a view (we offered a 'can't choose' option on the questionnaire). So, while there is general support for such a measure, among people who express a view, there can hardly be said to be great enthusiasm yet in either Britain or Northern Ireland.

Catholics in the RUC

One factor that has been thought to influence perceptions of the administration of justice in Northern Ireland has been the low participation of Catholics in the security forces. Analyses of occupational data in the 1981 Census, and more recent monitoring by the Fair Employment Commission suggest that one of the most important differences is the proportions of male Protestants and Catholics in security-related occupations (Osborne and Cormack, 1987; Gallagher, 1991; FEC, 1991). We asked respondents in Northern Ireland whether they felt it would be better for Northern Ireland if there were more Catholics in the RUC. The answers suggest a high level of consensus: 53 per cent of Protestants and 63 per cent of Catholics support greater participation by Catholics in the RUC.

This raises the obvious question, which we raised with respondents, as to why so few Catholics currently join the RUC. We offered a range of possible reasons and asked people to indicate which they felt were the two most important (which is why answers exceed 100 per cent).

	All[*]	Religious affiliation	
		Protestant	Catholic
% saying that Catholics are put off joining the RUC because ...			
... other Catholics put pressure on them not to join	80	87	68
... they do not want to join because they feel they will be treated badly by the RUC	46	46	41
... they try to join but they are not chosen because they are Catholic	14	10	20

[*] Includes those who have no religion. A fourth option was offered to respondents: "they are not as well qualified as Protestants to join the RUC". This was rated as most or next most important by 3 per cent overall (5 per cent of Protestants and 1 per cent of Catholics). 5 per cent overall said that none of these reasons was most or next most important (4 per cent of Protestants and 9 per cent of Catholics).

There is a fair measure of agreement among Protestants and Catholics on the explanations given; for instance, both communities believe that pressure from other Catholics is the most plausible reason, though with different force. (In fact, 77 per cent of Protestants and 55 per cent of Catholics rate it as the *most* likely explanation.) It is noteworthy also that while few respondents (even among Catholics) believe that the RUC directly discriminates against Catholics in recruitment, close to half in both communities believe that Catholics are put off joining because they feel they would be badly treated by the RUC once recruited.

Policing the police

Current arrangements for dealing with complaints against the police in Northern Ireland are essentially that the Chief Constable is responsible for dealing with complaints against junior officers, and the Police Authority for Northern Ireland is responsible for complaints against senior officers (see Note 10 at the end of this chapter, and Dickson and Millar (1990) for fuller details).
     We have already seen that Catholics and Protestants disagree fundamentally on the view that "when the police or the army commit an offence in Northern Ireland, they usually get away with it". So of particular interest are responses to two further questions on the procedures for dealing with complaints against the police in Northern Ireland (Weitzer, 1986; Brewer, 1991). The first question asked which body was responsible for looking into a complaint against the police. Many more Protestants than Catholics give the correct answer. A half of Protestants but only a third of Catholics name the Police Authority while a further 20 per cent of Protestants and 16 per cent of Catholics say it is the Chief Constable.

The second and more interesting question asked respondents which of these bodies *should* be responsible for looking into a complaint against the police.   If any single body were to receive a high degree of endorsement by both religious communities, it would suggest that it is seen as relatively impartial. But this was not the case. Among Catholics, the answers are more or less evenly divided among the six options offered (including 'don't know'). A majority of Protestants in contrast, opt for the Police Authority or the Chief Constable as the appropriate body.

	All[*]	Religious affiliation	
		Protestant	Catholic
% saying that a complaint against the police in Northern Ireland should be the responsibility of:	%	%	%
The Police Authority of Northern Ireland	28	38	14
The Chief Constable of the RUC	17	20	13
The Northern Ireland Office	15	16	13
The Home Office	11	7	17
The courts	11	7	17
Don't know	9	7	12
None of these	5	3	6

[*]   Includes those who have no religion.

Weitzer (1986) has argued that the RUC engages in a type of policing that may serve to encourage complaints, and points to evidence that the number of complaints has increased over the years. Discussing this, Brewer (1991) suggests that the procedures that are in place make the RUC more accountable than police forces in other divided societies. While this may be true, however, a majority of Catholics in Northern Ireland certainly do not think that the RUC is currently accountable enough. In addition, our survey highlights a central dilemma for those who seek to increase Catholic confidence in the police - that there appears to be no single existing institution which would currently be seen by Catholics as able to police the police effectively and equitably.

Conclusions

This chapter reports findings from the second annual survey in the current *NISA* series. Comparison across both years confirms a continuing long-term decline, tentatively identified in the 1989 survey, in the dominance of religion in Northern Ireland. The latest survey also suggests that views within the province about possibilities for constitutional change remain as polarised as ever along the religious divide. A parallel gulf exists between views in Northern Ireland and those in Britain. For instance, while the majority in Northern Ireland prefer the province to remain within the United Kingdom, the majority in Britain would prefer it to leave. And we now see for the first time some emerging differences between Northern Ireland and Britain on the expected consequences of the break-up of the Union. Overall a majority believes that withdrawal of the British troops would lead to an *increase* in bloodshed in the short-term. However, while the predominant view in Northern Ireland is that withdrawal would lead to an increase in bloodshed in the long-term as well, in Britain the largest group, nearly two in five, believe withdrawal would lead to a decrease in bloodshed in the long-term.

Respondents to both the 1990 *BSA* and *NISA* surveys were asked about their perceptions of crime, the police, safety on the streets and the powers of the judiciary. Despite the high level of political violence in Northern Ireland, 'ordinary' crime seems to be less of a problem there than in Britain. People in Northern Ireland feel less threatened than the British do by crime, and feel that the area where they live is safer. And, surprisingly, although the Northern Irish are highly policed, they still appear to have somewhat less contact with the police on average than their British counterparts do.

On almost all the questions which refer to the conflict in Northern Ireland there are important differences in perceptions between Protestants and Catholics. In general, unlike Protestants, most Catholics do *not* believe that the security forces operate in an evenhanded manner. Nor do they feel that any of a wide range of security measures currently in force are applied impartially. Our evidence suggests therefore that one of the expressed objectives of the Anglo-Irish Agreement of 1985, to increase confidence in the administration of justice, has so far had limited success.

On a range of civil libertarian issues, our findings suggest that Catholics in Northern Ireland are more libertarian than Protestants. But two factors seem to influence this pattern of responses. On the one hand, more Catholics than Protestants in Northern Ireland appear to be suspicious of the state and thus less prepared to endorse wider state powers; this is undoubtedly linked to their perceptions that most state agencies are not evenhanded. On the other hand, Protestants in Northern Ireland appear to be less concerned with defending certain civil liberties because they are more concerned with maintaining the *status quo;* to this end they seem prepared to accept greater powers for the state.

In considering measures which might increase confidence in the administration of justice in Northern Ireland, a general view, among Catholics and Protestants alike, is that Northern Ireland would be better off if more Catholics joined the RUC. But the most frequently mentioned barrier to increased Catholic participation is pressure from other Catholics, an obstacle which may be difficult to remove in the absence of a wider political resolution to the conflict and in a society where residential segregation is still widespread (Curtice and Gallagher, 1990, p.210). A significant proportion of Catholics and Protestants in Northern Ireland also believe that Catholics would be badly treated by the RUC if they did join. This may well be a circular problem. But, on our evidence, the RUC will have to be much more successful in demonstrating its evenhandedness before Catholics generally begin to feel they would be welcome within its ranks.

Finally, and perhaps most worryingly, there is no obvious single existing body which would come even close to receiving widespread endorsement from Catholics for dealing with complaints against the police or alleged abuses by other members of the security forces. To many members of the minority community, the legal system is seen as flawed, and there appears to be a long way to go before confidence in its institutions can be established.

Notes

1. See Hadden and Boyle (1989) pp.38-40 and 85-6. There is conflicting evidence as to the extent of public confidence in the police. For example, in his Annual Report for 1988, the then Chief Constable of the Royal Ulster Constabulary cited survey data which showed that 70 per cent of those questioned said the police did a good or very good job and described the "so-called alienation of the police and the public", as "often a political manipulation of the facts" (Hermon, 1989).

2. The Continuous Household Survey (CHS), conducted by PPRU, shows only two per cent of respondents claiming to have "no religion". A likely explanation is that the CHS is primarily a factual survey, so that the question receives a factual answer related to the respondent's background. In *NISA*, on the other hand, the response represents a statement of the respondent's current religious "persuasion" (Sweeney, 1991).

3. For a recent examination of Northern Ireland's image abroad, see Goldring (1991). A French academic who has long had an interest in Irish affairs, Goldring combines his comments on Northern Ireland's international image with acute observations of the ways in which the violence there influences everyday life.

4. Ryder (1989) suggests that, while the RUC has obtained some useful information *via* the confidential telephone it has been used also to lure security forces into booby-traps and ambushes.

5. By 1987 the local security forces comprised almost 13,000 RUC officers (including Reservists), all but 13 per cent of whom were full-time. In addition, the Ulster Defence Regiment had around 9,000 full- and part-time members (Northern Ireland Annual Abstract of Statistics, No.7, 1988). Currently there are 5.2 full-time police officers for every 1,000 people in Northern Ireland (rising to 8.9 per 1,000 if the UDR is included). In contrast, there are 2.4 full-time police officers per 1,000 people in England and Wales (Smith and Chambers, 1991).

6. The widely differing feelings about the UDR are revealed by responses to a further question in which we asked respondents to rate the effectiveness of the RUC, the British Army and the UDR in dealing with sectarian crime. A majority (77 per cent) - and almost as many Catholics as Protestants - rated the RUC as the most or next most effective. In stark contrast, only 2 per cent of Catholics rate the UDR as most or next most effective in respect of sectarian crime, in comparison with 33 per cent of Protestants.

7. Vehicle checkpoints are common on main arterial routes in Northern Ireland and are thus encountered by most people at some point, while random searches of pedestrians or house searches are used mainly in areas from which paramilitary activity is believed to originate.

8. Items on state power are drawn from the self-completion questionnaires and refer to questions 2.05 and 2.34 from the Northern Ireland questionnaire, and questions 2.05, 2.37 and 2.38 from the British Version L questionnaire. Items on the right to dissent are also drawn from the self-completion questionnaires (Northern Ireland and British Version L) and refer to questions 2.02, 2.03 and 2.04. See **Tables 4.1** and **4.2**

9. A goodness-of-fit (r^2) can be calculated for each regression equation. This runs from zero to one and measures the extent to which the plotted points lie on the regression line: the closer r^2 is to unity, the higher the goodness-of-fit of the regression line.

10. Complaints may be made to the Chief Constable at any police station or to the Independent Commission for Police Complaints (ICPC). The Chief Constable is responsible for dealing with complaints against junior officers. If the complaint is against a senior officer the Chief Constable must refer it to the Police Authority for Northern Ireland, the body given the general duty by the Police Act (Northern Ireland) 1970 to maintain an adequate and efficient police force in Northern Ireland. The ICPC was created by the Police (Northern Ireland) Order 1987 to serve as an independent monitor of the way in which complaints against the police are handled. The ICPC may supervise all complaints if it so wishes, but there are some investigations which it must supervise.

References

ARTICLE 19, *No Comment: Censorship, Secrecy and the Irish Troubles,* Article 19, London (1989).

BARCLAY, G.C., (ed), *A Digest of Information on the Criminal Justice System: Crime and Justice in England and Wales,* Research and Statistics Department, HMSO, London (1991).

BOYLE, K., HADDEN, T. and HILLYARD, P., *Law and State: The Case of Northern Ireland,* Martin Robertson, London (1975).

BOYLE, K., HADDEN., T. and HILLYARD, P., *Ten Years on in Northern Ireland: The Legal Control of Political Violence,* Cobden Trust, London (1980).

BREWER, J.D. with MAGEE, K., *Inside the RUC: Routine Policing in a Divided Society,* Clarendon Press, Oxford (1991).

COMMITTEE ON THE ADMINISTRATION OF JUSTICE (CAJ), *Making Rights Count: Discussion, Analysis and Documentation of International Charters of Rights and their Application to Northern Ireland,* CAJ, Belfast (1990).

CURTICE, J. and GALLAGHER, T. 'The Northern Irish dimension', in Jowell, R., Witherspoon, S. and Brook, L., (eds), *British Social Attitudes: the 7th report,* Gower, Aldershot (1990).

DAVIS, J.A., 'British and American attitudes: similarities and contrasts', in Jowell, R., Witherspoon, S. and Brook, L., (eds), *British Social Attitudes: the 1986 Report,* Gower, Aldershot (1986).

DICKSON, B., (ed), *Civil Liberties in Northern Ireland: the CAJ Handbook,* Committee on the Administration of Justice, Belfast (1990).

DICKSON, B. and MILLAR, R., 'Complaints against the police', in Dickson, B., (ed), *Civil Liberties in Northern Ireland: the CAJ Handbook,* Committee on the Administration of Justice, Belfast (1990).

DWORKIN, P., *A Bill of Rights for Britain*, Chatto and Windus, London (1990).

EWING, K.D. and GEARTY, C.A., *Freedom Under Thatcher: Civil Liberties in Modern Britain*, Clarendon Press, Oxford (1990).

FAIR EMPLOYMENT COMMISSION (FEC), *A Profile of the Workforce in Northern Ireland: a Summary of the 1990 Monitoring Returns*, Research Report No.1, FEC, Belfast (1991).

GALLAGHER, A.M., *Majority Minority Review 2: Employment, Unemployment and Religion in Northern Ireland*, University of Ulster, Coleraine, (1991).

GOLDRING, M., *Belfast: from Loyalty to Rebellion*, Lawrence and Wisehart, London (1991).

GREER, S.C. and WHITE, A., *Abolishing the Diplock Courts*, Cobden Trust, London (1986).

HADDEN, T. and BOYLE, K., *The Anglo-Irish Agreement: Commentary, Text and Official Review*, Sweet and Maxwell, London (1989).

HADDEN, T., BOYLE, K. and CAMPBELL, C., 'Emergency law in Northern Ireland: the context', in Jennings, A., (ed), *Justice Under Fire: the Abuse of Civil Liberties in Northern Ireland*, Pluto Press, London (1988).

HERMON, J.C., *Chief Constable's Annual Report 1988*, HMSO, Belfast (1989).

HILLYARD, P., 'Political and social dimensions of emergency laws in Northern Ireland', in Jennings, A., (ed), *Justice Under Fire: the Abuse of Civil Liberties in Northern Ireland*, Pluto Press, London (1988).

McKEOWN, M., *Two Seven Six Three: an Analysis of Fatalities Attributable to Civil Disturbances in Northern Ireland in the Twenty Years between July 13, 1969 and July 12, 1989*, Murlough Press, Ireland (1989).

MOXON-BROWNE, E., *Nation, Class and Creed in Northern Ireland*, Gower, Aldershot (1983).

NORTHERN IRELAND OFFICE, *Guide to the Emergency Powers*, HMSO, Belfast (not dated).

NORTHERN IRELAND OFFICE, *A Commentary on Northern Ireland Crime Statistics 1987*, HMSO, Belfast (1988).

O'BOYLE, M.P., 'Emergency situations and the protection of human rights: a model derogation provision for a Northern Ireland Bill of Rights', *Northern Ireland Legal Quarterly*, vol.28, no.2 (1977), pp.160-87.

OSBORNE, R.D. and CORMACK, R.J., *Religion, Occupations and Employment 1971-81*, Fair Employment Agency, Belfast (1987).

ROSE, R., *Governing Without Consensus*, Faber, London (1971).

RYDER, C., *The RUC: A Force Under Fire*, Methuen, London (1989).

SMITH, D.J., *Equality and Inequality in Northern Ireland, Part 3: Perceptions and Views*, Policy Research Institute, London (1987).

SMITH, D.J. and CHAMBERS, G., *Inequality in Northern Ireland*, Clarendon Press, Oxford (1991).

SWEENEY, K., 'Technical details of the survey', in Stringer, P. and Robinson, G., (eds) *Social Attitudes in Northern Ireland*, Blackstaff Press, Belfast, 1991.

THORNTON, P., *Decade of Decline: Civil Liberties in the Thatcher Years*, National Council for Civil Liberties, London (1989).

WALSH, D.P.J., *The Use and Abuse of Emergency Legislation in Northern Ireland*, Cobden Trust, London (1983).

WALSH, D.P.J., 'The Royal Ulster Constabulary - A law unto themselves?' in Tomlinson, M., Varley, T. and McCullagh, C. (eds), *Whose Law and Order? Aspects of Crime and Social Control in Irish Society*, Sociological Society of Ireland, Belfast (1988).

WEITZER, R., 'Accountability and complaints against the police in Northern Ireland', *Police Studies*, no. 9 (1986), pp.99-109.

Acknowledgements

The *BSA* investigators, our colleagues at the Policy Planning and Research Unit (PPRU) and at the Centre for Social Research at Queen's University Belfast are grateful for the funding from the Central Community Relations Unit and the Nuffield Foundation, which enabled us to extend the *British Social Attitudes* survey series to Northern Ireland. PPRU continues to carry out the fieldwork with its usual skill and efficiency, and this expertise has contributed significantly to the success of this initiative.

In addition, the editors are grateful to Kevin Sweeney and Edgar Jardine of PPRU, and their colleagues, and to Peter Stringer of the Centre for Social Research, for their help in developing the Northern Ireland version of our questionnaire.

4.1 'LIBERTARIANISM' IN RELATION TO STATE POWER

	% giving 'libertarian' response			
	Britain	Northern Ireland		
Q.2.34(NI); L2.37 and L2.38(Britain)	All	All	Protestants	Catholics
a. People on probation or parole should be be fitted with an electronic tag *(disagree)*	19	23	12	39
b. On duty police officers should carry guns *(disagree)*	67	18	5	38
c. Convicted criminals are let off lightly *(disagree)*	6	10	4	20
d. A retracted confession should not be enough to convict someone *(agree)*	74	65	56	78
e. Police should be allowed to question suspects for a week with no solicitor *(disagree)*	80	69	56	88
f. Political refugees should always be welcome *(agree)*	22	36	28	48
g. Complaints against the police should be investigated by an independent body *(agree)*	92	79	70	90
h. Every adult should have to carry an identity card *(disagree)*	40	39	32	51
i. If a suspect remains silent it should count against them in court *(disagree)*	42	37	21	62
j. Prisons contain people who should be given a lighter punishment *(agree)*	48	37	30	47
k. Police should not need a warrant to search suspects' homes *(disagree)*	73	65	53	79

Q.2.05(NI); L2.05(Britain)

i. Police should be allowed to keep a suspect under surveillance *(not allow)*	8	10	8	16
ii. Police should be allowed to tap a suspect's telephone *(not allow)*	58	53	43	66
iii. Police should be allowed to open a suspect's mail *(not allow)*	72	69	60	78
iv. Police should be allowed to detain a suspect overnight for questioning *(not allow)*	32	28	19	40

4.2   'LIBERTARIANISM' IN RELATION TO DISSENT

Q.2.02(NI); L2.02(Britain)	Britain All	Northern Ireland All	Protestants	Catholics
		% giving 'libertarian' response		
a. Organising public meetings to protest against the government *(should be allowed)*	88	79	76	80
b. Publishing pamphlets to protest against the government *(should be allowed)*	84	75	71	78
c. Organising protest marches and demonstrations *(should be allowed)*	70	64	59	68
d. Occupying a government office and stopping work there for several days *(should be allowed)*	10	10	6	11
e. Seriously damaging government buildings *(should be allowed)*	1	1	1	2
f. Organising a nationwide strike of all workers against the government *(should be allowed)*	31	32	23	41

Q.2.03(NI); L2.03(Britain)				
i. Revolutionaries holding public meetings to express their views *(should be allowed)*	48	40	33	49
ii. Revolutionaries publishing books expressing their views *(should be allowed)*	58	52	47	55

Q.2.04(NI); L2.04(Britain)				
i. Racists holding public meetings to express their views *(should be allowed)*	26	27	28	24
ii. Racists publishing books expressing their views *(should be allowed)*	3	34	34	29

5 House and home

John Curtice [*]

For much of the 1980s both public policy and the private market favoured the owner-occupier. Expansion of the private sector was stimulated by the government's policy of selling council houses at discounted prices to existing tenants: between 1979 and 1990 well over one and a half million public sector dwellings were sold off. Tax relief on home loans was raised from £25,000 to £30,000 in 1983. The proportion of the housing stock in Britain which was owner-occupied rose from 55 per cent at the end of 1978 to 67 per cent by 1989, while the proportion which was rented from local authorities fell from 32 per cent to 23 per cent over the same period (Housing and Construction Statistics, 1990). Ministers proclaimed the creation of a 'property-owning democracy'.

Meanwhile most owner-occupiers saw large increases in the market value of their properties. For most of the decade house prices rose faster than either retail price inflation or real average incomes. On an index where 1985 prices represent 100, house prices in the UK rose on average from 73 in 1982 to 202 in 1989 (CSO, 1991a). In the south-east the rise was even steeper. Particular beneficiaries were those who bought their council houses at a discount. Although only a minority of owner-occupiers was able to realise these gains in wealth, many were able to raise loans on the strength of the value of their homes - one of the main sources of the growth in consumer credit during the economic boom of the late 1980s.

---

[*] Senior Lecturer in Politics and Director of the Social Statistics Laboratory, University of Strathclyde

Owner-occupation flourished to some extent at the expense of the council renting sector. Investment in public sector housing declined, and local authorities were not allowed to use the income they received from the sale of their properties to build new accommodation. During the 1970s, local authorities built on average 111,000 new homes a year; by 1989 this figure had fallen precipitously to 17,000 homes a year. Meanwhile, council house rents were going up substantially, especially in the first half of the decade when they outpaced both average mortgage payments and the retail price index (CIPFA). Together with the increase in the amount of mortgage interest relief that had been given to home-owners,[1] these changes constituted a significant shift in resources away from the local authority sector and towards owner-occupation.

But by the end of the decade, the economic climate had changed. In an attempt to curb the growth in consumer credit which had stoked inflation following the 1987 general election, and to prop up a falling currency, the government increased interest rates to the highest level since November 1981. The 1988 Budget limited relief on mortgage interest rates to £30,000 per property, rather than per mortgagor, and the rush to buy before the August deadline pushed up house prices still further, particularly in London. Between May 1988 and May 1989, base rates nearly doubled from seven and a half per cent to 14 per cent, and they remained very high until the spring of 1991. The impact on many owner-occupied households was severe: the number of mortgages in arrears by more than 12 months doubled between 1988 and 1990 (CSO, 1991b.). House prices stagnated and then fell in London, the south-east, East Anglia and the south-west. Further north the impact was less severe, but even so average house prices across the UK as a whole fell marginally in the last twelve months of the decade.

So, both housing policy and the housing market saw very considerable changes during the 1980s. Since the British Social Attitudes series started in 1983, it has carried a number of questions on housing issues. In addition to some standard items about the kind of accommodation respondents occupy and their satisfaction with it, we have also included detailed questions exploring attitudes towards public sector housing and the sale of council houses, and towards the advantages and disadvantages of owner-occupation. So we can use data from all seven surveys to chart changes in attitudes and try to discover how they relate to changes in the housing market during the 1980s.

We focus on two issues. First, have there been changes in the kinds of people in different forms of housing tenure? Secondly, what impact, if any, do changes in policy and their effect on the housing market appear to have had on public attitudes towards housing? In addressing these issues we will concentrate our analysis on two academic controversies about housing policy which have arisen in the course of the 1980s.

Two controversies

The first controversy, initiated by critics of the Conservative governments' housing policies, has focused attention on the alleged disadvantages of the 'right to buy' policy for those who *remain* council tenants. Forrest and Murie (1983; 1986; 1988), for example, have argued that people who have bought their council homes are atypical of council tenants in general; and that the properties they bought are atypical of the stock of local authority housing. Buyers, they argue, tend to be better off, and the houses they have bought are on the more desirable estates rather than the unpopular 'deck access' flats on peripheral estates.

According to this argument then, council housing has been 'residualised': local authorities are no longer expected to be mass providers of social housing at an affordable rent, but instead to supply only a safety net for those who are too poor or too old or who are otherwise unable or unwilling to provide for themselves. Consequently, the argument runs, those who remain in council properties tend increasingly to be from the poorest and the most disadvantaged sections of society. And the housing they occupy under this new regime is declining in quality owing to lack of resources and a paucity of new investment. In short, the social and economic gap between local authority tenants and owner-occupiers is being widened as a direct result of housing policy. Selling council houses may be advantageous for the relatively well-off, but for the majority who remain council tenants it brings about a material reduction in the quality of their housing and consequently in their social and economic resources (Clapham *et al*, 1990).

In contrast, the second controversy has been initiated by advocates of the Conservative government's housing policies. Particularly important has been the contribution of Peter Saunders who has argued that, for the majority of people, owner-occupation has two important advantages over renting:

> Two important claims are mentioned time and time again when people are asked why they prefer to own rather than rent their homes. One is financial - buying is seen as cheaper in the long run, or rent is seen as a waste of money, or rising house prices are seen as a means of saving for the future or accumulating capital. The other has to do with the sense of independence and autonomy which ownership confers - the freedom from control and surveillance by a landlord and the ability to personalise the property according to one's tastes (Saunders, 1990, p.84).

Most importantly, Saunders believes that owner-occupation *always* has these advantages. He argues not only that owner-occupiers have made long-term financial gains throughout the twentieth century, and that such gains are likely to continue for the foreseeable future, but that, of the various forms of housing tenure, only owner-occupation can satisfy what is a biologically-determined impetus to possess material objects which provide the security and autonomy we need. Home ownership, the argument runs, provides legal protection against interference by others. Tenants, in contrast, will always be subject to the power of their landlords.

So, according to Saunders, owner-occupation is popular because it satisfies a natural 'desire to own'. In consequence, it will always be preferred to any other form of tenancy, regardless of changes in people's social and economic circumstances.

In challenging this viewpoint, Forrest et al (1990) make two main points. Firstly, they say, as owner-occupation expands, it becomes a more heterogenous sector. In particular, not all owner-occupiers make a substantial financial gain from their homes; it varies by time, location and type of house. Some fail to realise any gain at all. Secondly, they point out that the "meanings and characteristics of home ownership have changed over time" (p.179): the popularity of owner-occupation, far from being uniform, varies according to social and economic circumstances. Its current popularity reflects not an intrinsic appeal, but rather a choice conditioned by a particular set of opportunities and constraints - such as the availability of mortgage finance, tax relief on interest repayments, council house waiting lists, security of tenure and so on.

Our data enable us to address both these controversies. We can examine how far there is evidence of a 'residualisation' of council housing during the 1980s. And we can see how robust attitudes towards owner-occupation actually are in the face of the much less favourable economic climate which existed by the time of our fieldwork in the spring of 1990.

Tenure profiles

To examine these issues, we shall look at trends across the 1980s. But to enable us to get our bearings we first identify the profiles from our 1990 data of council tenants, owner-occupiers and private renters.[2] There are a number of major differences between the sorts of people in the three main forms of tenure (for earlier figures see Bosanquet, 1986).

Age by housing tenure

Age	All %	Owner-occupiers %	Council tenants %	Other renters[3] %
18-34	32	30	33	48
35-44	20	23	13	10
45-64	29	31	25	23
65+	19	16	28	21

Firstly we see that a much higher proportion of council tenants than of owner-occupiers are in the oldest age group (65 and over). With over a quarter of council tenants in this age group (and over a quarter of this age group in council tenancies), the importance of local authority housing for elderly people is clear.

The largest single group of council tenants, however, is those aged under 35. But the proportion of owner-occupiers from this age group is almost equally high - it is in the private rental sector where the proportion of young people is unusual. Nearly one-half of all those renting privately are under 35. Of course, for many of these young people the private rental sector is only a staging-post. Over half of all private renters moved into their present accommodation within the previous two years, and over half expect to move out within the following two years. Many will eventually become owner-occupiers or council tenants, depending on the subsequent course of their careers and on their family circumstances.

Among owner-occupiers we found that outright owners are, not surprisingly, much older on average than those with a mortgage. Just under three in four mortgage holders are aged below 45 compared with just under one in four outright owners.

There are also marked differences between owner-occupiers and council tenants in terms of social class. Nearly one-half of all council tenants are in semi- or unskilled manual occupations, while only one in twenty are members of the salariat.[4]

Goldthorpe class schema[*] by housing tenure

Social class:	Owner-occupiers %	Council tenants %	Other renters %
Salariat	32	5	28
Routine non-manual, petty bourgeoisie, supervisors and foremen	39	28	33
Skilled working class	10	17	7
Semi- and unskilled working class	16	46	24

But while council tenants are typically working class, the working class are not typically council tenants. In 1990 just over a half of semi- and unskilled manual workers owned their own homes.

Indeed, owner-occupiers and council tenants differ not so much in terms of the class they belong to, as according to whether or not they have a paid job. Just over forty per cent of council tenants are either themselves currently in paid work (of 10 or more hours a week) or have a spouse who is, compared with just over half of those renting privately (many of

---

[*] We have used the Goldthorpe 'compressed schema' (see Appendix 1) but combined the routine non-manual, petty bourgeoisie, and manual supervisors and foremen categories, while retaining the distinction in the full schema between skilled working class and semi- and unskilled working class.

whom are in full-time education) and nearly three-quarters of owner-occupiers. As we might have anticipated from their age profile, nearly one-quarter of council tenants are retired,[5] compared with 15 per cent of owner-occupiers. As many as 12 per cent of council tenants are both unemployed themselves and do not have a working spouse or partner, while only 3 per cent of owner-occupiers are in this position. As many as a half of the unemployed respondents interviewed in 1990 lived in council accommodation.

In consequence, council tenants are much more reliant upon the state for their income as well as for their housing. The table below shows the proportion in each kind of tenure who report having received certain state welfare payments within the previous five years. As is immediately apparent, council tenants are far more likely than owner-occupiers to have received each of these benefits.

State benefit receipt, household income and housing tenure

	All %	Owner-occupiers %	Council tenants %	Other renters %
% living in household with a member in receipt of:*				
Unemployment benefit	16	13	22	21
One-parent benefit	4	2	11	6
Family credit	3	1	12	3
Income support	12	6	26	25
Housing benefit (rate or rent rebate)	15	6	43	34
Income quartile:	%	%	%	%
Lowest	25	16	60	33
Highest	25	29	6	28

* The question was asked about the respondent 'or anyone in this household ... during the last five years'.

Moreover, the difference between owner-occupiers and council tenants in their employment status is clearly reflected in their household income. As many as 60 per cent of council tenants live in a household with a total income in the lowest quartile, ten times as many as are in the highest quartile.[6]

Council tenants differ from owner-occupiers not only in their socio-economic characteristics, but also in the kind of accommodation they live in. There are hardly any council tenants living in detached houses. In addition, while less than one in twenty owner-occupiers lives in a purpose-built flat, over a quarter of council tenants do so. In short, the stock of owner-occupied properties contains more of the kind of accommodation generally thought to be desirable.

The private rental market also contains hardly any detached houses but is most distinctive for its relatively high proportions of converted flats and 'non-self-contained' accommodation.

Accommodation type by housing tenure

Accommodation type:	All %	Owner-occupiers %	Council tenants %	Other renters %
Detached house	21	28	*	10
Semi-detached house	38	40	37	19
Terraced house	27	26	34	24
Purpose-built flat	10	4	27	24
Converted flat	3	2	2	17
Room(s)	*	*	*	4

* = less than one half of one per cent

'Residualisation'

Council tenants are then, in general, less well-off, less likely to be in paid work and (if they have a job) more likely to be in a manual occupation. But how far is this a new phenomenon? Did the socio-economic gap between council tenants and owner-occupiers widen during the 1980s? In short, has there been a 'residualisation' of council housing?

There are clear signs from the *British Social Attitudes* data that there has. Let us look first of all at the types of council dwellings that have been sold. We regularly ask all owner-occupiers whether or not they have previously rented their present house from the local authority. We can thus see whether or not council accommodation bought under the 'right to buy' scheme is typical of the general stock of local authority housing by comparing it with that lived in by those who have not (as yet anyway) bought their council houses.[7] (To ensure an adequate sample base we have combined data from the 1989 and 1990 surveys.)

'Right to buy' and council housing stock

Accommodation type:	Bought home from council %	Current council tenant %
Detached house	2	1
Semi-detached house	47	33
Terraced house	42	31
Purpose-built flat	7	33

Whereas one in three council tenants live in a purpose-built flat, only one in fourteen of those who have bought their accommodation do so. Moreover, nearly one-half of those who have bought their property from the council live in semi-detached houses, compared with one-third of current local authority tenants.

There is also evidence of 'residualisation' when we compare the demographic and socio-economic characteristics of those who have exercised their 'right to buy' and those who have not. For example, just over one-half of those who have bought their home from the council are currently aged between 35 and 64 (and thus likely to be at the height of their earning power) compared with fewer than forty per cent of those who are now local authority tenants (see also Kerr, 1988). We show below the resultant changes in the age profile of council tenants during the period 1983-1990.

Combined data from surveys conducted in ...

	1983-1985	1986/1987	1989/1990
% of council tenants aged:	%	%	%
18-34	29	33	32
35-44	12	15	13
45-64	33	30	26
65+	25	24	29

Younger and older people who are less likely to have bought their council accommodation, now constitute a larger proportion of council tenants than they did in the early 1980s. Of the above age groups, only *one* (people aged 45-64), has reduced its incidence among the population of council tenants.

There is evidence too that the gap between owner-occupiers and council tenants has widened in terms of their labour-market position. While the proportion of unemployed people living in council dwellings has not declined at all during the 1980s, the proportion of those in work has declined sharply.

% living in council housing, 1984-1990

	1984	1985	1986	1987	1989	1990
Economic position:	%	%	%	%	%	%
In paid work	19	20	16	14	14	12
Registered unemployed	49	56	54	47	59	50

Other groups for whom the state is commonly a major source of income have remained dependent on council housing. Around one-half of single parents with dependent children live in council properties, as do around

40 per cent of the permanently sick.[8] Above all, there is clear evidence
of a growing gap in the household income levels of owner-occupiers and
council tenants. Whereas in 1983 just under half of council tenants aged
under 60 were living in households with incomes in the bottom quartile,
by 1990 around 60 per cent did so.[9]

This widening gap between council tenants and owner-occupiers is not,
however, simply the consequence of the sale of council properties to more
affluent tenants. Other government policies have played a part too. For
example, the real value of social security payments - upon which, as we
have seen, council tenants are especially dependent - has not kept up with
average incomes (Department of Social Security, 1991). And other
policies, unrelated to housing, such as widening share ownership, have
also had differential impacts on the two tenure groups. Although share
ownership has just about doubled in both sectors, the resultant gap has
also nearly doubled: now, around 40 per cent of owner-occupiers are
share-owners, while only around 10 per cent of council tenants are:

% owning shares in each tenure type

	1985	1986	1987	1989	1990
Owner-occupiers	20	22	32	33	38
Council tenants	3	5	8	7	8

However, we should not exaggerate the impact of residualisation. For
example, a third of council house purchasers (in our 1989 and 1990
surveys combined) are in the semi- and unskilled working class.   In
contrast, and contrary to the stereotype of the typical council house
purchaser popularised by the media, purchasers from the skilled working
class constitute just one in seven of all purchasers. The proportion of
semi- and unskilled workers who are council tenants has fallen by nine
percentage points since 1984-5; although, even so, the proportion of
buyers from the semi- and unskilled working class is still lower than the
proportion of council tenants from this class.[10] The 'residualisation' of
council housing has been less important in intensifying traditional class
divisions than it has in widening the gap between all those in paid jobs
and a so-called 'underclass' who depends upon the state rather than on
the labour market for most or all of its income.

Perceptions of 'residualisation'

Is there any evidence that this change in the profile of council tenants has
had any impact upon popular attitudes and perceptions? Firstly, there is
only inconclusive evidence that people nowadays are more likely than in
1983 to believe that those on high incomes benefit most from government
housing support. True, the trend is upward but is by no means linear,

and our question was by no means simple, reflecting the complexities of government policies in the housing field.

> *Central government provides financial support to housing in two main ways. First, by means of allowances to low income tenants; second by means of tax relief to people with mortgages. On the whole, which of these three types of family would you say benefits **most** from central government support for housing - families with **high** incomes, families with **middle** incomes, or families with **low** incomes?*

The table below shows that while the proportion thinking that those on high incomes benefit most rose between 1986 and 1989, in 1990 the proportion fell back again considerably . It could well be that responses to this question fluctuate in response to variations in the share of the owner-occupied market. For the rise in the proportion believing that high-income households were the main beneficiaries coincided with the period of large increases in property values, and the fall in 1990, with the end of the property boom. We return to the issue of confidence in the property market towards the end of the chapter.

Perceived gainers from government housing policies, 1983-1990

	1983	1984	1985	1986	1987	1989	1990
Families with:	%	%	%	%	%	%	%
High incomes	32	37	33	33	40	42	37
Middle incomes	27	20	20	22	20	20	22
Low incomes	39	38	43	40	36	35	38

Similarly, support for the government's policy on council house sales has fluctuated over the decade; but now seems to have declined from the high level it reached in the mid-1980s. At the time of our first reading in 1983, 54 per cent supported the unrestricted 'right to buy'; by 1986 support peaked at 63 per cent; by 1990 it had declined substantially to 53 per cent.

Finally, while public support for extra government spending on health and education may have increased during the 1980s, even at the expense of a heavier tax burden, (see Chapters 2 and 3), there has been no parallel rise in enthusiasm for increased government expenditure on social housing. The proportion of respondents nominating housing as a first or second priority for extra state spending has remained consistently at 20 per cent since 1983. Admittedly it is the third most popular item for extra expenditure, but it has always been a poor third behind health and education and it is now trailing even further behind.

So while government policy may have served in practice to residualise council tenants, the impact of this on public attitudes has clearly been only marginal. Public concern over the health and education services appears to be much greater. Of course health care in particular is a universal service, which social housing has never been and is now even less so.

The popularity of home ownership

We now look at attitudes to owning and renting. In particular we try to establish how popular home ownership is, and whether its popularity is constant over time or varies according to people's social and economic circumstances. How far are Saunders' claims for home ownership supported by our evidence?

One broad though very crude measure included in the *BSA* survey is a simple measure of satisfaction with one's present accommodation. Not unexpectedly the vast majority of respondents express satisfaction, but the dissatisfied minority is much more prevalent among tenants (council and private) than among owner-occupiers.

Housing satisfaction by tenure, 1990

	All %	Owner-occupiers %	Council tenants %	Other renters %
Very satisfied	44	49	32	30
Quite satisfied	44	44	43	44
Neither satisfied nor dissatisfied	5	4	6	8
Quite dissatisfied	5	3	10	12
Very dissatisfied	3	1	9	6

Further, the level of satisfaction expressed by owner-occupiers with their accommodation has remained consistently high throughout the 1980s - evidence, perhaps, in support of Saunders' general thesis that it is an inherently superior form of tenure. But we have already seen that the housing stock in the owner-occupied and rental sectors differs considerably. For instance, hardly any council tenants live in detached houses, while few owner-occupiers live in flats; and, as we shall see, people's satisfaction with their accommodation varies considerably according to the type of accommodation they live in. So we need to investigate whether it is the type of property which matters rather than its tenure type. The table below shows the proportion of people who are very satisfied with their accommodation, taking into account both tenure and type of housing. The figures have been derived from all five of the *British Social Attitudes* surveys conducted between 1985 and 1990, since by combining the datasets we are able to ensure adequate numbers in the rarer combinations of housing type and tenure.

Housing tenure, 1985-90 surveys combined

	Owner-occupiers	Council Tenants	Other Renters
% saying very satisfied			
Detached house	61	(-)	(-)
Semi-detached house	47	26	29
Terraced house	38	27	17
Purpose-built flat	43	24	41
Self-contained flat	37	(-)	24

(-) = fewer than 100 cases

Owner-occupiers, whether in a detached house, a semi-detached one, a terraced house or a flat, are much more likely to be very satisfied than are council tenants or private renters (except for those in purpose-built flats). So the tenure of a property does, it appears, matter greatly. So owner-occupation appears to bring its beneficiaries greater satisfaction than those in other forms of tenure irrespective of the type of the accommodation they occupy.

Further evidence of the appeal of owner-occupation is that the proportion of council tenants expecting eventually to buy their present home has actually *increased* over the years, despite the fact that council tenants have become relatively poorer. Nearly one in four now say that it is 'very' or 'quite' likely that they will buy their council property 'at some time in the future' compared with just one in eight in 1983. Government policy has, of course, encouraged purchase throughout the period and has made the terms increasingly favourable by, for example, increasing discounts to purchasers and relaxing conditions on eligibility. On our evidence, these incentives seem likely to maintain a steady pace of council house sales for the foreseeable future,[11] especially if the economic climate becomes more favourable. After all, as many as two-thirds of all tenants (council and private) say that, if they had a free choice, they would opt to buy.

So owner-occupation is a goal for many households. But this is not the whole story. True, when we present tenants (council and private) with a set of reasons why people might not want to buy their own home and ask, for each, whether it applies to them, financial reasons - such as inability to afford a deposit, get a mortgage or keep up with repayments - predominate. But other reasons also come into play. Approximately two-thirds say they simply do not want to be in debt, and over half that buying a home would be "just too much of a responsibility"; nearly half say they are too old to change. These answers suggest that for a substantial body of the tenant population there are cultural as well as financial obstacles to becoming an owner-occupier.

Nonetheless, most of the evidence so far appears to support Saunders' arguments about the *popularity* of owner-occupation. But are the *reasons* that Saunders gives for the popularity of owner-occupation correct?

Some evidence that they may not be is provided by responses to a pair of questions asked in the 1987 survey. Respondents were asked:-

> *Thinking now just of council estates (SCOTLAND: or housing schemes). What do you think are the good things about living on a council estate (SCOTLAND: or housing scheme)?*

and

> *And what do you think are the bad things about living on a council estate (SCOTLAND: or housing scheme)? ***

The questions ask about council *estates* rather than about council housing in general. But since 85 per cent of council tenants say they live on an estate they are relevant to most council tenants, and as such the answers are interesting. Council estates are clearly not popular - around three in ten of the sample could not nominate anything good about them, compared with only about one in ten who could not nominate anything bad (one in five of council tenants). But the concerns that Saunders identified - about lack of autonomy, or control by the landlord, for instance - were scarcely mentioned among the bad features of council estates. Rather, their main disadvantages were seen to be the social environment, such as excessive noise and the nuisance of petty crime. These were more likely to be mentioned by council tenants themselves than by owner-occupiers, who were rather more inclined to say that tenants failed to look after their estates properly.

Bad things about living on a council estate, 1987

% of respondents mentioning:	All %	Owner-occupiers %	Council tenants %
Hooliganism, noise	33	31	38
Vandalism, graffiti	23	22	25
Neglect by tenants	19	23	12
Poor design	14	16	9
% saying nothing is bad	11	9	20

Since respondents could give more than one answer, the columns may add up to more than 100 per cent.

Virtually no council tenants, or owner-occupiers for that matter, nominated lack of choice, and only five per cent nominated lack of

---

* The questions were open-ended, so respondents were free to answer in their own words.

privacy - factors which would appear much more germane to Saunders' arguments.

Ironically, the social environment - in the form of friendly neighbours - was also seen as an *attraction* of living on a council estate, especially by council tenants themselves. But also relatively high on the list of good points - according to owner-occupiers at any rate though not so much to council tenants themselves - are that the landlord undertakes repairs quickly and cheaply, and that the allocation policy takes needs into account - that is, attributes which are unique to a successful social housing policy.

Good things about living on a council estate, 1987

% of respondents mentioning:	All %	Owner-occupiers %	Council tenants %
Friendliness/neighbourliness	32	29	44
Good/quick/free repairs	16	17	11
Provides housing for those in need	12	15	3
Good facilities	11	9	15
Cheap(ish) rents	10	11	3
% saying nothing is good	29	39	31

Since respondents could give more than one answer, the columns may add up to more than 100 per cent.

The relatively poor quality of the council tenant's social environment is underlined further by responses to a series of questions asked in the 1990 survey about whether or not a number of specified social problems were common in their area. Council tenants (and to a lesser extent those who were renting privately) are more likely than owner-occupiers to say that each problem is common. In particular, the proportion of council tenants reporting incidents of vandalism, properties in bad condition, graffiti and noisy neighbours is considerably higher than that of owner-occupiers.

Social problems in the neighbourhood, 1990

% saying each was very or fairly common:	All	Owner-occupiers	Council tenants	Other renters
Rubbish/litter	40	38	48	46
Teenagers in street	35	33	46	35
Vandalism	19	15	35	25
Homes/gardens in bad condition	16	11	32	26
Graffiti	14	11	25	16
Noisy neighbours	13	9	23	19
Drunks/tramps	9	6	14	17

Trends in the popularity of home ownership

Saunders claims further that the popularity of owner-occupation is largely unaffected by changes in social and economic circumstances. Problems in the economy may depress the housing market, he argues, but they do not dampen people's desire to own their own home. Evidence from our surveys challenges this claim, since the less favourable economic climate enjoyed by home-owners since the autumn of 1989 does seem to have dented the popularity of home ownership and brought about a re-evaluation of the relative merits of owner-occupation and tenancy.

This trend is seen in responses to a range of questions on attitudes towards home ownership asked in the 1986, 1989 and 1990 surveys. First we asked respondents whether they would recommend that a newly-wed young couple, both with steady jobs, should buy a home as soon as possible, wait a bit, or not plan to buy a home at all. While in 1986 and, still more so, in 1989 the overwhelming weight of advice was that they should buy as soon as possible, the proportion who would give this advice has fallen considerably in the less buoyant housing market of 1990. For some people, the desirability of home ownership in the long term is, perhaps for the time being at least, outweighed by the riskiness of the investment in the short term. This appears to be true among owner-occupiers themselves, for whom the drop in support for buying has been sharpest.

% advising to buy as soon as possible

	1986	1989	1990
All	74	78	70
Owner-occupiers	83	88	78
Council tenants	53	50	47

In the same three years we followed up this question with another, asking respondents what they might say to this hypothetical newly-wed couple about the advantages and disadvantages of home ownership.[12] Responses to this question too show a sharp decline since 1986 in the extent to which home ownership is regarded as a desirable goal, and once again the fall has been particularly marked between 1989 and 1990 when higher mortgage interest rates were really beginning to bite. The change is evident among both owner-occupiers and council tenants. So the worsening housing market within a worsening economic climate seems to have brought about some re-evaluation: for example, between 1989 and 1990 there has been an eight percentage point increase in the proportion who regard home-ownership as a risky investment and an equivalent fall in the number who strongly agree that owning is cheaper than renting.

Attitudes towards home ownership
'Positive' statements

	1986	1989	1990
% strongly agreeing that:			
Buying a home works out cheaper than paying rent	44	41	33
Owning own home gives you freedom to alter it	40	36	31
Your own home will be something to leave to your family	39	41	34
Owning a home makes it easier to move	27	28	19

'Negative' statements

	1986	1989	1990
% strongly agreeing that:			
Couples who buy their own home would be wise to wait before starting a family	23	25	18
Owning a home is too much of a risk for couples without secure jobs	24	24	26
% agreeing that:			
Owning your home is just too much of a responsibility	12	11	9
Owning your home can be a risky investment	25	26	34
Owning your home ties up money you may need for other things	35	35	37
Owning your home is a big financial burden to repair and maintain	50	54	55

More importantly, perhaps, this re-evaluation extends to areas fundamental to the claim that home ownership provides greater freedom and autonomy than does renting. There have been significant falls, for instance, between 1989 and 1990 in the proportion strongly endorsing the positive claims that home-ownership allows one to move when one wants to, or to alter one's home at will.

Meanwhile council tenants appear to see their housing costs as rather less of a burden nowadays than they did in the mid 1980s. In 1986, when council rents had just risen more sharply than mortgage interest rates, just over half of council tenants felt that the rent they paid for their accommodation was on the high side. In 1990 only one-third of council tenants take this view. Further, whereas in 1983 and in 1986, one in four of *all* respondents felt that council tenants paid low rents, by 1990 only one in three take this view.

By 1990 too, council tenants are also much less likely than they were five years earlier to want to move from their present home "if they had a free choice"; indeed they are no more likely to want to do so than are owner-occupiers. Of course, this may be due partly to the fact that an appreciable proportion of former council tenants who wanted to move have already done so, in addition to the fact that a rising proportion (as we reported earlier) expect to buy their present homes. But it is also probably due in part to a greater degree of caution among council tenants about moving from the public sector into the private sector, in the financial climate of the early 1990s.

% who would choose to stay in their present home, 1985-1990

	1985	1986	1989	1990
Outright owners	58	71	73	67
Owners with a mortgage	59	63	60	60
Council tenants	51	55	60	65
Private renters	55	47	50	40

Conclusions

Owner-occupation is by far the most popular form of housing tenure. Two-thirds of tenants would prefer to own their own homes if they had a free choice. But the growth in owner-occupation at the expense of council tenancy together with the impact of other government policies to reduce dependency on the state has had the effect of widening the gap between owner-occupiers and council tenants in terms of both their socio-economic positions and the quality of their housing. One consequence is that many tenants are currently unable to fulfil their aspirations - fewer than one in five actually expect to buy in the next two years. But support for the 'right to buy' policy is still widespread, despite some evidence that it may have passed its peak.

But the popularity of owner-occupation is conditional, not immutable. It appears to have been dented, at least for the time being, as a consequence of the adverse economic climate experienced by many owner-occupiers since 1989. The attraction of home-ownership seems to wane as its potential reduces and as its costs increase. While it may provide autonomy and security, these attributes are apparently not enough to sustain its appeal (at the same level) when the economic advantages of ownership change.

If attitudes to housing vary according to the economic climate, then there seems no reason that they will necessarily be unresponsive to political changes either. Indeed, Conservative governments under Mrs Thatcher were highly successful in promoting the benefits of owner-occupation. But a future government could be equally successful in promoting the cause of social housing, albeit not necessarily provided by local authorities. Attitudes towards housing, like other social goods, are socially constructed and not biologically conditioned.

Notes

1. This was the consequence of three factors: an increase in the number of households with mortgages, the rise in house prices and, in some years, higher interest rates.
2. Strictly speaking, our data refer to individuals *living in* owner-occupied and council dwellings, who are not themselves necessarily legally owners or tenants, since respondents are asked whether their *household* owns or rents their accommodation. The shorter nomenclature is used for ease of style. It should be noted that, unlike many statistics published on housing issues, our figures do indeed refer to *individuals* and not households.
3. 'Other renters' is a residual category for all those respondents who are neither owner-occupiers nor council tenants. So besides including those renting their property from a private individual or from a firm, it also includes those renting from a housing association or living rent-free. Some properties at present managed by housing associations have recently been transferred from the local authority sector with the encouragement of central government. Our data suggest that there are some similarities in profile and attitudes between the occupants of the two forms of tenure, but the number of sample members renting from housing associations is too small to allow us to report the results separately with any confidence. Tenants renting from New Town Development Corporations are included with local authority tenants.
4. Respondents have been classified according to their present occupation (or last occupation if they were retired or unemployed). If, however, they were below retirement age and not economically active or retired, but married to someone who *was* economically active or retired, they were then classified on the basis of their spouse's occupation.
5. This figure includes respondents who are themselves not in paid work and are not retired (such as looking after the home) but whose spouse is retired.
6. The *British Social Attitudes* surveys do not attempt to collect data on exact household income; rather respondents are asked to place themselves in a gross annual income band. As a result, it is not possible to identify precisely which respondents fall into the bottom or top income quartiles. Our method was to identify those respondents in each type of tenure who were clearly in each of the two quartiles; and then to add in the required proportion of council tenants in the next income band up or down (that is, to bring the proportion up to 25 per cent or down to 75 per cent exactly). For example, if an adjacent band included those whose incomes were between the 22 per cent and the 28 per cent mark, half the respondents in this band were included in the bottom quartile. Those aged over 60 have been excluded in order to remove the impact of retirement which usually brings with it a substantial drop in household income.
7. Some respondents may, of course, have bought their council home, but subsequently moved in to new owner-occupied accommodation. We did not ask the necessary questions to enable us to identify these respondents (if, indeed, there were any) but leaving them out should not seriously invalidate our comparison. (This omission has been rectified in the 1991 questionnaire.)
8. Unfortunately it is not easy to chart over time the likely impact of council house sales on the profile of remaining council tenants in receipt of state benefit. The relevant

question was first asked in the 1986 survey, thus giving us only a short time-series. Moreover, in 1988 radical changes were made to the social security system which affected eligibility for benefit. Nonetheless, our data certainly show no sign of a consistent decline in the proportion of council tenants who have received income support, housing benefit or family credit (or their predecessors) within the previous five years.

9. For the calculation of the bottom quartile, see Note 6 above. The 25 per cent cut-off point in each period lay within the following bands: 1983-4, £5,000-£5,999; 1985-7, £5,000-£6,999; 1989-90, £10,000-£11,999.

10. Indeed the percentage point fall in the number of council tenants between 1984/5 and 1990 has been the same in each social class. However, we should note that this means that approximately one in two of the salariat who had lived in a council house switched tenures during the second half of the 1980s compared with one in four of those in the semi- and unskilled working class. Thus in a *relative* sense even the class gap has widened. Thus, for example, the odds ratio for the salariat: semi- and unskilled working class/owner occupier: council tenant has doubled over the period from 8.4 to 16.8.

11. Although the level of local authority property sales in 1990 was, at 130,000, approximately 50,000 below that for 1988 and 1989, it was still 30,000 above the level typical of the mid-1980s (Housing and Construction Statistics, 1990).

12. This series of questions has also been asked in the 1991 survey. In future *Reports* in this series we shall be able to see whether the 1989/91 recession continues to affect attitudes towards home ownership.

References

BOSANQUET, N., 'Interim report: housing', in Jowell, R., Witherspoon, S. and Brook, L., *British Social Attitudes: the 1986 Report,* Gower, Aldershot (1986).

CENTRAL STATISTICAL OFFICE (CSO), *Economic Trends: 1991, Annual Supplement,* HMSO (1991a.).

CENTRAL STATISTICAL OFFICE (CSO), *Social Trends 21,* HMSO, London (1991b.).

CIPFA, *Housing Rents Statistics,* Chartered Institute of Public Finance Accountants, London (annually).

CLAPHAM, D., KEMP, P. and SMITH, S., *Housing and Social Policy,* Macmillan, Basingstoke (1990).

DEPARTMENT OF SOCIAL SECURITY, *Social Security Statistics 1990,* HMSO, London (1991).

FORREST, R. and MURIE, A., 'Residualisation and Council Housing: aspects of the changing social relations of housing tenure', *Journal of Social Policy,* vol.12 (1983), pp.453-68.

FORREST, R. and MURIE, A., 'Marginalization and subsidized individualism: the sale of council houses in the restructuring of the British welfare state', *International Journal of Urban and Regional Research,* vol.10 (1986), pp.46-66.

FORREST, R. and MURIE, A., *Selling the Welfare State: The Privatisation of Public Housing,* Routledge & Kegan Paul, London (1988).

FORREST, R., MURIE, A. and WILLIAMS, P., *Home Ownership: Differentiation and Fragmentation,* Unwin Hyman, London (1990).

HOUSING AND CONSTRUCTION STATISTICS: GREAT BRITAIN, HMSO, London (1990).
KERR, M., *The Right to Buy: A National Survey of Tenants and Buyers of Council Homes,* HMSO, London (1988).
SAUNDERS, P., *A Nation of Home Owners,* Unwin Hyman, London (1990).

Acknowledgement

Since 1985, the Department of the Environment has provided funding to enable us to field questions on housing issues. We are grateful to them for their steadfast financial support, and to Alan Holmans in particular for his advice on new questions to refresh the module.

6 Shades of green

Ken Young [*]

During the 1970s public concern in western countries about the quality of the physical environment increased. Britain was no exception, although the shaping of public debate began more quietly and ran a different course from that in, say, Sweden or Germany. In 1972 *The Ecologist* published a comprehensive environmental programme for Britain under the title *The Blueprint for Survival*. The following year a small group of people adopted *The Blueprint* for a new environmentalist party, campaigning from 1975 as the Ecology Party. Only meagre political success followed, and in 1985 the party conference voted for a change of title to the Green Party both to signify a closer alignment with the markedly more successful European Greens and to sharpen the distinctiveness of their identity in the face of gradual adoption of pro-environment stances by the mainstream parties (Frankland, 1990).

In the European Parliament elections of 1989 the British Greens won 15 per cent of the vote, finishing second in six Euro-constituencies and beating the Liberal Democrats in all but one. The British Green Party's performance was the best in Europe in terms of share of the national vote, and under proportional representation they would have formed the largest national contingent in a Green bloc. Although their electoral fortunes have waned since, and they appear as yet to be a very long way from achieving any British parliamentary representation under the present voting system, the upsurge of support for their uniquely unambiguous policy position testifies to the seismic shift in environmental awareness that the *British Social Attitudes* series has regularly charted.

---

[*] Professor of Politics, Queen Mary and Westfield College, University of London.

The green world view

Although the use of the term 'ecology' to denote the relationship between a species and its habitat can be traced to the 1870s, public concern over the potentially harmful impact of people's activities upon their environment at both local and global levels is very recent and emerged mainly during the 1970s and 1980s (Simpson, 1990). Previous *Reports* in this series have shown how very high and widespread are levels of concern about, for example, industrial pollution, traffic fumes and the cumulative threat to the global environment posed by the discharge of 'greenhouse' gases into the atmosphere. As we shall see, the results from our 1990 fieldwork confirm these findings and show the extent to which the identification of new issues by scientific research and by campaigning bodies has evoked a response among a population for whom a paucity of scientific knowledge is apparently no obstacle to growing feelings of concern and the corresponding belief that 'something must be done'.

But by whom: government, industry, the individual or by some combination of these? The three main parties have been quick to adopt green policy positions. For instance, Mrs Thatcher followed her 1988 Royal Society speech with a claim that "we Conservatives are not merely friends of the earth, we are its guardians and trustees for years to come". The subsequent White Paper provided an account of her government's stewardship of environmental matters. Both of the main opposition parties now give their environmental policies a high profile, aided by the mass media. Meanwhile environmental groups excoriate all the main parties for the shallowness and opportunism of their commitments.

Yet unlike many other major national and international political issues, green issues give ordinary people a chance to express their political concerns through their own personal actions. At one level, environmental protection is part of the arcane world of intergovernmental congresses and agreements; yet at another level, people are able to make a direct intellectual connection between their own purchases or practices and their supposed contribution to the overall state of the planet.

The environmental movement has increasingly stressed this connection: as *The Friends of the Earth Handbook* puts it, "individually accepting responsibility for the way we live, and collectively taking action to do something about it, allows us to restore a sense of balance between ourselves and the economic order in which we operate" (Friends of the Earth, 1987, p.16). The connection is consolidated in such popular publications as the *Green Consumer Guide* (Elkington and Hailes, 1988), *Cruelty-free Shopper* (Howlett, 1989), or *How to be Green* (Button, 1990).

So the movement goes beyond narrowly-based politics to a more far-reaching green world view. It aims not only to influence the outcome of electoral contests but to achieve broader cultural change. While industry and government tend to have short-term financial and political horizons, the environmental movement continues to warn about consequences that will not materialise for twenty years or two hundred years or more. Environmental groups aim to achieve cultural change which would influence attitudes, behaviour and understanding of the everyday world. The green world view embodies environmentally appropriate behaviour that is founded upon chains of personal, industrial and governmental responsibility. So distinctive and explicit are these precepts that they might fairly be seen as constituting a model of green citizenship.

That a culture shift with respect to environmental values is taking place is almost beyond dispute. Views differ, however, on its causes. Some attribute it narrowly to green campaigning; others link it to a wider value re-orientation, notably the 'postmaterialist' rejection of the consequences of economic growth (Inglehart, 1990); others see it as part of the growth of feminism (King, 1989); others see it as the first stirrings of a new secular religion: Mary Douglas' observation that the same conditions that affect belief in a denominational god also bear upon environmentalism (Douglas, 1975) casts a provocative light upon such popular titles as *Green Pages: the Business of Saving the World* (Elkington, Burke and Hailes, 1988).

Certainly the green world view is an ambitious (if still slightly obscure) project, setting itself an 'eco-political task' that "redefines economic and social behaviour along more sustainable lines" (Simpson, 1990, p.17). It encompasses a specific vocabulary, a distinctive set of beliefs to which it gives expression, and a concomitant life style. In John Button's words, it

> stresses the importance of respect for the earth and all its inhabitants, using only what resources are necessary and appropriate, acknowledging the rights of all forms of life, and recognising that all that exists is part of one interconnected whole (Button, 1988, p.190).

This general statement takes us some way towards identifying the components of a green world view in which four dimensions may be distinguished: recognition of the existence of a global ecosystem and threats to it; concern for and commitment to global well-being; a sense of connectedness with nature; and the willingness to adjust personal patterns of behaviour and consumption to protect the environment.[1]

This chapter explores the extent to which a green world view and the elements of green citizenship can be discerned from our 1990 survey. We will be particularly attentive to lines of social division which may be expected to correspond with differing attitudes to the environment: principally social class, income, education, gender, and religion. There is an ever-present risk when measuring attitudes to a subject on which a new consensus is emerging that we will over-represent (or at least over-report) 'approved' attitudes or patterns of behaviour. Allowance should be made for this, although it is not so much a problem when considering either year-on-year changes or comparisons between sub-groups within the sample.

Another intractable problem is the possible ambiguity of the responses we obtain. There is always a temptation to infer environmentalist values from what appear to be environmentalist practices. But the frequent confluence of personal interests - whether in the form of healthy eating, household economies or social conformity - with environmentally sound practices makes it impossible to identify which 'came first'. The danger of over-interpreting and thereby over-estimating the strength and stability of green attitudes and practices must be constantly borne in mind.

Threats to the ecosystem and global well-being

The first step in our investigation of the green world view is to ask how far our respondents perceive that environmental deterioration is a threat. It is commonplace to claim that problems are most clearly perceived when they are close to home. Pollution in the immediate neighbourhood, for example, might be expected to evoke a sharper response than would the abstractions of global environmental change. Yet there is little reason to credit this view. Popular response to complex scientific phenomena may well be strong when the phenomena are either easily portrayed or able to be grasped at the symbolic level. It is not so much the scientific reality but the "image" that is important in shaping perceptions (Boulding, 1957).

This is apparently the case with environmental change. In each of the issues we explore, some notion of ecosystem - a set of mutually sustaining and interacting phenomena which are vulnerable to unintended and long-term damage - appears to underlie the pattern of responses.[2] Recognition of the actual or potential seriousness of environmental damage is one indicator of this; so too is willingness to support policy interventions that constrain public or private choices in the interests of environmental quality or safety.

Environmental hazards and pollution

We ask respondents how concerned they are about a range of environmental issues. The three issues below - the use of chemicals in agriculture, the disposal of sewage, and the quality of drinking water - address the basic ecosystem notion of chains of effects which may threaten health. All three are widely recognised as hazards.

		Very concerned	A bit concerned	Not very concerned	Not at all concerned
Level of concern about:					
Disposal of sewage	%	69	25	3	2
Insecticides, fertilisers and chemical sprays	%	57	34	6	2
Quality of drinking water	%	51	31	13	4

Subgroup differences in responses to these questions are marked. In demonstrating this, we concentrate on those reporting themselves to be 'very concerned'. In our previous explorations of environmental issues we have found notable differences between men and women in different age groups and relatively few differences between people in different social classes, despite the popular representation of environmental awareness as a middle-class stance.

	Age and sex						Social class	
	Men			Women			Non-	
	18-34	35-54	55+	18-34	35-54	55+	manual	Manual
% very concerned about:								
Disposal of sewage	60	66	65	70	79	74	71	67
Insecticides, fertilisers								
and chemical sprays	39	51	64	43	72	70	59	56
Quality of drinking								
water	43	46	46	53	58	57	52	50

These responses to new questions could have been anticipated on the basis of our previous findings. Earlier *Reports* have highlighted the distinctiveness of women in the middle age group in their concern for the environment. Even so, the size of the differences between women and men and, in particular, women over 35, is remarkable. Does it suggest once again that women have a greater awareness of those ecological chains which were first brought into popular awareness by Rachel Carson's *Silent Spring* (1962)?[3]

Surprisingly perhaps, given the oft-cited connection between eco-feminism and nurturing, we found relatively few differences between women with young children, those with older children and those who have never had children. The sole example - and it is a striking one - is attitudes to chemicals in agriculture where mothers are much more concerned than women who have never had children. We found bigger differences based on religion. First, those who profess *any* religious attachment register higher levels of concern about these threats to the environment than do those who do not, and, on agricultural chemicals, religious *attendance* (such as churchgoing) rather than professed *belief* is the more powerful discriminator.

	Religious attenders	Religious non-attenders	Non-religious
% very concerned about:			
Disposal of sewage	73	72	64
Insecticides, fertilisers			
and chemical sprays	67	58	50
Quality of drinking water	53	51	49

In order to probe respondents' general assessment of environmental trends, we asked first how exaggerated or not the statement is that "within the next twenty years, damage to the environment will be the biggest single problem facing Europe". Half of the respondents think it is more or less true, with a further third believing the prospect to be only 'slightly exaggerated'. As few as ten per cent of respondents believe the statement to be 'highly exaggerated'. Secondly, we asked about acid rain, a problem from which Britain suffers relatively little since air pollutants originating here tend to be precipitated over Scandinavia. But it is a growing problem in Europe and has been given extra publicity by the development of closer economic ties with the former communist-bloc countries. In any event, just over one-half of respondents rate acid rain as a 'very serious' environmental concern, and a further one-third as 'quite serious'. These are high levels of expressed concern by any standards about an issue that poses no immediate direct threat to the sample members.

Energy options and the risks of nuclear power

We have asked a series of questions about nuclear power and the disposal of nuclear waste since the first *BSA* survey in 1983. The following table brings together responses to several questions which show trends in the perceived risks of nuclear power.

	1983	1986	1989	1990
% agreeing that:				
Waste from nuclear power stations has very or quite serious environmental effects	83	90	89	90
A serious accident at a British nuclear power station is very or quite likely in next ten years	45	59	58	59
Nuclear power stations create very or quite serious risks for the future	63	78	73	74

As we will see in respect of other environmental hazards, the overall picture is one of increasing concern since 1983, although in this case there have been more marked fluctuations, largely reflecting the sharp rise in concern in 1986, immediately following the disaster at Chernobyl. On the other hand, concern about nuclear waste has remained at very high levels in recent years.[4] These overall perceptions of risk feed directly into the majority preference for a non-nuclear energy policy. Ronald Inglehart, in his most recent (1990) reference to environmental aspects of postmaterialism, argues that the concern of postmaterialists for efficient resource use should lead them to favour nuclear power over other, non-renewable energy options. They do not; rather, the association of environmental conservationism with anti-nuclear views - which was established in the United States even before the Three Mile Island incident reshaped patterns of American opinion - is echoed here.

But this does *not* imply the cognitive inconsistency that Inglehart claims. Our findings, based on an unusually extensive range of questions, suggest that opposition to nuclear power generation by no means implies support for the continuing consumption of fossil fuels. Rather, since our first survey in 1983 support has shifted decisively away from the construction of new coal-fired power stations towards a preference for making do with existing capacity. Although support for nuclear power fluctuates somewhat, it has been low since 1983 and is now still lower. In contrast, there has since 1983 been an equally fluctuating but seemingly inexorable trend away from expanding coal-fuelled power stations towards making do with what power-generating capacity we already have. Between 1987 and 1990, both trends have been decisive.

	1983	1984	1985	1986	1987	1989	1990
% agreeing that:	%	%	%	%	%	%	%
We should make do with the power stations we have already	32	38	34	34	25	44	55
We should build more coal-fuelled power stations	47	44	41	52	48	37	28
We should build more nuclear power stations	19	15	23	11	22	16	14

Do those figures suggest an increasingly sophisticated public, cautious about the risks of nuclear power - in which waste disposal is probably the most persistent source of reservations - while at the same time increasingly aware that the principal source of greenhouse gases is the burning of fossil fuels in power stations? Could the position of no change in capacity, favoured by just over half the sample, be indicative of a growing public adoption of what might be termed an 'energy strategy'? These may be tempting inferences to draw but they would be quite unjustified. The questions above probably do little more than tap general attitudes, and a further series of questions are necessary before we can explore in any depth either the energy policy preferences of our respondents or their likely level of support for conservationist policies. We refer later to a series of questions about the extent to which individuals themselves act in environmentally-conscious ways - a better method, perhaps, of tapping potential support for active conservationist measures.

Concern for the planet

The environmental problems we deal with range from the irritating and mildly harmful to the potentially life-threatening. Their impact extends from the local (traffic noise) to the regional (nuclear waste) to the international (industrial effluent and acid rain). Of a different order are threats to the ecosystem itself, matters of global significance for reasons either of interdependence (population growth) or of the universal nature of exposure to them (climatic change).

We begin with levels of concern about such global threats. Of those shown below, the two threats that refer to major atmospheric changes - ozone depletion and the build-up of greenhouse gases - occasion more alarm than do the two that refer to world resource issues of fuel supplies and population growth.

		Very concerned	A bit concerned	Not very/ Not at all concerned
Level of concern about:				
Thinning of the ozone layer	%	57	30	10
The 'greenhouse effect'	%	46	36	15
Using up earth's remaining coal, oil and gas	%	37	38	23
Growth in world population	%	30	39	29

These are all issues where knowledge of the existence of hazards might be expected to feed concern for their effects, with the more educated respondents displaying the highest levels of concern. But this is not true, except insofar as respondents with *no* educational qualifications express less concern. Otherwise it is difficult to distinguish people with A'levels or O'levels/CSEs from those with degrees in any consistent way. Similarly, associations with religion are not strong either in respect of denomination or of attendance, except unsurprisingly, that Catholics are notably less concerned about world population growth.

We also put a specific question about global warming, asking respondents in effect how far-fetched they thought it was that "within twenty years, life on earth will be seriously damaged by a rise in the world's temperature". About one half think that the statement exaggerates the real position, while the other half think it is more or less true. Men of all ages, but particularly older men, are more disposed than their female counterparts to dismiss the statement as 'highly exaggerated'.

Gender differences in perceptions of these more cataclysmic environmental threats are quite strong, and are also reflected in assessments of the seriousness of those processes which are believed to contribute to the greenhouse effect, depletion of the ozone layer and climate change. We asked specifically about three: cutting down of tropical rainforests, industrial fumes in the air and aerosol chemicals in the atmosphere. As the table below shows, women tend to be slightly

more concerned about pollution threats than men are, and concern tends
to diminish with age.

		Men			Women		
% saying very serious:	Total	18-34	35-54	55+	18-34	35-54	55+
Cutting down tropical rainforests	68	74	71	57	69	70	67
Industrial fumes in the air	58	59	57	47	62	65	53
Aerosol chemicals in the atmosphere	51	54	47	40	60	58	48

Protecting flora and fauna

Recognition of a global ecosystem is mostly a matter of knowledge rather
than value systems. In contrast, the issue of protecting species and their
habitats, given the limited evidence as to the working of eco-balances, is
less of a scientific issue than a moral one.[5] Respect for non-human forms
of life requires a degree of empathetic projection, a quality which Herbert
Spencer defined as "the greatest civilising force". That projection involves
grasping the notion that sentient creatures care what is done to them. In
Dawkins' memorable example, there is a moral difference between
demolishing York Minster and hacking to death a whale, precisely
because the whale cares what we do to it (Dawkins, 1989, p.57).

In practice, respect for the natural world and for the preservation of
species is likely to originate more from a kind of generalised
conservationism that deplores the loss of any species than from an
intrinsic respect for life as such. Few take a fundamentalist position
which concedes an equality of right to life between human beings and
other species.

Our questions provide a point of entry to all of these issues, covering
attitudes to the loss of plant and animal species, expenditure to protect
rare species, the use of animals for both cosmetic and medical
experimentation, and even the issue of fox-hunting. However, in no case
do they probe deeply enough to discover underlying beliefs. The
complexities of these matters would require their own module of
questions to explore them fully.

The processes of species elimination are complicated, and their
consequences uncertain or ambiguous (Myers, 1989). Nonetheless,
deforestation and the use of chemical pesticides in agriculture are now
recognised as liable to threaten the survival of some species.

First, we asked respondents to indicate the strength of their agreement
or disagreement with the proposition that "too much money is spent trying
to protect rare plants and animals". Overall, fewer than 15 per cent

agree, while over half disagree (54 per cent); almost a third neither agree nor disagree, suggesting that many people have not considered the issue.

Secondly, we asked them to indicate the strength of their concern over the loss of plant and animal species. As many as 88 per cent of the sample declare themselves to be concerned, two-thirds of these saying 'very' concerned. Differences between men and women and between the different age groups and social classes appear as before, and in the expected directions.

While most of our questions have a 'protective' focus, centring on practices which seek to mitigate hazards or counter destruction, we also approached the issue from another direction with a question first asked in 1983 on whether "fox-hunting should be banned by law." The results are striking, with over two-thirds in favour and only 16 per cent of our respondents disagreeing. Support for a ban has risen substantially since 1983 when just 45 per cent were in favour.

These apparently clear findings are nonetheless difficult to interpret, as the question of fox-hunting taps a wide range of feelings, from the sanctity of animal life through class hostility to a Wildean aestheticism. Considering that fox-hunting might well be a potent symbolic issue, it is surprising that class differences are not greater: even among those in Social Classes I and II only 22 per cent oppose a ban. On the other hand, party differences are more clear cut, with Conservative identifiers (22 per cent) more opposed to a ban than Labour and Liberal Democrat supporters (12 per cent each). Sympathy with fox-hunting is most noticeable among the very small number of respondents who live in the countryside itself; but even here, only 27 per cent oppose a ban. Women, particularly younger women (under 35), tend to be more hostile than men towards fox-hunting. The overall pattern promises popular sympathy for the Labour Party's new policy on field sports, which would, if enacted, ban the hunting of foxes for sport.

We also repeated two other questions first included in 1983, asking respondents to indicate the strength of their agreement or disagreement with the propositions that "it is acceptable to use animals for testing and improving cosmetics", and then "it is acceptable to use animals for testing medicines if it could save human lives".

The use of animals for cosmetic purposes is strongly rejected throughout our sample, with only five per cent agreeing with the statement, and one-half of the sample registering 'strong' disagreement. This opposition has grown since 1983 when 12 per cent agreed. Men, except young men, are less concerned than women.

However, people do distinguish clearly between the use of animals in cosmetic testing and their use in medical research. Where human lives, rather than appearances, are at stake, people come down heavily in favour of animal experimentation; only a quarter of the sample disagrees. However, once again we found a substantial minority who would not express a view either way on what is after all a complex and inevitably over-simplified ethical question.

Perhaps the most striking feature of the table below is the social class differences - respondents in Social Classes I and II are ten percentage points more likely to support animal experiments for medical research than are those in Social Classes IV and V - and the gender gap within the different age groups.   There is, for instance, a gap of almost 20 percentage points between middle-aged women and men; the gap diminishes sharply, as is often the case, among older and younger people.

It is acceptable to use animals for testing medicines

		Agree strongly/ Agree	Disagree/ Disagree strongly
% agreeing or disagreeing:			
Age within sex:			
Men 18-34	%	57	27
35-54	%	67	25
55+	%	62	23
Women 18-34	%	58	25
35-54	%	48	28
55+	%	56	25
Social Class:			
I/II	%	62	23
III non-manual	%	59	22
III manual	%	59	25
IV/V	%	51	32
All	%	58	26

Environmental action

In this section of the chapter we move from examining essentially cost-free protestations of concern for the environment to issues of practical action.   Here we are dealing with people's practices as they report them to us, and with their views on the allocation of responsibility for environmental protection.   That is, we are concerned here less with what people feel generally than with what they do specifically, or are prepared to do - including what they are prepared to pay for.

One unequivocal expression of concern for, or interest in, the natural world is membership of environmental or 'nature' organisations such as the National Trust, the RSPB, the Worldwide Fund for Nature and Friends of the Earth. Although the proportion of the sample belonging to any one such organisation is small, almost one in five of the sample belong to at least one environmentally-orientated body. Membership carries a financial cost, and as expected members of most of these bodies are drawn from the higher income households: as many as one-third of the 118 National Trust members in our sample are drawn from the highest income group (£23,000 or over a year). This lends support to the notion that what distinguishes the better-off from the less well-off is their behaviour rather more than their attitudes.

Individual responsibility or government action?

A central tenet of the 'green world view' is the acceptance of a greater degree of personal responsibility for the environment. We asked our respondents whether or not they agreed that "science can solve environmental problems without any need for people to change their behaviour". This proposition - which may well be measuring faith in science rather than the assumption of personal responsibility - is overwhelmingly rejected, with just 13 per cent agreeing. People in the manual social classes and with no educational qualifications are far more inclined than others to give science the benefit of the doubt. Science also enjoys greater authority among older people.

We also asked about the respective responsibilities for the environment of government, industry and 'ordinary people'; each of the statements we put to respondents recognised that action involved costs. Respondents were asked to record their agreement or disagreement with each statement on a five-point scale:

> *The government should do more to protect the environment, even if it leads to higher taxes*
>
> *Industry should do more to protect the environment, even if it leads to lower profits and fewer jobs*
>
> *Ordinary people should do more to protect the environment, even if it means paying higher prices*

This set of questions would repay analysis in greater depth. For the moment we find, first, a very high proportion of people (between two-thirds and three-quarters) who agree or agree strongly with *each* of the three statements. Second, we find the now expected associations with age, income, social class and education. Third, as the table below shows, we do not however find the familiar gender effect. Men in virtually all age groups are more inclined than women to support all three types of action despite the costs.

	Protection of the environment		
% agreeing strongly or agreeing	Government should do more	Industry should do more	Ordinary people should do more
All	66	75	75
Men			
18-34	64	72	71
35-54	74	80	80
55+	71	83	77
Women			
18-34	57	65	67
35-54	68	82	83
55+	66	68	70

Car use and transport

A third area in which we explored willingness to accept (or allocate) responsibility for environmental protection was private transport. We asked our respondents how much they agreed or disagreed with two statements:

For the sake of the environment, car users should pay higher taxes

If the government had to choose, it should improve roads rather than public transport

The following table shows the overall distribution of responses:

		Agree strongly	Agree	Neither agree nor disagree	Disagree	Disagree strongly
Car users should pay higher taxes	%	5	18	21	41	12
Government should improve roads first	%	7	30	20	31	12

The very high degree of perceived threat from lead in petrol exhausts, reported earlier, does not carry over into support for higher taxation for car users, but opinion on the (forced) choice between road improvements and public transport is more divided. Moreover, as the next table shows, there is, surprisingly, an *inverse* relationship between income and support for public transport. Thus, those in households with incomes below £12,000 a year - where levels of car ownership are notably lower - are *less* keen on public transport expenditure than their circumstances might lead us to expect.

Government should improve roads rather than public transport

	Under £7,000	£7,000- £11,999	£12,000- £17,999	£18,000- £22,999	£23,000 or more
	%	%	%	%	%
Agree strongly or agree	44	41	35	28	31
Neither agree nor disagree	17	15	21	21	17
Disagree or disagree strongly	37	44	43	50	52

These results are startling enough to demand a closer analysis by use of, or access to, a car. Here we find again that the relationships are in the opposite direction from that which reasoning might suggest, with those having the use of a car being less keen on road improvements (35 per cent) than those in non-car households (41 per cent). Either the question was misunderstood, which does not seem likely in this case, or there is some other explanation. Two come to mind. First, could the high cost and poor service of present public transport provision have convinced its users of the virtues of car travel, to the extent that most non-car users nowadays are aspiring ones? Secondly, perhaps car users believe that if public transport were improved, fewer other drivers would use the roads leaving them clearer for themselves; and the same calculus could be made by public transport users in the opposite direction. But these are speculations. We will investigate this apparent conundrum in more detail in future modules on the environment to see if it stands up to scrutiny.

Not surprisingly, those with low to middle incomes (between £7,000 and £17,999 a year) are less enthusiastic about increased taxes for car users than are the better off. In this case, however, access to a car does prove a more powerful discriminator. Those in households which do not have the use of a car or van are more ready to impose taxes for the sake of the environment. Nevertheless, the relatively large proportion of respondents with no view on this matter suggests that the process by which policy would bite - by raising the price of car ownership and use, thus reducing car usage - may not have been recognised by many respondents. If it had been we suspect that more people would have taken a view one way or the other.

For the sake of the environment, car users should pay higher taxes	With access to car	Without access to car
	%	%
Strongly agree or agree	21	35
Neither agree nor disagree	20	26
Disagree or disagree strongly	58	35

In a culture which places a high value on mobility, the freedom to travel which the car confers appears to overcome the otherwise consistent concern for the quality of the environment. Here perhaps is the crunch, the point where cost-free environmental attitudes meet the real personal costs of mobility constraint. This, and the apparent deafness to recent transport policy debates, might be seen as the principal (and arguably most   important)   qualification   upon   the   otherwise   ubiquitous environmental enthusiasm of our respondents.

The position is unlikely to remain static.   Research carried out regularly in (West) Germany since 1960 shows an initially marked, then steady, decline in the percentage of car owners claiming that they drive because they enjoy it (from 64 to 41 per cent), rather than because they have to. Wolfgang Sachs has analysed the gratifications of motoring with great insight, commenting that:

> it is just a tiny, privileged minority who can afford to give up the car altogether, because only privileged minorities are in a position to freely choose their daily speed and distance. All others are left tied up with the heritage of their past desires (Sachs, 1984, p.276).

Environmental activism

We now turn to examine our data on everyday environmental behaviour. We asked a range of questions about the extent to which respondents engage in environmentally-sensitive and resource-conscious behaviour. We deal first with three aspects of behaviour that do not involve changing purchasing habits, with respect to saving energy, recycling and cutting back on driving. We also added a question to each of these to ascertain how far they were contemplating changing their habits.

		Does now	Intends to do
Make a conscious effort to save electricity	%	71	7
Return bottles etc for recycling	%	60	15
Cut back on driving*	%	35	5

* Base excludes those replying that the question does not apply to them.

Practices which represent *personal economies* - saving electricity and cutting back on driving - are more strongly associated with income, suggesting, perhaps, that the environmental benefits of such behaviour are secondary to the financial ones. On the other hand, the practice here which reveals a level of *environmental consciousness* and incurs a degree of personal cost - recycling household waste - is more positively associated with social class and education.* These findings are broadly congruent

---

* We also asked respondents whether they "choose to eat less meat." This question is not reported here, however, since responses appear to be more closely related to attitudes to diet, which are influenced by class and educational level, than to environmental concerns.

with those from a major US study which found that cutbacks were associated with low household incomes while those on higher incomes spend them on energy efficiency measures (Dillman, Rosa and Dillman, 1984).

The widespread (if possibly over-reported) practice of conserving resources cannot necessarily be interpreted as evidence of environmental concern. Research in the Netherlands concluded that in respect of reducing home energy consumption, for example, conservation behaviour is complex and may well derive from goals other than conservation, and that "a general [conservation] disposition does not exist" (Midden and Ritsema, 1984, p.135). A US study, reported in the same volume, reviewed evidence from a range of conservation studies, concluding that "a generalised conservation tendency is present among only a fraction of the population, [and] even here the motivation does not appear to be entirely one of social responsibility" (Painter, *et al*, 1984, p.151).

When we turn to consumer behaviour, however, we see a more direct trade-off between the supposed environmental benefits of 'environment-friendly' products and the personal costs of using them. Even where prices are lower, the consumer may be obliged to meet some higher cost in convenience.

Market research studies have indicated that environmental consciousness *does* translate into a willingness to accept higher costs. They suggest a widespread acceptance on the part of many consumers that there is an 'environmental premium' to pay for goods (Mintel, 1989), and that increased environmental concern is increasingly translating itself into purchasing patterns (Mackenzie, 1991). Our findings confirm these conclusions and suggest that further changes in some aspects of purchasing behaviour may well be in prospect.

		Does now	Intends to
Purchases:			
Environment friendly aerosols	%	77	3
Toiletries and cosmetics not tested on animals	%	58	8
Products made out of recycled materials	%	57	9
Environment-friendly washing powders	%	49	12
Unleaded petrol*	%	45	27
Organically-grown fruit and vegetables	%	39	12

* Base excludes those replying that the question does not apply to them.

These proportions are surprisingly high, and the relationships are striking, though once again in the expected directions. There is a notable association between 'green consumerism' and both education and income (see **Table 6.1**), although the income threshold at which the switch seems to be made to 'green' purchases is perhaps surprisingly low; it is only those with the very lowest incomes who refrain from buying green, presumably because these products tend to be more expensive or because the shops they use do not stock them (or label them) as enthusiastically.

'Green' consumer or 'new' consumer?

Our findings appear to confirm the premise that 'green' consumers certainly exist, but they are still difficult to define (see, for example, Eden, 1990). Nonetheless, strong evidence now exists to suggest that people are willing to accept some personal costs for the sake of improving or protecting environmental quality while at the same time believing that government and industry have a major part to play. Mackenzie's conclusion from her review of recent market research surveys is pertinent:

> consumers recognise that their actions as individuals alone can only go so far. The blame for causing environmental problems in the first place is laid squarely [on] industry, and alleviating the problems is regarded as a task for industry and the government. Consumers are happy to make a contribution, but expect this to be made easy for them to do. In many areas, individual action is considered to be effective only if everyone else does it too, and this is felt unlikely to happen without some inducement from legislation, from the development of appropriate infrastructure, or from the true participation of manufacturers in developing real solutions (Mackenzie, 1991, p.73)

Consumer behaviour is however notoriously fickle, and green consumerism is no panacea for manufacturers. Evidence is growing of scepticism among consumers (and the trade press) as to the validity of the claims made for 'green' products.[6] In any event, there are the murmurings here of a 'new consumerism'; that is, a better informed and more assertive form of consumer behaviour, in which people use their purchasing power to achieve social or economic goals. As far as environmental goals are concerned, there would need to be a better consolidation of beliefs, values and actions than at present exists before such power could be exercised effectively. In particular, it seems, there would need to be a greater degree of consistency than we have found which could flow only from a stronger grasp of realities.

We have seen in *The 6th Report* that the doubts and uncertainties inherent in major scientific controversies are not reflected in popular attitudes, where fixed ideas tend to prevail; Evans and Durant conclude that "public ignorance of some of the findings of science is very great," (Evans and Durant, 1989). Perhaps the most sobering of recent research findings has been the very weak association between the perception of global problems and their solution through appropriate individual behaviour. As Cope and Winward conclude, "consumers in general appear to have very little understanding of the true connection between specific environmental problems and the consumer behaviour which can ameliorate these problems" (1991, pp.83-86).[7]

Conclusions

This review attempts to answer two questions. First, does a 'green world view' prevail within a wider group than that of green activists? Secondly, are some social groups 'greener' than others?

We have found only a weak association between attitudes to a range of distinct issues. The holism and internal consistency found in the pronouncements of green activists is scarcely reflected by respondents to our survey. They take utilitarian approaches to issues which greens see as fundamental, and weigh up personal advantage against social costs to a greater degree than green activists would approve.

Is 'green' then a useful concept in the interpretation of social attitudes? Until very recently it has been conventional to see environmentalism either as an aspect of postmaterialism (Inglehart, 1990) or as an aspect of middle class radicalism (Cotgrove, 1976; Cotgrove and Duff, 1980). Both interpretations involve processes of social change - rising wealth, eroding class identities, greater assertiveness - that are likely to increase support for environmentalism in the long term; yet each overstates the distinctiveness of environmentalism, while understating its current prevalence. Our findings suggest that positive attitudes to the environment lack the coherence claimed by both accounts; at the same time they have a far wider social base than is consistent with either account. Green consumerism, on the other hand, is a different phenomenon, part of a wider trend towards more demanding and aware consumer behaviour.

Should environmental activists take heart from the rise of green consumerism? Certainly, it can be represented as introducing a vast audience to the idea that they are responsible for the consequences of their purchasing decisions - a central tenet of the green world view. There remains, however, a major obstacle to further greening, imposed by the nature of consumerism itself.

The green world view as represented by John Button (1988), Friends of the Earth (1987) and other activists stresses 'necessity' and 'appropriateness' in the use and consumption of resources. This minimalist approach to consumption is clearly at odds, not just with the expansionary dynamic of a market economy, but also with the common desire to improve the material well-being of everyday life. While the green perspective caricatures normal patterns of consumption into an ideology - "consumerism equates more possessions with greater happiness. You are what you own, and the more you own, the happier you will be" (Irvine 1989) - probably few of our respondents would describe their own impulses in these terms; rather, as Sachs conjectures, yesterday's desires have become today's necessities, thereby subverting the greens' case for 'appropriate' consumption. To that extent, green consumerism is something of a contradiction in terms.

Modern Britain, then, has certainly become somewhat green and may become greener yet. But the process appears to be one of wider permeation rather than one of a deepening of commitment. Even this cursory review of the data suggests that while generalised environmental concern is to be found in all social groups, the intensity with which people express it varies greatly.

This, of course, is what might have been expected prior to the emergence of the current composite notion of environmentalism. Much of what passes for correct behaviour in a green age would have been seen earlier as a matter of life-style (vegetarianism, interest in conservation), as a matter of income (home energy conservation), as a matter of education (familiarity with scientific debates), or as a matter of ideology (nuclear politics and animal rights). Increasingly, we weave these separate strands together into a green world view, encouraged to do so by the flood of green popular literature. More subtly, and perhaps more realistically, we may expect to find limited spillover effects, as the adoption of one attitude or practice lowers the barriers to the adoption of another.

Much more work, particularly on attitude change, must be done. Future surveys in this series may throw light upon the robustness and stability of the attitudes we have described. It is notable that such differences in attitudes on environmental issues as exist between the supporters of the three main political parties are generally small, no doubt partly reflecting the lack of clear policy differences on these issues between the parties. The environment may have become a political issue in recent years but it has not (yet) become a party political issue in the way that, for example, health and education have become. Similarly, any assessment of who is greenest must be an interim judgement, based on shifting patterns of support for distinguishable options and practices.

Yet there are signs that a social base does exist for deeper green environmentalism. We began by examining a coherent and cohesive world view, which, while it fails to pervade the wider society in quite that form, nevertheless offers what may well be an increasingly appealing means of interpreting, and thus coping with, a world of threat and rapid change. All such world views (or assumptive worlds) bring a degree of certainty, or at least expectability, to everyday life; they bring order and purpose and hope. To that extent, the green world view plays much the same role as do the traditional religions.

It is notable, therefore, that on a number of counts, those who profess and practice *any* religion consistently register a higher degree of environmental awareness than those who do neither. Theological notions of man's dominion over the earth as told in Genesis may vary, but most Christians (at least) probably incline to some notion of environmental responsibility (or *stewardship*) in preference to the notion of divinely sanctioned exploitation. Respect for the earth and its inhabitants, the appropriate use of resources, acknowledgement of the rights of life and the recognition of the interconnected wholeness of existence - as proclaimed by green activists - sounds like a universalistic religion for an ecumenical age.

Moreover, the green world view tends to be a more 'feminine' world view. Younger to middle-aged women, in 1990 as in previous years, have shown themselves distinctive in the extent to which they care about environmental issues. It is safe to say that women in that age group are well established as by far the greenest social group in Britain. In addition, the generalised formulations of the popular green handbooks are given a cutting edge by 'ecofeminist' theory. Not all of this writing has the rigour and persuasive power of Patricia Hynes' *The Recurring Silent Spring* (nor indeed that of its prototype), but the feminist appeal of the green world view has also been characterised as the appeal of "no dogma, no authorized texts or beliefs and no authoritative body to authorize anything" ('Starhawk', 1989, p.175). Not all of the women in our sample are likely to identify themselves as feminists in this sense, but in striving to make sense of our findings it may be fruitful to explore further the persistence of such feminine images in the green world view.

Notes

1. These may be more formally understood as the four components - beliefs, values, cathexes and interventions - of a coherent green 'assumptive world' as described briefly in *The 5th Report* (Young, 1988) in relation to countryside change, and more fully in Young (1979).

2. Geertz (1963, p.3) characterises an ecosystem as a "community of interrelated organisms together with their common habitat and can range in size, scope and durability from a drop of pond water together with the micro-organisms which live within it to the entire earth with all of its plant and animal inhabitants". The term is generally adopted in order to avoid the crude dualism of man-environment relations and to introduce instead ideas of 'the balance of nature' as a dynamic equilibrium. That said, popular and campaigning usages often revert to a static and unstable equilibrium in stressing the adverse effects of industrialisation upon the global ecosystem. We use the term 'ecosystem' here when referring to the notion of a green world view, reverting to the term 'environmental interdependence' when discussing our own, more limited, findings.

3. A commemorative volume derived from a conference designed to reassess Carson's work after 20 years concluded that while "there seems no likelihood of completely eliminating chemical controls in the near future ... virtually all the issues Rachel Carson explored are in some stage of correction" (Marco, Hollingsworth and Durham, 1987, p.198). These qualifications of course apply only to pesticide, and not fertiliser, use. For a radically different assessment, see Hynes (1989).

4. Roman Catholics and non-Christian believers register very much higher levels of concern about the general threat from nuclear power and about the hazards of nuclear waste than do Protestants and those with no religion, a suggestive finding that should prompt further analysis of religiosity and pollution threats; see also Douglas (1966), Greeley (1991).

5. Freedman's introduction to environmental ecology distinguishes between philosophical (sic), utilitarian and ecological reasons for seeking species preservation, but his examples are entirely utilitarian; Freedman (1989) pp.267-8.

6. A useful review of press and trade journal commentary on the green consumer is to be found in Eden (1990).

7. Not purchasing CFC-based aerosols is incorrectly cited by respondents as the most
    effective way of avoiding global warming, and recycled packaging as the most
    effective means of protecting the tropical rainforests.

References

BOULDING, K., *The Image*, University of Michigan Press, Ann Arbor
(1957).
BUTTON, J., *A Dictionary of Green Ideas*, Routledge, London (1988).
BUTTON, J., *How to be Green*, Century Hutchinson, London (1990).
COPE, D. and WINWARD, J., 'Information Failures in Green
Consumerism', *Consumer Policy Review* 1(2), (April 1991) pp.83-6.
COTGROVE, S., 'Environmentalism and Utopia', *Sociological Review*,
(New Series) 24, (1976), pp.23-42.
COTGROVE, S. and DUFF. A., 'Environmentalism, Middle-class
Radicalism and Politics', *Sociological Review*, (New Series) 28 (2), (1980),
pp.333-51.
DAWKINS, M.S., 'Attitudes to Animals' in Friday, L. and Laskey, R.,
(eds), *The Fragile Environment: the Darwin College Lectures*, Cambridge
University Press, Cambridge (1989).
DILLMAN, D.A., ROSA, E.A. and DILLMAN, J., 'Lifestyle and Home
Energy Conservation in the United States: the Poor Accept Lifestyle
Cutbacks while the Wealthy Invest in Conservation', in Ester, P., *et al*,
(eds), *Consumer Behavior and Energy Policy*, Elsevier, Amsterdam (1984).
DOUGLAS, M., *Purity and Danger*, Routledge and Kegan Paul, London
(1966).
DOUGLAS, M., 'Environments at Risk', in Douglas, M., *Implicit
Meanings: Essays in Anthropology*, Routledge, London (1975).
EDEN, S.E., *Green Consumerism and the Response from Business and
Government*, University of Leeds School of Geography, Working Paper
542 (1990).
ELKINGTON, J. and HAILES, J., *The Green Consumer Guide*, Gollancz,
London (1988).
ELKINGTON, J., BURKE, T. and HAILES, J., *Green Pages: the Business
of Saving the World*, Routledge, London (1988).
EVANS, G. and DURANT, J., 'Understanding of Science in Britain and
the USA', in Jowell, R., Witherspoon, S. and Brook, L., (eds), *British
Social Attitudes: special international report (6th Report)*, Gower, Aldershot
(1989).
FRANKLAND, E.G., 'Does Green Politics Have a Future in Britain?',
Green Politics One, Edinburgh University Press, Edinburgh (1990).
FREEDMAN, B., *Environmental Ecology: The Impacts of Pollution and
Other Stresses on Ecosystem Structure and Function*, Academic Press, San
Diego (1989).
FRIENDS OF THE EARTH, *The Friends of the Earth Handbook*,
Optima, London (1987).

GEERTZ, C., *Agricultural Involution: the Processes of Ecological Change in Indonesia*, University of California Press, Berkeley (1963).

GREELEY, A., *Religion and the Environment*, Working Paper, NORC, Chicago, (1991).

HOWLETT, L., *Cruelty-free Shopper*, Bloomsbury, London (1989).

HYNES, H.P., *The Recurring Silent Spring*, Pergamon Press, Oxford (1989).

INGLEHART, R., *Culture Shift in Advanced Industrial Society*, Princeton University Press, Princeton, NJ (1990).

IRVINE, S., *Beyond Green Consumerism*, Discussion Paper No.1, Friends of the Earth, London (1989).

KING, Y., 'The Ecology of Feminism and the Feminism of Ecology', in Plant, J., (ed), *Healing the Wounds: the Promise of Ecofeminism*, Green Print, London (1989).

MACKENZIE, D., 'The Rise of the Green Consumer', *Consumer Policy Review* 1(2) (April 1991) pp.68-75.

MARCO, G.J., HOLLINGWORTH, R.M. and DURHAM, W., 'Many Roads and Other Worlds' in Marco, G.J., Hollingworth, R.M. and Durham, W., (eds), *Silent Spring Revisited* American Chemical Society, Washington DC, (1987).

MIDDEN, C.J.H. and RITSEMA, B.S.M., 'The Meaning of Normative Processes for Energy Conservation' in Ester, P., *et al*, (eds), *Consumer Behavior and Energy Policy*, Elsevier, Amsterdam (1984).

MINTEL, *The Green Consumer*, Mintel Publications, London, 1989.

MYERS, N., 'The Future of Forests' in Friday, L. and Laskey, R., (eds), *The Fragile Environment: the Darwin College Lectures*, Cambridge University Press, Cambridge (1989).

PAINTER, J., SEMENIK, R. and BELK, R. 'Is There a Generalized Energy Conservation Ethic? A Comparison of the Determinants of Gasoline and Home Heating Energy Conservation,' in Ester, P., *et al*, (eds), *Consumer Behavior and Energy Policy*, Elsevier, Amsterdam (1984).

SACHS, W., 'Are Energy-intensive Life-images Fading?', Ester, P., *et al*, (eds), *Consumer Behavior and Energy Policy*, Elsevier, Amsterdam (1984).

SIMPSON, S., *The Times Guide to the Environment: a Comprehensive Handbook to Green Issues*, Times Books, London (1990).

'STARHAWK', 'Feminist Earth-based Sprituality and Ecofeminism', in Plant, J., (ed), *Healing the Wounds: the Promise of Ecofeminism*, Green Print, London (1989).

YOUNG, K., '"Values" in the Policy Process' in Pollitt, C., (ed), *Public Policy in Theory and Practice*, Hodder and Stoughton, London (1979).

YOUNG, K., 'Interim Report: Rural Prospects', in Jowell, R., Witherspoon, S. and Brook, L., (eds), *British Social Attitudes: the 5th Report*, Gower, Aldershot (1988).

Acknowledgements

SCPR is grateful to the Countryside Commission for their steadfast support of this survey series and particularly to Jeremy Worth for his advice and help, and to the Economic and Social Research Council who became joint funders of this module in 1990. Together, they enable us to continue monitoring attitudes to environmental and countryside issues.

6.1 GREEN PURCHASING (Y127)
by household income, highest educational qualification and age within sex

% purchasing regularly or sometimes:	Annual household income				
	Under £7,000	£7,000-£11,999	£12,000-£17,999	£18,000-£22,999	£23,000 or over
Environment-friendly aerosols	63	76	83	90	89
Toiletries and cosmetics not tested on animals	43	64	65	67	68
Products made out of recycled materials	48	60	61	62	68
Environment-friendly washing powders	43	55	48	57	58
Unleaded petrol*	36	45	39	55	53
Organically-grown fruit and vegetables	37	42	34	36	51

* Base excludes those replying that the question does not apply to them

% purchasing regularly or sometimes:	Highest educational qualification				
	Degree	Professional	A'level	O'level/CSE	None
Environment-friendly aerosols	93	87	87	82	62
Toiletries and cosmetics not tested on animals	72	66	62	63	47
Products made of recycled materials	80	68	64	59	44
Environment-friendly washing powders	63	61	63	46	40
Unleaded petrol*	56	52	46	43	37
Organically-grown fruit and vegetables	62	47	41	35	33

* Base excludes those replying that the question does not apply to them

% purchasing regularly or sometimes:	Age within sex					
	Men			Women		
	18-34	35-54	55+	18-34	35-54	55+
Environment-friendly aerosols	80	78	59	91	88	62
Toiletries and cosmetics not tested on animals	49	49	35	81	80	50
Products made of recycled materials	54	49	48	66	68	52
Environment-friendly washing powders	46	50	42	58	57	40
Unleaded petrol*	40	45	50	45	40	51
Organically-grown fruit and vegetables	31	40	39	34	48	38

* Base excludes those replying that the question does not apply to them

7 Working mothers: Free to choose?

Sharon Witherspoon and Gillian Prior [*]

The proportion of women under retirement age in Britain who are in paid work has been going up since the second world war; it has increased by over ten per cent in the last ten years alone. According to the latest available official figures, 66 per cent of women aged 16-59 in Britain are now in paid work, but this includes fewer than 40 per cent of women with children under five (Employment Gazette, 1990, p. 630).

Women with pre-school age children have to choose between devoting themselves full-time to the care of their children, or combining childcare with paid work. For most women, taking care of young children is doubtless rewarding and enjoyable, particularly in comparison with the low-paid and routine part-time work that is often the only option open to women with childcare responsibilities. Moreover, the expectation among couples that the man should provide most of the family income and that the woman should perform most of the domestic work is still widespread, buttressed by a logic of comparative economic advantage as well as by traditional gender attitudes.

But it seems far-fetched to suggest that most mothers of young children are actually engaging in a rational calculation, examining the alternatives open to them and then deciding freely whether it is better for them and their families to stay at home with their children or to get paid work

---

[*] Sharon Witherspoon was formerly a Research Director at SCPR and a Co-director of the *BSA* survey series and is now a graduate student at the State University of New York at Stony Brook. Gillian Prior is a Researcher at SCPR, and a Co-director of the *BSA* survey series.

outside the home. In particular, it is unlikely that most women are aware of the potential costs of their specialisation in childcare. In cash terms, it has been estimated that the average mother of two, with the typical patterns of economic inactivity and part-time work, has lifetime earnings about £122,000 lower than her childless counterpart, "almost exactly half of her possible earnings after the age of 25" (Joshi, 1990, pp. 52-3). In addition, over one-third of new marriages nowadays is likely to end in divorce, and lone parenthood among women is associated with a significant decrease in household income. So women who stay at home are, in some sense, gambling that their marriages will last. There is also some evidence that women who continue to do paid work while their children are young receive a larger share of family income than women who do not (see Morris and Ruane, 1989, pp.60-75), and have a stronger voice in family decision-making (see Spitze, 1988; Huber and Spitze, 1983; Pahl, 1989).

There are, of course, also disadvantages for mothers of young children who *do* go out to work (leaving aside the question of whether or not their children are as well cared for). In particular, most women with full-time jobs outside the home still do the bulk of the domestic work in addition to most of the childcare, as our own data demonstrate vividly (see Witherspoon, 1988). So there are pulls and pushes in both directions for mothers of young children. And their choices are constrained further by the absence of affordable and suitable childcare arrangements in Britain. It is not surprising, therefore, that most of the growth in women's employment in Britain has been in the form of part-time work, an arrangement viewed by many as allowing women to have the best of both worlds - continued participation in the labour market *and* the opportunity to spend some time with their children.

Increasingly, however, there is doubt as to whether part-time working is, after all, such a panacea. In the first place, the move to part-time working after the birth of a child is often associated with downward occupational mobility, since higher-level jobs are not usually available on a part-time basis. Secondly, part-time pay rates are often lower than those for similar full-time work. Finally part-time work is probably a significant factor in the occupational segregation of women, itself a source of much of the obstinate gap in men's and women's pay (see Martin and Roberts, 1984; Dex and Shaw, 1986; Dex, 1987; Joshi, 1990; Marsh, 1991).

Current government policy on women's working patterns is officially one of *laissez faire*. However, the recent decisions to raise child benefit for the first time in several years and to exempt employer-provided childcare from tax, together with mounting concern about potential labour shortages in the 1990s owing to demographic changes, suggest that a *laissez faire* policy may not last. So far, however, the government has taken only halting steps to help mothers stay in the labour market. The recent tax concessions on employer-provided nurseries have been accompanied by leaflets and a campaign generally aimed at convincing employers that they need to retain women workers (see Hansard, 10 May

1991). But public funding of nursery places for pre-school children is still well below the European Community average. And the government itself is not neutral when it comes to part-time working. For instance, successive governments have offered employers incentives to use part-timers. In particular, the lower limits on liability for national insurance, and the thresholds at which redundancy pay and other entitlements come into play, mean that part-time workers are relatively cheaper to employ than full-time workers, and that many part-time working women do not have the same benefits and rights as are offered to their full-time counterparts.   Against this background, we sought to find out more about what women themselves want, about the importance *they* attach to the availability and adequacy of alternative forms of childcare. Would significant numbers of women who are now full-time 'homemakers' prefer to have paid work, or are most women largely content with the choices open to them? Would women welcome help from outside the home with childcare, and would the availability of such provision be likely to affect their patterns of paid work? These are the sorts of issues we have addressed in the 1990 *British Social Attitudes* survey.

Flexible working arrangements for employees

Although much of the policy debate about childcare provision centres on women's actions and preferences, many men are also potential beneficiaries of greater flexibility in work arrangements. Indeed, as Marsh (1991) points out, British men work longer hours than their counterparts in most other European Community countries. And, she concludes, "There seems no way in which a work pattern involving such a long commitment to paid employment could be emulated by anyone who had a major responsibility for children" (p. 80).

The 1990 *British Social Attitudes* data show that 29 per cent of men worked more than 50 hours in the week preceding the interview; fewer than five per cent of women worked such long hours. Men who are professionals or employers, or skilled manual workers, are particularly likely to work more than 50 hours a week. Men too may thus have an interest in reducing their working hours, or at least in increasing the flexibility of their working arrangements and thereby their choices about their family roles.

As many as 31 per cent of male employees and 21 per cent of female employees say they would prefer to work fewer hours each week. On the other hand, if we make the fairer comparison between *full-time* men and *full-time* women employees, we find that virtually the same proportion (around one in three) would prefer to work fewer hours each week, compared with only 4 per cent of those women working 10-29 hours a week.[1]

Still, if as many as one in three full-time (male or female) employees were to reduce their working hours, the question remains as to who would pay. Employers are naturally reluctant to cut working hours without also cutting wages, and cite Britain's comparative uncompetitiveness as a reason why they cannot afford shorter working hours.[2] And *British Social Attitudes* data show that men, unlike women, are extremely unwilling to work shorter hours in exchange for a reduction in pay. Only 12 per cent of the men who want a reduction in working hours would actually choose this option if it meant earning less money as a result; the comparable figure for women is three times higher (38 per cent). This is not surprising since full-time working women have much less leisure-time than full-time working men (Social Trends, 1988, pp.157-158); we might have expected them, therefore, to be more serious than their male counterparts about reducing the hours they work outside the home.

Against this background, the period since the mid-1980s has seen much speculation that firms will begin to offer more flexible working arrangements, in addition to part-time working, in order to retain a trained labour force, minimise labour costs and operate efficiently (Horrell and Rubery, 1991; Hakim, 1987). There is as yet little evidence of any such trend. Still, the projected effect on the labour market of demographic trends was proving difficult for the government to ignore[3] (see, for example, Employment Gazette, 1988, p. 429): the number of young people entering the labour market has been decreasing as a result of declining birthrates, so the total labour pool would stagnate or decline unless women were brought into the labour force in larger numbers. Partly because women and young people share a labour market, both being more likely to work in the service sector, in less-skilled jobs, at low hourly rates, and so on (see Ermisch, 1983), the government at last began to take steps to alert employers to these demographic trends, encouraging them to consider initiatives to recruit and retain women workers in order to avoid labour shortages. But are employers offering working arrangements that help women combine paid work and childcare? If so, who is taking advantage of them?

We included a new series of questions in the 1990 survey about the availability and use of flexible working arrangements. A number of the arrangements we asked about were *general* benefits, potentially useful to all employees, whether men or women, parents or not parents (for example, flexible hours, working from home, job-sharing). Others were targeted specifically at those responsible for looking after children. We asked *all* men and women employees whether each arrangement was available to them at their workplace and whether they used it, or would do so if it were available. For each arrangement, they were given the following answer categories:

> Not available - and I would *not* use it if it were
> Not available - but I *would* use it if it were
> Available - but I do *not* use it
> Available - and I *do* use it

This allows us to derive three useful measures: how widely available each arrangement is, how much is it used, and a crude measure of suppressed demand for it. (This latter measurement is crude in part because it is hypothetical: employees with children may not know whether they would use any of the working arrangements, and those who do not have children may be doubly unsure. Even so, it is a useful baseline measure of the relative potential popularity of various working arrangements aimed at helping with childcare.)

The following table shows the results for all employees under retirement age, including those working under 10 hours a week who were otherwise classified as looking after the home.

Availability and use of flexible working arrangements

General arrangements	All employees	Men employees	Women employees	Women employees with a child under 12
Part-time working	%	%	%	%
Available at all	44	21	67	79
Do use	20	2	39	64
Would use if available	12	12	11	10
Flexible hours	%	%	%	%
Available at all	31	27	34	38
Do use	24	20	27	33
Would use if available	43	42	44	42
Job-sharing schemes	%	%	%	%
Available at all	16	9	22	24
Do use	3	1	3	9
Would use if available	18	12	23	30
Working from home	%	%	%	%
Available at all	16	18	14	12
Do use	12	14	11	11
Would use if available	29	29	28	31
Arrangements aimed at helping with childcare				
Term-time contracts	%	%	%	%
Available at all	13	7	18	27
Do use	6	3	10	21
Would use if available	27	25	29	51
Workplace nurseries	%	%	%	%
Available at all	5	4	6	8
Do use	*	*	*	1
Would use if available	25	24	27	48
School holiday care	%	%	%	%
Available at all	2	1	3	5
Do use	*	*	1	3
Would use if available	25	25	27	48
Childcare allowances towards the costs of childcare	%	%	%	%
Available at all	1	1	2	3
Do use	*	*	*	2
Would use if available	32	29	36	70

As can be seen, the most widely-available of these arrangements is part-time working, here defined as working 'less than the full working day'. Our figures are broadly in line with official estimates from the Labour Force Survey, showing that around two in five women employees work part-time. Our figures also show that among mothers with a child aged less than twelve, around two-thirds work part-time. In contrast, fewer than 2 per cent of men employees work part-time, but, perhaps surprisingly, 12 per cent say they *would* do so, given the opportunity.

The proportion of mothers of young children in paid work has increased by nearly 10 per cent since 1985 (Cohen, 1990; Employment Gazette, 1990), and much of this increase has been due to the growth in the number of part-time jobs available. But despite the large numbers of women already working part-time, our data suggest that there may still be further demand. For instance, among the women professionals, managers and employers in our sample, only about ten per cent work part-time, but as many as an additional 20 per cent say they would if they could. Moreover, more than one-quarter (28 per cent) of full-time working women with a child under 12 say they would work part-time if that option were made available by their employers. Still, the widespread availability of part-time work is virtually the only evidence from our survey that employers do have working arrangements that specifically attract women workers.

The next most available arrangement is flexible hours, defined as allowing the employee to "adjust their own daily working hours". About one-third of all employees say that flexible hours are available, and about one-quarter make use of them; this figure rises to one-third of women with children under 12. But when we take a closer look at the data we find that flexible hours are available principally to people working in non-manual jobs and, among women, especially to those in part-time jobs. Moreover, a recent survey of working hours (Marsh, 1990) confirms that this flexibility is usually an informal arrangement, allowing the individual's daily time of arrival at work to vary only within a relatively narrow range, which falls far short of true 'flexi-time'.

Other forms of work flexibility are distinctly minority affairs. About one in ten mothers of children under 12 take part in job-sharing schemes, "where part-timers share one full-time job", and this arrangement is most common in the public sector, particularly among clerical workers. Indeed, job-sharing is fairly widespread in the public sector, where there is in any case evidence that jobs have been systematically reviewed in order to increase women's participation (Metcalf, 1990). Our data suggest that many working women, but particularly those with a child, would welcome an expansion of job-sharing schemes, perhaps recognising that it can open up job opportunities that are not normally available on a part-time basis. Around 15 per cent of the *part-time* women employees in our sample are already job-sharing, but a further 30 per cent or so say they would use a job-sharing scheme if it were available. In addition, the expansion of job-sharing schemes might enable some full-time workers to switch to part-time work. Nearly one in three full-time working mothers with a child under 12 also say they would make use of job-sharing (and thus switch to part-time work) if the option were available.

Working from home "at least some of the time" is available to around one in six employees and has a take-up rate of 75 per cent, one of the highest found. But, as might be expected, this form of flexible working is almost wholly confined to those working in higher level non-manual jobs and is, perhaps, an example of a 'Matthew effect' - "to those that have shall be given" (Merton, 1973).

So these general forms of work flexibility are less prevalent than might have been expected. However, we find that employers are even *less* likely to provide forms of flexible working specifically designed to help women combine paid work and childcare. Metcalf's conclusion that "only a small growth in measures affecting female retention may be confidently expected" appears to be well-founded (Metcalf, 1990, p.8). As the table shows, no form of special arrangement designed to make childcare easier was used by more than 6 per cent of employees.

The most common of these specific arrangements is term-time contracts, an option taken up by one in ten women employees and by one in five of those with a child under 12. Yet term-time working (defined as "allowing parents special time off during the school holidays") is available partly because education authorities are an important source of women's employment, rather than because many other employers are introducing it. When we exclude nursery workers, teachers and lecturers in higher and further education from this figure, the proportion of mothers of children under 12 working on term-time contracts drops from 21 per cent to 15 per cent. Nearly two-thirds of those mothers who are working full-time (and nearly one-half of those working part-time) would work on term-time contracts if they could - further evidence that options that help mothers to spend more time with their young children might lead to a diminution, rather than an increase, in the total amount of time spent in paid work. On the other hand, this might be offset by an increase in *total* female participation in the labour market if these options were available.

The three benefits we asked about which provide *direct* help with childcare are each available to fewer than one in twenty employees. Among working mothers of under-fives, only 4 per cent had a workplace nursery available. They are available to about 9 per cent of women working in the public sector, and to about 3 per cent of those working in the private sector. Workplace nurseries are not, of course, a panacea; they are useful only when children are very young and for the mother who has a fairly easy journey to work. Even so, about three-quarters of working mothers of under-fives (and nearly half of working mothers with a child under 12) say they would use workplace nurseries if they were available.

Workplace childcare, though, is by no means the most popular option we asked about. Not surprisingly, fully 70 per cent of mothers of under-twelves would like to have childcare allowances towards covering the costs of childcare. Obviously, this would be equivalent to a pay rise, but the point about such an allowance is that it would help the woman and her family *choose* the kind of childcare they prefer.[4] It seems highly unlikely, however, that many employers would offer such an allowance unless it became an established part of collective bargaining or was required by law. And there are few signs that the government will offer positive incentives to employers to adopt such schemes.

We also asked women employees about the availability of career breaks, "keeping women's jobs open for a few years so that mothers can return to work after caring for young children". About one-quarter of women employees say that career breaks are available to them, and about one in ten mothers of children under 12 have used such an arrangement. But, a further 50 per cent of those with children under 12 say they would use this option if it were available.

A recent report documents the extent to which women have access to paid maternity leave, and the extent to which provision beyond the statutory minimum is available (McRae and Daniel, 1990). We asked, however, about *paternity* leave, "allowing fathers extra leave when their children are born", and found that one in ten of men employees have used paternity leave, and another 16 per cent say it is available to them. A further third would make use of it if it were available. Paternity leave is equally common in the public and private sectors.

Overall, then, there is evidence of suppressed demand for greater flexibility in working arrangements which would help parents combine paid work and childcare. Some mothers would reduce their working hours, while others would increase them, if they had the option.

Childcare: provision and preference

We went on to ask *all* mothers of children under 12 what childcare arrangements they were using. We asked those in paid work (including mothers working less than 10 hours a week) about their use of a number of different arrangements, and we asked those classified as looking after the home about a shorter list of possible childcare arrangements.[5] We confined these questions to women only because we were interested here in the relationship between childcare and *women's* availability to work outside the home. The table below shows the relative importance of each of a number of childcare arrangements for those in paid work.

Women employees with a child under 12

Women's present childcare arrangements:	All %	Age of youngest child		Working status	
		Under 5 years %	5 to 11 years %	Part-time %	Full-time %
A relative looks after them	57	64	52	59	55
A friend or neighbour looks after them	10	1	16	10	10
They go to a childminder	14	17	12	7	25
A mother's help or nanny looks after them at home	4	7	2	3	6
Mother works only while children are at school	25	8	34	32	12
Children look after themselves until mother is home	11	-	17	8	25
Mother works from home	4	5	3	6	-
The children go to a day-nursery	7	17	1	6	9
The children go to a workplace nursery	1	-	1	-	2

Because we asked women to mention *all* the arrangements they used, the percentages add to more than 100.

Relatives are by far the most important providers of childcare, irrespective of the age of the youngest child. We know from the 1980 Women and Employment Survey (Martin and Roberts, 1984) that husbands and grandmothers are the relatives mentioned most often as helping with childcare. But the use of some forms of childcare varies according to the age of the youngest child. Thus, only a handful of mothers of under-fives arrange for a friend or neighbour to look after their children, while 16 per cent of those with school-aged children do so. The proportions are virtually reversed in the case of day-nurseries. And though none of the mothers of under-fives say they allow their children to look after themselves, over one in six mothers of children between 5 and 11 do so.

There seems to have been little change in the use of paid childcare in the ten years since the Women and Employment Survey; childminders, day-nurseries and mother's helps or nannies are all used to more or less the same extent as they used to be in 1980 (Martin and Roberts, 1984, p.39). The estimated number of registered nursery places available in Britain in 1988 (including local authority, private and voluntary nurseries) would cater for about two per cent of under-fives (Cohen, 1990, pp.12-22), a level of provision which is changing very slowly in the light of the potential demand revealed by our survey.

Of the small proportion of women employees in our sample (eight per cent) who use any form of nursery or creche provision, about half say they use private provision. Full-time workers are more likely than part-time workers to use a private nursery and are generally more likely to pay for childcare. This doubtless reflects not only the fact that they are more able to afford it than are part-timers, but also that they are less available themselves (for instance, after school hours).

Of course, mothers who do not go out to work make use of childcare too. So we asked those with children under 12 about any forms of childcare they use regularly during the day. Three-quarters use *no* form of regular childcare, and eight per cent (including 12 per cent of mothers of under-fives) use day nurseries. These mothers are obviously more able to make informal arrangements: thus 14 per cent of mothers of under twelves arrange regularly for a relative, friend or neighbour to look after their children. Clearly, mothers without paid jobs are in fact working in the home caring for their children. But the fact that 21 per cent also regularly use a form of childcare is a reminder that the availability of childcare is important for reasons *other* than increasing women's availability for paid work. Mothers may, for instance, want childcare in order to spend time with their children individually, or to make time for household work or other domestic responsibilities, or simply to create leisure-time.

We asked members of our sample who were using any form of childcare how convenient and satisfactory they found their child-care arrangements. We should treat the answers cautiously, since feelings of dissatisfaction might have been suppressed in case they signified inadequate parenting. Nonetheless, around two in every three working mothers, find their childcare arrangements convenient and satisfactory, as the table below shows.

Women employees with a child under 12

	All	Age of youngest child		Working status	
		Under 5 years	5 to 11 years	Part-time	Full-time
Childcare arrangements are:	%	%	%	%	%
Very convenient	63	61	66	64	63
Fairly convenient	32	32	32	32	32
Not very/not at all convenient	5	8	4	4	7
Overall assessment of childcare arrangements:	%	%	%	%	%
Very satisfied	69	63	71	71	65
Fairly satisfied	26	27	23	24	27
Not very/not at all satisfied	7	10	6	7	9

Moreover, there is little apparent difference in satisfaction between mothers of pre-school children and other mothers, or between full-time and part-time working mothers. Although the numbers are small, our evidence suggests that mothers of 5-11 year-olds whose children look after themselves are the least happy about their childcare arrangements; they are most likely to say that their arrangements are 'not at all convenient' and that they are 'not at all satisfied'.

On this evidence then, there appears to be little dissatisfaction among working mothers with the childcare arrangements they use; but when we look at the answers to a follow-up question to mothers in paid work about their preferences, we find a more complex picture:

*Suppose you could choose from **any** of the types of childcare on the card. Which would be your first choice for childcare while you are at work, and which would be your second choice?*

The table below shows the *combined* first and second choices.

Women employees with a child under 12

Preferred arrangements for looking after children while at work:	All	Age of youngest child		Working status	
		Under 5 years	5 to 11 years	Part-time	Full-time
	%	%	%	%	%
A relative would look after them	58	64	55	59	57
Mother would work only while they were at school	55	39	64	59	46
Mother would work from home	17	17	19	17	21
A friend or neighbour would look after them	17	8	23	18	15
They would go to a workplace nursery	13	20	8	12	14
A mother's help or nanny would look after them at home	10	11	9	5	20
They would go to a childminder	9	8	10	9	9
They would go to a council-funded day nursery	8	14	5	9	6
They would go to a private day-nursery	5	14	-	4	7
They would look after themselves until their mother came home	3	-	4	3	2

Because first and second preferences are combined, percentages add to more than 100.

These answers show that most mothers are strongly committed to caring for their children themselves or within their families. Indeed, if we take only first choices, this preference is even clearer, with 41 per cent saying they would work only while their children were at school, and an additional 30 per cent saying they would prefer a relative to look after them. They also show an unmet demand for nursery provision, especially for workplace nurseries, perhaps because they enable mothers to be near their children. One in five working mothers of pre-school children would choose workplace nurseries as their preferred childcare arrangement if they were available. Since fewer than one per cent of the mothers in our sample actually use a workplace nursery, the gap between preferences and practice is very large. Workplace nurseries are the most popular of the nursery options offered. Council nurseries are preferred over private nurseries among all groups except full-time working mothers, who already use (and can afford) private nurseries more than part-timers do.

We had designed this question about childcare preferences among working mothers so as to allow them to say they would prefer to look after their children themselves; otherwise, we felt, we might artificially inflate the size of the unfulfilled demand for alternative forms of childcare. But to complete the picture, we also needed to ask mothers who were *not* currently working outside the home what, if any, form of childcare would enable them to do so.

> *Suppose you decided to take a paid job outside the home, and you could choose from **any** of the types of childcare on this card. Which would be your first choice for childcare while you were at work, and which would be your second choice?*

The answers suggest that women who do not work outside the home are even more strongly of the view that children are best looked after by their mothers or families. This pattern is clearest when we compare the answers given by mothers of pre-school children in paid jobs with those given by their counterparts not in paid work.

	Mothers of pre-school children	
Preferred arrangements for looking after children while at work:	In paid work %	Not in paid work %
A relative would look after them	64	33
Mother would work only while they were at school	39	51
Mother would work from home	17	27
A friend or neighbour would look after them	8	19
They would go to a workplace nursery	20	20
A mother's help or nanny would look after them at home	11	6
They would go to a childminder	8	15
They would go to a council-funded day-nursery	14	8
They would go to a private day-nursery	14	10
They would look after themselves until their mother came home	3	2

Percentages add to more than 100 because first and second preferences are combined

Mothers who are looking after the home are much more likely than those in paid work to say that they would work only when their children were at school, or that they would work from home, or that a friend or neighbour would look after their children. Also popular among mothers not in paid work (indeed as popular among them as among those in paid work) are workplace nurseries, again suggesting that proximity to their children may be an important factor for mothers. It also suggests that the wider availability of childcare at or near the workplace might indeed tempt more women back to paid employment.

To get a better sense of whether the availability of more suitable childcare would lead women to work longer hours than now, or, if they were not working at present, to return to or take up paid work, we asked mothers in paid work:

And if you did have the childcare arrangement of your choice would you prefer to work more hours than now, work fewer hours than now, or are you happy with the hours you work at present?

A follow-up question to those part-time working mothers who felt they *would* work longer hours asked if they might then work full-time or not.

And we asked mothers who were not working outside the home:

*And if you did have the childcare arrangement of your choice, would you prefer to work part-time, work full-time, or would you choose **not** to work outside the home?*

As the table below shows, a substantial minority of part-time working mothers say that having better childcare would lead them to work more hours, and a small minority say it might enable them to work full-time. This suggests that, for all its flexibility, some women work part-time partly because it is all that employers offer.[6] (See Dex and Shaw, 1986; and Cohen, 1990, for a further analysis of the supply of part-time working.) A substantial majority (two in three) of mothers who are not currently in paid work say they would be likely to go out to work, mostly part-time.

	Mothers of a child under 12		
	Working full-time	Working part-time	Looking after home
If had childcare **arrangements of choice**	%	%	%
..would work more hours, [but still] part-time	2	14	52
..would work full-time	-	16	13
..would work fewer hours/ would not work for pay	23	4	27

If these hypothetical answers were indeed accurate predictors of behaviour, the likely outcome would be a substantial increase in the total number of hours women spend in paid work. True, nearly one quarter of full-time working mothers would work fewer hours (perhaps because of the difficulties of combining full-time paid employment, childcare, and domestic duties), but nearly one-third of the much greater number of part-time working mothers would work longer hours. And although the answers given by those not in paid work about their propensity to go out to work are probably less likely to be a guide to their actual behaviour (since the question is even more hypothetical in their case), any increase in their working hours owing to the provision of the right kind of childcare would lead to an increase in women's overall participation within the labour market.

As a final hypothetical question about women's future participation in paid work, we asked mothers of children under 12, both employees and those looking after the home, what they might do when their children were older.

> When all your children have gone to secondary school, which do you think you are most likely to do: work full-time, work part-time, or not have a paid job at all?

The answers suggest that women's plans are influenced by their own current positions in the labour force, itself a product of their varying skills, opportunities and commitment to paid work.

	Mothers of a child under 12		
	Working full-time now	Working part-time now	Looking after home now
When children are in secondary school, most likely to:	%	%	%
Work full-time	88	41	37
Work part-time	6	55	43
Not have paid work	4	1	14

The implication of these figures is that women's participation rate in the labour market is likely to rise. According to the 1989 Labour Force Survey, current participation rates among women whose youngest child is 11 to 15 are much lower than our sample predicts about themselves. Our figures do not include mothers who are currently unemployed or self-employed, but even with an allowance for the upward bias these omissions would produce, British women may be planning (or hoping?) to return to full-time work in increasing numbers in the 1990s, if jobs are available. In 1989, 31 per cent of mothers of secondary school children were in full-time paid work; in our sample, 48 per cent of mothers of a child aged under 12 said they *expected* to work full-time when their children were in secondary school. In any event, increasing divorce rates,

better educational opportunities for women and the growth in service
sector work are eventually likely to lead to an increase in the proportion
of women who will wish to work full-time when their children are in
secondary school. Whether they will find work is another matter.

Why women stay at home - pleasures and constraints

By concentrating on paid work for women, we have neglected so far the
reasons women may have for *not* going out to work. Many women enjoy
staying at home or looking after their children full-time. And in any case,
women still do most of the work around the home, and many women feel
that mothers of pre-school children *ought* to stay at home with them -
although the proportion of working-age women who feel this way has
declined sharply in the last 25 years (Witherspoon, 1988, p.192).
Nevertheless, we wanted to explore the relative weight given to the belief
that mothers ought to stay at home with young children, and to the
assessment that it was simply too difficult to combine paid work and
childcare.

The *British Social Attitudes* series has long included an open-ended
question asking women their reasons for not having a paid job outside the
home. As the table below shows, most women give family responsibilities
as their main reason.

		Women aged 18 - 59 who are looking after the home[*]		
Main reason for not having a paid job	All	Youngest child under 5	Youngest child 5-11	No child under 12
	%	%	%	%
Looking after children at home	59	89	70	16
Prefer to look after home and family	27	12	36	38
Husband or partner against it	3	3	-	5
High cost of childcare	3	7	5	-
Not qualified for available jobs	3	1	8	3
Poverty trap - would lose benefit if in paid job	3	1	5	5
No jobs available	2	2	-	5
Pregnant or in ill-health	10	7	2	20
Too old to work	3	-	-	7

[*] Those who did not answer this question are excluded from the base

Women with young children, especially under-fives, are much more likely
than other women to say it is because they are looking after their

children. A small minority also give negative reasons, such as the cost of childcare, the lack of available jobs, or a disapproving husband.

We also asked mothers of a child under 12 who were looking after the home how important a number of specific reasons were to them for not having a paid job. Their answers are shown below.

Women aged 18 - 59 with a child under 12 who are looking after the home

	Very important	Fairly important	Not very important	Not at all important[*]
'Positive' reasons				
It's better for the children if I am at home	% 76	18	3	3
I enjoy spending time with my children more than working	% 73	18	4	2
'Negative' reasons				
I cannot find the kind of work I want with suitable hours	% 36	16	9	36
It would cost too much to find suitable childcare	% 35	22	11	28
My life would be too difficult if I had to combine childcare and paid work	% 28	3	14	11
I cannot find the kind of work I want near my home	% 27	21	9	39
I cannot find the kind of childcare I would like	% 24	20	11	41
My husband or partner would not want me to work	% 23	14	14	46

[*] Includes those answering 'does not apply'

Once again positive reasons for staying at home are comfortably the most popular ones. But as many as half of these mothers of young children say that the cost of suitable childcare, the difficulty of finding convenient work near home, and the difficulty of combining paid work with childcare are 'very' or 'fairly' important reasons for them personally - a further sign that the greater availability of affordable childcare might enable them to look for paid jobs outside the home. The importance attributed to a job with 'suitable hours' suggests again that part-time work is preferred when children are young.

Using factor analysis, we tried to determine empirically whether there were any underlying relationships between these answers. Was it simply, perhaps, that people tended to agree more with the positive reasons than with the negative ones?   Or were work and childcare issues separate sources of constraint?

Our analysis shows that women's answers to three of the eight statements (the first, the second and the last) tend to correlate with one another, tapping attitudes towards both positive and negative effects of the woman's working on both her children and her husband or partner. Answers to the other five statements - about the constraints on finding both suitable work and childcare - are also related. The analysis suggests therefore that many women who are considering whether or not to work outside the home have to balance, on the one hand, their obligations towards and their enjoyment of their families, and, on the other hand, the advantages of paid work and the obstacles to it.

We then created two scales by combining the items within each factor, and investigated whether different groups of women choose to stay at home for different reasons. We found in particular that women with educational qualifications beyond O'level are much less likely than other women to attribute importance to the three family reasons: only eight per cent of them said 'very important' to all three, compared to about one in four women with lower or no educational qualifications. Yet these more educated women are also less likely (by about the same margin) to attribute great importance to the difficulties of finding suitable jobs. They may be implying that they have chosen to stay at home with their young children, rather than that they do so because of labour market conditions or because their spouse wishes them to.

Women's values

So far we have focused mainly on women's experiences of and attitudes towards the childcare they have arranged for their own children. But the survey also asks about people's general beliefs about gender roles and different forms of childcare. This enables us to explore the relationship between women's experiences and their more general views about traditional gender roles.

Younger women (under 35), and women with higher educational qualifications, are particularly likely to be less 'traditionalist' in their views on a wide range of gender-related issues (see Witherspoon, 1988). But these subgroups contain large numbers of women who do not (yet) have children, and whose views have not (yet) been coloured by their own decisions about childcare and related domestic matters. We wanted to find out the extent to which women with young children go out to work *despite* feeling that it may not be best for their children, or whether they believe that their children are at least as well-off as if the mother stayed at home.   Listed below are the statements we asked respondents to evaluate, with the proportion of mothers taking a *strongly* non-traditionalist stance, as well as the overall proportion who held non-traditionalist views at all (either strongly or moderately).

Women aged 18 - 59

| | All | Mothers of a child under 12 | | |
		Working full-time	Working part-time	Not in paid work
A husband's job is to earn money; a wife's job is to look after the home and family				
% strongly non-traditionalist	30	49	33	24
% non-traditionalist at all	71	88	78	63
A working mother can establish just as warm and secure a relationship with her children as a mother who does not work				
% strongly non-traditionalist	20	47	27	8
% non-traditionalist at all	57	86	66	38
A job is all right, but what most women really want is a home and children				
% strongly non-traditionalist	19	39	20	11
% non-traditionalist at all	55	76	62	44
Having a job is the best way for a woman to be an independent person				
% strongly non-traditionalist	10	10	9	5
% non-traditionalist at all	55	69	51	42
All in all, family life suffers when the woman has a full-time job				
% strongly non-traditionalist	11	29	9	3
% non-traditionalist at all	43	69	41	22
A pre-school child is likely to suffer if his or her mother works				
% strongly non-traditionalist	9	18	16	3
% non-traditionalist at all	41	61	56	28
A woman and her family will all all be happier if she goes out work				
% strongly non-traditionalist	3	4	5	2
% non-traditionalist at all	17	29	37	11

As the table shows, full-time working mothers of young children are particularly likely to be non-traditionalists on all but one of these issues. Nearly nine in ten reject the view that the husband should be the breadwinner and the wife's job is to look after the home; more than three-quarters dispute that what most women want is a home and children; more than two-thirds feel that a job is the best way for a woman to be independent, and disagree that family life suffers when the mother has a full-time job; nearly as many disagree that a pre-school child suffers if his or her mother works. Indeed, the only item on which non-traditionalists are in a minority among full-time working mothers is the one in which the *woman's* happiness is at issue: fewer than one-third believe that a woman and her family will be happier if she works. This item shows the smallest difference between the answers of full-time working mothers and of mothers who do not work outside the home.

In addition, the views of mothers who are not in paid work are strikingly different from those of mothers who work outside the home, particularly in respect of statements which ask about the effect of the mother's working on her family or children.   Only on the first item, which is arguably the most extreme formulation of the traditional view about gender roles, is there a non-traditionalist majority among those not in paid work; on all the other items, the proportion of non-traditionalist 'homemakers' ranges between around 10 per cent and 45 per cent.

As might be expected, on most items the views of mothers with part-time paid jobs are around midway between those of mothers with full-time jobs and those without paid jobs, but there are exceptions. First, on the item about a job being the best way for a woman to be an independent person, and the one about family life suffering when a woman has a full-time job, the answers of part-time working mothers are closer to those of mothers without paid jobs, suggesting that part-timers are less likely to be committed to pursuing careers in the way that full-timers are.   But secondly, part-timers are *more* likely than full-time working mothers to believe that a woman and her family will be happier if she works. Again this suggests that the burden felt by full-time working mothers is particularly heavy.

Yet even those mothers with non-traditional beliefs have some reservations about the effect a mother's work has on family relationships. The proportion of those taking a *strongly* non-traditionalist view drops to below one-third even among mothers with full-time jobs when we ask about family life or pre-school-age children. Views on this issue are also linked to plans for future labour market participation. Among those who believe that family life suffers if a woman works full-time, 38 per cent plan to work full-time (and 51 per cent part-time) when their children are in secondary school; yet among those who dispute this view, as many as two-thirds plan to work full-time (and around a quarter part-time). Whether beliefs are a consequence of behaviour, or *vice versa*, these items nonetheless discriminate strongly between mothers who work outside the home and mothers who do not: the former are simply much less likely than the latter to believe that a mother's work adversely affects her relationships with her children.

This is clearly the crux of the matter, since there is relatively little disagreement in principle about the relative merits of different forms of childcare. We asked about the suitability of various forms of childcare for a (putative) child under three years old "whose parents both have full-time jobs".[7] Women with higher educational qualifications and younger women tended to be slightly more favourable towards nursery provision - whether local authority, private or in the workplace.   But these differences are small compared with the differences in beliefs about traditional gender roles. More notable is the difference between what is believed to be suitable childcare and the actual childcare used by working mothers of under-fives.

The most striking thing about the table below is the discrepancy between the high proportion who judge a workplace nursery as 'very suitable' for a child, and the fact that no mothers of under-fives in our sample used one (largely due to the fact that only four per cent had access to one). Indeed, the shortfall of nursery provision of all kinds, judged against its perceived suitability, is very marked. All groups of women agree broadly about the suitability of nurseries, yet few working mothers are actually using nurseries of any sort. This is perhaps the most persuasive evidence we found of unmet demand.

Women aged 18 - 59

	% saying arrangements very suitable for child under three	% of working mothers of under-fives using arrangement
Workplace nursery	51	-
Relative	44	64
Private nursery	34	8
Local authority nursery	27	9
Childminder	21	24[*]
Neighbour or friend	12	1

[*] Includes nanny or mother's help as 'babysitter'

Finally, we asked respondents whether, in a range of specified circumstances, they thought women should work outside the home full-time, part-time or not at all. As the table below shows, there is general agreement that women should go out to work before there are children, and a fair amount of agreement that they should do so after the children leave home. But there is little agreement about what mothers of young children should do.

Women aged 18 - 59

Should the woman work ...	All %	Mothers of a child under 12		
		Working full-time %	Working part-time %	Not in paid work %
... after marrying, before there are children?				
Work full-time	85	88	90	88
Work part-time	6	4	4	4
Stay at home	2	-	-	2
... when there is a child under school age?	%	%	%	%
Work full-time	5	18	1	1
Work part-time	33	35	55	27
Stay at home	51	41	34	64
... after the youngest child starts school?	%	%	%	%
Work full-time	19	43	12	7
Work part-time	66	47	47	77
Stay at home	5	-	1	11
... after the children leave home?	%	%	%	%
Work full-time	70	84	67	70
Work part-time	17	6	17	21
Stay at home	1	-	2	2

Among mothers of under-twelves we find large differences according to current working status. Nearly one in five full-time working mothers with children under twelve think mothers of pre-school children *should* work full-time,[8] compared to only one per cent of mothers not in paid work who take this view; this disparity is even greater in respect of school-aged children (43 per cent and 7 per cent respectively). Full-time working mothers are less ambivalent than other mothers about juggling domestic roles and paid work when their children are at school.

Conclusions

We have found little evidence to suggest that most women who look after their children full-time are deeply dissatisfied with their lot, or that a majority wishes to join the labour market instead. We have, however, seen that a minority of them might well choose to work outside the home if more suitable forms of childcare were available, and that a majority of women with young children who already work outside the home want to see more flexibility and improved provision of childcare alternatives, particularly at their workplace.

We have also found evidence that in future, women may be more likely than they are now to seek full-time work once their children are in secondary school. This is an important finding because other studies (Martin and Roberts, 1984; Dex and Shaw, 1986; Becker, 1981) have already shown that younger women, women with higher educational qualifications, and women who live in societies characterised by high rates of divorce, are increasingly likely to expect to work continuously, and to display career or job commitments similar to those of men. As Harding has argued, changes in attitudes towards the family are likely to presage changes in behaviour, and may indeed be more reliable than projections from existing behaviour. Moreover, he argues, "governments are able - though fiscal and other policies - to provide help with the responsibilities and financial burdens of childbearing, and so increase the attractiveness of that sort of lifestyle" (Harding, 1989, p. 151). Governments therefore need to be aware of women's views on these issues if they are not to be taken by surprise at the choices women make in future.

Looking abroad for hints about these choices, we know that Britain has one of the lowest employment participation rates in the European Community among mothers of under-fives, and the participation rate of women working full-time is even lower (Cohen, 1990, p. 10). Britain also provides fewer publicly-funded childcare services for pre-school children than do most of its European partners (Coote, Harmon and Hewitt, 1990, p. 19).

How would a society that was concerned about the disproportionate burden that the domestic division of labour places on women, re-arrange its affairs? It would surely consider some or all of these policies: an increase in nursery provision at or near women's workplaces, and tax incentives (beyond the current concession) to encourage employers to provide such help; an increase in publicly-funded local day nurseries and creches; provision of some sort of childcare tax allowance in addition to increases in child benefit; the extension of employers' national insurance liability to all part-time work, and the extension of employment protection to these jobs. These changes would provide women and their families with a much wider choice than now.

This is one side of the family equation. But it is hard to ignore the other, less visible one: the role of men. Controversial work by Nancy Chodorow (1978) has examined the psychological legacies for children of part-time fathering; other studies (also controversial) have documented the effects on children brought up with little or no contact with their fathers in the aftermath of marital breakdown (Burgoyne, Ormrod and Richards, 1987; MacLean and Wadsworth, 1988). But even where fathers live at home, the evidence is that childcare is still largely the woman's responsibility.

And our data suggest that men are considerably more likely than women to believe that this *should* be the case. Looking only at parents of children under twelve, just over one-half of fathers disagree with the view that a husband should be the breadwinner and the wife should look after the home and children, compared to nearly three-quarters of mothers; just over half of fathers agree that pre-school children suffer if their mothers work, while just over one-third of mothers take this view; and fathers (59 per cent) are more likely than mothers (50 per cent) to believe that the mothers of pre-school children should not work outside the home. Whatever talk there is of the 'New Man', he is much rarer than the 'New Woman'. This gap in attitudes has consequences for family life in general, as well as for women's decisions to work outside the home.

In the absence of changes in men's attitudes, or in their working hours outside the home, or in their contribution within the family towards childcare and domestic duties, it seems unlikely that even a greater availability of childcare outside the home would alter domestic arrangements greatly. Indeed, without these changes, it is conceivable that many useful forms of work flexibility which might be offered to women - such as job-sharing, career-breaks, special sick-leave, or term-time working - might serve to reinforce rather than mitigate the already formidable level of occupational segregation based on gender, to women's longer-term disadvantage.

Notes

1.   For most purposes, the survey treats as employees only those working at least ten hours a week. Since the questions about childcare are clearly relevant to all part-time women workers, in some sections of this chapter 'part-time' includes those working at least one hour a week. Where this is the case, it is clearly noted.

2.   In fact men in all of Britain's successful European competitor countries work a shorter working week; Britain has by far the largest proportion of men working

long hours of any of the EC countries. The level in, for instance, (West) Germany is about one-third the British level, see Eurostat, 1990.

3.   Political concern about this demographic issue has subsided somewhat in the wake of the 1989-91 recession, but the underlying secular trend is still evident.

4.   As the authors of an IPPR paper on family policy point out, this would not in the short-term guarantee the *supply* of high-quality childcare (Coote, Harmon and Hewitt, 1990, pp.41-42).

5.   We also asked self-employed women about the childcare they used while working, but the numbers are too small to analyse separately, so they are excluded from the discussion here.

6.   The use of part-time workers working below a certain number of hours a week lowers employers' direct costs, since they do not pay National Insurance, and their indirect costs, since these workers have fewer pension, holiday, sick leave, redundancy and other employment protection entitlements.

7.   The question allowed respondents to say that each form of childcare was 'not at all suitable'; thus those who felt strongly that mothers of young children should not work outside the home could answer accordingly.

8.   This proportion would be even larger if we looked at the views of mothers of pre-school children separately. Many mothers currently working full-time did not, of course, do so when their children were younger.

References

BECKER, G., *A Treatise on the Family*, Harvard University Press, Cambridge, Mass. (1981).

BURGOYNE, J., ORMROD, R. and RICHARDS, M., *Divorce Matters*, Penguin, Harmsworth (1987).

CENTRAL STATISTICAL OFFICE, *Social Trends 18*, HMSO, London (1988).

CHODOROW, N., *The Reproduction of Mothering: Psychoanalysis and the Sociology of Gender*, University of California Press, Berkeley (1978).

COHEN, B., *Caring for Children: the 1990 Report*, Report for the European Commission's Childcare Network on Childcare Services and Policy in the United Kingdom, London (1990).

COOTE, A., HARMON, H. and HEWITT, P., *The Family Way: A New Approach to Policy-Making*, Institute for Public Policy Research, London (1990).

DEX, S., *Women's Occupational Mobility: A Lifetime Perspective*, Macmillan, Basingstoke (1987).

DEX, S. and SHAW, L.B., *British and American Women at Work: Do Equal Opportunities Policies Matter?* Macmillan, Basingstoke (1986).

EMPLOYMENT DEPARTMENT, 'Women in the labour market: Results from the 1989 Labour Force Survey', *Employment Gazette*, HMSO, London (December 1990), pp. 619-643.

EMPLOYMENT DEPARTMENT, 'Employers alerted to youth shortage', *Employment Gazette*, HMSO, London (August 1988), p.429.

ERMISCH, J.F., *The Political Economy of Demographic Change: causes and implications of population trends in Great Britain*, Heinemann, London (1983).

EUROSTAT, *Labour Force Survey,* Office for Official Publications of the European Communities, Luxembourg (1990).

HAKIM, C., 'Trends in the flexible workforce' in *Employment Gazette,* HMSO, London (November 1987), p.529.

HANSARD, HMSO, London (10 May 1991).

HARDING, S., 'Interim Report: The Changing Family', in Jowell, R., Witherspoon, S. and Brook, L., (eds.), *British Social Attitudes: special international report,* Gower, Aldershot (1990).

HORRELL, S. and RUBERY, J., *Employers' Working-Time Policies and Women's Employment,* HMSO, London (1991).

HUBER, J. and SPITZE, G., *Sex Stratification: Children, Housework and Jobs,* Academic Press, New York (1983).

JOSHI, H., 'The Cash Opportunity Costs of Childbearing: An Approach to Estimation using British Data', *Population Studies,* 44, (1990).

MACLEAN, M. and WADSWORTH, M., 'Children's Life Chances and Parental Divorce' in *International Journal of Law and the Family,* Vol. 2 (1988), pp.155-166.

MARSH, C., *Hours of Work of Women and Men in Britain,* HMSO, London (1991).

MARTIN, J. and ROBERTS, C., *Women and Employment: A Lifetime Perspective,* HMSO, London (1984).

McRAE, S. and DANIEL, W., *Maternity Rights: the Experience of Women and Employers,* Policy Studies Institute, London (1991).

MERTON, R.K., 'The Matthew Effect in Science', in *The Sociology of Science: Theoretical and Empirical Investigations,* University of Chicago Press, Chicago (1973).

METCALF, H., *Retaining Women Employees: Measures to Counteract Labour Shortages,* Institute of Manpower Studies Report No. 190, Brighton (1990).

MORRIS, L. and RUANE, S., *Household Finance Management and the Labour Market,* Avebury, Aldershot (1989).

PAHL, J., *Money and Marriage.* Macmillan, Basingstoke (1989).

SPITZE, G., 'Women's Employment and Family Relations: A Review' in *Journal of Marriage and the Family,* 50 (August 1988), pp. 595-618.

WITHERSPOON, S., 'Interim Report: A Woman's Work', in Jowell, R., Witherspoon, S. and Brook, L., (eds.), *British Social Attitudes: The 5th Report,* Gower, Aldershot (1988).

Acknowledgement

SCPR is grateful to the Employment Department whose financial support for the survey series since 1984 has enabled us to continue to ask questions on labour market and workplace issues. We would like to thank Jenny Dibden, Gillian Smith and Jenny White of the Department, in particular, for their assistance in designing the 1990 questionnaire module.

8 Smoking and health

Yoav Ben-Shlomo, Aubrey Sheiham and Michael Marmot [*]

Over the past decade, the number of smokers in Britain, already declining during the 1970s, has continued to fall. Some population subgroups are, however, more resistant to change than others (Pierce, 1989). The image of smoking as a sophisticated, cultured or 'macho' activity has also changed. This may well have a lot to do with the restrictions on advertisers, now no longer allowed to depict positive images of smoking associated with sport and the outdoor life, and with health education campaigns which have emphasised the dirty and anti-social aspects of the habit. More recently, there has been growing concern over the dangers of passive smoking with the publication of several reports highlighting the risks associated with ambient tobacco smoke (for instance, Office on Smoking and Health, 1987; Wald *et al.* 1991). Smoking in public places has also become increasingly restricted (for example, the bans on London Transport tube trains and buses).

For the first time in 1990, the *British Social Attitudes* survey carried a module on attitudes to smoking, including questions about people's intentions to give up smoking, and the factors that inhibit or promote giving up. We tried to assess the importance people attach to different health messages in relation to smoking and to the way people perceive

[*] Yoav Ben-Shlomo is a Wellcome Research Fellow in Clinical Epidemiology at University College and Middlesex School of Medicine, London, where Aubrey Sheiham is Professor of Dental Public Health and Michael Marmot is Professor of Epidemiology and Public Health. Michael Marmot is also Professor of Epidemiology at the London School of Hygiene and Tropical Medicine.

the dangers of passive smoking, restrictions on smoking in public places, and advertising and sponsorship by tobacco companies. We also investigated public attitudes towards action against smokers such as whether they should be discriminated against when seeking life or health insurance.

The results will provide benchmark measures against which to measure changes in attitudes. They will, we hope, also make it easier in future to assess the likely impact of any further restrictions proposed on smoking in public and at the workplace.

Who smokes and who does not?

The table below summarises for a number of demographic and social groups the proportions who have never smoked, who used to smoke, and who smoke now.[*] Our sample is confined to adults aged 18 and over.

		Never smoked	Ex-smokers	Current smokers
All	%	42	28	27
Men:				
18-34	%	51	17	31
35-54	%	32	30	34
55+	%	21	56	19
Women:				
18-34	%	54	14	33
35-54	%	53	22	25
55+	%	49	33	18
Highest educational qualification:				
Degree/Professional	%	47	28	22
A'/O' level	%	49	23	26
CSE/Other/None	%	38	32	29
Social Class:				
I/II	%	44	33	20
III non-manual	%	51	26	23
III manual	%	36	34	30
IV/V	%	38	23	37

Our results, confirmed by those of other studies, show that current smoking is least common among the oldest age group. Women are on the whole also less likely to be smokers than are men, but not in the age group under 35. This is clearly a change, since many more women than men have never smoked, and many more men than women have given up.

---

[*] In this and other analyses, the very small number of (exclusively male) current pipe and cigar smokers is excluded.

So the trend towards smoking among younger women is strongly upward; men, on the other hand, are becoming less likely to be smokers. Smoking is rather more common among the working-classes and the less qualified than among the educated middle-classes. Moreover people in Social Classes I and II have been especially successful in giving up. More surprisingly, perhaps, people in Social Class III manual seem also to be relatively successful nowadays in giving up smoking, accounting partly for the major fall in male smoking.

We then looked at the characteristics of 'lighter' and 'heavier' smokers ('heavier' being defined as fifteen or more cigarettes a day). We find that women in all age groups smoke less heavily than men, and that people in the middle age-group (35-54) - men *and* women - are the heaviest smokers. Older smokers may, of course, cut down because of ill-health, or because of shortage of money, while smokers under 35 may not yet have peaked in their habit. There is no clear pattern according to education, but skilled manual workers appear to be conspicuously heavier smokers than people in the other social classes.

Our sample bases tend to become too small when we divide respondents into manual and non-manual workers and then look separately at smoking habits by age and gender. There is a suspicion, however, that younger middle-class women (18-34) are nowadays more likely to smoke than are their equivalent male cohort. In any event, the relatively high numbers of young female smokers appear to reflect both an increased uptake of smoking among women and a lower rate of quitting. Later we will discuss differences in attitudes to giving up, which might help to explain some of these differences.

So far our results are comparable with longitudinal data from several developed countries on trends in smoking behaviour (Pierce, 1989). In all the countries there has been a marked decline in the habit over the last twenty years, but among the manual social classes and the less well-educated the fall has been less steep. This evidence therefore suggests that the longstanding differences between the social classes in smoking-related morbidity and mortality will persist.

Trend data from the USA also suggest that smoking may soon become more prevalent among women generally than among men (Pierce *et al,* 1989). Although smoking among British women has declined more sharply than among American women, a recent study (Marmot *et al,* 1991) suggests that the American pattern may repeat itself here. Carried out between 1985 and 1988 among British civil servants, the study shows that a higher proportion of women than men in all grades except the lowest grade, were smokers, with the largest gap appearing in the highest grade - 18 per cent of women, compared with 8 per cent of men. Our findings show too that, in the 'higher' socio-economic groups, men appear to have taken the 'no smoking' message more seriously than have women. Attempts to discourage people from starting the habit, or to encourage smokers to give up, will therefore have to take these gender, class and educational differences even more seriously than hitherto.

Who intends to give up smoking and who does not?

Cross-sectional surveys such as *British Social Attitudes*, can of course explore intentions, but they cannot tell us, at the individual level, whether they are fulfilled.   Prospective studies have, however, shown a clear relationship between the resolve to give up smoking and success in doing so (Pierce *et al*, 1987; Marsh and Matheson, 1983). So we can, to an extent, take expressed intentions to predict future trends in behaviour. In any case, information about the sorts of people likely to give up smoking, and about their apparent motives, may help guide health educationalists towards the most effective ways of persuading people not to smoke.

We asked current cigarette smokers: "how likely is it that you will try to give up smoking within the next two years or so?" About three in five claimed that it was 'very' or 'fairly' likely that they would try. As the following table shows, distinctive patterns of responses emerged:

Likelihood of trying to give up smoking in near future

		Very/Fairly likely	Not very/Not at all likely
Men:			
18-34	%	72	25
35-54	%	58	39
55+	%	(48)	(48)
Women:			
18-34	%	62	38
35-54	%	59	38
55+	%	(49)	(46)
Highest educational qualification:			
Degree/Professional	%	76	23
A'/O' level	%	65	33
CSE/Other/None	%	49	44
Social Class:			
I/II	%	71	24
III non-manual	%	64	35
III manual	%	54	41
IV/V	%	49	48
Cigarette consumption:			
Smokers: 1-14 per day	%	66	34
15+ per day	%	55	45

Bracketed percentages are based on sub-group cells of fewer than 50 respondents.

We see that younger men (18-34 year olds), but not younger women, are markedly more likely than older ones to say they will try to give up. There are also clear gradients according to social class and educational qualifications; and, hardly surprisingly, heavier smokers are less optimistic

about giving up than are lighter smokers. These 'intentions' are all the
more credible because they reflect the behaviour patterns we have
already reported.

Among 'reluctant smokers', optimism still prevails: thus, people who
have tried to give up more than once are much more likely than those
who have not to say they will try again. Three in five of those who have
attempted but failed to quit the habit say they will try again, while only
two in five of those who have never tried say they will try to do so 'within
the next two years or so'.

Why give up smoking?

We asked current and ex-smokers whether and why they wanted to give
up, or had given up. Health is the reason cited most often (around two-
thirds say that it is 'very' or 'fairly' important), followed by cost and family
pressures, each mentioned as important by around one in five. As we can
see from the table below, while similar proportions of men and women
cite health, cost and family pressures, women tend to attach more
importance than do men to peer group social pressures, such as mixing
more with non-smokers, the smell of smoke and the fact that smoking has
become less fashionable nowadays.

Reasons given by current and ex-smokers for wanting to give up smoking*

% saying very or fairly important	Total	Men	Women
For health reasons	87	85	89
It costs too much to continue smoking	51	49	54
My family wants me to give up	43	40	47
I do not want tobacco smoke on my clothes and hair	34	30	44 **
More of the people I mix with are non-smokers	25	21	29 **
Smoking is less fashionable	17	13	23 **
There are more places where I can't smoke	16	14	20

* Those current smokers who say they do not want to give up smoking are
excluded from the calculation.
** On these items, the difference between men and women is statistically
significant.

People who cite several reasons as important ones for trying to stop might
be thought to have a more powerful incentive to do so than those who

give only one reason. And this is indeed the case. Smokers in this group are more likely to have tried to give up, to want to stop, and to say they intend to give up. Moreover, this association holds good across all social classes, and among those at all levels of educational attainment.

Reasons for smoking

Of course, reasons for wanting to give up may be more than outweighed by the perceived benefits of smoking. Table 8.1 shows the importance attached by current and ex-smokers to a range of reasons for smoking. Enjoyment, and the difficulty of giving up, are those cited most often as 'very important' (by around two in five current and ex-smokers), and in this respect there are no differences between men and women. On the other hand, more women than men feel that smoking helps them keep their weight down and cope with everyday life, while men are a little more likely than women to feel that it helps them concentrate.

We can classify reasons for smoking as either *positive* (for example, "smoking is simply something I enjoy"), or *negative* (for example, "smoking is just a hard habit to give up"). Interestingly, a mere two per cent of smokers give only positive reasons, while around one-half (52 per cent) give a combination of positive and negative reasons, and 18 per cent give only negative reasons. The remaining one-quarter or so (whom we classify as 'indifferent') do not rate any of the offered reasons for smoking as important. Note 1 at the end of this chapter provides further details of this classification. The table below shows the association between people's reasons for smoking and their previous attempts to give up, their desire to, and their intentions.

	Reasons given as important ones for smoking		
	Negative only	Positive and negative	None ('Indifferent')
Tried to give up	%	%	%
Often or a few times	53	57	34
Only once or never	47	43	66
Want to give up	%	%	%
Very much or quite a lot	67	66	39
Not very much or not at all	33	34	61
Will try to give up	%	%	%
Very or fairly likely to	78	60	48
Not very or not at all likely to	22	40	52

Members of the 'indifferent' group seem to differ from the others, in that they have the least desire or intention to stop smoking, and have tried to give up on fewer occasions. They are also especially likely to be lighter smokers.

An important and encouraging finding for health educationalists is that smokers who intend to try to give up smoking are more aware than others are of the health hazards of smoking. We asked respondents to rank, in order of importance, possible factors that might adversely affect the general health of a (hypothetical) young person. Two-thirds (68 per cent) of smokers who said that they would try to give up named smoking as the most important factor, compared to 59 per cent of those who did not think they would try. Of course, some smokers who intend to give up may already have a smoking-related illness, which would influence their answers (we cannot investigate this as we did not collect data on people's health). One finding which supports this view is that a higher proportion of older people than younger people believe smoking to be an important contributory factor to ill-health. Even so, over half of the youngest age-group (18-34) also cite smoking as the most important factor affecting a person's health.

Another factor which might affect people's motivation to give up smoking is a 'fatalistic' attitude to health. Some commentators have suggested not only that this might explain some of the social class differences in response to health-promotion campaigns, but also that 'fatalism' might be the critical obstacle to changing lifestyles (for example, Lewis et al, 1989). We used responses to two statements ("good health is just a matter of luck" and "if heart disease is in your family, there is little you can do to reduce your chances of getting it")[*] to classify people as 'fatalists' and 'non-fatalists' (see Note 2 at the end of this chapter for further details). As predicted, in comparison with their counterparts, fatalists had less of a wish to give up smoking and were less likely to try to give up. Smokers were more likely than non-smokers to be fatalists as were older people (aged 55 and over), the less well-educated and those in the manual social classes, but there were no differences according to gender. These associations with social class and education were evident among non-smokers too.

These findings, confirmed by the results of a logistic regression model we used with the same background variables (which we will report elsewhere) and the results of much recent research, all suggest that the less well-qualified and, to a smaller extent, the manual social classes generally, are less inclined to give up smoking than are the rest of the population. This in turn suggests that the difference between the middle classes and working classes in the prevalence of smoking will continue to grow. Women are also rather less likely than men, and heavier smokers less likely than lighter smokers, to express the wish to give up, although in the latter case it is of course possible that smokers who wish to quit, cut down as a prelude to stopping. Moreover, from the evidence available it appears that both the wish to give up *and* the number of

---

[*] Responses to these two questions were highly correlated ($r = 0.52$, $p < 0.001$).

reasons advanced for giving up are both predictive of trying to stop smoking.

So, campaigns aimed at trying to persuade smokers to give up will need to focus on the less well-qualified, and to emphasise the many different disadvantages of smoking.

Perceptions of the risks of smoking

As a way of exploring health beliefs, all respondents (not just smokers) were asked to imagine that they were advising a young person on how best to improve his or her health in general, and then how to avoid getting heart disease.

As the table below shows, being a non-smoker is seen as by far the most important factor in improving general health; cutting down on fatty foods comes a comfortable second place. For avoiding heart disease, however, cutting down on dietary fat is seen as a little more important than smoking, with stress (just above exercise) in third place.

The most important way to ...[*]

	... improve health generally	... avoid getting heart disease
	%	%
Not to smoke	61	37
Eat less fatty food	11	44
Eat more fruit and vegetables	11	2
Take more exercise	9	7
Reduce stress	4	8

[*] Only the five most frequently mentioned ways are shown

No clear patterns emerge according to sex or age, although younger women (aged 18-34) are more likely than other groups to nominate eating less fat as more important, and being a non-smoker as less important. Smokers *and* non-smokers rated being a non-smoker as important - in fact smokers (40 per cent) more so than non-smokers (33 per cent).

Fatty foods were more likely to be nominated as harmful by the less-qualified, who, as we have noted, are less likely to regard smoking as especially harmful, whilst stress and lack of exercise are identified as rather more of a danger by the better qualified. In any event, the message that smoking can harm health and the heart appears to have got through to people whatever their level of education, confirming the findings of other studies that awareness of the dangers of smoking is widespread.

Marsh and Matheson (1983) showed that the proportion believing that smoking was related to heart disease had increased substantially between 1964 and 1981. The emphasis nowadays on dietary fat as a cause of heart disease is interesting, as it probably reflects the influence of the mass media rather than of medical advice. Doctors still tend to place greater emphasis on cutting down or stopping smoking, rather than on reducing dietary fat (Lichtenstein *et al*, 1985). Moreover, a survey on the prevention of heart disease, carried out in 1982, found that only seven per cent of those questioned said that cutting out fat would be helpful, compared with 39 per cent who mentioned cutting down or stopping smoking (Research Surveys of Great Britain, 1982).[*] In the *Heart-beat Wales* project, carried out in 1985, a rather higher proportion of respondents thought that smoking (70 per cent) rather than animal fats (61 per cent) contributed to heart disease (Welsh Heart Programme, 1986). So our results suggest a possible recent change in public attitudes to heart disease, with rather greater concern nowadays about the dangers of fat in the diet than about smoking.

Is the public getting the right health messages? The Whitehall study (Reid *et al*, 1976) found that heavy smokers had a 75 per cent greater risk of dying from coronary heart disease than non-smokers, while people whose blood cholesterol was in the top quintile had a 33 per cent greater risk than those whose blood cholesterol was in the lowest quintile. Other data also support the finding that heavy smoking may be a greater risk factor for heart disease than high blood cholesterol (The Pooling Project Research Group, 1978). However, in Japan where cigarette consumption is high, but where fat consumption is low, there is a low rate of heart disease. And among the Japanese who emigrate to the USA and begin to consume a relatively high fat diet, the proportion getting heart disease increases (Marmot and Davey Smith, 1989). It is not clear from the evidence whether to label either smoking or diet as the more important in preventing heart disease. As both are important, health education messages about the perils of dietary fat and of smoking should not focus on one to the detriment of the other.

The risks of passive smoking

To assess perceived risks of passive smoking, that is exposure to other people's tobacco smoke, we asked:

*Suppose a non-smoker lives, or works closely, with a heavy smoker. How risky is it for the **non-smoker**?*

The risks are seen as serious by around three-quarters of respondents; almost a quarter regard it as a 'very serious' health risk. Women in all age groups are considerably more likely than men to perceive passive smoke exposure as serious, but they are also more likely to regard most

---

[*] A further option offered was 'to improve your diet', which might have also implied eating less fat. If this category is combined with the 'cut out fat' category, the combined total climbs to 33 per cent.

environmental risks as more serious (see Chapter 6). In other respects too, the differences in perceptions of passive smoking as being risky are fairly predictable, as the table below shows.

% saying that passive smoking is a ...		Very or fairly serious health risk
Age and sex:		
Men:	18-34	75
	35-54	62
	55+	60
Women:	18-34	84
	35-54	81
	55+	75
Social class:		
Non-manual		77
Manual		69
Smoking status:		
Never smoked		86
Ex-smokers		74
Cigarette consumption:		
Smokers:	1-14 per day	58
	15+ per day	51

The social class difference in perception remains, even when we control for smoking behaviour. Thus, as the table below shows, the middle classes are less tolerant of passive smoking than are the working classes regardless of whether or not they smoke themselves.

	Never smoked		Ex-smoker		Current smoker	
	Non-manual	Manual	Non-manual	Manual	Non-manual	Manual
Passive smoking is:	%	%	%	%	%	%
A very or fairly serious risk	88	84	78	74	59	50
Not much of a risk or no risk at all	13	16	22	26	41	50

These findings about passive smoking are only a little less striking than those in the USA, where in 1986, 88 per cent believed that exposure to passive smoke was generally harmful to health (MMWR, 1990).

Attitudes towards smoking in public places

In addition to asking about possible health risks from passive smoking, we also asked respondents if they were ever bothered by other people's tobacco smoke. Just under two-thirds (63 per cent) say that they were bothered either 'often' or 'sometimes', rising to nearly a quarter (73 per cent) of non-smokers. Other people's smoke is obviously less annoying if you are smoking yourself, or if you are accustomed to inhaling smoke; yet a third of smokers also complain of being bothered on occasions. Over half of non-smokers (and just over a quarter of smokers) say that they sometimes avoid places or events because of the smoky atmosphere. Lighter smokers are much more likely to say this than are heavier smokers (45 per cent than of the former, compared to only 19 per cent of the latter).

A Marplan survey (Smith *et al*, 1988) found similar proportions of non-smokers and smokers who were bothered by other people's smoke, as did a community-based survey in Ontario in 1985 (Pederson *et al*, 1987).

We then went on to ask specifically about whether or not smoking should be freely allowed in public places: for each of seven sites, we asked respondents if smoking should be 'freely allowed', 'restricted to certain areas', or 'banned altogether'. The full results are shown in **Table 8.2**, separately for smokers, ex-smokers and those who have never smoked. The sites we asked about were: hospitals, cinemas, restaurants, airlines, trains, workplaces and pubs. Proportions favouring complete bans are high, ranging between 72 per cent for hospitals and 26 per cent for pubs. Support for unrestricted smoking in *any* of the seven places, except pubs, is minimal, never exceeding 5 per cent; even in pubs only a quarter of respondents think that smoking should be freely allowed, around the same proportion who think it should be completely banned.

Our results are similar to those from other studies in Britain, the USA and Canada. For instance, the 1981 OPCS survey (Marsh and Matheson, 1983) asked about five similar public places, but permitted only a 'yes/no' response to the question. Clearly the inclusion in our survey of a compromise option ('restricted to certain areas') would lead fewer people to favour either complete freedom or a complete ban. Yet, while the proportion of smokers favouring a ban did decline, the proportion of non-smokers supporting a complete ban was fairly similar in the two surveys. These results must be viewed with some caution, since differences may be due to the different way in which the question was asked. Nonetheless they do suggest that non-smokers may have become less willing than before to tolerate smoking in public places.

Recent years have, of course, seen increasing provision of no-smoking areas at workplaces, in restaurants, on public transport and so on. This in itself would lead more people to support restrictions that have now become normative. Moreover, a study carried out in Australia has shown that smokers who had been opposed to restrictions on smoking at their workplaces came to accept and even welcome them once they had been introduced (Borland *et al*, 1990).

To examine the issue of 'public smoking' more closely, we classified respondents as belonging to one of two groups: a 'restrictive' group consisting of people who favour bans on smoking in at least four places and restricting it in the other three; and the rest who are more tolerant. As the figure below shows, women tend to be more restrictive than men and older people more so than younger people. Social class and education gradients are also apparent, with those in non-manual occupations and those who are better-qualified more likely to be in the restrictive category in public places. Non-smokers are, of course, far more likely to be in the restrictive category (60 per cent of non-smokers compared with 11 per cent of smokers). When we control for this, the relationship between sex and age remains, but the social class and education patterns (noted earlier) become less evident. These results are similar to those found by the OPCS survey carried out in 1981 (Marsh and Matheson, 1983).

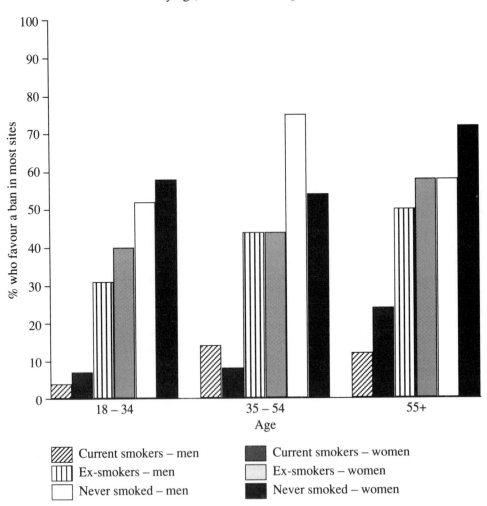

Attitudes to restrictions on smoking in public places
by age, sex and smoking status

People's attitudes to restrictions on smoking in public places also differ according to their perceptions of the health hazards of passive exposure to smoke. Only 16 per cent of those who think that passive smoking carried either 'no risk' or 'not much risk' fell into the restrictive category, compared with 71 per cent of those who feel passive smoking to be a 'very serious risk'. Even among smokers themselves, the more likely they are to regard passive smoking as risky, the more likely they are to favour restrictions. There is, however, no significant association between 'restrictiveness' and the perceived risks to health of smoking oneself.

**Attitudes to restrictions on smoking in public places
by perceived risk of passive smoking**

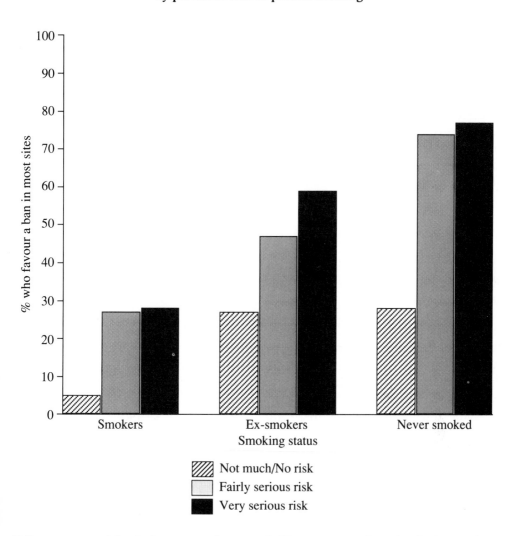

When we used logistic regression modelling to examine the independent effect of each of a number of factors on 'restrictiveness' (the results are presented in **Table 8.3** as 'odds ratios'), we found once again that the most important factors predicting 'restrictiveness' are age, perceptions of the risks of passive smoking and, above all, being a smoker or an ex-smoker. The gender differences noted above disappeared when these other factors were taken into account.

Although curbs on smoking in public places have increased enormously over the last decade only one-quarter of our sample (in response to a further question) thinks that there are already enough restrictions. Further controls might even gain widespread acceptance among many smokers.

Tobacco advertising and sponsorship

Nearly two-thirds of respondents feel that *all* cigarette advertising should be banned, around half of whom feel this strongly. Indeed, only 16 per cent oppose such a ban. However, opposition to sponsorship by tobacco companies of sporting and artistic events is much more muted: only 43 per cent and 35 per cent oppose sports and artistic sponsorship respectively by tobacco companies. Apparently sponsorship is seen in quite a different light from direct advertising, its benefits to sport and the arts apparently outweighing its possible harmful effects in promoting tobacco products. Naturally, 'restrictiveness' over smoking in public places and disapproval of advertising and sponsorship all go together.

Attitudes towards smokers

Finally, we asked several questions to try to discover how smokers are perceived in a society in which they are now in such a minority, and in particular whether or not measures ought to be taken against them.

Just over one half of respondents (53 per cent) believe that nowadays "most people look down on smokers". Interestingly, similar proportions of current smokers, ex-smokers and those who had never smoked share this assessment. Three in five respondents support much higher taxes on cigarettes (in common with a surprising one-third of smokers themselves). And nearly three-quarters (73 per cent) would support ('definitely' or 'probably') increases in life insurance premiums for smokers. In contrast, however, when asked if "NHS hospitals should give smokers low priority for heart or lung operations", only a quarter of respondents would go along with that degree of discrimination. Still this is a fairly large proportion in favour of such a drastic measure.

Clear differences emerge according to social class and education. Once more, those in the 'higher' social classes and the better qualified are particularly intolerant, tending to favour higher taxes on cigarettes and larger premiums for life insurance. Moreover these differences persist, irrespective of whether people are smokers or non-smokers. In addition, heavy and lighter smokers hold broadly similar views on these issues, except for the fact that lighter smokers are more in favour than heavier smokers of increased taxation on cigarettes. This may be because it would cost heavier smokers more and because, as we have seen, light smokers are more likely to want to quit.

According to the sparse evidence available, almost all arising from comparisons with the 1981 OPCS survey, public attitudes towards smokers have over time become less tolerant. A higher proportion than in 1981 (53 per cent compared with 47 per cent) feel that people look down upon smokers, and a considerably higher proportion (60 per cent compared with 47 per cent) now favour increased taxation on cigarettes. Virtually none of our results, however, supports the commonly-held notion that ex-smokers are more anti-smoking than those who have never smoked.

Conclusions

While smoking is on the decline in most developed nations, our findings, supported by others, indicate that the decline among the manual social classes is much slower. Better qualified people are more likely than others to try to give up. In addition, young women appear to be going against the general trend, to the extent that smoking may eventually become more common among them than among young men.

The findings also suggest that large and increasing majorities of the public favour restricting or banning smoking in public places. Smokers tend to support restrictions rather than outright bans. If the habit continues to decline and awareness of the dangers associated with passive smoking (already widespread) increases further, even more restrictions are therefore likely to be supported. These findings should give encouragement to those responsible for health policies aimed at reducing smoking. Even the complete banning of smoking advertisements is widely supported.

The abolition of sponsorship by tobacco companies is, however, more controversial; as the financial problems of the arts and of many sports increase, it is perhaps understandable that funding by tobacco companies is still tolerated, if not exactly welcomed.

The changing image of smokers is harder to evaluate, though our results certainly suggest it is becoming more negative. Punitive measures, such as increased taxation or larger insurance premiums for smokers, attract widespread support, but not (as yet, anyway) to the extent of discrimination against smokers in respect of health care.

Health education campaigns appear to have been successful in that the majority of the population - smokers and non-smokers - now perceive the habit to be harmful to health. Interestingly, excess fat in the diet is now thought to be more or less equally harmful as far as heart disease is concerned. Perception of the risk of passive smoke exposure is also widespread (but rather less so than in the USA). Smokers are, not surprisingly, less sensitive towards the harm that smoking may cause others and less in favour of restrictions on smoking in public places. Our evidence suggests that, as smoking becomes less common and people become more aware of the hazards of passive smoke exposure, attitudes towards smoking may continue to harden; this may help the reluctant smoker to finally give up.

Notes

1. Smokers were divided into four groups depending on how they rated both positive and negative reasons for smoking, at question Y141. **Positive reasons** were: a. "Helps me to relax"; c. "Helps me feel more confident with other people"; f. "Helps me cope with everyday life"; g. "Helps me concentrate"; i. "Is simply something I enjoy". **Negative reasons** were: b. "It is a very hard habit to give up"; h. "I don't have the willpower to give up".

    A 'positive' smoker rated the positive reasons 'very' or 'fairly' important on average, whilst not rating the negative reasons as 'very' important.

    A 'negative' smoker rated the negative reasons as 'very' or 'fairly' important, and did not rate any of the positive reasons as 'very' important.

    A 'positive and negative' smoker rated both the positive and the negative statements as 'very' or 'fairly' important, on average.

    An 'indifferent' smoker rated both the positive and the negative reasons as 'not very' important, or 'not a reason at all'.

2. 'Fatalists' and 'non-fatalists' were classified from responses to question Y2.22, g. "Good health is just a matter of good luck", and h. "If heart disease is in your family there is little you can do to reduce your chances of getting it." 'Fatalists' agreed with both statements, while 'non-fatalists' did not agree with both statements.

References

BORLAND, R., OWEN, N., HILL, D. and CHAPMAN, S., 'Changes in acceptance of workplace smoking bans following their implementation: a prospective study', *Preventive Medicine,* vol.19 (1990), pp.314-22.

LEWIS, P.A., CHARNY, M., LAMBERT, D. and COOMBES, J., 'A fatalistic attitude to health amongst smokers in Cardiff', *Health Education Research,* no.4 (1989), pp.361-65.

LICHTENSTEIN, M.J., ELWOOD, P.C., THOMAS, H.F. and SWEETNAM, P.M., 'Doctors' opinions on the prevention of myocardial infarction', *Journal of the Royal College of General Practitioners,* vol.35, (1985), pp.516-19.

MMWR, 'Leads from the MMWR. Passive smoking: beliefs, attitudes, and exposures -United States, 1986', in *The Centers for Disease Control. Smokers' beliefs about the health benefits of smoking cessation - 20 US communities, 1989; Journal of the American Medical Association,* vol.264 (1990).

MARMOT, M.G. and DAVEY SMITH, G., 'Why are the Japanese living longer?' *British Medical Journal,* vol.299 (1989), pp.1547-51.

MARMOT, M.G., DAVEY SMITH, G., STANSFELD, S., PATEL, C., NORTH, F., HEAD, J., WHITE, I., BRUNNER, E. and FEENY, A.,

'Health Inequalities among British Civil Servants: the Whitehall II Study', *The Lancet,* vol.337 (1991), pp.1387-1393.

MARSH, A. and MATHESON, J., *Smoking Attitudes and Behaviour,* HMSO, London (1983).

OFFICE ON SMOKING AND HEALTH, *The Health Consequences of Involuntary Smoking: a Report of the Surgeon-General,* CDC, Rockville, Maryland (1987).

PEDERSON, L.L., BULL, S.B., ASHLEY, M.J. and LEFCOE, N.M., 'A population survey in Ontario regarding restrictive measures on smoking: relationship of smoking status to knowledge, attitudes and predicted behaviour', *International Journal of Epidemiology,* vol.16 (1987), pp.383-91.

PIERCE, J.P., 'International comparisons of trends in cigarette smoking prevalence', *American Journal of Public Health,* vol.79 (1989), pp.152-57.

PIERCE, J.P., DWYER, T., CHAMBERLAIN, A., ALDRICH, R.N. and SHELLY, J.M., 'Targeting the smoker in an anti-smoking campaign'. *Preventive Medicine,* vol.16, (1987), pp.816-24.

PIERCE, J.P., FIORE, M.C., NOVOTNY, T.E., HATZIANDREU, E.J. and DAVIS, R.M., 'Trends in cigarette smoking in the United States. Projections to the year 2000', *Journal of the American Medical Association,* vol.261 (1989), pp.61-65.

REID, D.D., McCARTNEY, P.M., HAMILTON, P.J.S. and ROSE, G., 'Smoking and other risk factors for coronary heart disease in British civil servants', *The Lancet,* no.2 (1976), pp.979-83.

RESEARCH SURVEYS OF GREAT BRITAIN, *Heart Disease,* RSGB for the Health Education Council, London (1982).

SMITH, C., BERRY, J. and ROBERTS, J.L., 'Passive smoking - a survey of knowledge, attitudes and behaviour', *Health Education Journal,* vol.47 (1988), pp.100-02.

THE POOLING PROJECT RESEARCH GROUP, 'Relationship of blood pressure, serum cholesterol, smoking habit, relative weight and ECG abnormalities to incidence of major coronary events', *Journal of Chronic Diseases,* vol.31 (1978), pp.201-306.

WALD, N.J., BOOTH, C., DOLL, R., HOWARD, G., JARVIS, M., LANE, D.J., ROBERTSON, A. and VENITT, S., *Passive Smoking: a Health Hazard,* ICRF and CRC, Dewsbury (1991).

WELSH HEART PROGRAMME, *The Pulse of Wales: Heartbeat Report No. 4.* Heartbeat Wales, Cardiff (1986).

Acknowledgement

SCPR and the authors are grateful to the Health Education Authority for its financial support for the questionnaire module on attitudes to smoking.

8.1 IMPORTANCE OF REASONS FOR SMOKING (CURRENT AND EX-SMOKERS) (Y141)

		Very important reason	Fairly important reason	Not very important reason	Not a reason at all
Smoking is a very hard habit to give up					
	Total	% 42	25	16	16
	Men	% 44	24	17	14
	Women	% 40	25	15	18
Smoking is simply something I enjoy					
	Total	% 40	43	9	6
	Men	% 42	41	10	5
	Women	% 38	46	8	6
Smoking helps me relax					
	Total	% 25	44	17	12
	Men	% 24	45	18	12
	Women	% 27	43	16	13
I don't have the willpower to give up					
	Total	% 23	25	18	32
	Men	% 22	24	17	35
	Women	% 24	27	19	29
Smoking helps me cope with everyday life					
	Total	% 12	25	24	37
	Men	% 8	25	26	40
	Women	% 17	26	23	34
Smoking helps me keep my weight down					
	Total	% 10	16	22	49
	Men	% 6	13	23	56
	Women	% 16	21	21	41
Smoking is the normal thing to do among people I mix with					
	Total	% 9	25	22	42
	Men	% 10	25	22	42
	Women	% 9	25	22	42
Smoking helps me concentrate					
	Total	% 9	26	24	39
	Men	% 9	29	20	40
	Women	% 9	23	30	38
Smoking helps me feel more confident with other people					
	Total	% 6	16	29	47
	Men	% 5	19	27	47
	Women	% 7	13	32	47

8.2 ALLOWING SMOKING IN PUBLIC PLACES (Y2.17)
by smoking status

Smoking should be...	Total	Current smoker	Ex- smoker	Never smoked
	%	%	%	%
In hospitals				
...freely allowed	*	*	-	1
...restricted to certain areas	26	50	24	13
...banned altogether	72	47	76	86
In cinemas	%	%	%	%
...freely allowed	3	7	1	2
...restricted to certain areas	35	62	29	22
...banned altogether	61	28	70	75
At restaurants	%	%	%	%
...freely allowed	4	11	2	2
...restricted to certain areas	37	62	33	24
...banned altogether	57	24	64	73
On airline flights	%	%	%	%
...freely allowed	2	7	1	1
...restricted to certain areas	44	69	41	32
...banned altogether	52	21	57	67
On trains	%	%	%	%
...freely allowed	3	8	1	1
...restricted to certain areas	58	76	59	47
...banned altogether	38	14	40	51
At people's places of work	%	%	%	%
...freely allowed	5	13	2	2
...restricted to certain areas	60	75	63	48
...banned altogether	33	9	33	48
In pubs	%	%	%	%
...freely allowed	25	47	19	15
...restricted to certain areas	45	46	50	42
...banned altogether	26	3	26	39

8.3 ODDS RATIOS FOR LOGISTIC REGRESSION MODELS FOR RESTRICTING PUBLIC SMOKING

Explanatory variable	Univariate odds ratio (95% confidence interval)	Multivariate odds ratio (95% confidence interval)
Sex		
Women	1.0	1.0
Men	0.9 (0.7-1.1)	1.2 (0.9-1.5)
Age		
18-34	1.0	1.0
35-54	1.3 (1.0-1.7)	1.7 (1.2-2.4)
55+	1.9 (1.4-2.5)	2.4 (1.9-4.1)
Social class		
Non-manual	1.0	1.0
Manual	0.8 (0.7-1.1)	1.2 (0.8-1.6)
Highest educational qualification		
Degree/professional	1.0	1.0
A'/O'level	0.8 (0.6-1.1)	0.9 (0.6-1.3)
CSE/Other/None	0.8 (0.6-1.1)	0.8 (0.5-1.2)
Smoking status		
Current smoker	1.0	1.0
Ex-smoker	7.7 (5.1-11.5)	5.2 (3.3-8.1)
Never smoked	12.8 (8.6-18.9)	10.0 (6.5-15.2)
Perceived risk of passive smoke exposure		
Little or no risk	1.0	1.0
Fairly or very serious risk	5.6 (4.0-7.9)	4.3 (3.0-6.3)
Health is just luck		
Agree	1.0	1.0
Neither	1.3 (0.84-2.1)	0.9 (0.5-1.5)
Disagree	2.4 (1.7-3.4)	1.5 (1.0-2.3)

An odds ratio greater than 1 indicates that the subgroup was more likely to be in favour of restricting public smoking.

9 Interim report: Civil liberties

Lindsay Brook and Ed Cape[*]

Among the frustrations of this series is the repeated realisation that only a limited range of subjects can be covered thoroughly. An even greater frustration in the context of this chapter is that we did not introduce a module on civil liberties seven years earlier, especially as the 1980s have seen such interesting changes and the elevation of civil liberties into a controversial political issue. As Dworkin's polemic on Britain in the 1980s has it:

> Intellectual liberty [has become] just another commodity, to be enjoyed when there is no commercial or administrative price to be paid for it, but abandoned, with no evident grief, when that price begins to rise. That is not despotism. But it cheapens liberty and diminishes the nation. (Dworkin, 1988, quoted in Ewing and Gearty, 1990, p.16).

Yet looking back on our data, we do have a serviceable body of trend data to provide background to the findings of the 1990 module reported here. As we shall see, for instance, there have been mounting worries about the powers of government, especially in relation to the perceived inability of trade unions to respond (see Millward, 1990, p.28). Confidence in the police and prison service is low and falling, and the public is rather more cautious now than it was about derogating powers to the police.

---

[*] Lindsay Brook is a Research Director at SCPR and a Co-director of the *BSA* survey series; Ed Cape is Senior Lecturer in the Department of Law, Bristol Polytechnic.

We have included in the module more questions than we will cover here. We asked, for instance, about the right to strike, eliciting an intriguing set of responses which we hope to report in a future chapter on attitudes to trade unions. Questions about the blasphemy law go unreported here, though Chapter 4 includes a range of civil liberties issues such as these in respect of British and Northern Irish respondents. We are also able to take only a first look here at the many interesting subgroup differences that exist, hoping that other users of the dataset may care to look further.

Setting the context

How free a society do people perceive Britain to be in comparison with other countries, and how 'open' do they think its government is? We asked these questions about six nations including Britain: three other liberal democracies (Canada, West Germany* and the USA), and the Soviet Union* and China.* All, unlike Britain, have written constitutions. While large majorities believe that all four liberal democracies protect citizens' rights and that they enjoy open government, Britain is rated best among them in respect of protecting rights and worst on 'open government', with as many as a quarter of the sample questioning British credentials on this count.

% saying for each nation:	Britain %	West Germany %	USA %	Canada %
Citizens' rights very or fairly well protected	85	70	73	78
Citizens' rights not very or not at all well protected	11	8	12	2
Don't know	4	22	15	20
% saying for each nation:				
It is very or fairly open	71	61	76	72
It is not very or not at all open	25	19	13	6
Don't know	4	19	11	21

More worryingly, perhaps, only eight per cent of respondents rate Britain both as 'very' open *and* as 'very' respectful of its citizens' rights.

These views on Britain are shared by most subgroups within the population. Men, older people and Conservative identifiers tend to show more confidence in Britain, graduates and Labour identifiers less. But

---

* Germany was, of course, still divided at the time of the 1990 fieldwork round; the Soviet Union was, of course, not; our fieldwork took place some ten months after the Tiananmen Square killings.

the picture is one of consensus rather than of division. The more marked differences, especially along the political divide, emerge in respect of the openness of government. Fewer than two in three Labour identifiers, compared with over four in five Conservatives, believe that Britain enjoys 'very' or 'fairly' open government. But both Labour identifiers and graduates tend to be more sceptical about the record of the other three liberal democracies too.

Evidence of unease about Britain's civil libertarian record comes also from a recent MORI opinion poll on the 'State of the Nation' (reported in Dunleavy and Weir, 1991), which found that the British public believed that citizens' rights were less respected here than in the rest of the European Community. So, alongside a degree of approval of Britain's record, there is a sense of disquiet, hardly echoing Hume's view of Britain in the mid-eighteenth century as "the bastion of the general liberties of Europe and patron of mankind".

While the public's impressions of what happens in other countries are likely to come mainly from the media, since few people will have answered from expert knowledge or personal experience, informed commentators would nonetheless probably agree with respondents' assessments. Canada's 1982 Charter of Rights and Freedoms, the United States Constitution and the West German *Grundgesetz* (Basic Law) which begins with an extensive bill of rights (Topf *et al,* 1989) are all, in different ways, models of their kind. That China and the USSR have written constitutions has not prevented widespread abuse of human rights there, and respondents' answers show they are aware of this (only nine per cent and 10 per cent respectively believing that citizens are protected in China and the Soviet Union, and still fewer (seven per cent) believing that each enjoys open government). But things have changed dramatically since 1990, in the Soviet Union anyway, and we shall look for changes in respondents' perceptions when we repeat these questions in 1993.

Cornerstones of civil libertarianism

How libertarian are the British? The answer depends, of course, on how one defines libertarianism, especially in a modern liberal democracy. We looked at five issues (three general, two more specific) out of the many we could have chosen, all of which are central to current civil libertarian debates in Britain, and the first three of which have been at the core of civil libertarianism over the centuries:

> Rights of political protest
> The claims of conscience against the law
> Protection against wrongful conviction at the risk of letting the
>   guilty go free
> The reinstatement of the death penalty
> The introduction of compulsory identity cards

Rights of political protest

The right to engage in peaceful forms of protest is a fundamental article
of all human rights conventions. In 1990, we repeated a question that
had been first asked in 1985, as part of the *International Social Survey
Programme's* (ISSP) 'role of government' questionnaire module, asking
whether people should be allowed to engage in each of six forms of
protest "against a government action they strongly oppose". We show only
the 1990 figures below since there has been little change since 1985 in the
distribution of answers. Large majorities uphold people's rights to
organise public meetings, to publish pamphlets and to hold marches and
demonstrations. Indeed, most of those saying these actions should be
allowed say 'definitely' rather than 'probably'. But only around a third
would approve of the legal right to organise a "nationwide strike of all
workers against the government" (only 12 per cent without any
reservation), and only a handful would support protest that involved
damage (or even potential damage) to property.

% saying it should definitely or
probably be allowed:

Public protest meetings	88
Protest pamphlets	84
Marches and demonstrations	70
Nationwide political strike	31
Occupation of government buildings	10
Serious damage to government buildings	1

In 1986, Parliament enacted the Public Order Act introduced in the wake
of the miners' strike. The government's case was that the Act was
necessary in order to replace a 'complex and fragmented law'; critics
argue that the law is now even more complex and that the Act has added
unnecessarily to "the extensive list of police public order powers" (Ewing
and Gearty, 1990, p.117).

Ironically, the only respect in which public attitudes appear to have
moved over the five years on this issue is that a *smaller* proportion in
1990 (43 per cent) than in 1985 (52 per cent) would 'definitely' oppose a
nationwide protest strike as a form of political protest. Strike action of
this kind has effectively been outlawed by a series of labour relations Acts
during the 1980s: nonetheless a substantial minority of the population as
a whole (and a bare majority among graduates and Labour identifiers)
see a political strike as a legitimate weapon, perhaps of last resort, against
a government that is seen as having gone too far.

Conservative identifiers are noticeably less enthusiastic than adherents
of the other major parties about the right to all forms of protest and,
perhaps predictably, hardly any see a strike as a legitimate form of
political protest. On the other hand, while Liberal Democrat identifiers
are slightly *firmer* than Labour identifiers in their support for peaceful
forms of protest, they become more cautious as the type of protest gets

more confrontational. So any Liberal Democrat campaign, such as to win proportional representation, is destined, it seems, to be fought in a very orderly manner.

In 1990, we added a new question to the ISSP module, which tried to establish whether or not there was a link between supporting the *right* to political protest and sympathy for political protest *per se.* We asked respondents how favourable or unfavourable they were in general towards "people who organise protests against a government action they strongly oppose". A true libertarian, it may be argued, ought to be indifferent both to the protesters' political stance and to the extent of sympathy they engender. As the table below shows, however, especially in respect of the more confrontational forms of protest, there is a strong link between one's civil libertarian resolve and one's sympathy for protesters generally.

	Feelings about political protesters	
	Favourable	Unfavourable
Public protest meetings	%	%
Should definitely or probably be allowed	95	68
Should probably or definitely *not* be allowed	2	28
Marches and demonstrations	%	%
Should definitely or probably be allowed	85	28
Should probably or definitely *not* be allowed	12	69

Only one in seven respondents 'disapprove' of protesters generally, but few of them would go along with Voltaire and "defend to the death [their] right" to express their views in any but the most innocuous way.

The claims of conscience

A more difficult dilemma for the civil libertarian is the primacy of the law against the dictates of conscience. Some would argue that, in a liberal democracy, laws passed by an elected parliament should always be respected: the way to change them is through the ballot box or through peaceful political campaigns. Others would say that conscience is paramount: if individuals regard a law as oppressive and unjust, they have a duty to challenge it and if necessary to defy it - a well-tried method over the centuries and one by which countless injustices have been rectified.

We asked two questions about the primacy of the law. The first, a repeat of one asked in 1985, posed a simple choice (with an option to say 'can't choose'). The second was in the form of an 'agree/disagree' scale.

As we see, the balance of opinion differed according to the way the dilemma was put. The first question ran:

In general, would you say that people should obey the law without exception, or are there exceptional occasions on which people should follow their consciences, even if it means breaking the law?

	1985	1990
% saying:	%	%
Obey the law without exception	37	41
Follow conscience on occasions	58	52
Can't choose or not answered	5	7

By a small majority then, respondents say that people should put their consciences first (we did not ask them what they themselves might do), although the majority seems to have weakened somewhat over the past five years. But when we put the same dilemma in a different way in 1990 (using a five-point scale with a neutral mid-point), around a quarter of respondents chose the mid-point. This seems to have had the effect of depressing the claims of conscience, while having little impact on the overall proportion who support the claims of the law.

The law should always be obeyed, even if a particular law is wrong

	%
Agree strongly	10
Agree	36
Neither agree nor disagree	25
Disagree	26
Disagree strongly	3

Public attitudes are divided then, but (judging by the volatile pattern of responses to the two questions) it does not appear that the dilemma is one of great public concern - at least at present. Conformity with the law increases with age (twice as many in the youngest age group - 18-34 years - as in the oldest - 65 and over - say that people should follow their conscience) and decreases with education. We might, however, have expected the attitudes of Conservative identifiers to be particularly distinctive on this issue. After all, Conservative politicians frequently attack their Labour counterparts for declining to take disciplinary action against members (including some MPs) who elect to follow their conscience over, for example, poll tax payments. Yet opinion among Conservatives was relatively evenly split.

Protecting the innocent

In Britain, as in many other (but not all) liberal democracies, the formal burden of proof in court lies with the prosecution. Nonetheless, that the accused is 'innocent until proved guilty' always carries the attendant danger that some of the guilty will be acquitted, especially in view of the burden of proof 'beyond reasonable doubt'. To the committed civil libertarian this is an acceptable and necessary risk. Three in five respondents agreed. Our question, asked in 1985 and 1990, was:

> *All systems of justice make mistakes, but which do you think is worse ...*

	1985 %	1990 %
... to convict an innocent person,	67	62
or, to let a guilty person go free?	20	19
(Can't choose)	12	19

The majority taking the libertarian stance is substantial (especially among graduates and Labour identifiers, yet surprisingly rather less so among 18-24 year olds), and has remained more or less stable over the last five years. Still, around one person in five is prepared to risk the conviction of an innocent person rather than taking the opposite risk, and a further one in five (in 1990) has no view on the matter. These findings may give the libertarian cause for concern.

Reintroduction of capital punishment

The *British Social Attitudes* series has carried a standard question since 1983, worded in such a way as to reflect the terms in which the debates about the reintroduction of capital punishment have been conducted since abolition (in 1969):

> *Are you in favour of or against the death penalty for (1) murder in the course of a terrorist act? (2) murder of a police officer? (3) other murders?*

Decisive majorities are still in favour of the reintroduction of the death penalty in all three circumstances although there does appear to have been some softening of attitudes in the last five years.

	1983	1985	1990
% in favour of capital punishment for:			
Murder in the course of a terrorist act	74	77	70
Murder of a police officer*	70	71	67
Other murders	63	66	61

* In 1983 and 1985 'murder of a policeman'.

This change may have something to do with the succession of IRA cases, notably the 'Guildford Four', the 'Birmingham Six' and the 'Maguire Seven', which were much in the news just before and during fieldwork in spring 1990. Many respondents must have been alerted to the implications of a succession of unsafe verdicts for crimes that had once been capital offences. Nonetheless, the death penalty still appears to have a symbolic importance which outweighs all other factors. As expected, the younger respondents are, the more educated and the more left-wing, the less likely they are to support the death penalty in any circumstances.

The introduction of identity cards

Civil rights groups in Britain have long been wary of the introduction of mandatory identity cards. In 1988, the then Home Secretary asked the police to assess the case for a national compulsory system of identity cards. There were many objections, primarily in respect of the potential of such a system for abuse by state agencies. As Thornton (1990) put it: "a unique personal number could lead to access to a wide range of data bases. ...There is much evidence from other countries that [identity cards are] inconvenient, unnecessary and an invasion of privacy" (pp.30,32). We placed our question on this subject towards the end of a series dealing with a wide range of civil libertarian issues to avoid its being associated only with, say, football hooliganism.

Public attitudes are fairly evenly split, with 37 per cent for and 40 per cent against the introduction of compulsory identity cards in Britain. As many as one in five, once again, have no opinion either way. Moreover, only around 20 per cent feel strongly about the matter (dividing equally for and against). Nor is this an issue that divides people much along age or gender lines. Graduates are the most resistant to the idea of identity cards: even so, only 17 per cent of them are 'strongly' opposed. It is certainly not an issue then on which the nation appears to be polarised.

Looking at the range of answers given so far on all these issues, committed civil libertarians might well feel rather despondent. The public appears at best to be ambivalent and at worst to be unconcerned about certain rights and freedoms and protections that are at the core of a libertarian society. On the other hand, we must remember that many libertarian concerns we have touched on so far are about protections for minorities of one sort or another; for the bulk of the population the issues are therefore somewhat abstract and hypothetical. Those who are not directly affected may believe that the checks and balances are acceptable, and that, 'ordinary' people are able to get on with their day-to-day lives with no discernible infringement by the state upon their rights as citizens; some encroachment on minority rights is therefore acceptable if it leads to a more stable society.

We shall turn later to a series of less abstract issues to see how the British public has responded to some of the recent changes in the law.

A secretive society?

The Official Secrets Act of 1989 was introduced to 'achieve maximum clarity' in a law that, before the 1980s, had fallen largely into disuse and, during the 1980s, into some disrepute. In particular, a number of prosecutions under the all-embracing Section 2 of the 1911 Act caused concern on two main counts: first, that the Act was not an "appropriate vehicle for dealing with many of [the] cases brought before the courts"; and secondly (and more importantly) that it was being used "not to protect national security, but to protect the government from future political embarrassment" (Ewing and Gearty, 1990, p.139). Two cases against civil servants in 1984 caused particular controversy: that of Sarah Tisdall for leaking to *The Guardian* a document concerning the delivery of cruise missiles to Greenham Common; and that of Clive Ponting for sending documents to an MP about the Falklands war. Sarah Tisdall was imprisoned, Clive Ponting acquitted. The jury in the Ponting case had apparently accepted the defence argument that the leak did not compromise national security; rather it was in the public interest that the documents should have been published. Later, the government's worldwide campaign to prevent publication of Peter Wright's *Spycatcher* served only to intensify concern that the moving force behind all these cases was the protection not of national security but of the government itself. The new Official Secrets Act, by removing the 'public interest' defence, was widely criticised as a significant move towards further control of information by government.

In this respect the concerns of the civil libertarian lobby are, it seems, shared by those of the public at large as the responses to our question about the comparative 'openness' of British society has shown: only 13 per cent see Britain as a 'very open' society. Answers to a more detailed series of questions reveal the focus of these concerns.

The following question was asked in 1985 (not repeated in 1990):

Suppose a newspaper got hold of confidential government papers about defence plans and wanted to publish them ... should the newspaper be allowed to publish the papers, or should the government have the power to prevent publication?

A second parallel question (also asked in 1985 only) dealt with 'economic plans'.

	1985	
	Defence plans	Economic plans
	%	%
Newspapers should be allowed to publish	24	58
Government should have power to prevent publication	69	34

While the freedom of the press to disclose defence plans is widely opposed, there is majority support for their right to publish economic plans. These somewhat pragmatic responses are shared by people in other countries (see Taylor-Gooby, 1989). But in 1990 we introduced three new scenarios, asking whether the government should or should not be allowed to stop publication in each case:

Suppose...

... there was a minor leak of radiation from a nuclear power station which was unlikely to have harmed anyone

... the government decided to start developing a new weapons system

... a cabinet minister was asked to resign for having used his position to make a lot of money

Again, the public judged each case on its merits and was most censorious about disclosure of defence information. Only one in four would approve of a government cover-up over a radiation leak, and only a handful over the reasons behind a ministerial resignation.

The government should be:	Radiation leak %	Weapons system %	Cabinet resignation %
Definitely allowed to keep it* secret	10	26	3
Probably allowed	16	22	4
Probably not allowed	16	15	16
Definitely not allowed	57	34	75

* Keep 'the reason' secret in the case of the cabinet resignation.

Interestingly, a British government *would* have the power to keep all three matters out of the public domain. Unauthorised disclosure of matters such as these would almost certainly be in contravention of the new Official Secrets Act. Indeed, in 1987 the government went to some lengths to try to suppress the showing of a BBC documentary about the Zircon surveillance project - an action that Roy Jenkins, then MP for Edinburgh Hillhead, memorably described as that of "a second-rate police state, infused equally with illiberalism and incompetence". Our evidence suggests that these sorts of cover-up evoke very little sympathy and that, on the whole, the British public is in favour of more open government. Indeed, even on the vexed question of disclosure of information which could compromise national security (such as a new weapons system) the public is more or less evenly divided.

In response to a further question about whether a civil servant should be allowed to reveal the truth about "a cabinet minister [who] gives false information to parliament about an important national issue", more than four in five (83 per cent) of respondents favour the right of civil servants to disclose the correct facts; only seven per cent say that they should be legally required to keep silent.

The overriding impression then is of a public that has a strong distaste for government powers that enable it to protect its own interests rather than those of the state. The public's perception of where the dividing line should be drawn is clearly not where the government would draw it. For instance, the Armstrong memorandum (see NCCL, 1985) sets out guidelines stipulating that civil servants' loyalties are to the government of the day and to the minister in charge of their department. Breach of contract in disclosing information could lead to disciplinary measures, including dismissal (see Zellick, 1990). The public, however, seems to see civil servants more as public servants than as government servants alone.

Protection from prosecution of journalists who are unwilling to reveal the source of confidential information has long been regarded as an important safeguard against attempts by government to curb debate on 'sensitive issues'. The Contempt of Court Act 1981 was thought to give journalists just such protection, yet in a number of recent cases the courts have decided that it is "in the interests of justice" to order disclosure. The 1989 Official Secrets Act makes the media liable to prosecution "if they have reasonable cause to believe that the information" they have received is confidential. Our question asked specifically about the right of a newspaper to keep its sources confidential in the following circumstances:

Suppose a person leaked secret defence plans to a newspaper, and the government wanted to find out who it was. [Should] the paper have the legal right to keep the person's name secret, or not?

	%
Definitely should	16
Probably should	17
Probably should not	21
Definitely should not	43

We also asked about a firm wanting to discover the name of someone who had "leaked secret plans about a new commercial invention" and the distribution of answers was similar.

So, by a two-to-one majority the public's view is that newspapers *should* have to disclose their sources in these circumstances. At first reading, this may appear to be something of a paradox, since we found earlier that opinion was fairly evenly divided over whether government secrecy (about a new weapons system) should be respected in the first place. Now, by denying journalists the right to protect their sources, a majority appears, in effect, to wish to inhibit publication. Perhaps some respondents failed to make this connection; or perhaps 'secret defence plans' sounded more central to national security than did 'a new weapons system'. Or perhaps suspicion about the integrity of the press outweighs concern about government secrecy: we know from other *British Social Attitudes* data that journalists are certainly not held in high esteem (Jowell and Topf, 1988, pp.111-12). The issues are, of course, very complex ones, and not likely to be ones that many people think a great deal about. That there is widespread ambivalence is therefore not all that surprising. To most people these are not necessarily matters of principle anyway.

Freedom of expression

We have already noted the widespread public tolerance of orderly political protest. A more exacting test of libertarian values is, perhaps, the extent to which people tolerate free expression of explicitly 'extreme' views. We asked about various forms of freedom of expression for "people who want to overthrow the government by revolution" and for "people who believe that whites are racially superior to all other races" (in our shorthand 'revolutionaries' and 'racists') in two parallel questions first asked in 1985. We also introduced three new questions in 1990 about the rights of "people who support acts of terrorism in the UK". Committed civil libertarians would naturally support the normal freedoms of expression for such minorities, although they might be in favour of some restraint - such as outlawing incitement to racial hatred - to protect vulnerable minorities. Less committed libertarians, however, would tend to judge each case differently according to the views of the 'extremists' in question, or perhaps be more likely to impose blanket barriers against public exposure to extremist views of any kind.

In 1985 we found that respondents tended to be restrictive in respect of the rights of racists to express their views, but fairly evenly divided about the rights of revolutionaries. By 1990, we see more censoriousness about revolutionaries and *much* greater censoriousness about racists. The proportion prepared to allow racists to hold public meetings to express their views has dropped by 12 percentage points, and the proportion tolerating the publication of books expressing white supremacist views has dropped by no less than 16 percentage points in five years.

% agreeing that each group should probably or definitely be able to express their views by:	Revolutionaries		Racists	
	1985	1990	1985	1990
Holding public meetings	52	48	38	26
Publishing books	64	58	50	34

It is perhaps surprising that people are much more relaxed about the activities of 'revolutionaries' than about 'racists': on the face of it, "people who want to overthrow the government by revolution" might seem to represent a more pervasive threat to society at large. Yet the reality is that, in Britain, 'revolutionaries' have never posed a threat comparable to that of, say, the Baader-Meinhoff group in West Germany or the Red Army faction in Italy.* In contrast, marches by the National Front in racially-mixed parts of inner cities (or by the Fascist Party in Jewish areas during the 1930s) have been more in evidence over the years. Again, therefore, the responses suggest a pragmatic stance rather than a principled one: if 'revolutionaries' were actually to become a threat, we suspect that the fairly widespread tolerance of their right to freedom of expression would quickly evaporate.

Firm evidence for this is provided by responses to our new questions on the rights of "people who support acts of terrorism in the UK" to express their views in the media. In October 1988, the Home Secretary took action under the Broadcasting Act 1981 to ban from television or radio "any words spoken whether in the course of an interview or discussion or otherwise" by representatives or supporters of eight proscribed organisations (including the IRA and the Ulster Volunteer Force) and three legal ones (including Sinn Fein and the Ulster Defence Association). Such organisations, the government claimed, thrived on publicity for their views: to deny them access to television and radio would cut off this source of potential support for their respective causes. Opponents were dismayed at the arbitrary nature of the ban, notably against legal political parties, especially as they felt that the BBC and IBA had in the past responded to public concern and to government pressures, for instance the BBC agreed not to screen the *Real Lives* programme in 1985.

By a majority of around two to one, respondents would deny 'terrorists' access to the mass media (see also Chapter 4), as the government has done in respect of spokespersons of the named organisations. We asked about television interviews, newspaper interviews and the publication of books.

---

* The terrorist movements in Northern Ireland are not revolutionary groups in the same sense; their purpose is much more specific and can hardly be said to constitute 'left-wing' threats in the way that the question intended.

Access of 'terrorists' to the media

The law should:	Television interviews %	Newspaper interviews %	Publication of books %
Definitely or probably allow it	29	32	29
Probably or definitely not allow it	66	63	66

As the table above shows, respondents are more or less as censorious about the rights of 'terrorists' as they proved to be about the rights of 'racists'. Indeed, they would go further than the government; they would extend the ban to cover interviews with the press and the publication of books. We did not ask whether there would be support for similar measures against 'racists' - but on present evidence we suspect there would be.

The problem with questions such as these is that they do not discriminate between respondents who are tolerant because of their libertarian principles and those who are tolerant because they are actually sympathetic to the group in question. To disentangle this, we tried to elicit people's general disposition towards racists and revolutionaries, just as we had done earlier towards political protesters. We were somewhat thwarted by the fact that too few people looked favourably upon revolutionaries and racists for us to be able to examine their views separately, so we added in those who said that they felt 'neither favourable or unfavourable'. Even so, these groups comprise rather less than one fifth of respondents. As the table below confirms, there is still much less support for freedom of expression for racists - even among those who are sympathetic or neutral - than there is for revolutionaries. But 'tolerance' does increase substantially *with* sympathy, suggesting that libertarianism *per se* is even rarer than we had first suspected: for instance, only one in three of those who feel hostility towards racists would concede their right to publish books about their views, and only one in five would allow them to hold public meetings.

	Feelings about each group	
	Favourable/ Neutral	Unfavourable
% saying revolutionaries should be allowed to:		
Hold public meetings	75	42
Publish books	79	54
% saying racists should be allowed to:		
Hold public meetings	44	22
Publish books	51	31

Evenhandedness of society

A further test of a libertarian society is its treatment of minority groups. We wanted to explore not only whether people were tolerant of, say, ethnic or religious minorities, or of different social classes or income groups, or of those whose lifestyle is unorthodox, but also whether they rejected institutionalised prejudice and discrimination against them. In other words, we wanted to test the extent to which people support the notion that only "membership of society - citizenship - [should be] the basis of the common good, and hence indispensable to any social morality or good society" (Jordan, 1989, quoted in Lister, 1990, p.69). Our questions are far from comprehensive, and the responses reported here give only indications of the sorts of concerns that people feel about injustices to minority groups.

Perhaps the most salutory feature of our findings is the fact that substantial proportions of the sample believe that these minority groups *are* treated unfairly by society. For instance, well over half of respondents think that people of Asian and West Indian origin are discriminated against when looking for jobs. One in five believes that this happens to West Indians 'a lot'. Moreover, perceptions of racial discrimination have changed little over the decade. Consistently, around two-thirds of people have supported legislation against it - although we did not ask whether or not the present Race Relations Act of 1976, frequently criticised for being too weak (for example, CRE, 1990, p.14), should be strengthened. Other inequities were also perceived to be widespread. For instance, the existence of poverty in Britain is seen to be growing: in 1989, 63 per cent acknowledged that 'there is quite a lot of real poverty in Britain today', and almost a third attributed poverty to 'injustice in our society' rather than to the fault of the poor themselves (see Taylor-Gooby, 1990). And as Chapter 2 shows, there is substantial support for narrowing the gap between rich and poor.

Are these perceived inequalities seen to be embodied in the legal system? After all, equality before the law is held to be another of the cornerstones of a libertarian society: "The main purpose of the criminal law is to impose certain minimum standards of behaviour for the benefit of the community as a whole .... a universal set of principles to determine who is guilty and who is innocent" (Poulter 1990, p.14). Is this the way the British public sees it as working? We asked:

> *Suppose two people - one white, one black - each appeared in court charged with a crime they did **not** commit. What do you think their chances are of being found **guilty** ...?*

A parallel question was asked about "another two people from different backgrounds - one rich, one poor". The table below summarises the results:

% saying:	%
The white person is more likely to be found guilty	3
Both have the same chance	49
The black person is more likely to be found guilty	42

% saying:	%
The rich person is more likely to be found guilty	2
Both have the same chance	38
The poor person is more likely to be found guilty	56

These results are remarkable, suggesting very widespread public scepticism about the fairness of the judicial system. Only around one-half of the population believes the legal system is indifferent to colour and fewer than four people in ten believe it is indifferent to economic circumstances. These are strong indictments, especially in view of the fact that legal aid rates paid to solicitors taking on criminal work have declined in real terms, so jeopardising the quality of representation for people who cannot afford to pay for themselves. There is also a growing body of evidence (the most recent from NACRO, 1991) that black people are more likely than white people to be arrested, remanded in custody, and sent to prison if convicted. Indeed, the government incorporated a clause in the Criminal Justice Act, 1991, requiring the courts to deal with all cases without discrimination.

It is of course true that the vast majority of criminal defendants are worse off than average, and that those who sit in judgement upon them are much better off than average, and rather unlikely to come from ethnic minority backgrounds. Nonetheless, people from all backgrounds tend more or less equally to the view that the administration of justice in Britain is not evenhanded, just as many in Northern Ireland (see Chapter 4) felt that evenhandedness is lacking there.

But we must be cautious about drawing too hasty conclusions from these findings. There is clearly a widespread view nowadays that blacks and Asians in Britain are not treated fairly and that racism towards them should not be tolerated; however, this tendency towards liberal attitudes certainly does not extend to new immigration. Successive immigration and nationality Acts (dating back to the 1960s) have, of course, already reduced new immigration to a trickle. In theory, these measures are not racially discriminatory: immigration officers can be disciplined if they display racial prejudice. In practice, the rules and discretionary powers discriminate against black and Asian would-be immigrants, and it is evident that public opinion strongly favours these sorts of controls. On balance, the public would like to see the controls tightened in respect of black and Asian immigration. Our time-series allows us to look at trends

since 1983, and to compare attitudes to white and black would be
entrants. The question was in this form:

*Britain controls the numbers of people from abroad that are allowed
to settle in this country. Please say, for **each** of the[se] groups,
whether you think Britain should allow more settlement, less
settlement, or about the same amount as now.*

	% saying more settlement		% saying less settlement		% saying about the same as now	
	1983	1990	1983	1990	1983	1990
Indians and Pakistanis	2	2	71	62	26	35
West Indians	2	2	67	58	28	39
Australians and New Zealanders	16	9	28	31	55	69
People from European Community countries*	7	7	44	41	47	51

* In 1983, 'people from common market countries'.

Few people favour relaxation of controls for *any* of the four groups, but
there is much greater support for tightening up on black immigration than
on white. Of course, this is not a 'knowledge' question: few respondents
would know what current immigration levels in each category are. But
the fact that more people in 1990 than in 1983 favour the *status quo* (and
fewer favour 'less' settlement) surely reflects an awareness that controls
are much stricter now. In response to a further question, we find that the
public is not even prepared to concede more generous settlement rights
to the *families* of recent immigrants; over half (56 per cent) would like to
see stricter controls on them too, a third are content with things as they
are, and only one in ten favours relaxation of the regulations.

To find out whether there was greater sympathy for refugees than for
'voluntary' immigrants, we also asked respondents whether they agreed or
disagreed with the view that "refugees who are in danger because of their
political beliefs should always be welcome in Britain". Only 15 per cent
felt strongly on the matter either way; 29 per cent neither agreed nor
disagreed. Of those who did have an opinion, two-thirds were against an
unreserved welcome for political refugees. On this evidence, the
government clamp-down on refugees, started in the mid-1980s, will find
favour among many. Of course, asylum-seekers tend, nowadays anyway,
to be black or Asian (Sri Lankan Tamil, Somali and Iraqi Kurdish
refugees were in the news before or during the 1990 survey period). And
the number of applicants increased very substantially in the late 1980s
with evident strains upon local authorities, government agencies and
voluntary bodies. Other western European countries, traditionally more
welcoming to refugees than Britain in post-war years, have also
introduced new restrictions. As far as public attitudes are concerned,
however, this is surely a case in which a hypothetical question such as
ours might prove to be a wholly unreliable guide as to how people *would*
react when faced by a potential entry of people who were in grave danger

or distress. But then our questions seek to measure attitudes and values, not potential behaviour - which is frequently different.

Court powers and procedures

Earlier we noted a strong current of concern about the fairness of the judicial system. We now see whether or not this concern extends to a number of specific court powers, procedures for dealing with suspects, and sentencing policy more generally.

Two questions dealt with police questioning and trial evidence. Both issues had been much in the news in connection with a series of trials of suspected terrorists. Respondents were asked to say how much they agreed or disagreed with each of two statements:

*A confession made during police questioning and later withdrawn should **not** on its own be enough to convict someone.*

If someone remains silent under police questioning, it should count against them in court.

	Retracted confession should not be enough to convict %	'Remaining silent' should count against suspect %
Agree strongly	18	5
Agree	55	26
Neither agree nor disagree	17	25
Disagree	7	34
Disagree strongly	1	8

Almost three-quarters of respondents are unhappy about the admissibility of uncorroborated (and retracted) confessions of guilt. These are, of course, legally sufficient for a conviction, subject to the same burden of proof that applies to any other evidence. But views about an accused person's right to remain silent are much more ambivalent, underlined by the fact that one in four people have no opinion either way. Both sets of responses, however, suggest a sense of unease about the administration of justice, prompted perhaps by the unprecedented publicity the issues have attracted in recent years. The 'right to remain silent' has been debated since the early 1970s; the 1972 Criminal Law Revision Committee recommended its abolition (Criminal Law Revision Committee, 1972), but the Royal Commission on Criminal Procedure came to the opposite conclusion (Royal Commission on Criminal Procedure, 1981). Both these matters are now to be considered by the Royal Commission on Criminal Justice announced in March 1991, following the successful appeal by the 'Birmingham Six'.

The right to trial by jury is considered to be one of the bastions of our criminal justice system. Yet the vast majority of trials are held in magistrates' courts. Admittedly, most serious cases are tried by jury, but the list of offences that cannot be referred to Crown Courts (and thus not be heard by a jury) is ever-lengthening. The latest changes, in 1988, have taken away from an estimated ten thousand defendants a year the right to jury trial, at a considerable cost saving. We confined our attention to the question of whether "people charged with serious crimes" should have the right to a jury trial even "when the jury might be in danger". This was an extreme formulation, pushing people away from an automatic endorsement of such an established system; even so, as many as a half of respondents still insist that trial by jury for serious crimes is sacrosanct compared to 38 per cent who feel in these circumstances that the right should be waived. Experts are divided as to whether, in fact, the jury system ensures a fairer trial, but there has been something of a media onslaught on the jury system in recent years (see Enright and Morton, 1990). So it is notable that such a high proportion of the public still support it, even when the question wording was designed to discourage them from doing so.

The last aspect of the judicial system we investigated dealt with sentencing policy. We asked respondents how much they agreed or disagreed with the two statements below.

	Agree strongly	Agree	Neither agree nor disagree	Disagree	Disagree strongly
Too many convicted criminals are let off lightly by the courts	% 36	43	15	5	1
The prisons contain too many people who ought to be given a lighter punishment	% 9	39	27	20	3

The responses suggest that only a minority of people have much confidence in the custodial sentencing practices of courts. On the other hand, these opinions may have something to do with a lack of confidence in the prison service too: the Strangeways riot was on television screens daily at the height of our 1990 fieldwork. In any event the balance of public opinion seems to be that courts are both too light on serious offenders and too severe on minor offenders.

Police powers

As will be seen, there are public concerns too about the nature and exercise of police powers, though these worries are slightly more focused. Stronger measures to prevent crime and disorder are widely supported, and the public is more willing in 1990 (50 per cent) than it was in 1985 (38 percent) to see more resources devoted to law enforcement. This trend must be seen in conjunction with the greater fear nowadays about the likelihood of neighbourhood crime (76 per cent in 1990 compared with 69 per cent in 1983 said that they worried that they or another household member might be the victim of crime).

So people want more policing and imply they are prepared as taxpayers to finance it. But that is not the same as a vote of confidence in the police. By any standards, the police have been well served over the last decade: they are relatively better paid than they were at the end of the 1970s (see Ewing and Gearty, 1990, pp. 17-18), and their powers have been substantially increased. But this has not been matched by a rise in public esteem. Our data show a sharp drop (of 11 percentage points - from 77 per cent to 66 per cent) between 1983 and 1987 in the proportion thinking that the police are 'well run', and a similar fall between 1983 and 1990 in the proportion saying they are 'very satisfied' with the way "the police in Britain do their job".

However, this decline in confidence appears to be in the *institution*, not in individual officers with whom respondents are in contact. Similar proportions of our sample in 1983 and 1990 reported having gone to the police to report crimes or accidents, or to seek help or advice. And similar proportions (the great majority) as seven years earlier had found them helpful and polite. So it is apparently not what people experience in their encounters with the police that reduces their confidence; rather it is what they read or hear about the institution that seems to cause concern.

So far we have found, not surprisingly, that increasing numbers of people are concerned about crime and want something done about its inexorable rise. But are they prepared to tolerate measures which might help prevent crime but would involve a diminution of civil liberties? We asked a number of questions that addressed this age-old conflict.

First we asked about the introduction of video surveillance in public places. We put the question like this:

*Some people say that video cameras ought to be installed in public places to detect criminals. Others think that this will cut down on everyone's privacy. Do you think that video cameras **should** or **should not** be allowed ...*

Video cameras	% saying definitely be allowed	% saying definitely/ probably be allowed*
At football grounds to detect troublemakers	88	98
On roads to detect speeding drivers	55	82
On housing estates to detect vandals	53	82
At political demonstrations to detect people taking part	40	63

* The items have been reordered according to the proportion saying each should 'definitely be allowed'. The two other categories on the four-point scale were 'probably not be allowed' and 'definitely not be allowed'.

As may be seen from the table, people's answers seem to depend somewhat on *whose* civil liberties are likely to be infringed. There is, for instance, near unanimity about the desirability of surveillance at football matches. Worries begin to appear over closed-circuit television systems to catch speeding drivers or vandals, but again the overwhelming majority support the idea. A smaller proportion supports surveillance at political demonstrations "to detect people taking part". Still, it is surprising that approaching two-thirds of respondents would allow people's presence at political demonstrations to be recorded on video (40 per cent unreservedly). On the other hand this figure may well be exaggerated by a flaw in the preamble to our question, which specified the use of video surveillance "to detect criminals". We shall try to rectify this in future rounds, and see if it makes a difference.

Home Office guidelines exist on the use of video equipment by police, but no parallel regulations govern its use by local authorities, shops, banks or private security firms. Civil liberty lobbyists do not oppose video surveillance *per se*, but argue strongly for tight statutory controls (Liberty, 1989). They urge, among other safeguards, proof that surveillance systems are justified, informing the public that they are being deployed, restrictions on access to tapes, and their erasure after a specified period (unless needed for court proceedings). These measures, they argue, would help cut down on improper intrusions into privacy and reduce the risk of abuse. Yet such worries do not (yet) appear to be shared by the great majority of respondents: effective crime prevention and detection seem to outweigh any libertarian concerns they might have.

But video surveillance systems are not targeted at individuals, and we see a very marked shift in attitudes when we turn to another set of questions about measures against a *particular* suspect. To test the public's civil libertarian resolve to its limit, we introduced a suspect with a "long criminal record":

Suppose the police get an anonymous tip that a man with a long criminal record is planning to break into a warehouse, should the police be allowed, without a court order ...

	% saying definitely	% saying definitely/probably[*]
... to keep the man under surveillance	62	90
... to detain the man overnight for questioning	28	64
... to tap his telephone	14	37
... to open his mail	9	23

[*] The items have been reordered according to the proportion saying each should 'definitely' be allowed. The other answer categories (not shown here) were 'probably not', 'definitely not' and 'can't choose'.

Once again, surveillance - which is already permitted without a court order - is a broadly acceptable form of crime prevention. But when it comes to police powers in respect of an individual - even one with a criminal record - the public makes distinctions between legitimate and illegitimate measures. There is ambivalence about overnight detention - perhaps to a surprising degree, since this again would already be allowed following arrest in connection with attempted burglary. And there are emphatic majorities against telephone tapping or interception of mail without a court order to do so. Telephone tapping and opening mail are not, of course, routinely available measures: the Secretary of State has to issue a warrant (not a court order) for either and the number or warrants issued is not very great (around 500 were in force in 1990).[1] But there appears to be a cultural distaste for this sort of 'snooping', detected also by a survey carried out for the Committee on Privacy (HMSO, 1972, p. 230). In addition, people may not be willing to give powers to the police that have already been criticised publicly for being inadequately regulated: in 1985, for instance, Cathy Massiter, a retired MI5 official, revealed that members of several legal organisations (including trade unions and CND) were under unauthorised surveillance by the security services.

These questions on surveillance, detention and interception were first asked in 1985, and there has been a marked rise in the five years in the proportions unable to choose an answer category for each proposition. There seems therefore to have been an increase in uncertainty over the five years as to the sorts of powers the police should have, underlining again the possible conflict people feel between their desire on the one hand to bolster police power in an attempt to fight crime more effectively and, on the other, their fear of ceding more power to the police, especially in view of the diminishing public confidence they enjoy.

The widespread opposition we have seen to interception of telephone conversations and letters intensified when we asked about three other police powers: searching suspects' homes without a warrant, always carrying arms on duty (a move that the Police Federation itself opposes), and withholding a suspect's right to see a solicitor for up to a week.

		Agree strongly/ Agree	Neither agree nor disagree	Disagree/ Disagree strongly
The police should not need a warrant to search the homes of suspects	%	16	9	73
On-duty police officers should always carry guns	%	14	18	67
The police should be allowed to question suspects for up to a week without letting them see a solicitor	%	9	9	80

The police have fairly wide powers anyway to enter and search premises without a warrant, but denial of a suspect's right to see a solicitor for such a long period would be a considerable extension of their present powers (see Hurwitt and Thornton, 1989, pp. 132-134, 147-148). Despite these differences, the spread of answers to the three propositions was broadly the same. Decisive majorities would deny the police all three powers. Indeed, scarcely anyone agrees 'strongly' that any of these three powers should be granted.

A recent opinion poll found a very similar pattern of responses to those reported here: scant endorsement for police powers covertly to gather information about individuals, only minority support for greater powers to detain and question suspects, but substantially more for measures *not* directed at a particular individual but intended to assist in serious crime detection (Gallup, 1991).

Little wonder then that we find overwhelming public support for the proposition that "serious complaints against the police should be investigated by an independent body, not by the police themselves". Only two percent disagree. Of course the Police Complaints Authority, set up under the Police and Criminal Evidence Act 1984, does have an independent element, but it supervises only a small minority of investigations (five per cent in 1989), and the actual investigations are still carried out by the police themselves. There is also evidence (Maguire and Corbett, 1991) that an overwhelming majority of complainants whose grievance has been investigated are dissatisfied. Grounds for dissatisfaction seem plentiful: for instance, only a very small percentage of complaints are substantiated (three per cent in 1989); over 30 per cent of complainants reported that the police had tried to dissuade them from going ahead; and only half would complain again in similar circumstances. But change may be on the way. The Police Federation now supports a fully independent investigating authority (memorandum to the Home Affairs Committee, 11 July, 1989). And in its Triennial Review 1989-91, the Police Complaints Authority itself proposed a "radical departure from existing procedures", while still stopping short of recommending independent investigations.

In any event, the strong public endorsement of an independent system is perhaps a further sign that confidence in the police nowadays is less than full-hearted.

Constitutional safeguards

Those concerned about the protection of civil liberties in Britain have put forward a number of proposals to reverse what they see as their erosion in recent years. For instance, Ewing and Gearty (1990) have proposed a system of parliamentary scrutiny (modelled on the Standing Committee of the Australian Senate) of the civil liberties and human rights implications of all proposed legislation. An alternative idea, first proposed in 1971, is a British Human Rights Commission. But the most well-publicised campaign has been for a Bill of Rights, especially since the publication of Charter 88 (NSS, December 1988). The signatories to the Charter and others (see, in particular, Holme and Elliott, 1988) advocate a written constitution, without which they believe that civil liberties in Britain cannot be adequately protected.[*] On their agenda too is electoral reform, devolution, an elected upper house and a Freedom of Information Act. Others have more recently added to this agenda, urging fixed-term parliaments and (oddly perhaps) compulsory voting (Dunleavy and Weir, 1991).

We only touched on this issue with a question that is less than ideal for such a complicated matter. In any case no single question would be sufficient to address this subject (or more or less any other subject).[2] But we did not have space for further questions. Still, the results are decisive.

Some people support a Bill of Rights for Britain which would give the **courts rather than Parliament** *the final say on any laws or government actions which threaten basic freedoms. Others say it is better to leave things as they are.*

	%
Definitely	27
Probably	30
Probably not	13
Definitely not	6
(Can't choose)	23

Three times as many people support the idea as oppose it, but as with other questions of this sort, almost as important a finding perhaps is that one in four people have no opinion either way. As on many civil rights issues of this kind, a Bill of Rights is particularly popular among the highly qualified and among Labour identifiers: twice as many Labour as Conservative identifiers think that there should definitely be a Bill of Rights, but part of this difference may be accounted for by the fact that there is currently a Conservative government. Some of the issues included in Charter 88, such as a Freedom of Information Act and, of course, proportional representation, are also distinctive party political issues, and they seem likely to become even higher profile ones than before.

---

[*] For a draft Bill of Rights for Britain and a cogent argument for its implementation, see Lester *et al* (1990).

Conclusion

In this interim report we have only skimmed the surface of a rich dataset which will bear much further detailed analysis. Still, even a cursory look at the data suggests that people of 'principle' on either side of the libertarian divide will find little to cheer them up. Public attitudes, predictably perhaps, tend to be pragmatic rather than doctrinaire, even in respect of what might be called the cornerstones of British democracy.

So, while freedoms of speech and assembly are clearly supported by British public opinion, the support does depend to a large degree on the viewpoints being expressed. The right to advocate unpopular causes (or to protest against popular ones) is much less firmly defended by the public than are *abstract* rights of freedom of expression. Moreover, when it comes to organisations which advocate terrorism, there is strong public support for the government's 1988 ban on television interviews with their spokespersons; indeed sizeable majorities would go further and outlaw newspaper interviews and their right to publish books too.

There is, however, little ambivalence about the public's desire for open government. Not only do people tend to think of Britain as more secretive than other liberal democracies, but they also disapprove of such secrecy except in relation to national security matters. The wider 'public interest' argument in favour of 'closed' government is given fairly short shrift, being interpreted by many as usually serving the government's, not the public's interests.

Perhaps the feature of the data of most concern is the widespread public scepticism we found about the fairness of the British judicial system. Fewer than one-half of respondents believe that either black people or poor people have an equal chance before the law, and there is considerable disquiet about extending the powers of the police, *despite* increasing worries about the growth in crime. The high public esteem which the police have reputedly enjoyed seems to be waning somewhat nowadays. And the courts do not come out well either, being seen as neither evenhanded nor particularly effective: the public's verdict is that judges and magistrates are too severe on minor offenders and too lenient on serious offenders.

There are then authoritarian streaks ('bring back the death penalty') and libertarian streaks ('no guns for the police') in British society, but the overriding impression is one of an absence of dogma on these matters. Indeed, as we remark on occasions throughout this chapter, quite large proportions (often around one in four) of respondents decline to express a view one way or another on many issues. This is heartening for the researcher (since we certainly do not discourage 'don't knows' when that is the appropriate answer), but it must be slightly disheartening for the committed libertarian or, for that matter, for the authoritarian.

We have not yet conducted detailed analyses of subgroup differences and their interrelationships. Nor have we referred repeatedly in this chapter (on every occasion that we established it) to the fact that graduates stand out as being the most libertarian on almost all of the issues we covered - from freedom of speech to freedom of information, from wariness of police powers to support of constitutional safeguards. Those with no educational qualifications tend to be the least libertarian. Of course libertarian attitudes are by no means the monopoly of the highly-educated, but they are certainly in the vanguard on most of the issues we covered.

Age and party identification are important as well, but their influence is rather more selective. For instance, younger people are especially supportive of the right to protest, wary of police surveillance and sympathetic to ethnic minorities. On the other hand, their views are not markedly different from those of older people on other aspects of police powers, or on freedom of information or on constitutional matters. Instead, these last two issues divide people along party lines: Labour identifiers are especially keen on a Bill of Rights and on 'open' government, and especially cautious about extending police powers and about curbing the right to political protest. Our overall conclusion then is that the British may perhaps most accurately be described as fainthearted libertarians.

Notes

1.   Although one warrant can cover many telephone lines, and press reports suggest that as many as 35,000 are tapped in any one year.

2.   The 'State of the Nation' poll question had as its preamble: "Britain needs a Bill of Rights to protect the liberty of the individual", and there was no 'status quo' alternative offered as an answer category. Seventy-two per cent of respondents agreed with the statement, an increase of 12 percent on those agreeing in a similar poll in 1989.

References

COMMITTEE ON PRIVACY, *Report*, ['the Younger Report'], Cmnd. 5012, HMSO, London (1972).

CRIMINAL LAW REVISION COMMITTEE, *Eleventh Report - Evidence (General)*, Cmnd.4991, HMSO, London (1972) .

DUNLEAVY, P. and WEIR, S., 'Left for rights', *New Statesman and Society*, no. 148 (April 1991).

DWORKIN, R., 'Devaluing liberty', *Index on Censorship, Britain* (17) (1988).

ENRIGHT, S. and MORTON, J., *Taking Liberties: the Criminal Jury in the 1990s*, Weidenfeld and Nicolson, London (1990).

EWING, K.D. and GEARTY, C.A., *Freedom under Thatcher: Civil Liberties in Modern Britain*, Clarendon Press, Oxford (1990).

GALLUP, Gallup Political and Economic Index, Report 336, Dod's Publishing and Research, London (February, 1991).

HOLME, R. and ELLIOTT, M. (eds) *1688-1988: Time for a New Constitution*, MacMillan, London (1988).
HURWITT, M. and THORNTON, P., *Civil Liberty: the Liberty/NCCL Guide*, (4th ed.), Penguin, Harmondsworth (1989).
JORDAN, B., *The Common Good: Citizenship, Morality and Self-interest*, Basil Blackwell, Oxford (1989).
JOWELL, R. and TOPF, R., 'Trust in the establishment', in Jowell, R., Witherspoon, S. and Brook, L., (eds), *British Social Attitudes: the 5th Report*, Gower, Aldershot (1988).
LESTER, A., CORNFORD, J., DWORKIN, R., GOODHART, W., HEWITT, P., JOWELL, J., LACEY, N., PATCHETT, K. and SPENCER, S., *A British Bill of Rights*, Constitutional Paper No.1, Institute for Public Policy Research, London (1990).
LIBERTY, 'Who's watching You? Video surveillance in public places', *Briefing No. 16*, Liberty (October, 1989).
LISTER, R., *The Exclusive Society: Citizenship and the Poor*, Child Poverty Action Group, London (1990).
MAGUIRE, M. and CORBETT, C., *A Study of the Police Complaints System*, HMSO, London (1991).
MILLWARD, N. 'The State of the unions', in Jowell, R., Witherspoon, S. and Brook, L., (eds), *British Social Attitudes: the 7th Report*, Gower, Aldershot (1990).
NACRO, *Black People's Experience of Criminal Justice*, National Council for the Rehabilitation of Offenders, London (1991).
NCCL, *The Purging of the Civil Service*, National Council for Civil Liberties (with Trade Union Liaison Committee), London 1985 (especially Appendix A. 'The Duties and Responsibilities of Civil Servants in Relation to Ministers' by Robert Armstrong, Cabinet Office, 25 February 1985).
NSS, 'Charter 88', *New Statesman and Society* (2 December, 1988).
POULTER, S., 'Cultural pluralism and its limits: a legal perspective', in *Britain: A Plural Society*, CRE, London (1990).
ROYAL COMMISSION ON CRIMINAL PROCEDURE, *Report*, Cmnd.8092, HMSO, London (1981)
TAYLOR-GOOBY, P., 'The role of the state', in Jowell, R., Witherspoon, S. and Brook, L., (eds), *British Social Attitudes: Special International Report*, Gower, Aldershot (1989).
TAYLOR-GOOBY, P., 'Social welfare: the unkindest cuts', in Jowell, R., Witherspoon, S. and Brook, L., (eds), *British Social Attitudes: the 7th Report*, Gower, Aldershot (1990).
TOPF, R., MOHLER, P. and HEATH, A., 'Pride in one's country: Britain and West Germany', in Jowell, R., Witherspoon, S. and Brook, L., (eds), *British Social Attitudes: Special International Report*, Gower, Aldershot (1989).
THORNTON, P., *Decade of Decline: Civil Liberties in the Thatcher Years*, NCCL, London (1989).

WOOD, J. and CRAWFORD, A., *The Right of Silence: the Case for Retention*, The Civil Liberties Trust, London (1989).
ZELLICK, G., 'To whom do civil servants owe loyalty?', *New Law Journal*, vol. 140 (1990), p.1412.

Acknowledgements

SCPR is grateful to The Nuffield Foundation for new funding to enable us to include a module of questions on civil liberties, which we will repeat in 1993; and to the ESRC for supporting the *International Social Survey Programme* (ISSP) on which some of our analyses have been based. We are also grateful to James Cornford, Jeffrey Jowell and Anthony Lester for their helpful comments on the draft questionnaire.

10 Interim report: Economic outlook

Bridget Taylor [*]

Between 1983, when the *British Social Attitudes* survey series began, and the latest round in 1990, there were marked fluctuations in economic conditions.

In 1983 Britain was recovering from the serious economic recession of 1979-1981 when unemployment[1] and inflation[2] had risen rapidly while output - particularly manufacturing output[3] - had fallen. By 1986 output had recovered somewhat, and inflation had fallen (to around 3 per cent), but unemployment had continued to rise, albeit more slowly. The boom was beginning which helped to return the Conservative Party to office in 1987 and lasted long after the election.

Indeed, economic growth was sustained and fairly rapid up to 1989. Many people did well during this period; most of those in employment had found their incomes rising in real terms,[4] and home-owners were especially likely to feel more prosperous. The service sector had expanded rapidly,[5] much more than had manufacturing output.[6] Official unemployment figures remained very high until mid-1986, and then began to fall rapidly. Meanwhile, tax and benefit changes had contributed to increasing inequality in incomes.

By the time of our fieldwork in the spring of 1990, year-on-year inflation had accelerated sharply again to reach nearly 10 per cent, and the balance of payment deficit had grown to record levels, both having been fuelled (in part) by a consumer spending boom. Interest rates had been rising sharply in the preceding two years[7] with serious consequences for

---

[*] Bridget Taylor is a researcher at SCPR and a Co-director of the *BSA* survey series.

many mortgage-holders, and growth in the economy had begun to falter.[8] In short, Britain was entering another recession.

The government's aims over the decade had been to increase competition and flexibility in the economy to try to make it more efficient and stronger and to reduce dependence on government, while at the same time increasing choice for individuals. Critics (for example Coutts *et al,* 1990) argue that the decade has in fact seen a fundamentally weakened economy, in particular as a result of the decline in manufacturing, lack of investment, and the costs of high unemployment.

The 1990 survey included a large number of questions about the economy and the labour market, on most of which we have time-series, often going back to 1983. In this chapter, we confine ourselves to a brief review of principal attitude movements on some key issues, with a cursory glance at subgroup differences. We look first at respondents' assessments of Britain's economic prospects over the years, followed by their assessments of their *own* economic prospects. Then we look at changing public attitudes to a wide range of economic policy options - such as the relative priority that should be accorded to inflation and unemployment - which have been and continue to be the subject of much political and economic controversy.

Economic and industrial expectations

Inflation and unemployment

As we have noted, both the rate of inflation and the level of unemployment have fluctuated markedly since 1983. Each year we have asked respondents whether, in a year from now, they expect prices to have gone up, to have stayed the same or to have gone down, and we have asked the same question about unemployment. As we see from the table below, public expectations have also fluctuated markedly, varying from the mildly pessimistic or, perhaps more accurately, from the somewhat gloomy to the realistic.

	1983 %	1984 %	1985 %	1986 %	1987[*] %	1989[*] %	1990 %
In a year from now prices will have:							
Gone up by a lot	24	31	40	26	26	45	46
Gone up by a little	56	52	48	49	52	43	40
Stayed the same	12	13	8	17	17	8	8
Gone down by a little or a lot	5	3	3	6	3	4	6

[*] Note there was no *British Social Attitudes* survey in 1988, so there is a gap in this time-series and others in many of the tables in this chapter.

In a year from now, unemployment will have:	1983 %	1984 %	1985 %	1986 %	1987 %	1989 %	1990 %
Gone up by a lot	31	25	33	29	17	10	18
Gone up by a little	37	31	34	37	23	16	29
Stayed the same	17	31	23	25	32	37	34
Gone down by a little or a lot	13	12	9	8	25	35	16

Quite realistically, the British public has become inured to price inflation: large majorities in each of the seven years have anticipated price rises, few have anticipated stability, and only a handful have ever expected prices to fall. Pessimism about inflation rose sharply between 1983 and 1985, then abated, then rose again between 1987 and 1989 (and continued into 1990), by when nearly one-half of respondents expected prices to rise by 'a lot' over the coming year.

Similarly, the public seems to have become inured to unemployment, though less so. Indeed, there was a brief period between 1987 and 1989, when a higher proportion of respondents thought that unemployment had stabilised or would fall than thought it would continue to rise. But this moment of optimism had passed by the time of our 1990 fieldwork round.

When public expectations about inflation and unemployment are plotted against the official year-on-year trends (changes in the Retail Prices Index (RPI) and unemployment levels), the correspondence between the trend-lines is impressive (see Witherspoon and Taylor, 1990).[9] It seems that concern about price rises tends to move slightly ahead of the actual movement in the RPI. This suggests that respondents' expectations for price inflation over the year ahead are sensitive to other economic conditions likely to bear upon prices, so that public expectations about price rises are a fairly good predictor of changes in RPI. However, respondents' predictions of the level of unemployment are not as impressive. Unlike inflation, it appears that public expectations about changes in unemployment tend to follow rather than to anticipate actual changes. This is not surprising, perhaps, since everyone has a personal interest in price trends, whether they are in the labour market or not, whether they are threatened by unemployment or not. But only a minority of the population has such a strong personal interest in unemployment levels. Most people are likely, therefore, to have made a link between certain economic messages and the likelihood of impending price rises, while the only message they receive about unemployment levels tends to be an historical one.

The contrasts in expectations between subgroups are striking, as the table below shows.[10] We confine our attention to those believing that prices and unemployment will rise by 'a lot'.

	% saying prices will rise by a lot	% saying unemployment will rise by a lot
All	46	18
Economic status:		
Employee	43	15
Self-employed	36	19
Unemployed	63	33
Looking after home	54	24
Retired	47	20
Annual household income:		
Under £7,000	57	26
£7,000 - £22,999	45	17
£23,000 or over	36	11
Party identification:		
Conservative	31	9
Liberal Democrat	49	16
Labour	57	26

Looking *across* the table at the two columns, we find that in 1990 people in every subgroup were gloomier about the prospects for inflation than about those for unemployment. Looking *down* the table, however, the clear relationship between both sets of expectations and economic status, income and party identification (obviously associated characteristics) is striking. As Anthony Harrison wrote in *The 1984 Report,* "the poorer one's own economic circumstances are, the gloomier are one's expectations about both unemployment and inflation" (p.48). Thus, the unemployed were the most pessimistic of all. Even so, despite their own current experience of unemployment, almost twice as many of them expected prices to rise substantially as expected unemployment to rise substantially. In contrast, employees with incomes of over £23,000 were the least pessimistic about both inflation and unemployment. Indeed, there is a clear gradient in pessimism on both counts according to household income. Indeed, employees with low incomes were nearly as pessimistic as respondents who are unemployed.

It is not surprising either to find that Labour Party identifiers were much more pessimistic about the prospects for both inflation and unemployment than were Conservatives, with the views of Liberal Democrats in between, but closer to those of Labour than of Conservative identifiers. This may be because Conservative identifiers were more likely to believe that their party's economic policies would bear fruit, or because their party political preferences predisposed them simply to hope for the best for 'their' government. Probably both factors were at work.

Industrial performance

We have asked respondents each year whether they think Britain's general industrial performance will improve, stay much the same or decline over the following year. In fact, employment in manufacturing industry has fallen both in terms of absolute numbers and as a proportion of the workforce throughout the period covered by the *BSA* surveys. Output from manufacturing had been rising slowly but turned downwards at about the time of the 1990 survey. Meanwhile, Britain's balance of payments deficit had reached around £20 billion in 1989, the largest ever recorded, and was still high (though improving) at the time of the 1990 survey.

As the table below shows, the proportions predicting an improvement in Britain's industrial performance has varied, declining substantially between 1984 and 1985, increasing between 1986 and 1987, and then plummeting to reach its lowest level in 1990, when just one in five respondents anticipated some improvement. In 1990 for the first time, the proportion predicting a decline exceeded that predicting an improvement.

	1983 %	1984 %	1985 %	1986 %	1987 %	1989 %	1990 %
Over the next year, Britain's industrial performance will:							
Improve a lot	5	4	3	3	7	5	3
Improve a little	39	34	25	22	29	25	16
Stay much the same	34	41	44	47	41	47	50
Decline a little	13	11	15	16	12	12	19
Decline a lot	4	4	6	7	6	4	7

We must be cautious about interpreting responses to this question as a direct indication of public feelings about the state of British industry. After all, measures of improvement such as this depend on one's base. In 1983, for instance, it may be that industrial performance was perceived as so poor that it could only improve. On the other hand, it hardly seems likely that the growth in pessimism towards the end of the decade reflected a view that British industry was in such a healthy state that it could only get worse. Moreover, the suggestion in the 1990 figures of a growing malaise is buttressed by the corresponding growth in pessimism we reported in respect of unemployment levels.

Again respondents who were in paid work were more sanguine about Britain's industrial prospects than are others, notably the unemployed - who displayed the largest rise in pessimism of any group between 1989 and 1990. Even the self-employed, however, who were generally more optimistic than others about Britain's economic situation, split equally between more predicting decline and improvement. Overall, we find that the decrease in optimism between 1989 and 1990 had been sharpest among those groups who had expressed the greatest optimism in earlier years; thus, in 1990, those with the highest household incomes (£23,000 or over a year) were slightly *more* likely than others to predict a decline in industrial performance.

Perhaps not surprisingly, respondents currently employed in the public sector were more pessimistic about Britain's industrial prospects than were those employed in the private sector, employees in manufacturing were more gloomy than those in the service sector, and people living in Scotland were somewhat more pessimistic than those living elsewhere in Britain. More striking, however, was the marked decline in optimism among those in the Midlands - the most optimistic region in 1989 - where the proportion predicting some improvement fell by 18 percentage points in one year, compared with between 8 and 11 percentage points in other regions.

We have also regularly asked self-employed respondents about their *own* businesses. Perhaps the most telling finding from this group is the decline in the proportion of self-employed who had set up their businesses within the last 12 months. In 1987 and 1989, it had been between 12 and 13 per cent; in 1990, in contrast, the proportion was just seven per cent. Does this figure represent the beginning of the decline in the 'enterprise culture' or just the start of the recession? Certainly, optimism among the self-employed had diminished between 1989 and 1990: although well over twice as many still predicted improvement (35 per cent) as decline (14 per cent), the outlook was less bullish than it had been in previous years.

Individual economic circumstances

Income levels

The responses reported so far relate to expectations about the economy, but we also asked respondents about their *own* circumstances and prospects. Our findings have an added interest in the light of work by Sanders (1991) which suggests a strong link between personal economic expectations, the level of interest rates and government popularity. Sanders explains a great deal of the variance in government popularity between January 1987 and November 1990 in terms of these two factors.

During the period of our survey series, most people in employment at least have found their incomes rising faster than inflation. On the other hand, those dependent on non-wage incomes have, on average, experienced falling real incomes.

We ask respondents to rate their own income on a three-point scale from 'high' to 'low'. Not surprisingly, perhaps, their ratings correspond loosely to their actual household incomes - at least as far as the poor are concerned. Thus in 1990, 84 per cent of those with the lowest household incomes (under £7,000 a year)* described their income as low, and only 8 per cent of those with the largest household incomes (£23,000 a year or more) did so. More modestly, however, only one in ten respondents with the highest household incomes describe their incomes as 'high'. Of course how wealthy people *feel* depends on their outgoings as well as their income, and we did not ask about disposable income. Nonetheless, the figures indicate a marked reluctance to admit to being financially comfortable. Indeed, a mere three per cent of all employees described their incomes as high.

When we ask employees to rate the relative level of their own wages or salary (as we do each year), we see the same exaggerated modesty. Only a handful of respondents describe their pay as 'on the high side'. However, there is evidence of a recent shift among employees in their sense of satisfaction with their pay: while in 1987 some 42 per cent described their pay as 'very' or 'a bit' low, this proportion had dropped to 35 per cent by 1990. Even so, this shift was smaller than might have been expected from the increase in real wages during the period, indicating that expectations about pay levels may have risen along with real pay increases.

In contrast, retired people have become more pessimistic during the 1980s about the purchasing power of their pensions. By 1990, only one in four pensioners, compared with 40 per cent in 1983, believed the state pension would keep up with price rises, and nearly two-thirds expected it to fall behind, compared with less than half in 1983.

Responses to another question about how respondents are coping on their present income have, however, remained remarkably constant since it was first asked in 1984: one-quarter said they were 'living comfortably', one-half said they were 'coping', and one-quarter said they were finding it 'difficult' or 'very difficult'. So although *employees* appeared to be slightly more content than they used to be about their *pay*, this seems to have had no discernible impact on how people generally felt they were *managing* on their income, perhaps because their expenditure had risen in line with incomes. Perhaps partly for the same reason, respondents' feelings about how they were managing were not all that closely related to their actual income levels. Thus only half of those with under £7,000 a year said they were finding it 'difficult' or 'very difficult' to manage, and only half of those with the largest incomes (£23,000 or more) said they were 'living comfortably'.

In contrast, economic status was a powerful correlate of feelings about income. Respondents who were unemployed were three times more likely to describe their incomes as low as were those in paid work, and, as noted, pensioners were also particularly likely to be dissatisfied with their incomes. This is particularly important because, in virtually all

---

* The question on household income asks about "income from *all* sources before tax".

survey measures, pensioners tend to express greater contentment with their circumstances than do younger people.

Each year since 1984 we have asked two questions to assess, first, perceived past changes in respondents' household income: and, secondly, expected changes. We asked whether over the last year household income has 'fallen behind prices', 'kept up with prices' or 'gone up by more than prices', and then a similar question about the year ahead.

	1984	1985	1986	1987	1989	1990
Over the last year household income has:	%	%	%	%	%	%
Fallen behind prices	46	55	47	45	49	52
Kept up with prices	44	37	41	44	40	37
Gone up by more than prices	8	7	9	9	10	9
Over the next year household income will:	%	%	%	%	%	%
Fall behind prices	43	49	44	39	45	50
Keep up with prices	45	39	43	46	41	38
Go up by more than prices	8	8	9	10	10	8

It is remarkable that in not a single year has more than one in ten respondents reported that their household income has risen by more than prices, despite the fact that throughout this period the percentage rise in personal disposable income has exceeded price inflation.[11] Furthermore, the proportions throughout the period have remained surprisingly constant, relative to the variations in the actual rate of inflation. In all six surveys, the proportion reporting a relative decline over the previous year has exceeded, albeit by a small margin, the proportion predicting a decline over the following year, indicating perhaps a modicum of optimism.

The pattern of subgroup differences in 1990 was similar to that for expectations about unemployment and inflation. Three-quarters of the unemployed reported a fall, and two-thirds predicted a further decline, in real incomes; and pensioners were nearly as pessimistic about the year ahead. In the case of the unemployed, however, the despondency was recent: between 1987 and 1989, they had become more optimistic, perhaps in response to the falling unemployment levels.

Even after employment status has been taken into account, differences between identifiers with different political parties persist, suggesting that responses do not reflect objective judgments alone. In all the main employment status subgroups, Labour identifiers were much more likely than Conservative identifiers to predict that their incomes would fall behind inflation. For instance, among employees 52 per cent of Labour identifiers predicted a decline in real income compared with 32 per cent of Conservatives; among those looking after the home the proportions were 66 per cent and 35 per cent respectively; and among the retired, 80 per cent and 54 per cent respectively.

Level of actual household income - itself clearly related to economic status - produced even larger differences, with those on low incomes much more despondent than the better-off about their past and future purchasing power. About three-quarters of those with incomes under £7,000 a year reported *and* anticipated a decline in real income, compared with less than one-third of those with £23,000 or over. And younger respondents, aged under 25, were noticeably more sanguine about changes in their real incomes than were their elders, justifiably so since those in employment should reasonably expect their pay to increase faster than prices in their early years at work.

Jobs

As we have noted, unemployment levels had risen slowly between 1983 and 1986 to reach over one in ten of the labour force but had then fallen sharply to 1990 and had stabilised by the time of our 1990 fieldwork. However, vacancies at jobcentres had begun falling steadily from mid-1988.[12] We have also noted that manufacturing industry over the whole period had been shedding labour while the service sector was expanding both in absolute terms and as a proportion of the labour force.

Each year we ask employees for their predictions about staffing levels at their workplace over the following year. Changes in responses from year to year have been small, but the figures for 1990 do suggest a renewed pessimism about future staffing levels, although not (yet) at the level it had reached in 1983 and 1984.

Over coming year expect workplace will	1983 %	1984 %	1985 %	1986 %	1987 %	1989 %	1990 %
Increase number of employees	16	18	22	21	23	26	23
Number will stay the same	54	51	52	54	52	53	50
Reduce number of employees	29	29	24	23	22	20	25

These year-on-year trends, as expected, are loosely related to trends in predictions about unemployment in Britain generally. The recent increase in pessimism about people's workplaces coincides with the gloom about unemployment levels generally.

There were striking differences in 1990 in the expectations of public and private sector employees. As many as 40 per cent of public sector workers predicted a reduction in the number of employees at their workplaces over the coming year, compared with about one in six of those in the private sector. In fact, private sector employees were more than twice as likely as those in the public sector to predict an *increase* in staffing levels (27 per cent against 13 per cent). Moreover, expectations in the two sectors had diverged markedly since 1989, surprisingly in view of the fact that the private service sector has in the event been hit particularly hard by the current recession. Within the public sector, employees in services remained more optimistic than those in manufacturing and transport. The same pattern appeared in the private sector, but the differences here were much smaller.

Perhaps the starkest measure of confidence in the economy is derived from the answers of unemployed people to questions about their chances of finding work. Optimism about their chances of finding a job to match their qualifications had fallen markedly: in 1990 37 per cent said that they were 'very' or 'quite' confident compared with 46 per cent in 1989 (though confidence was higher in 1990 than it was in 1984). Even more worryingly, in 1990 just 41 per cent of the unemployed felt that there was a real chance of finding a job in their area, compared with 62 per cent a year earlier. This underlines the point made earlier, that the most accurate predictions about economic trends appear to come from those to whom the figures are of the greatest personal importance.

Economic policy options

Government intervention

In 1990, as in previous years, we asked respondents whether they support or oppose a number of macroeconomic policies which a government might use to help solve Britain's economic problems.[*] We have continually found widespread enthusiasm for active government intervention in the economy, and there are few signs that this enthusiasm is declining. For instance, in 1990 not only did public opinion support controls on credit (82 per cent), and import controls (72 per cent), but there has also been persistent support for Keynesian policies of combating unemployment through setting up construction projects to create more jobs (83 per cent). There has been consistently less support, but majorities nonetheless, for other 'unfashionable' remedies, control of prices by law (56 per cent), and more government subsidy to industry again (56 per cent).

Moreover, when we asked respondents whether it should or should not be the *government's* responsibility to provide industry with the help it needs to grow, nine in ten said 'yes', and almost as many thought the

---

[*] In 1989 we dropped an item on devaluation of the pound and added questions about interest rate policy and controls on credit.

government should be responsible for keeping prices under control. Fewer, but again still a substantial majority (60 per cent), said that it should be the government's responsibility to "provide a job for everyone who wants one".

However, although in general a *laissez faire* approach to economic management does not seem to have caught the public's imagination, neither has intervention in the form of state ownership of industry. Fewer than one in five people in 1990 supported more nationalisation, and this included fewer than one in three Labour identifiers. Nonetheless, support for *further* privatisation had been falling, to a low of 16 per cent in 1990. The strong public preference was for the *status quo.*

Inflation and unemployment

Control of inflation has been a central plank - even *the* central plank - of successive Conservative governments' economic policy during the 1980s. As we have seen, the rate of inflation has fluctuated widely during this period and, with it, the level of public concern. In particular, as inflation accelerated sharply during the spring of 1990, so the growth in concern was reflected in responses to our latest survey.

Control of inflation and control of unemployment are often presented as mutually exclusive alternatives, and we have long included two questions which set them up as such, as a way of assessing respondents' priorities.

> *If the government **had** to choose between keeping down inflation and keeping down unemployment, to which do you think it should give highest priority?*

> *Which do you think is of most concern to **you and your family** - inflation or unemployment?*

These questions allow us to examine both current policy preferences and changes in priorities over time. However, as the table below shows, responses reveal a substantial gap between what respondents have said the government's priority ought to be, and what has been of greater concern to themselves and their families. Consistently respondents have seen unemployment as a greater priority for government than as a threat to most of them personally.

	1983	1984	1985	1986	1987	1989	1990
Government priority:	%	%	%	%	%	%	%
Inflation	27	26	22	20	23	39	49
Unemployment	69	69	73	75	73	57	47
Household concern:	%	%	%	%	%	%	%
Inflation	N/A	52	51	51	55	67	70
Unemployment	N/A	44	44	45	41	30	26

The trends are instructive. In 1990, for the first time in our time-series, when asked to choose between inflation and unemployment as the greater priority for government, public opinion was evenly divided. The proportion choosing of inflation as the higher priority had risen by 26 percentage points since 1987, with a corresponding drop in the proportion nominating unemployment. Similarly, while a majority of respondents throughout the period has said that inflation is the greater concern to them personally, the proportion rose sharply (by 15 percentage points) between 1987 and 1990.

The size of these changes is dramatic. From a majority of more than three to one between 1985 and 1987 in the proportions nominating unemployment as the higher priority than inflation, opinion in 1990 was evenly divided. Concern about inflation - both as a government priority and as a personal threat - was at its highest level since 1983. Even so, nearly twice as many respondents nominated unemployment as the government's priority as regarded it as a greater concern to them personally. Since the 1990 survey, of course, inflation levels have fallen and unemployment levels have risen, and these trends in public priorities might well change once more.

While the proportions giving priority to inflation at recent rounds have of course risen sharply among respondents in all subgroups, different interests were nonetheless apparent. For instance, the views of the self-employed and those of retired people - who understandably feel unemployment to be less important - were distinguishable from other groups, such as those in work. As the table below shows, in 1990 these two groups were much more likely both to nominate inflation as the government's priority, and to rate inflation as the greater concern to them personally. In view of the high and rising level of unemployment since the 1990 fieldwork round and the record level of business failures[13], it will be interesting to see whether this pattern persists among the self-employed.

		Economic status			
	Employee	Self-employed	Un-employed	Looking after home	Retired
Government priority:	%	%	%	%	%
Inflation	47	56	41	48	54
Unemployment	50	39	57	46	40
Household concern:	%	%	%	%	%
Inflation	67	78	43	72	81
Unemployment	30	20	52	23	15

Among employees there was a predictable gradient in concern according to household income: those on lower incomes were more likely than the better-off to nominate unemployment as their greater personal concern; and, equally predictably, unemployed people were especially likely to nominate unemployment as the government's priority as well as their own greater concern. Even so, it is notable that only just over half of the jobless in 1990 said that unemployment was of greater concern to them personally - testimony to the universal concern at that time about inflation and the universal impact of inflation.

While concern about inflation had increased in 1990 among identifiers with all the main political parties, marked differences in priorities remained. A substantial majority (64 per cent) of Conservative identifiers nominated inflation, rather than unemployment, as the government's priority compared with around two in five Labour identifiers and Liberal Democrats. Similarly, and more surprisingly perhaps, as many as four in five Conservative identifiers nominated inflation as the greater concern to them personally, compared with around two-thirds of Labour identifiers and Liberal Democrats. In respect of the conflict between inflation and unemployment then, Labour identifiers and Liberal Democrats were almost indistinguishable.

Taxation

During the period since 1983 there has been a major shift from direct to indirect taxation in the contribution to central government revenue. Both the basic rate and the higher rates of income tax have been reduced substantially, most notably in the 1988 budget which reduced the basic rate from 27 to 25 per cent and the top rate from 60 per cent to 40 per cent. Overall, the chief beneficiaries of the 1988 tax changes were, according to Keegan (1989, p.221), the top five per cent of income earners. Meanwhile VAT had remained at a uniform 15 per cent since 1979. It did not go up until a year after our 1990 fieldwork, though its range had been extended in the meantime. Among the net effects of these and other changes in the structure of taxation over the period is that the overall tax burden has continued to shift away from the rich.

As noted in Chapter 2, a majority of respondents in 1990 prescribed tax increases in order to spend more on health, education and social benefits; there was also widespread support for many economic policy options (as well as for social and welfare measures) which might involve increases in public expenditure - and hence taxation.

How should the tax burden (and any increase in it) be shared among the population? We repeated a question in 1990 that we had asked in 1985 and 1986 about progressive taxation policies or, as we put it, whether those with high incomes should pay a *larger* proportion of their earnings in taxes than those who earn low incomes, the *same*, or a *smaller* proportion. As the table below shows, a majority in each year had said high income-earners should pay 'a larger' or 'much larger' share, and this proportion (now 82 per cent) had risen in the five years, with a corresponding decline in support for 'the same proportion'.

	1985	1986	1990
Proportion of income those on	%	%	%
high incomes should pay in tax:			
A much larger proportion	24	21	21
A larger proportion	50	56	61
The same proportion	22	19	14
A smaller or much smaller			
proportion	1	1	1

Not surprisingly, there was a clear gradient by income in the proportion saying 'much more', those on the lowest incomes (under £7,000) being more than twice as likely to give this response as those on the highest incomes (33 per cent against 14 per cent). There were also predictable differences between the identifiers with different political parties, the views of Liberal Democrats again being closer to those of Labour identifiers than Conservatives.

Since 1983 we have also asked respondents for their views on current tax levels for each of three income groups - defined only as high, middle and low. (Although the question does not specifically refer to income tax, it is likely that respondents' answers refer to this rather than to indirect taxes, notably VAT, or to the total tax burden.) The table below shows remarkable changes in public perceptions since 1983, but especially between 1987 and 1989, the period during which there were major reductions in direct taxes particularly (but not exclusively) for high-earners. Until 1987 the balance of opinion was that taxes for *everyone,* including high-earners were 'about right' or 'too high'. In 1989, however, the balance in respect of high-earners shifted markedly towards the view that they were not taxed highly enough. To some extent, sympathy for middle-income groups diminished too. These views were stable between 1989 and 1990. It remained the case that as many as one-half of respondents believed that taxes for those on high incomes should be increased; more surprisingly, perhaps, given the general antipathy to taxes, only around a quarter thought that taxes for those on middle incomes were too high; in contrast approaching one-half in 1983 took that view. Amid all this turbulence, the public perceptions of taxation levels for those on low incomes (that they are too high) had remained remarkably stable.

	1983 %	1986 %	1987 %	1989 %	1990 %
Taxes for those on high incomes:					
Too low or much too low	32	37	39	52	50
About right	36	35	37	33	35
Too high or much too high	29	23	21	12	13
Taxes for those on middle incomes:	%	%	%	%	%
Too low or much too low	4	5	5	6	6
About right	50	52	56	64	64
Too high or much too high	44	40	36	27	28
Taxes for those on low incomes:	%	%	%	%	%
Too low or much too low	3	2	2	2	3
About right	16	15	14	15	19
Too high or much too high	79	81	82	80	76

Predictable differences between various income groups occur, but the largest differences are according to political affiliation. Just one-third of Conservative identifiers considered that tax levels for those on high incomes should be increased, compared with around 60 per cent of Labour identifiers and Liberal Democrats. In respect of those on low incomes, Conservative identifiers were twice as likely as Labour identifiers and Liberal Democrats to say that tax levels are about right (28 per cent and 14 per cent each respectively). Still, as many as two-thirds of Conservative identifiers believed taxes for those on low incomes still to be excessive.

Each year we have asked respondents whether the gap between those with high incomes and those with low incomes is 'too large', 'about right' or 'too small'? A striking 81 per cent in 1990 believed that the gap was too large, a noticeably higher proportion than in 1983 (72 per cent). A mere handful of respondents each year had said that it is too small. Similarly, when we asked employees about the gap between the highest and lowest paid people at their workplaces, the proportion saying the gap is 'too big' had risen in recent years, from 39 per cent in 1986 to 47 per cent in 1990.

Conclusions

While between 1983 and 1989 optimism about both Britain's economic performance and respondents' own economic circumstances generally increased, there was a sharp downturn in 1990. The less well-off economically had become particularly pessimistic. The unemployed emerged as the most gloomy on many measures and the self-employed as the most sanguine. Conservative identifiers remained much more optimistic about the economy than either Labour identifiers or Liberal Democrat.

Nonetheless all subgroups, including Conservative identifiers, supported a wide range of policies involving further government intervention in the economy and the labour market. People persisted in believing it was the government's responsibility to ensure that everyone who wants a job has one, to the extent of creating jobs through construction projects. On the other hand, it seems that combating unemployment remains a top priority only when inflation appears to be more or less under control. When inflation is high and rising, as it was in 1990, respondents tend to switch their priority towards that target, and away from unemployment.

As far as taxation policies are concerned, there was clearly a degree of public unease, as we found in relation to public expenditure policies, that the main beneficiaries in recent years have been those who were already better off rather than the less well-off.

Notes

1. The sources of figures on unemployment cited or referred to in this chapter, including those by economic sector, are CSO (July 1991a.) table 21, p.38 and the graph on p.39; various issues of the *Employment Gazette* (Employment Department) and CSO (July 1991b), tables 3.9, 3.10 and 3.11, pp.27-29.
2. Figures on inflation are derived from CSO (1991) table 1, p.7 (annual indices) and table 2, p.8 (monthly - percentage changes over 12 months).
3. Figures on output by sector refer to the period from 1984 onwards and are derived from CSO (1991) table 16, p. 28 and the graphs on p.29.
4. Figures on average earnings refer to the period from 1986 onwards and are derived from CSO (July 1991a.) table 23, p.42 and the graph on p.43; they have been compared with figures on inflation to derive estimates of the real value of earnings.
5. Figures on employment by sector refer to the period 1984 onwards and are derived from CSO (July 1991a) table 21, p.38.
6. Figures on the balance of payments refer to the whole period covered by the surveys and are derived from CSO (July 1991a) table 27, p.50 and the graphs on p.51.
7. Figures on interest rates refer to base rates for the period from 1984 onwards, and are derived from CSO (July 1991a) table 39, p.68.
8. Figures on growth are for GDP for 1988 to 1991, and are derived from OECD (1991) table 29, p.111.
9. We plotted for 1983 to 1990 (and for 1983 to 1989 in Witherspoon and Taylor 1990, p.13 and p.19) the proportion of respondents expecting inflation to rise by 'a lot' over the year *ahead* and the percentage change in the Retail Prices Index over the *previous* 12 months (averaging the monthly figures for April and May each year - the modal months for interviewing on this survey); and the proportion expecting unemployment to rise by 'a lot' over the *coming* year with the percentage change in the number unemployed over the *previous* 12 months. The scales for the two sets of figures in each case were of course different.

10. For further analyses by subgroups of these and other questions reported in this chapter, see Taylor and Prior (1991).
11. On an index where 1985 = 100, real personal disposable income rose to 124 in 1990, the largest increase occurring between 1988 and 1989 (CSO July 1991a. table 4, p.12).
12. Figures on vacancies at jobcentres - annual from 1984 and quarterly from mid-1988 - are derived from CSO (July 1991a.) table 21, p.38.
13. In 1990 there were over 4,500 business failures compared with around 2,150 in 1988 and 2,600 in 1989; and in the first half of 1991 alone there were over 3,800 failures (Trade Indemnity, 1991, p.6).

References

CENTRAL STATISTICAL OFFICE (CSO), *Retail Prices 1914-1990*, HMSO, London (1991).

CENTRAL STATISTICAL OFFICE (CSO), *Economic Trends*, no.453, HMSO, London (July 1991a).

CENTRAL STATISTICAL OFFICE (CSO), *Monthly Digest of Statistics*, no.547, HMSO, London (July 1991b).

COUTTS, K., GODLEY, W., ROWTHORN, B. and ZEZZA, G., *Britain's Economic Problems and Policies in the 1990s*, IPPR Economic Study No.6, London (1990).

DONALDSON, P. and FARQUHAR, J., *Understanding the British Economy*, Penguin, London (1991).

EMPLOYMENT DEPARTMENT, *Employment Gazette*, various editions, HMSO, London (monthly).

HARRISON, A., 'Economic policy and expectations', in Jowell, R. and Airey, C., (eds), *British Social Attitudes: the 1984 report*, Gower, Aldershot (1984).

KEEGAN, W., *Mr Lawson's Gamble*, Hodder and Stoughton, London (1989).

MAYNARD, G.W., *The Economy under Mrs Thatcher*, Blackwell, Oxford (1988).

OECD, *OECD Economic Outlook*, OECD, Paris (1991).

SANDERS, D., 'Government popularity and the next general election', *Political Quarterly*, vol.62, no.2 (April-June 1991).

TAYLOR, B. and PRIOR, G., *British Social Attitudes 1990 Survey: A Report for the Employment Department*, SCPR, London (1991).

TRADE INDEMNITY, *Quarterly Business Review, July to September 1991*, Trade Indemnity plc, London (1991).

WITHERSPOON, S. and TAYLOR, B., *British Social Attitudes 1989 Survey: A Report for the Employment Department*, SCPR, London (1990).

Acknowledgement

We are grateful to the Employment Department for their support of those questions reported here that deal with labour market attitudes and expectations.

Appendix I
Technical details of the surveys

British Social Attitudes

In 1990, as in 1989, 1987 and 1986, the generosity of the Sainsbury Family
Charitable Trusts enabled us to interview around 3,000 respondents, a
substantial increase from the 1,700 to 1,800 interviewed in the first three
years of the *British Social Attitudes* survey series. So we were again able
to cover more topics in the questionnaire. Core questions were asked of
all respondents, and the remaining questions were asked of a half sample
of around 1,500 respondents each - version L of one half, version Y of the
other.* The structure of the questionnaire is shown in Appendix III.

Sample design

The survey was designed to yield a representative sample of adults aged
18 or over living in private households in Britain.
   For practical reasons, the sample was confined to those living in private
households whose addresses were listed in the electoral registers. People
living in institutions (though not in private households at such institutions)
were excluded, as were households whose addresses were not on the
electoral registers. Fieldwork was timed to start in mid-March, so the

---

* The two questionnaires were labelled 'L' and 'Y' in 1990, according to the colour of
their cover ('L' for lilac, 'Y' for yellow), to allow easier identification by interviewers.

sample was drawn from the 1989 registers, which were just reaching the end of their period of currency.

The sampling method involved a multi-stage design, with four separate stages of selection.

Selection of parliamentary constituencies

One hundred and seventy-six parliamentary constituencies were selected from all those in England, Scotland and Wales. In Scotland, the four constituencies north of the Caledonian Canal were omitted for reasons of cost.

Before selection, the constituencies were stratified according to information held in SCPR's constituency datafile. This datafile is a compilation of information gathered from OPCS *Monitors*, and includes a variety of social indicators such as population density, percentage of Labour vote at the 1987 general election, percentage of those holding professional qualifications, percentage of male unemployment and so on. The stratification factors used in the 1990 survey were:

- Registrar General's Standard Region
- Population density (persons per hectare) with variable banding used according to region, in order to make the strata roughly equal in size[1]
- Ranking by percentage of homes that were owner-occupied, from the 1981 Census figures.

Constituencies were then selected systematically with probability of selection proportionate to size of electorate. To compensate for the use of old registers, the size of the electorate in each constituency was updated to its 1990 level, using the figures from *Electoral Statistics* prior to the selection of constituencies.

Selection of polling districts

Within most of the selected constituencies a single polling district was chosen. Any polling district with fewer than 500 electors was combined with one or more other polling districts before the selection stage, so that in some constituencies a combination of polling districts was selected. Polling districts were chosen with probability proportionate to size of electorate.

Selection of addresses

Twenty-six addresses were selected in each of the 176 polling districts. The sample issued to interviewers was therefore 176 x 26 = 4576 addresses.

The addresses in each polling district were selected by starting from a random point on the list of electors and, treating the list as circular, choosing each address at a fixed interval. The fixed interval was calculated for each polling district separately to generate the correct number of addresses.

By this means, addresses were chosen with probability proportionate to their number of listed electors. At each sampled address the names of all electors given on the register were listed, and the name of the individual on which the sampling interval had landed was marked with an asterisk. (This person is known as the 'starred elector'.) Each starred elector was allocated a serial number.

Questionnaire versions

Alternate serial numbers were allocated to the L or Y half of the sample. Odd serial numbers were allocated to the L sample, and even serial numbers to the Y sample, so that each questionnaire version was assigned to 2288 addresses. This meant that each interviewer (and each sampling area) had both L and Y addresses. In fact the L version was used in all 176 areas but, due to interviewer error, the Y version was used in 175 areas.

Selection of individuals

The electoral register is an unsatisfactory sampling frame of *individuals,* although it is regarded as reasonably complete as a frame of *addresses.* So a further selection stage was required to convert the listing of addresses into a sample of individuals.

Interviewers were instructed to call at the address of each starred elector and to list all those eligible for inclusion in the sample - that is, all persons currently aged 18 or over and resident at the selected household.

In households where the list of people eligible to take part in the survey was the same as the electoral register listing, the interviewer was instructed to interview the starred elector. Where there was a difference between the household members named in the register and those eligible to take part in the survey (because there had been movement into or out of the address after the compilation of the electoral register, or because some people were not registered) the interviewer selected one respondent by a random selection procedure (using a 'Kish grid'). Where there were two or more households at the selected address, interviewers were required to identify the household of the starred elector, or the household occupying the part of the address where he or she used to live, and to select a household using a Kish grid; then they followed the same procedure to select a person for interview.

Before analysis, the data were weighted to take account of any differences between the number of people listed on the register (which determined the initial selection probability) and the number found at the address. Such differences were found in 26 per cent of addresses, in each of which data were weighted by the number of persons aged 18 or over currently living at the address divided by the number of electors listed on the register for that address. The vast majority of such weights was between 0.25 and 2.0. In only 8 cases were weights below 0.20 assigned, and in only 13 cases were weights greater than 2.0. At 74 per cent of addresses the number of persons listed on the register and the number found at the address matched, so that the effective weight was one. The unweighted base (the number of persons interviewed) was 2,797 and the weighted base was 2,698.

Fieldwork

Interviewing was carried out mainly during March, April and May 1990, with 13 per cent of interviews taking place later.

Fieldwork was conducted by 174 interviewers drawn from SCPR's regular panel. The 87 interviewers who had not worked on a previous *British Social Attitudes* survey attended a one-day briefing conference to familiarise them with the selection procedures and questionnaires. Eighty-seven interviewers who had worked on a *BSA* survey before did not attend a briefing, but were sent detailed instructions about the project. The average interview length was, for version L of the questionnaire, 62 minutes, and for version Y, 59 minutes.

The final response achieved is shown below:

	Number	%
Addresses issued	4576	
Vacant, derelict, other out of scope	174	
In scope	4402	100
Interview achieved	2797	63.5
Interview not achieved	1605	36.5
Refused	1177[2]	26.7
Not contacted	255[3]	5.8
Other non-response	173	3.9

The response rate achieved with the L version of the questionnaire was 63 per cent, and with the Y version, 64 per cent. Response rates ranged between 74 per cent in the North of England and 55 per cent in Greater London and 52 per cent in the East Midlands.

As in earlier rounds of the series, respondents were asked to fill in a self-completion questionnaire which was, whenever possible, collected by the interviewer. Otherwise, the respondent was asked to post it to SCPR. If necessary, up to three postal reminders were sent to obtain the self-completion supplement.

Three hundred and sixty-seven respondents (13 per cent of those interviewed) did not return their self-completion questionnaire. Version L of the self-completion questionnaire was returned by 86 per cent of respondents, and version Y by 88 per cent. Non-respondents to the self-completion questionnaire included a higher proportion of unskilled manual workers, residents of Greater London and Scotland, respondents with no educational qualifications, and respondents aged 65 or over. However, since the overall proportion returning a self-completion questionnaire was high we decided against additional weighting to correct for non-response.

Analysis variables

A number of standard analyses have been used in the tables that appear both in the text and at the end of the chapters of this report. The analysis groups requiring further definition are set out below.

Region

The Registrar General's 10 Standard Regions have been used, except that we have distinguished between Greater London and the remainder of the South East. Sometimes these have been grouped into what we have termed 'compressed region': 'Northern' includes the North, North West and Yorkshire and Humberside. East Anglia is included in the 'South', as is the South West.

Social class

Respondents are classified according to their own social class, not that of a putative 'head of household'. The main social class variable used in the analyses in this report is the Registrar General's, although Socio-Economic Group (SEG) has also been coded, and so can by used by secondary analysts with access to the datatape.

Each respondent's social class is based on his or her current or last occupation. So all respondents in paid work at the time of the interview, or waiting to take up a paid job already offered, or retired, or seeking work, or looking after the home, have their occupation (present, future or last as appropriate) classified into Occupational Unit Groups, according to the OPCS *Classification of Occupations 1980.* This method has been adopted on each survey, except for that of 1983 when we separately classified those looking after the home. The combination of occupational classification with employment status generates the six social classes:

I	Professional	⎫
II	Intermediate	⎬ 'Non-manual'
III (Non-manual)	Skilled occupations	⎭
III (Manual)	Skilled occupations	⎫
IV	Semi-skilled occupations	⎬ 'Manual'
V	Unskilled occupations	⎭

In this report we have usually collapsed them into four groups: I & II, III Non-manual, III Manual, IV & V.

The remaining respondents are grouped as 'never worked/not classifiable', but are not shown in the tables. For some analyses, it may be more appropriate to classify respondents according to their *current* social class, which takes into account only their present employment status. In this case, in addition to the six social classes listed above, the remaining respondents not currently in paid work fall into one of the following categories: 'not classified', 'retired', 'looking after the home', 'unemployed' or 'others not in paid occupations'.

In some chapters, John Goldthorpe's schema is used. This system classifies occupations by their 'general comparability', considering such factors as sources and levels of income, economic security, promotion prospects, and level of job autonomy and authority. We have developed a programme which derives the Goldthorpe classification from the five-digit Occupational Unit Groups combined with employment status. The full Goldthorpe schema has 11 categories but the version used in this report (the 'compressed schema') combines these into five classes:

- Salariat (professional and managerial)
- Routine non-manual workers (office and sales)
- Petty bourgeoisie (the self-employed, including farmers, with and without employees)
- Manual foremen and supervisors
- Working class (skilled, semi-skilled and unskilled manual workers, personal service and agricultural workers).

There is a residual category of those who have never had a job or who have given insufficient information, but this is not shown in any of the analyses in this report.

Industry

All respondents whose occupation could be coded were allocated a Standard Industrial Classification (SIC, 1980). Two-digit class codes were applied. Respondents were also classified as working in public-sector services, public-sector manufacturing and transport, private-sector manufacturing or private-sector non-manufacturing, by cross-analysing SIC categories with responses to a question about the type of employer for whom they worked. As with social class, SIC may be generated on the basis of the respondent's current occupation only, or on his or her most recently-classifiable occupation.

Party identification

Respondents can be classified as identifying with a particular political party, or party grouping, on one of three counts: if they consider themselves supporters of the party (Q.2a,d), or as closer to it than to others (Q.2b,d), or as more likely to support it in the event of a general election (Q.2c). The three groups are generally described respectively as *partisans, sympathisers,* and *residual identifiers.* The three groups combined are referred to in both text and tables as 'identifiers'.

Liberal Democrat identifiers (in spring 1990) include those nominating the Social and Liberal Democrat Party, the Liberal Party, the Alliance or the Social Democrat Party. Respondents saying "Alliance" were asked whether this meant Liberal Democrat or SDP (Owen).

Other analysis variables

These are taken directly from the questionnaire, and to that extent are self-explanatory. The principal ones used in the in-text and end-of-chapter tables are:

Sex (Q.901a)	Highest educational qualification obtained (Q.908)
Age (Q.901b)	Marital status (Q.900)
Household income (Q.918a)	Religion (Q.118a)
Economic status (Q.23)	Religious attendance (Q.119)

Sampling errors

No sample precisely reflects the characteristics of the population it represents because of both sampling and non-sampling errors. If a sample were designed as a random sample (if every adult had an equal and independent chance of inclusion in the sample) then we could calculate the sampling error of any percentage, p, using the formula:

$$s.e\ (p) = \sqrt{\frac{p(100\text{-}p)}{n}}$$

where n is the number of respondents on which the percentage is based. Once the sampling error had been calculated, it would be a straightforward exercise to calculate a confidence interval for the true population percentage. For example, a 95 per cent confidence interval would be given by the formula:

$$p \pm 1.96 \times s.e.(p)$$

Clearly, for a simple random sample, the sampling error depends only on the values of p and n. However, simple random sampling is almost never used in practice because of its inefficiency in terms of time and cost.

As noted above, the *British Social Attitudes* sample, like that drawn for most large-scale surveys, was clustered according to a stratified multi-stage design into 176 polling districts (or combinations of polling districts). With a complex design like this, the sampling error of a percentage giving a particular response is not simply a function of the number of respondents in the sample and the size of the percentage; it also depends on how that percentage response is spread within and between polling districts.

So, in the case of a complex sample design, we need to calculate the complex standard error, taking into account how percentage response is spread between different areas. The underlying principle is that, since the areas themselves are now samples, the clustering of responses in areas is in itself a source of response variation.

Estimates of complex sampling errors for the 1990 survey were made using the same procedure as that followed for 1989. First, we chose a range of questions and then looked at the proportions answering in a certain way (for example "expect inflation to go up"), separately for each of the 176 different sampling points. These sampling points were then treated as if they were a sample of areas, and we calculated the variance of the proportions between areas. This gives an unbiased estimate of the complex sampling error for the sample as a whole. That this estimate takes into account neither the fact that different areas had different response rates, nor the improvements in precision due to stratification, means that the estimates will tend to overstate the size of the complex error, though the size of this overstatement is likely to be small.

However, this procedure does not allow us to calculate the *components* of sampling variation - that is, how much of it would have occurred as a result of random sampling variation even if there had been no clustering, and how much is due to clustering. This means that we cannot calculate design factors which give us a yardstick for comparing our sample with the efficiency obtained using simple random sampling. Nonetheless, we can see which variables have larger or smaller confidence intervals, which helps us interpret responses.

The table below gives examples of the complex standard errors and confidence intervals calculated. In the case of most attitudinal questions asked of the whole sample, we can see that the confidence interval is usually around plus or minus two per cent of the survey proportion; so we can be 95 per cent certain that the true population proportion is within two per cent (in either direction) of the proportion we report. However, for certain variables (those most associated with the area a person lives in) we find the confidence interval is plus or minus three per cent or more. This is particularly so for party identification and housing tenure. For instance, Labour identifiers and local authority tenants tend to be concentrated within certain areas; consequently there is proportionately more variation in a clustered sample than there would be in a simple random sample. But for most variables, especially attitudinal ones, the use of standard statistical tests of significance (based on the assumption of simple random sampling) is unlikely to be misleading. The table below also shows that, when questions were asked of only half the sample, confidence intervals are correspondingly greater.

Classification variables		% (p)	Complex standard error of p (%)	95 per cent confidence interval	Weighted n
Q.2	**Party identification**				
	Conservative	34.9	1.46	32.04 - 37.76	943
	Liberal Democrat	7.8	1.59	6.58 - 9.02	210
	Labour	38.6	0.62	35.48 - 41.72	1041
Q.24	**Self-employed**	14.9	0.62	13.69 - 16.11	221
L154/ Y146	**Housing tenure**				
	Owns	72.3	1.75	68.87 - 75.73	1950
	Rents from local authority	18.5	1.72	15.13 - 21.87	500
	Rents from housing association	1.7	0.34	1.04 - 2.36	46
	Other renting	6.3	0.75	4.83 - 7.77	169
Q.907	**Age of completing continuous full-time education**				
	16 or under	68.4	1.39	65.68 - 71.12	1846
	17 or 18	16.5	0.85	14.83 - 18.17	444
	19 or over	12.3	0.93	10.47 - 14.13	331
L113a/ Y118a	**Religion**				
	No religion	36.3	1.23	33.89 - 38.71	981
	Protestant	48.5	1.35	45.86 - 51.14	1309
	Catholic	8.9	0.82	7.29 - 10.51	240

Attitudinal variables		% (p)	Complex standard error of p (%)	95 per cent confidence interval	Weighted n
Q.7	Britain should rid itself of nuclear weapons	27.6	1.00	25.63 - 29.57	745
Q.12	Expect inflation to go up	85.0	0.82	83.39 - 86.61	2294
Q.13	Expect unemployment to go up	47.0	1.19	44.66 - 49.34	1267
Q.108	Government should increase taxes and spend more on health, education and social benefits	54.3	1.26	51.83 - 56.77	1465
L148a	Nationalisation/privatisation				
	Favour more nationalisation	19.2	1.39	16.48 - 21.92	260
	Favour more privatisation	16.0	1.16	13.72 - 18.28	216
	Things should be left as now	57.5	1.79	54.00 - 61.00	1778
Y125	Concern about environmental issues				
	Very concerned about the greenhouse effect	45.5	1.52	42.52 - 48.48	612
	A bit concerned about the greenhouse effect	36.3	1.40	33.56 - 39.04	488
	Not very concerned about the greenhouse effect	11.5	1.12	9.31 - 13.69	155
	Not at all concerned about the greenhouse effect	3.7	0.63	2.46 - 4.94	50

These calculations are based on the total sample from the 1990 survey (2698 weighted, 2797 unweighted), or on L respondents (1353 weighted, 1397 unweighted) or Y respondents (1345 weighted, 1400 unweighted). As the examples above show, sampling errors for proportions based only on the Y or L sample, or on subgroups within the sample, are somewhat larger than they would have been, had the questions been asked of everyone.

Notes

1. The population density bands used were as follows:

Region	Density banding (persons per hectare)
North North West	} Under 6; 6-13; over 13
Yorks and Humberside	Under 8; 8-21; over 21
West Midlands	Under 5; 5-34; over 34
East Midlands East Anglia South West	} Under 2; 2-10; over 10
South East	Under 4; 4-8; over 8
Greater London	Under 40; 40-65; over 65
Wales Scotland	} Under 2; 2-10; over 10

2. 'Refusals' comprise refusals before selection of an individual at the address, refusals to the office, refusal by the selected person, 'proxy' refusals (on behalf of the selected respondent) and broken appointments after which the selected person could not be recontacted.
3. 'Non-contacts' comprise households where no-one was contacted, and those where the selected person could not be contacted (never found at home, known to be away on business, on holiday, in hospital, and so on).

Northern Ireland Social Attitudes

1990 was the second year in which the extension of the *British Social Attitudes* survey to Northern Ireland was carried out, with funding from the Nuffield Foundation and the Central Community Relations Unit in Belfast. Funding was also assured for a third *Northern Ireland Social Attitudes* survey in 1991. In 1990, as in 1989, core questions were asked in both surveys, but in addition there was a special module in the Northern Ireland questionnaire; in 1990 this module covered crime, law and order in Northern Ireland (Qs. 78-100). Some of these questions were asked in Britain too,[*] so allowing us to compare the attitudes of those living in Northern Ireland with the attitudes of people in Britain. The structure of the Northern Ireland questionnaire, and its relationship to the British questionnaire, is shown in Appendix III.

   An advisory board consisting of representatives from Social and Community Planning Research, the Policy Planning and Research Unit (PPRU) in Belfast (which also carried out the sampling and the fieldwork), the Centre for Social Research at Queen's University in Belfast (which had responsibility for special analyses), the Central

---

[*] Version L: Qs. 124-134.

Community Relations Unit and the academic community met several times in the months before fieldwork to plan the survey and design the module on community relations. As with all questionnaire modules, however, final responsibility for its coverage and wording remains with SCPR.

Sample design

The survey was designed to yield a representative sample of all adults aged 18 or over living in private households in Northern Ireland.

The sample was drawn from the rating list, the most up-to-date listing of private households, and made available to PPRU for research purposes. People living in institutions (though not in private households in such institutions) are excluded.

A combination of the small geographical size of Northern Ireland, the generally low population density (outside the Greater Belfast area) and the extent of coverage of PPRU's fieldforce mean that it is not necessary to cluster addresses within areas. The sample was therefore a simple random sample of all households listed on the rating list. Addresses were selected from a computer-based copy of the rating list using a NAG random-number-generation routine. The addresses selected for all surveys conducted by PPRU are excluded from further sampling for a period of two years. Before addresses were selected, the rating list file was stratified into three geographical areas: Belfast, East Northern Ireland and West Northern Ireland. Within each of these strata a simple random sample of addresses was selected, with probability proportionate to the number of addresses in that stratum. The issued sample was 1400 addresses.

Selection of individuals

The rating list provides a good sampling frame of *addresses*, but contains no information about the number of *people* living at an address. So a further selection stage was required to convert the listing of addresses to a listing of individuals.

Interviewers were instructed to call at each address issued in their assignments. They then had to list all people resident at the address who were eligible for inclusion in the sample: that is, all persons currently aged 18 or over living at the address. From this listing of eligible adults, the interviewer selected one respondent by a random selection procedure (using a computer-generated Kish grid).

In Northern Ireland, addresses could not be selected with probability proportionate to the size of the household (as with the electoral register sampling used in *British Social Attitudes*). So before the analysis, the data were weighted to adjust for the fact that individuals living in large households had a lower chance than individuals in small households of being included in the sample. This means that the weights applied to the Northern Ireland sample are, in general, larger than those applied to the British one. All the weights fell within a range between one and seven, and the average weight applied was 2.06. In order to retain the actual number of interviews, the weighted sample was scaled back to the size of the unweighted sample, yielding a total of 896 interviews and an average scaled weight of 1. The distribution of weights used is shown below:

No. of adults 18 and over	Weight	No.	%	Scaled weight
1	1	290	32.4	0.511
2	2	436	48.7	1.021
3	3	110	12.3	1.532
4	4	43	4.8	2.042
5	5	13	1.5	2.533
6	6	2	0.2	3.063
7	7	2	0.2	3.574

Thus, 32 per cent of households had only one adult present, 49 per cent were two-adult households, and so on.

Fieldwork

Fieldwork in Northern Ireland began in late February 1990. Over 90 per cent of interviews were carried out in February and March, 1990, with the remaining 84 interviews carried out in April.

Fieldwork was conducted by 55 interviewers drawn from PPRU's panel. All interviewers attended a one-day briefing conference to familiarise them with the selection procedures and the questionnaires. The interview took on average 68 minutes to administer.

Overall response achieved was:

	Number	%
Addresses issued	1400	
Vacant, derelict, other out of scope	123	
In scope	1277	100
Interview achieved	896	70
Interview not achieved	381	30
Refused	293	23
Not contacted	56	4
Other non-response	32	3

A response rate of 69 per cent was achieved in Belfast; it was also 69 per cent in East Northern Ireland and 73 per cent in West Northern Ireland.

As in the *British Social Attitudes* survey, respondents were asked to fill in a self-completion questionnaire which was, whenever possible, collected

by the interviewer. Otherwise, the respondent was asked to post it direct
to a Northern Ireland Post Office box from which it was forwarded,
through PPRU, to SCPR. If necessary, up to two postal reminders were
sent to obtain the self-completion questionnaire from those who had not
returned it.   In all, 772 respondents returned the self-completion
questionnaire, 86 per cent of those interviewed.

Advance letter experiment

As an experiment to test the effect on response rates, a letter was sent to
a random half of the selected households in the *Northern Ireland Social
Attitudes* sample (those with even serial numbers) shortly before
fieldwork began. This briefly described the purpose of the survey and the
coverage of the questionnaire, and asked for cooperation when the
interviewer called. In the event, the effect of the advance letter on overall
response was negligible.[*]

Analysis variables

Analysis variables were the same as used in the British survey, though of
course the questions about party identification included Northern Irish
political parties.

Sampling errors

Because the *Northern Ireland Social Attitudes* survey is drawn as a simple
random sample, there are no complex sampling errors to calculate. The
sampling error of any percentage, *p*, can be calculated using the formula:

$$s.e\ (p) = \sqrt{\frac{p(100\text{-}p)}{n}}$$

References

BROOK, L., TAYLOR, B. and PRIOR, G., *British Social Attitudes, 1990
Survey: Technical Report,* SCPR, London (1991).
SWEENEY, K., Technical details of the survey, in Stringer, P. and
Robinson, G., (eds), *Social Attitudes in Northern Ireland: the 2nd report,*
Blackstaff Press, Belfast (1992).

---

[*]   Further details of the advance letter experiment, as well as of the rest of the *Northern
Ireland Social Attitudes* survey, are in Sweeney (1992).

Appendix II
Notes on the tabulations

1. Figures in the tables are from the 1990 survey unless otherwise indicated.
2. Tables at the end of chapters and within the text are percentaged as indicated.
3. In tables, '*' indicates less than 0.5 per cent but greater than zero, and '-' indicates zero.
4. When findings based on the responses of fewer than 50 respondents are reported in the text, reference is made to the small base size. Any percentages based on fewer than 50 respondents (unweighted) are bracketed in the tables.
5. Percentages equal to or greater than 0.5 have been rounded up in all tables (eg. 0.5 per cent = one per cent, 36.5 per cent = 37 per cent).
6. In many tables the proportions of respondents answering 'don't know' or not giving an answer are omitted. This, together with the effects of rounding and weighting, means that percentages will not always add to 100 per cent.
7. 'Liberal Democrat' identifiers in the tables include those nominating (in spring 1990) the Social and Liberal Democrat Party, the Liberal Party, the Alliance or the Social Democrat Party, unless otherwise stated.
8. The self-completion questionnaire was not completed by 13 per cent of respondents in Britain and by 14 per cent of respondents in Northern Ireland (see Appendices I and III). Percentage responses to the self-completion questionnaire are based on all those who completed it.

Appendix III
The questionnaires

As explained in Appendix I, two different versions of the questionnaire were administered in Britain (each with its own self-completion supplement), and a separate questionnaire was administered in Northern Ireland (also with its supplement). The diagram on the next page shows the structure of the questionnaires and the topics covered (not all of which are reported in this volume).

All six questionnaires (interview and self-completion) are reproduced on the following pages. We have removed the keying codes and inserted instead the percentage distribution of answers to each question. We have also included the SPSS variable name, bracketed and in italics, beside each question. Percentages for the core questions are based on the total sample (2,698 weighted in Britain and 896 weighted and unweighted in Northern Ireland), while those for questions in versions L and Y are based on the appropriate subsamples (1,353 and 1,345 weighted). We reproduce first version L of the interview questionnaire in full; then those parts of version Y that differ; the two versions of the self-completion questionnaire follow. In the last part of Appendix III we reproduce the interview questionnaire administered in Northern Ireland and its self-completion supplement. Figures do not necessarily add up to 100 because of weighting and rounding, or for one or more of the following reasons:

(i) We have not always included percentages for those not answering (which are usually very small). They are, of course, included on the datatape.

(ii)   Some sub-questions are filtered - that is, they are asked of only a
       proportion of respondents. In these cases the percentages add up
       (approximately) to the proportions who were asked them. Where,
       however, a *series* of questions is filtered (for instance in the last part
       of Section 2 of the interview questionnaire), we have indicated the
       weighted base at the beginning of that series, and throughout derived
       percentages from that base.
(iii) If the (unweighted) base for a question is less than 50, frequencies
       (the *number* of people giving each response) are shown, rather than
       percentages.
(iv)   At a few questions, respondents were invited to give more than one
       answer and so percentages may add to well over 100 per cent.
       These are clearly marked by interviewer instructions on the
       questionnaires.

As reported in Appendix I, the *British Social Attitudes* self-completion
questionnaire was not completed by 13 per cent of respondents who were
successfully interviewed. To allow for comparisons over time, the answers
in the supplement have been repercentaged on the base of those
respondents who returned it (for version L: 1,163 weighted; for version
Y: 1,186 weighted). This means that the figures are comparable with
those given in all earlier reports in this series except in *The 1984 Report*,
where the percentages need to be recalculated if comparisons are to be
made.

   The *Northern Ireland Social Attitudes* self-completion questionnaire was
not completed by 14 per cent of respondents to the main questionnaire.
Again the answers in the supplement have been repercentaged on the
base of those who returned it (783 weighted).

   A module on the subject of the role of government, developed as part
of SCPR's involvement in the *International Social Survey Programme,* was
fielded on the self-completion supplement, on version L of the British
supplement (Qs. 2.01-19), and also on the *Northern Ireland Social Attitudes*
supplement (Qs. 2.01-19).

Structure of the questionnaires

Britain

Interview questionnaire

Both versions

Section 1.   Newspaper readership
              Party political identification
              International relations
              Defence

Section 2.   Economic issues and policies
              Perceptions of own household income
              Economic activity
              Labour market participation
              Flexible working arrangements/childcare
              New technology

Section 3.   Welfare State
              National Health Service

Version L	Version Y
Section 4. Religion Race Moral issues	Section 4. Education
Section 5. Crime and the police	Section 5. Religion
Section 6. Civil liberties	Section 6. Countryside and the environment
Section 7. Politics Poll tax European Community	Section 7. Smoking and health
Section 8. Housing (short)	Section 8. Housing (long)

Both versions

Section 9.   Demographics and other
              classificatory variables

Self-completion questionnaire

Version L	Version Y
Qs. 2.01-19 *ISSP* module: role of government	Qs. 2.01-02 National Health Service
Qs. 2.20-21 National Health Service	Qs. 2.03-05 Education
Qs. 2.22-23 Moral issues	Qs. 2.06-08 Women's work and childcare
Q. 2.24 Immigration	
Q. 2.25 Death penalty	Qs. 2.09-17 Countryside and the environment
Qs. 2.26-28 Women's work and childcare	Qs. 2.18-22 Smoking and health
Qs. 2.29-38 Civil liberties	Qs. 2.23-25 Housing
Qs. 2.39-40 New technology	Qs. 2.26-27 New technology
Q. 2.41 Left-Right scale	Q. 2.28 Left-Right scale
Q. 2.42 Liberal-Authoritarian scale	Liberal-Authoritan scale

Northern Ireland

Interview questionnaire

Section 1.   Newspaper readership
             International relations
             Defence

Section 2.   Economic issues and policies
             Perceptions of own household income
             Economic activity
             Labour market participation

Section 3.   Welfare State
             National Health Service

Section 4.   Social class*
             Religion
             Moral issues

Section 5.   Northern Ireland module:
                 Crime and the police
                 Reporting crime*
                 Evenhandedness of security forces*
                 Security operations*
                 Party political identification

Section 6.   Civil liberties

Section 7.   Countryside and the environment

Section 8.   Housing (short)

Section 9.   Demographics and other classificatory variables

Self-completion questionnaire

Qs. 2.01-19 *ISSP* module: role of government
Qs. 2.20-21 Moral issues
Q. 2.22   Immigration
Q. 2.23   Death penalty
Qs. 2.24-26 Northern Ireland: crime and the police*
Qs. 2.27-34 Civil liberties
Qs. 2.35-42 Countryside and the environment
Q. 2.43   Left-Right scale
Q. 2.44   Liberal-Authoritan scale

---

*   These modules were asked in Northern Ireland only; all others were also asked in Britain.

L

SCPR
SOCIAL & COMMUNITY
PLANNING RESEARCH

Head Office: 35 NORTHAMPTON SQUARE,
LONDON EC1V 0AX Telephone 01-250 1866

Field and DP Office: BRENTWOOD, ESSEX
Northern Field Office: DARLINGTON, CO. DURHAM

Spring 1990

P.1090/Britain

BRITISH SOCIAL ATTITUDES:

1990 SURVEY

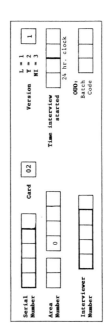

Serial
Number

Area
Number   0

Interviewer
Number

Card   02

Version   L = 1
           Y = 2
           NI = 3   1

Time interview
started
                24 hr. clock

OUO:
Batch
Code

Y & L   - 1 -

SECTION ONE

n = 2698
Qs. 1-23

[READPAP]

1.a) Do you normally read any daily morning newspaper at least 3 times a week?

%
Yes 68.1
No 31.9

IF YES [WHPAPER]
b) Which one do you normally read?
IF MORE THAN ONE ASK: Which one do you read most frequently?
ONE CODE ONLY

%
(Scottish) Daily Express 5.7
Daily Mail 7.8
Daily Mirror/Record 17.7
Daily Star 1.7
The Sun 13.8
Today 2.8
Daily Telegraph 4.3
Financial Times 0.6
The Guardian 2.7
The Independent 2.3
The Times 1.5
Morning Star 0.3
Other Irish/Northern Irish/Scottish regional or local daily morning paper (WRITE IN:) 4.4

Other (WRITE IN:) 0.3

More than one paper 2.1
(NA) 0.1

Y & L   - 2 -

n = 2698

2.a) ASK ALL [SUPPARTY]
Generally speaking, do you think of yourself as a supporter of any one political party?

%
Yes 50.9
No 48.9
(NA) 0.2

IF NO AT a) [CLOSEPTY]
b) Do you think of yourself as a little closer to one political party than to the others?

%
Yes 23.7
No 24.9
(NA) 0.6

IF NO AT b)
c) If there were a general election tomorrow, which political party do you think you would be most likely to support? CODE ONE ONLY UNDER c & d
IF ALLIANCE, PROBE: Liberal Democrat or SDP (Owen)?

IF YES AT a) OR b) [PTYALLEG]
d) Which one? CODE ONE ONLY UNDER c & d).
IF ALLIANCE, PROBE: Liberal Democrat or SDP (Owen)?

	n = 2698	c & d
	%	%
Conservative	23.0	34.9
Labour	22.8	38.6
(Social and) Liberal Democrat/Liberal/SLD	9.0	5.6
SDP/Social Democrat	9.6	2.1
Alliance (AFTER PROBE)		0.1
Scottish Nationalist		1.6
Plaid Cymru		0.5
Green Party/Ecology Party		2.5
Other party (WRITE IN)		0.2
Other answer (WRITE IN)		0.1
None		8.4
Refused/unwilling to say		3.0
(DK/NA)		2.4

IF ANY PARTY CODED AT c) & d) [LUSTRNG]
e) Would you call yourself very strong ... (QUOTE PARTY NAMED) ... fairly strong, or not very strong?

%
Very strong 10.9
Fairly strong 32.9
Not very strong 41.2
(Don't know) 0.3
(NA) 3.3

Y & L   - 3 -

n = 2698

ASK ALL   [CNTLCNCL]

3.a) Do you think that local councils ought to be controlled by central government more, less or about the same amount as now?

	%
More	20.3
Less	34.4
About the same	35.1
(Don't know)	10.0
(NA)	0.2

b) [RATES]
And do you think the level of local community charges - that is, the poll tax or rates - should be up to the local council to decide, or should central government have the final say?

	%
Local council	55.7
Central government	35.1
(Don't know)	8.5
(NA)	0.7

c) [RENTS]
How about the level of council rents? Should that be up to the local council to decide or should central government have the final say?

	%
Local council	75.5
Central government	14.9
(Don't know)	9.2
(NA)	0.5

4. Now a few questions about Britain's relationships with other countries. [EEC]

a) Do you think Britain should continue to be a member of the EC - the Common Market - or should it withdraw?

		%
EC:	Continue	75.9
	Withdraw	19.1
	(Don't know)	4.8
	(NA)	0.2

b) [NATO]
And do you think Britain should continue to be a member of NATO - the North Atlantic Treaty Organisation - or should it withdraw?

		%
NATO:	Continue	80.6
	Withdraw	10.4
	(Don't know)	8.9
	(NA)	0.1

Y & L   - 4 -

n = 2698

5. [NATION]
On the whole, do you think that Britain's interests are better served by ... READ OUT ...

	%
... closer links with Western Europe,	52.2
or - closer links with America?	18.4
(Both equally)	17.9
(Neither)	2.8
(Don't know)	8.7

6.a) [USANUKE]
Do you think that the siting of American nuclear missiles in Britain makes Britain a safer or a less safe place to live?

	%
Safer	35.1
Less safe	50.0
No difference	1.5
(Don't know)	13.0
(NA)	0.4

b) [OWNNUKE]
And do you think that having its own independent nuclear missiles makes Britain a safer or a less safe place to live?

	%
Safer	53.7
Less safe	32.6
(Don't know)	12.0
No difference	1.1
(NA)	0.6

7. CARD A   [UKNUCPOL]
Which, if either, of these two statements comes closest to your own opinion on Britain's nuclear policy?

	%
Britain should rid itself of nuclear weapons while persuading others to do the same	27.6
Britain should keep its nuclear weapons until it can persuade others to reduce theirs	69.1
(Neither of these)	2.7
(DK/NA)	0.6

8. [DEFPARTY]
Which political party's views on defence would you say comes closest to your own views?

CODE ONE ONLY

ONLY CODE ALLIANCE AFTER PROBE:
Liberal Democrats or SDP (Owen)?

	%
Conservative	39.8
Labour	23.9
(Social and) Liberal Democrat/Liberal/SLD	2.4
SDP/Social Democrat	1.2
Alliance (AFTER PROBE)	0.1
Other (WRITE IN:)	0.7
(Don't know)	26.1
None	3.7
Green Party	1.6
(NA)	0.4

Y & L   - 5 -

n = 2698

9. CARD B [PEACE]
    Which of the phrases on this card is closest to
    your opinion about threats to world peace?

	%
America is a greater threat to world peace than Russia	12.5
Russia is a greater threat to world peace than America	18.9
Russia and America are equally great threats to world peace	37.8
Neither is a threat to world peace	27.9
(Don't know)	2.7
(NA)	0.1

10.a) [NIRELAND]
    Do you think the long term policy for Northern
    Ireland should be for it ... READ OUT ...

	%
... to remain part of the United Kingdom,	28.7
or - to reunify with the rest of Ireland?	55.8
(Should be independent state)	0.6
(Up to Irish to decide)	4.1
(DK/NA)	9.9

b) Some people think that government policy towards
    Northern Ireland should include a complete with-
    drawal of British troops. Would you personally
    support or oppose such a policy? PROBE: Strongly
    or a little?
    [TROOPOUT]

	%
Support strongly	36.6
Support a little	23.3
Oppose strongly	17.7
Oppose a little	16.1
(Withdraw in the long term)	0.1
(Up to Irish to decide)	0.7
(OA)	0.2
(DK/NA)	5.3

11.a) [TROOPSHT]
    If British troops were withdrawn from Northern Ireland,
    do you think there would be more or less bloodshed in
    the short term, or would it make no difference?
    IF MORE/LESS: A lot (more/less) bloodshed or a little
    (more/less)?

	%
A lot more bloodshed	36.6
A little more bloodshed	20.6
A little less bloodshed	10.5
A lot less bloodshed	6.0
No difference	22.6
(DK/NA)	3.8

b) [TROOPLNG]
    And in the long term, if British troops were withdrawn,
    do you think there would be more or less bloodshed or
    would it make no difference?
    IF MORE/LESS: A lot (more/less) bloodshed or a little
    (more/less)?

	%
A lot more bloodshed	15.9
A little more bloodshed	12.6
A little less bloodshed	18.6
A lot less bloodshed	20.9
No difference	26.9
(DK/NA)	5.1

Y & L   - 6 -

n = 2698

SECTION TWO

Now I would like to ask you about two economic
problems - inflation and unemployment.

12. [PRICES]
    First, inflation: in a year from now, do you
    expect prices generally to have gone up, to
    have stayed the same, or to have gone down?
    IF GONE UP OR GONE DOWN:
    By a lot or a little?

	%
To have gone up by a lot	45.5
To have gone up by a little	39.5
To have stayed the same	7.9
To have gone down by a little	4.9
To have gone down by a lot	0.8
(Don't know)	1.2
(NA)	0.2

13. [UNEMP]
    Second, unemployment: in a year from now, do
    you expect unemployment to have gone up, to
    have stayed the same, or to have done down?
    IF GONE UP OR GONE DOWN:
    By a lot or a little?

	%
To have gone up by a lot	18.2
To have gone up by a little	28.8
To have stayed the same	34.1
To have gone down by a little	14.4
To have gone down by a lot	1.8
(Don't know)	2.4
(NA)	0.3

14.a) [UNEMPINF]
    If the government had to choose between
    keeping down inflation or keeping down
    unemployment, to which do you think it
    should give highest priority?

	%
Keeping down inflation	48.5
Keeping down unemployment	46.8
Other answer (WRITE IN:)	
Both equally	2.2
(DK/NA)	2.5

b) [CONCERN]
    Which do you think is of most concern
    to you and your family ... READ OUT ...

	%
... inflation,	70.4
or - unemployment?	26.2
Both equally	1.6
Other (WRITE IN:)	
(Don't know)	1.1
(NA)	0.3

Y & L
- 7 -

n = 2698

15. [INDUSTRY]
Looking ahead over the next year, do you think Britain's general industrial performance will improve, stay much the same, or decline?

IF IMPROVE OR DECLINE:
By a lot or a little?

	%
Improve a lot	3.0
Improve a little	15.6
Stay much the same	49.8
Decline a little	18.5
Decline a lot	6.7
(Don't know)	6.2
(NA)	0.2

16. Here are a number of policies which might help Britain's economic problems. As I read them out, will you tell me whether you would support such a policy or oppose it?
READ OUT ITEMS i)–x) AND CODE FOR EACH

			Support	Oppose	(DK/NA)
i)	[ECOHELP1]	Control of <u>wages</u> by law	%29.5	67.8	2.7
ii)	[ECOHELP2]	Control of <u>prices</u> by law	%56.1	41.6	2.3
iii)	[ECOHELP3]	Reducing the level of government spending on health and education.	% 8.2	90.6	1.2
iv)	[ECOHELP4]	Government controls to cut down goods from abroad	%72.4	24.2	3.4
v)	[ECOHELP5]	Increasing government subsidies for private industry	%56.3	37.3	6.4
vi)	[ECOHELP7]	Reducing government spending on defence	%64.5	32.2	3.3
vii)	[ECOHELP8]	Government schemes to encourage job sharing	%71.0	24.1	4.9
viii)	[ECOHELP9]	Government to set up construction projects to create more jobs	%83.2	14.2	2.6
ix)	[ECOHELPA]	Government action to cut interest rates	%88.7	7.5	3.7
x)	[ECOHELPB]	Government controls on hire purchase and credit	%81.8	14.7	3.5

17. [STATEOWN]
On the whole, would you like to see <u>more</u> or less state ownership of industry, or about the <u>same</u> amount as now?

	%
More	18.6
Less	24.3
About the same amount	53.2
(Don't know)	3.7
(NA)	0.2

18. [INCOMGAP]
Thinking of income levels generally in Britain today, would you say that the gap between those with high incomes and those with low incomes is ... **READ OUT** ...

	%
... too large,	80.5
about right,	14.9
or - too small?	2.5
(DK/NA)	2.1

Y & L
- 8 -

n = 2698

19. **CARD C**
Generally, how would you describe levels of taxation?
[TAXHI]
a) Firstly for those with <u>high</u> incomes? Please choose a phrase from this card. **RECORD ANSWER IN COL a) BELOW**
[TAXMID]
b) Next for those with <u>middle</u> incomes? Please choose a phrase from this card. **RECORD ANSWER IN COL b) BELOW**
[TAXLO]
c) And lastly for those with <u>low</u> incomes? Please choose a phrase from this card. **RECORD ANSWER IN COL c) BELOW**

	(a) High incomes	(b) Middle incomes	(c) Low incomes
Taxes are:	%	%	%
Much too high	3.5	2.7	26.6
Too high	9.5	24.8	49.5
About right	34.7	64.0	19.2
Too low	40.8	6.0	1.8
Much too low	8.9	0.1	0.7
(DK/NA)	2.7	2.3	2.2

20.a) [SHINC]
Among which group would you place yourself ... **READ OUT** ...

	%
... high income,	2.8
middle income,	53.4
or - low income?	42.6
(DK/NA)	1.2

b) **CARD D**
[HINCDIFF]
Which of the phrases on this card would you say comes closest to your feelings about your household's income these days?

	%
Living comfortably on present income	24.6
Coping on present income	50.9
Finding it difficult on present income	16.9
Finding it very difficult on present income	7.3
Other (**WRITE IN:**)	0.1
(DK/NA)	0.2

21. [HINCPAST]
Looking back over the last year or so, would you say your household's income has ... **READ OUT** ...

	%
... fallen behind prices,	52.3
kept up with prices,	
or - gone up by more than prices?	
(Don't know)	
(NA)	

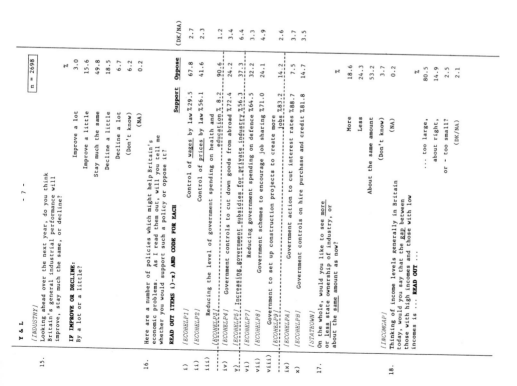

Y & L
- 9 -

		n = 2698 Qs. 22-23

[HINCXPCT]

22. And looking forward to the year ahead, do you expect your household's income will ...
READ OUT ...

	%
... fall behind prices,	49.9
keep up with prices,	38.3
or - go up by more than prices?	7.8
(Don't know)	3.8
(NA)	0.1

[RECONACT]
CARD E

23. Which of these descriptions applies to what you were doing last week, that is, in the seven days ending last Sunday? PROBE: Any others?
CODE ALL THAT APPLY IN COLUMN I
IF ONLY ONE CODE AT I, TRANSFER IT TO COLUMN II
IF MORE THAN ONE AT I, TRANSFER HIGHEST ON LIST TO II

	COL I	COL II ECONOMIC POSITION
		%
In full-time education (not paid for by employer, including on vacation)	A	2.8
On government training/employment scheme (eg. Employment Training, Youth Training Scheme, etc)	B	0.4
In paid work (or away temporarily) for at least 10 hours in week	C	54.9
Waiting to take up paid work already accepted	D	0.8
Unemployed and registered at a benefit office	E	3.2
Unemployed, not registered, but actively looking for a job	F	0.8
Unemployed, wanting a job (of at least 10 hrs per week) but not actively looking for a job	G	0.4
Permanently sick or disabled	H	2.4
Wholly retired from work	J	18.6
Looking after the home	K	15.7
Doing something else (WRITE IN:)	L	0.1

[HEMPLOYE]

24. IF IN PAID WORK OR AWAY TEMPORARILY (CODE 03 AT Q.23)
In your (main) job are you ... READ OUT ...

		n = 1480 Q. 24 only
		%
... an employee,		85.1
or - self employed?		14.9

Y & L
- 10 -

		n = 1260 Qs. 25-37

25. ALL EMPLOYEES (CODE 1 AT Q.24)
[ESRcBTIM]
In your present job, are you working ... READ OUT ...
RESPONDENT'S OWN DEFINITION

	%
... full-time,	79.8
or - part-time?	20.2

26. How many hours a week do you normally work in your (main) job?
(IF RESPONDENT CANNOT ANSWER, ASK ABOUT LAST WEEK)

ROUND TO NEAREST HOUR

[EcBHHOURS]

	MEDIAN:	3 9

[EcBHHRCAT]

	%
10-15 hours a week	5.5
16-23 hours a week	9.4
24-29 hours a week	4.5
30 or more hours a week	80.1
(DK/NA)	0.5

27.a) **[WAGENOW]**
How would you describe the wages or salary you are paid for the job you do - on the low side, reasonable, or on the high side? IF LOW: Very low or a bit low?

	%
Very low	9.8
A bit low	25.2
Reasonable	59.1
On the high side	5.5
Other answer (WRITE IN)	
(DK/NA)	0.4

b) **[PAYGAP]**
CARD F
Thinking of the highest and the lowest paid people at your place of work, how would you describe the gap between their pay, as far as you know? Please choose a phrase from this card.

	%
Much too big a gap	17.0
Too big	30.3
About right	41.2
Too small	2.7
Much too small a gap	0.2
(Don't know)	7.5
(NA)	1.0

- 11 -

Y & L

`n = 1260`

[WAGEXPECT]

28. If you stay in this job, would you expect your wages or salary over the coming year to ... **READ OUT** ...

	%
... rise by <u>more</u> than the cost of living,	16.4
rise by the <u>same</u> as the cost of living,	47.5
rise by <u>less</u> than the cost of living,	26.9
or – <u>not</u> to rise at all?	6.2
(Will not stay in job)	1.1
(Don't know)	1.7
(NA)	0.2

[NUMEMP]

29. Over the coming year do you expect your workplace will be ... **READ OUT** ...

	%
... increasing its number of employees,	22.8
reducing its number of employees,	24.7
or – will the number of employees stay about the same?	49.9
Other answer **(WRITE IN:)**	0.1
(DK/NA)	2.5

[LEAVEJOB]

30.a) Thinking now about your own job. How likely or unlikely is it that you will leave this employer over the next year for any reason? Is it ... **READ OUT** ...

	%
... very likely,	10.7
quite likely,	13.4
not very likely,	31.2
or – not at all likely?	44.4
(DK/NA)	0.3

IF VERY OR QUITE LIKELY AT a)

CARD G

b) Why do you think you will leave? Please choose a phrase from this card or tell me what other reason there is.

MORE THAN ONE CODE MAY BE RINGED

	%
[WHYG01] Firm will close down	1.4
[WHYG02] I will be declared redundant	2.3
[WHYG03] I will reach normal retirement age	1.1
[WHYG04] My contract of employment will expire	1.3
[WHYG05] I will take early retirement	0.8
[WHYG06] I will decide to leave and work for another employer	13.6
[WHYG07] I will decide to leave and work for myself, as self-employed	2.1
[WHYG010] I will leave to look after home/children/relative	1.8
Other answer **(WRITE IN:)** [WHYG08]	2.0
(DK/NA)	0.3

- 12 -

Y & L

`n = 1260`

[EUNEMP]

ASK ALL EMPLOYEES

31.a) During the last five years – that is since March 1985 – have you been unemployed and seeking work for any period?

	%
Yes	21.0
No	78.7
(NA)	0.2

[NUNEMP]

IF YES AT a)

b) For how many months in total during the last five years?

MEDIAN; MONTHS `0` `6`

[ESSELFEM]

ASK ALL EMPLOYEES

32.a) For any period during the last five years, have you worked as a self-employed person as your main job?

	%
Yes	5.0
No	94.7
(NA)	0.3

[ESSELFSEH]

IF NO AT a)

b) How seriously in the last five years have you considered working as a self-employed person ... **READ OUT** ...

	%
... very seriously,	5.4
quite seriously,	8.8
not very seriously,	13.7
or – not at all seriously?	63.9
(NA)	3.2

Y & L
   - 13 -

n = 1260

[PREFHOUR]
ASK ALL EMPLOYEES

33.a) Thinking about the number of hours you work each week including regular overtime, would you prefer a job where you worked ... READ OUT ...

	%
... more hours per week,	4.0
... fewer hours per week,	25.4
or - are you happy with the number of hours you work at present?	70.0
(Don't know)	0.7
(NA)	0.4

[MOREHOUR]
IF WOULD PREFER MORE HOURS PER WEEK (CODE 1 AT a)

b) Is the reason why you don't work more hours because ... READ OUT ...

	%
... your employer can't offer you more hours,	2.6
or - your personal circumstances don't allow it?	1.2
(Both)	0.2
Other reason (WRITE IN:)	-
(NA)	0.6

[FEWHOUR]
IF WOULD PREFER FEWER HOURS (CODE 2 AT Q.33a)

34.a) In which of these ways would you like your working hours to be shortened ... READ OUT ...

	%
... shorter hours each day,	9.3
or - fewer days each week?	15.7
Other (WRITE IN:)	0.2
(DK/NA)	0.8

[EARNHOUR]
b) Would you still like to work fewer hours if it meant earning less money as a result?

	%
Yes	5.9
No	18.6
It depends	0.8
(Don't know)	-
(NA)	0.7

Y & L
   - 14 -

n = 1260

ASK ALL EMPLOYEES
CARD H [EWRKARRA - EWRKARRL]

35. Please use this card to say whether any of the following arrangements are available to you, at your workplace... READ OUT a)-k) AND CODE ONE FOR EACH

	Not available- and I would not use it if it were	Not available- but I would use it if it were	Available- but I do not use it	Available- and I do use it	(Don't know)	(NA)
a) ...part-time working, allowing you to work less than the full working day?	%43.1	11.6	23.9	20.2	1.2	-
b) ...flexible hours, so that you can adjust your own daily working hours?	%25.3	42.8	6.8	23.7	0.8	0.5
c) ...job-sharing schemes, where part-timers share one full-time job?	%61.6	17.1	12.4	3.9	4.1	0.9
d) ...working from home at least some of the time?	%51.6	28.5	3.9	12.3	2.0	1.8
e) ...term-time contracts, allowing parents special time off during school holidays?	%52.7	26.6	6.0	5.5	7.2	2.0
f) ...nurseries provided by your employer for the young children of employees?	%66.0	24.8	4.5	0.2	3.5	1.0
g) ...arrangements by your employer for the care of children during school holidays?	%64.5	27.2	1.8	0.5	4.1	2.0
h) ...child care allowances towards the cost of child care?	%59.7	31.4	1.1	0.3	6.4	1.2

ASK WOMEN ONLY   n = 612

i) ...'career breaks', that is keeping women's jobs open for a few years so that mothers can return to work after caring for young children?	%36.9	27.6	18.1	4.9	9.3	2.8

ASK MEN ONLY   n = 648

j) ...paternity leave, allowing fathers extra leave when their children are born?	%32.3	30.2	16.0	10.0	10.2	1.1

ASK ALL EMPLOYEES

k) ...Any other arrangement to help people combine jobs and childcare? (PLEASE WRITE IN:)	%43.8	12.3	1.4	1.0	19.9	1.6
l) NEW CODE: Time off, either paid or unpaid, to care for sick children	% -	0.2	0.2	0.1	-	-
(None)	%20.0					

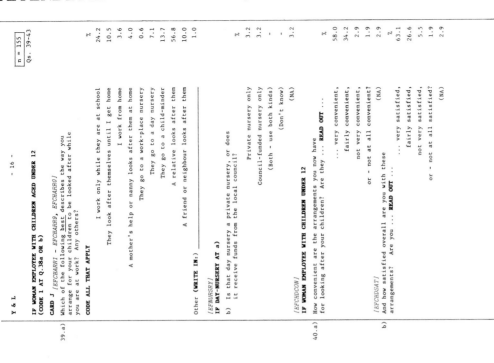

Y & L   - 16 -

		n = 155
		Qs. 39-43

IF WOMAN EMPLOYEE WITH CHILDREN AGED UNDER 12
(CODE 1 AT Q.38a OR b)

39.a) CARD J [EFCHARR1 - EFCHARR9, EFCHARRO]
Which of the following best describes the way you
arrange for your children to be looked after while
you are at work? Any others?

CODE ALL THAT APPLY

	%
I work only while they are at school	24.2
They look after themselves until I get home	10.5
I work from home	3.6
A mother's help or nanny looks after them at home	4.0
They go to a work-place nursery	0.6
They go to a day nursery	7.1
They go to a child-minder	13.7
A relative looks after them	56.8
A friend or neighbour looks after them	10.0
Other (WRITE IN:)	1.0

[EFNURSRY]
IF DAY-NURSERY AT a)

b) Is that day nursery a private nursery, or does
it receive funds from the local council?

	%
Private nursery only	3.2
Council-funded nursery only	3.2
(Both - use both kinds)	-
(Don't know)	-
(NA)	3.2

[EFCHDCON]
IF WOMAN EMPLOYEE WITH CHILDREN UNDER 12

40.a) How convenient are the arrangements you now have
for looking after your children? Are they ... **READ OUT** ...

	%
... very convenient,	58.0
fairly convenient,	34.2
not very convenient,	2.9
or - not at all convenient?	1.9
(NA)	2.9

[EFCHDSAT]
b) And how satisfied overall are you with these
arrangements? Are you ... **READ OUT** ...

	%
... very satisfied,	63.1
fairly satisfied,	26.6
not very satisfied,	5.5
or - not at all satisfied?	1.9
(NA)	2.9

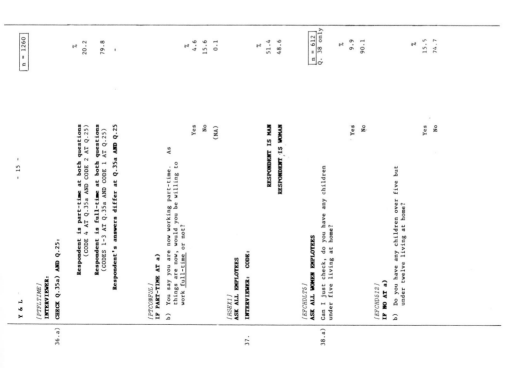

Y & L   - 15 -

		n = 1260

[PTFLTIME]
INTERVIEWER:
36.a) **CHECK Q.35a) AND Q.25:**

	%
Respondent is part-time at both questions (CODE 4 AT Q.35a AND CODE 2 AT Q.25)	20.2
Respondent is full-time at both questions (CODES 1-3 AT Q.35a AND CODE 1 AT Q.25)	79.8
Respondent's answers differ at Q.35a AND Q.25	-

[PTCONFUL]
IF PART-TIME AT a)

b) You say you are now working part-time. As
things are now, would you be willing to
work full-time or not?

	%
Yes	4.6
No	15.6
(NA)	0.1

[RSEX1]
ASK ALL EMPLOYEES
37. INTERVIEWER: CODE:

	%
RESPONDENT IS MAN	51.4
RESPONDENT IS WOMAN	48.6

[EFCHDLT5]
ASK ALL WOMEN EMPLOYEES

	n = 612
	Q. 38 only

38.a) Can I just check, do you have any children
under five living at home?

	%
Yes	9.9
No	90.1

[EFCHDS12]
IF NO AT a)

b) Do you have any children over five but
under twelve living at home?

	%
Yes	15.5
No	74.7

Y & L   - 17 -   n = 155

[EFCHDPR1, EFCHDPR2]
CARD K

41.   Suppose you could choose from any of the types of child-care
      on the card. Which would be your first choice for child-
      care while you are at work, and which would be your second
      choice? Please read the whole list before deciding.

      CODE ONE UNDER 'FIRST CHOICE'
      AND ONE UNDER 'SECOND CHOICE'

	First choice %	Second choice %
I would work only while they are at school	41.4	8.4
They would look after themselves until I got home	1.1	2.3
I would work from home	5.2	11.2
A mother's help or nanny would look after them at home	5.9	4.1
They would go to a work-place nursery	6.0	8.5
They would go to a council-funded day nursery	2.6	6.5
They would go to a private day nursery	1.3	4.5
They would go to a child-minder	3.2	5.6
A relative would look after them	29.9	26.5
A friend or neighbour would look after them	-	15.2
(Other)	0.8	4.6
(NA)	2.6	2.6

[EFPREWRK]

42.a) And if you did have the child-care arrangement
        of your choice, would you prefer to ... **READ OUT** ...

	%
... work more hours than now,	17.5
work fewer hours than now,	10.9
or - are you happy with the hours you work at present?	68.3
(Don't know)	0.6
(NA)	2.6

[RECONACE]
IF MORE HOURS AT a)

b) INTERVIEWER CHECK:

	%
Respondent works less than 30 hours a week (CODES 1, 2 OR 3 AT Q.26)	16.9
Respondent works 30+ hours a week (CODE 4 AT Q.26)	0.6
(NA)	3.2

[EFFTFULL]
IF CODE 1 AT b)

c) Do you think you might work full-time then,
    or not?

	%
Yes, might work full-time	11.2
No, would not	5.7
(Don't know)	-
(NA)	3.2

Y & L   - 18 -   n = 155

[EFSCFULL]
IF WOMAN EMPLOYEE WITH CHILDREN UNDER 12

43.   When all your children have gone to secondary school,
      which do you think you are most likely to do
      ... **READ OUT** ...

	%
... work full-time,	60.4
work part-time,	35.4
or - not have a paid job at all?	2.3
(NA)	1.9

n = 1260
Qs. 44-50

[EOLDRESP]
ASK ALL EMPLOYEES

44.a) Some people have responsibilities for looking
       after a disabled, sick, or elderly friend or
       relative. Is there anyone like this who depends
       on you to provide some regular care for them?

	%
Yes	8.9
No	90.8
(NA)	0.4

[EOLDAFHR]
IF YES AT a)

b) Does this responsibility ... **READ OUT** ...

	%
... prevent you from working longer hours in your job,	1.0
or - does it make no difference to your working hours?	7.8
(NA)	0.4

Y & L
- 19 -

n = 1260

ASK ALL EMPLOYEES

CARD L [WRKTEC1 - WRKTEC10]

Now I'd like to ask you about new technology at your workplace.

45.a) Which, if any, of these kinds of new technology are installed at your place of work? It doesn't matter whether you work with them or not, just tell me all that you know of at your workplace.

CODE ALL MENTIONED IN COL. a)

FOR EACH MENTIONED AT a) ASK b) [ETECWRK1 - ETECWRK8]
b) Do you yourself use, or does your own work involve the use of ... (ITEM MENTIONED AT a)?

CODE YES OR NO FOR EACH MENTIONED AT a)

	(a) At workplace	(b) Use/work with: YES	NO	(NA)
	%	%	%	%
Computer:				
Main frame computer	41.9	19.9	20.8	5.0
Telephone link to computer at another place	36.9	13.8	21.1	5.8
Micro/mini computer or computer network	44.4	23.8	19.4	5.0
Type of computer unknown	23.7	6.8	16.3	4.5
Word processor	56.6	20.2	34.0	6.2
Electronic memory typewriter	45.8	11.5	32.6	5.6
Computer controlled plant, machinery or equipment (including robots) used for design, assembly, handling, or production	22.1	8.2	12.8	4.9
Other new technology (WRITE IN)	5.9	3.4	1.5	4.8
One or more used at work		79.9%		
(NONE OF THESE)	15.8			
(Don't know)	3.6			

[ETECAFCT]
IF ANY NEW TECHNOLOGY AT WORKPLACE
(CODES 01-95 AT Q.45a)

46. Would you say that the use of new technology at your place of work has affected your own job ... READ OUT ...

	%
... for the better,	43.1
for the worse,	4.6
or - has it made no difference?	31.1
(DK)	0.4
(NA)	5.0

Y & L
- 20 -

n = 1260

47. Now thinking about all employees affected by new technology. Has new technology at your workplace generally meant ... READ OUT a)-c) AND CODE ONE FOR EACH

	More	Less	No Differ- ence	(Don't know)	(NA)
[TECHSKIL] a) ... that those affected by it have to work at a more or less skilled level, or has it made no difference?	% 37.0	6.3	30.9	5.0	5.0
[TECHRESP] b) ... that those affected by it have more or less responsibility in their work, or has it made no difference?	% 29.9	3.8	40.3	5.1	5.1
[TECHPAY] c) ... that those affected by it are paid more or less, or has it made no difference?	% 13.4	1.1	55.6	8.8	5.3

[TECHJOBS]
48.a) And has the use of new technology at your workplace meant that ... READ OUT ...

	%
... the organisation has increased the number of employees,	12.7
reduced the number of employees,	13.8
or - has it made no difference?	48.0
(Don't know)	4.6
(NA)	5.0

[TECHSAY]
b) And has the use of new technology at your workplace meant that those affected by it ... READ OUT ...

	%
... have more control over the pace of their work,	27.8
have less control over the pace of their work,	11.1
or - has it made no difference?	33.1
(Don't know)	7.0
(NA)	5.2

[TECHHWK]
c) And has the use of new technology at your workplace meant that those affected by it ... READ OUT ...

	%
... can work from home at least some of the time,	8.2
or - not?	65.8
(Don't know)	5.4
(NA)	4.9

Y & L — 21 —

n = 1260

[MPUNIONS]
ASK ALL EMPLOYEES

49.a) At your place of work are there unions, staff associations, or groups of unions recognised by the management for negotiating pay and conditions of employment?

	%
Yes	58.1
No	40.8
(NA)	1.1

[MPUNIONW]
IF YES AT a)

b) On the whole, do you think these unions or staff associations do their job well or not?

	%
Yes	35.2
No	19.5
(DK)	3.1
(NA)	1.4

[INDREL]
ASK ALL EMPLOYEES

50.a) In general how would you describe relations between management and other employees at your workplace ... READ OUT ...

	%
... very good	37.7
quite good,	44.4
not very good,	14.0
or - not at all good?	3.3
(DK/NA)	0.7

[WORKRUN]
b) And in general, would you say your workplace was ... READ OUT ...

	%
... very well managed,	25.6
quite well managed,	54.9
or - not well managed?	18.6
(DK/NA)	0.8

[SSRABPTIM]
ALL SELF-EMPLOYED (CODE 2 AT Q.24)

n = 221
Qs. 51-59

51. In your present job, are you working ... READ OUT ...

	%
... full-time,	83.0
or - part-time?	15.6
(NA)	1.4

RESPONDENT'S OWN DEFINITION

[SJBHOURS]
52. How many hours a week do you normally work in your (main) job?

(IF RESPONDENT CANNOT ANSWER, ASK ABOUT 'LAST WEEK')

ROUND TO NEAREST HOUR

MEDIAN: 4 5

[SJBHRCAT]
AND CODE:

	%
10-15 hours a week	5.3
16-23 hours a week	4.7
24-29 hours a week	2.6
30 or more hours a week	84.1
(DK)	0.5
(NA)	2.9

Y & L — 22 —

n = 221

[SUNEMP]
53. During the last 5 years - that is since March 1985 - have you been unemployed and seeking work for any period?

	%
Yes	19.0
No	80.5
(NA)	0.5

[SEMPLEE]
54. Have you, for any period in the last five years, worked as an employee as your main job rather than as self-employed?

	%
Yes	33.4
No	64.7
(NA)	1.9

[BUSIOK]
55. Compared with a year ago, would you say your business is doing ... READ OUT ...

	%
... very well,	10.1
quite well,	23.7
about the same,	44.4
not very well,	10.1
or - not at all well?	3.2
(Business not in existence then)	6.6
(NA)	1.9

[BUSIFUT]
56. And over the coming year, do you think your business will do ... READ OUT ...

	%
... better,	34.8
about the same,	43.9
or - worse than this year?	14.1
(Don't know)	0.5
Other (WRITE IN:)	4.9
(NA)	1.9

[SPARTNRS]
57. In your work or business, do you have any partners or other self-employed colleagues?

NOTE: DOES NOT INCLUDE EMPLOYEES

	%
Yes, have partner(s)	44.2
No	53.0
(NA)	2.8

[SNUMEMP]
58. And in your work or business do you have any employees, or not?

N.B. FAMILY MEMBERS MAY BE EMPLOYEES ONLY IF THEY RECEIVE A REGULAR WAGE OR SALARY.

	%
Yes, has employee(s)	33.4
No	65.1
(NA)	1.4

Y & L

- 23 -

n = 221

[RSEX2]
59. INTERVIEWER: CODE:

%
RESPONDENT IS MAN 74.7
RESPONDENT IS WOMAN 25.3

Q. 60 only   n = 56

[SFCHDLT5]
ASK ALL SELF-EMPLOYED WOMEN

60.a) Can I just check, do you have any children under five living at home?

%
Yes ... 13.7
No 86.3

[SFCHDS12]
IF NO AT a)

b) Do you have any children over five but under twelve living at home?

%
Yes ... 10.3
No 76.0

IF SELF-EMPLOYED WOMAN WITH CHILDREN AGED UNDER 12
(CODE 1 AT Q.60a OR b)

CARD J [SFCHARR1 - SFCHARR9, SFCHARR0]
61.a) Which of the following best describes the way you arrange for your children to be looked after while you are at work? Any others?

n = 13
Qs. 61-66

CODE ALL THAT APPLY

n
I work only while they are at school 5
They look after themselves until I get home 0
I work from home 8
A mother's help or nanny looks after them at home 4
They go to a workplace nursery 0
They go to a day nursery 0
They go to a child-minder 1
A relative looks after them 2
A friend or neighbour looks after them 0

Other (WRITE IN:) 0

[SFNURSY]
IF DAY-NURSERY AT a)

b) Is that day nursery a private nursery, or does it receive funds from the local council?

n
Private nursery only 0
Council-funded nursery only 0
(Both - use both kinds) 0
(Don't know) 0

Y & L

- 24 -

n = 13

[SFCHDCON]
IF SELF-EMPLOYED WOMAN WITH CHILDREN UNDER 12

62. How convenient are the arrangements you now have for looking after your children? Are they ... READ OUT ...

n
... very convenient, ... 8
fairly convenient, ... 4
not very convenient, ... 1
or - not at all convenient? 1

[SFCHDSAT]
63. And how satisfied overall are you with these arrangements? Are you ... READ OUT ...

n
... very satisfied, ... 7
fairly satisfied, ... 5
not very satisfied, ... 2
or - not at all satisfied? 0

[SFCHDPR1, SFCHDPR2]
CARD K
64. Suppose you could choose from any of the types of child-care on the card. Which would be your first choice for child-care while you are at work, and which would be your second choice? Please read the whole list before deciding.

CODE ONE UNDER 'FIRST CHOICE'
AND ONE UNDER 'SECOND CHOICE'

	First choice	Second choice
	n	n
I would work only while they are at school	4	2
They would look after themselves until I got home	0	0
I would work from home	3	2
A mother's help or nanny would look after them at home	1	1
They would go to a workplace nursery	0	0
They would go to a council-funded day nursery	2	0
They would go to a private day nursery	0	2
They would go to a child-minder	0	2
A relative would look after them	3	3
A friend or neighbour would look after them	0	1
(NONE OF THESE)		
(DK)	1	1

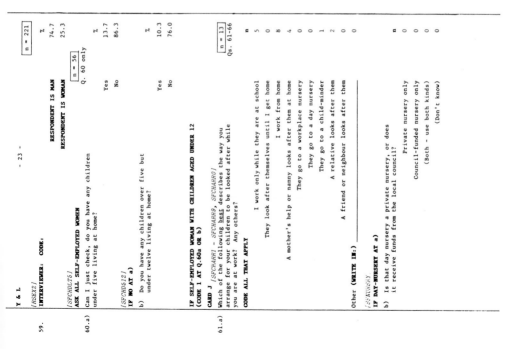

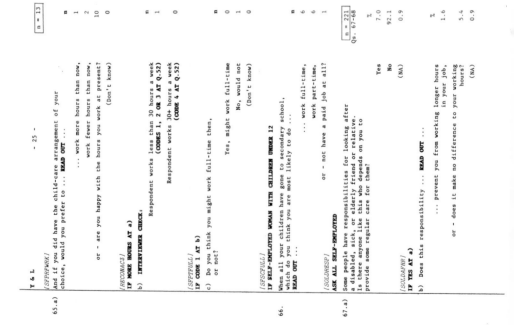

Y & L   - 25 -

[SPPREFWRK]
65.a) And if you did have the child-care arrangement of your choice, would you prefer to ... READ OUT ...

n = 13

	n
... work more hours than now,	1
work fewer hours than now,	2
or - are you happy with the hours you work at present?	10
(Don't know)	0

[RECOMAC3]
IF MORE HOURS AT a)
b) INTERVIEWER CHECK:

	n
Respondent works less than 30 hours a week (CODES 1, 2 OR 3 AT Q.52)	1
Respondent works 30+ hours a week (CODE 4 AT Q.52)	0

[SPPFFULL]
IF CODE 1 AT b)
c) Do you think you might work full-time then, or not?

	n
Yes, might work full-time	0
No, would not	1
(Don't know)	0

[SPSCFULL]
IF SELF-EMPLOYED WOMAN WITH CHILDREN UNDER 12
66. When all your children have gone to secondary school, which do you think you are most likely to do ... READ OUT ...

	n
... work full-time,	6
work part-time,	6
or - not have a paid job at all?	1

[SOLDRESP]
ASK ALL SELF-EMPLOYED
67.a) Some people have responsibilities for looking after a disabled, sick, or elderly friend or relative. Is there anyone like this who depends on you to provide some regular care for them?

n = 221
Qs. 67-68

	%
Yes	7.0
No	92.1
(NA)	0.9

[SOLDAFHR]
IF YES AT a)
b) Does this responsibility ... READ OUT ...

	%
... prevent you from working longer hours in your job,	1.6
or - does it make no difference to your working hours?	5.4
(NA)	0.9

Y & L   - 26 -

ASK ALL SELF-EMPLOYED
CARD L [STECWRK1 - STECWRK9]
68.a) Which, if any, of these kinds of new technology do you have or use in your work?
CODE ALL THAT APPLY

n = 221

	%
Computer: Telephone link to computer at another place	2.1
Main frame computer	6.5
Micro/mini computer or computer network	17.6
Type of computer unknown	2.6
Other: Word processor	15.6
Electronic memory typewriter	14.9
Computer-controlled plant, machinery, or equipment (including robots)	3.2
Other new technology (WRITE IN:)	1.4
(NONE OF THESE)	66.8

[STECAPCT]
IF ANY NEW TECHNOLOGY (CODES 01-95 AT a)
b) Would you say the use of new technology has affected your work ... READ OUT ...

n = 76
Q.69 only

	%
... for the better,	22.3
for the worse,	0.7
or - has it made no difference?	8.6
(NA)	1.6

[EDWORK10]
ALL IN FULL-TIME EDUCATION (CODE 01 AT Q.23)
69. And in the seven days ending last Sunday, did you have any paid work of less than ten hours a week?

n = 11
Q.70 only

	n
Yes	8
No	3

[GUNEMP]
ALL ON GOVERNMENT SCHEMES (CODE 02 AT Q.23)
70. During the last five years - that is since March 1985 - have you been unemployed and seeking work for any period?

	%
Yes	16.6
No	83.4

Y & L   - 27 -

71.a) [WWORK10]
ALL THOSE WAITING TO TAKE UP PAID WORK (CODE 04 AT Q.23)

n = 20
Q. 71 only

And in the seven days ending last Sunday, did you have any paid work of less than ten hours a week?

	n
Yes	1
No	19

b) [WWUNEMP]
During the last five years - that is since March 1985 - have you been unemployed and seeking work for any period?

	n
Yes	13
No	7

72.a) [UUNEMP1]
ALL UNEMPLOYED (CODES 05, 06, 07 AT Q.23)

n = 117
Qs. 72-75

In total how many months in the last five years - that is, since March 1985 - have you been unemployed and seeking work?

MEDIAN: [3][6] MONTHS

b) [CURUNEMP]
How long has this present period of unemployment and seeking work lasted so far?

MEDIAN: [2][4] MONTHS

73. [UWORK10]
And in the seven days ending last Sunday, did you have any paid work of less than ten hours a week?

	%
Yes	3.4
No	94.0
(NA)	2.6

74. [JOBQUAL]
How confident are you that you will find a job to match your qualifications ... READ OUT ...

	%
... very confident,	12.0
quite confident,	25.4
not very confident,	30.0
or - not at all confident?	29.9
(NA)	2.6

75.a) [UFINDJOB]
Although it may be difficult to judge, how long from now do you think it will be before you find an acceptable job?

MEDIAN: [0][3] MONTHS

	%
Never	14.8
(Don't know)	34.8
(NA)	4.1

b) [UJOBCHNC]
Do you think that there is a real chance now-adays that you will get a job in this area, or is there no real chance nowadays?

	%
Real chance	40.6
No real chance	54.6
(DK/NA)	4.8

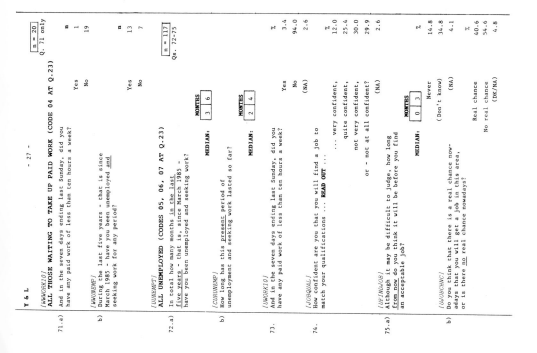

Y & L   - 28 -

76. [DWORK10]
ALL PERMANENTLY SICK OR DISABLED (CODE 08 AT Q.23)

n = 66
Q. 76 only

And in the seven days ending last Sunday, did you have any paid work of less than ten hours a week?

	%
Yes	-
No	100.0

77. [RWORK10]
ALL WHOLLY RETIRED FROM WORK (CODE 09 AT Q.23)

n = 501
Qs. 77-81

And in the seven days ending last Sunday, did you have any paid work of less than ten hours a week?

	%
Yes	2.7
No	96.8
(NA)	0.5

78. [EMPLPEN]
Do you (or does your husband/wife) receive a pension from any past employer?

	%
Yes	59.4
No	39.1
(NA)	1.5

79. [RETAGE]
(Can I just check) are you over (MEN:) 65 (WOMEN:) 60?

	%
Yes	91.2
No	8.6
(NA)	0.2

80.a) [RPENSION]
IF YES AT Q.79
On the whole would you say the present state pension is on the low side, reasonable, or on the high side?
IF 'ON THE LOW SIDE': Very low or a bit low?

	%
Very low	44.7
A bit low	29.5
Reasonable	15.4
On the high side	0.2
(DK/NA)	1.7

b) [RPEWINYR]
Do you expect your state pension in a year's time to purchase more than it does now, less, or about the same?

	%
More	1.4
Less	61.8
About the same	22.9
(Don't know)	
(NA)	3.8

81. [RETTRAGE]
IF NO AT Q.79
At what age did you retire from work?

MEDIAN: [5] YEARS

OR CODE: Never work...

Y & L

- 29 -

[IWORK10]
ALL LOOKING AFTER HOME (CODE 10 AT Q.23)

n = 423
Qs. 82-85

82.a) And in the seven days ending last Sunday, did you have any paid work of less than ten hours a week?

	%
Yes	9.9
No	89.9
(NA)	0.2

INCLUDE THOSE TEMPORARILY AWAY FROM A PAID JOB OF LESS THAN 10 HOURS A WEEK

[NOJOB1]+[NOJOB2]+[NOJOB3]
b) What are the main reasons you do not have a paid job (of more than 10 hours a week) outside the home? PROBE FULLY FOR MAIN REASONS AND RECORD VERBATIM

	%
Raising children	36.8
Retired/too old	16.7
Dependent relative	4.1
Prefer looking after home/family	18.6
'Poverty trap'	2.5
Already works (less than 10 hours a week)	2.3
No jobs available	1.8
Childcare costs	2.4
Unsuited for available jobs	2.3
Unpaid work/family business	0.7
Husband against working	0.7
Do volunteer work	1.8
(Other answer)	1.3
(DK)	0.1
Pregnancy/ill health	7.6
(NA)	20.7

[EVERJOB1]
83.a) Have you, during the last five years, ever had a full- or part-time job of 10 hours per week or more?

	%
Yes	33.1
No	66.2
(NA)	0.7

[EVERJOBT]
IF YES AT a)
b) How long ago was it that you left that job?

NO. OF MONTHS AGO

MEDIAN: | 2 | 4 |

[PTJOBSEH]
IF NO AT Q.83a)
84.a) How seriously in the past five years have you considered getting a full-time job?
... READ OUT ...

PROMPT, IF NECESSARY: FULL-TIME IS 30 HRS+ PER WEEK

	%
... very seriously,	2.1
quite seriously,	5.5
not very seriously,	6.0
or - not at all seriously?	52.4
(NA)	0.9

[PPJOBSEH]
IF NOT VERY OR NOT AT ALL SERIOUSLY AT a)
b) How seriously, in the past five years, have you considered getting a part-time job? ... READ OUT ...

	%
... very seriously,	1.5
quite seriously,	5.2
not very seriously,	7.5
or - not at all seriously?	44.1
(NA)	0.9

Y & L

- 30 -

85. ASK ALL LOOKING AFTER THE HOME [RECONACY]
INTERVIEWER CHECK:
RESPONDENT WORKS LESS THAN 10 HOURS A WEEK (CODE 1 AT Q.82a)

n = 423

	%
	9.9
ALL OTHERS	90.1

86. ASK THOSE LOOKING AFTER HOME AND WORKING LESS THAN 10 HOURS A WEEK
CARD H [TWRKARRA - TWRKARRL]
Please use this card to say whether any of the following arrangements are available to you, at your workplace ...

n = 42
Qs. 86-94

READ OUT a)-k) AND CODE ONE FOR EACH

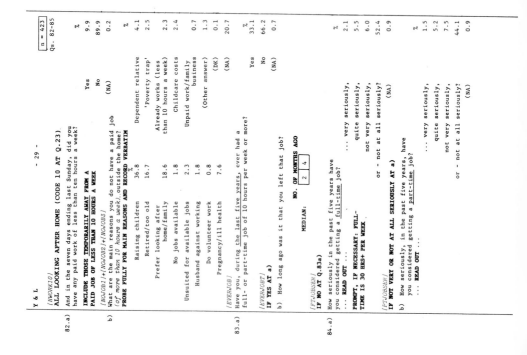

	Not available- and I would not use it if it were	Not available- but I would use it if it were	Available- but I do not use it	Available- and I do and I use it	(Don't know)	(NA)
a) ... part-time working, allowing you to work less than the full working day?	n 0	3	0	31	1	7
b) ... flexible hours, so that you can adjust your own daily working hours?	n 8	10	0	16	2	6
c) ... job-sharing schemes, where part-timers share one full-time job?	n 8	14	5	1	5	9
d) ... working from home at least some of the time?	n 21	8	2	4	2	6
e) ... term-time contracts, allowing parents special time off during school holidays?	n 7	4	6	14	3	8
f) ... nurseries provided by your employer for the young children of employees?	n 22	6	3	2	2	7
g) ... arrangements by your employer for the care of children during school holidays?	n 22	8	1	0	2	9
h) ... child-care allowances towards the cost of child care?	n 19	14	0	0	2	7
ASK WOMEN ONLY						
i) ... 'career breaks', that is keeping women's jobs open for a few years so that mothers can return to work after caring for young children?	n 15	12	4	0	3	8
ASK MEN ONLY						
j) ... paternity leave, allowing fathers extra leave when their children are born?	n 0	0	0	0	0	0
ASK ALL EMPLOYEES						
k) ... any other arrangement to help people combine jobs and childcare? (PLEASE WRITE IN:)	n 17	6	2	1	4	4
l) Time off, either paid or unpaid, to care for sick children NEW CODE	n 0	0	0	0	0	42
(None)	0	0	0	0	0	0

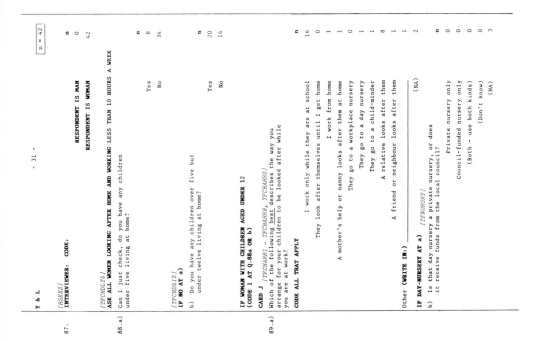

- 31 -

Y & L

[RSEX3]
INTERVIEWER: CODE:

	n = 42
RESPONDENT IS MAN	n
	0
RESPONDENT IS WOMAN	42

[TFCHDLT5]
ASK ALL WOMEN LOOKING AFTER HOME AND WORKING LESS THAN 10 HOURS A WEEK

88.a) Can I just check, do you have any children under five living at home?

	n
Yes	8
No	34

[TFCHDSI2]
IF NO AT a)

b) Do you have any children over five but under twelve living at home?

	n
Yes	20
No	14

IF WOMAN WITH CHILDREN AGED UNDER 12
(CODE 1 AT Q.88a OR b)

CARD J [TFCHARR1 - TFCHARR9, TFCHARRO]
89.a) Which of the following best describes the way you arrange for your children to be looked after while you are at work?
CODE ALL THAT APPLY

	n
I work only while they are at school	16
They look after themselves until I get home	0
I work from home	1
A mother's help or nanny looks after them at home	1
They go to a workplace nursery	0
They go to a day nursery	1
They go to a child-minder	1
A relative looks after them	8
A friend or neighbour looks after them	1
Other (WRITE IN:)	2

IF DAY-NURSERY AT a) [TFNURSRY]
b) Is that day nursery a private nursery, or does it receive funds from the local council?

	n
Private nursery only	0
Council-funded nursery only	0
(Both - use both kinds)	0
(Don't know)	0
(NA)	3

- 32 -

Y & L

[TFCHDCON]
IF WOMAN WITH CHILDREN UNDER 12

	n = 42

90.a) How convenient are the arrangements you now have for looking after your children? Are they ... **READ OUT** ...

	n
... very convenient,	22
fairly convenient,	3
not very convenient,	1
or - not at all convenient?	0
(NA)	2

[TFCHDSAT]
b) And how satisfied overall are you with these arrangements? Are you ... **READ OUT** ...

	n
... very satisfied,	23
fairly satisfied,	2
not very satisfied,	1
or - not at all satisfied?	0
(NA)	2

[TFCHDPR1, TFCHDPR2]
CARD K
91. Suppose you could choose from any of the types of child-care on the card. Which would be your first choice for child-care while you are at work, and which would be your second choice? Please read the whole list before deciding.
CODE ONE UNDER 'FIRST CHOICE' AND ONE UNDER 'SECOND CHOICE'

	First choice	Second choice
I would work only while they are at school	17	2
They would look after themselves until I got home	0	0
I would work from home	1	5
A mother's help or nanny would look after them at home	0	0
They would go to a work-place nursery	0	0
They would go to a council-funded day nursery	0	0
They would go to a private day nursery	0	2
They would go to a child-minder	0	9
A relative would look after them	6	5
A friend or neighbour would look after them	1	2
(NONE OF THESE)	0	3
(NA)	2	

[TFPRFWRK]
92.a) And if you did have the child-care arrangements of your choice, would you prefer to ... **READ OUT** ...

	n
... work more hours than now,	11
work fewer hours than now,	1
or - are you happy with the hours you work at present?	13
(Don't know)	0
(NA)	3

[TFPRFULL]
IF CODE 1 AT a)
b) Do you think you might work full-time then, or not?

	n
Yes, might work full-time	3
No, would not	8
(Don't know)	0
(NA)	3

Y & L - 33 - [n = 42]

[TFSCFULL]
IF WOMAN WITH CHILDREN UNDER 12

93. When all your children have gone to secondary school, which do you think you are most likely to do ... **READ OUT** ...

	n
... work full-time,	8
... work part-time,	17
or- not have a paid job at all?	0
(DK/NA)	3

[TOLDRESP]
IF LOOKING AFTER HOME AND WORKING UP TO 10 HOURS

94.a) Some people have responsibilities for looking after a disabled, sick, or elderly friend or relative. Is there anyone like this who depends on you to provide some regular care for them?

	n
Yes	5
No	35
(NA)	2

[TOLDAFHR]
IF YES AT a)

b) Does this responsibility ... **READ OUT** ...

	n
... prevent you from working longer hours in your job,	2
or - does it make no difference to your working hours?	3
(NA)	2

[HFCHDLT5]
IF LOOKING AFTER THE HOME AND NOT WORKING
(CODE 2 AT Q.85)

95.a) Can I just check, do you have any children under five living at home?

[n = 378]
Q. 95 only

	%
Yes	31.1
No	68.9

[HFCHDS12]
IF NO AT a)

b) Do you have any children over five but under twelve living at home?

	%
Yes	14.5
No	54.5

Y & L - 34 - [n = 173] Qs. 96-100

IF LOOKING AFTER HOME AND WITH CHILDREN AGED UNDER 12
(CODE 1 AT Q.95a OR b)
CARD M

96.a) Do you regularly use any of these childcare arrangements for your child or children during the day?

	%
YES: [HFCHARR4] A mother's help or nanny looks after them at home	0.6
[HFCHARR6] They go to a day-nursery	4.9
[HFCHARR7] They go to a child-minder	1.0
[HFCHARR8] A relative looks after them	1.7
[HFCHARR9] A friend or neighbour looks after them	2.3
[HFCHARR0] Other (**WRITE IN:**)	-
NO: NONE OF THESE	75.3
(NA)	3.8

[HFNURSRY]
IF DAY-NURSERY AT a)

b) Is that day-nursery a private nursery, or does it receive funds from the local council?

	%
Private nursery only	0.4
Council-funded nursery only	4.3
(Both - use both kinds)	-
(Don't know)	-
(NA)	3.9

[HFCHDCON]
IF LOOKING AFTER HOME AND USING CHILD-CARE REGULARLY
(CODES 1-7 AT Q.96)

97.a) How convenient are the arrangements you now have for looking after your children? Are they ... **READ OUT** ...

	%
... very convenient,	7.7
fairly convenient,	11.1
not very convenient,	1.6
or - not at all convenient?	0.6
(NA)	3.8

[HFCHDSAT]
b) And how satisfied overall are you with these arrangements? Are you ... **READ OUT** ...

	%
... very satisfied,	9.2
fairly satisfied,	9.3
not very satisfied,	2.0
or - not at all satisfied?	0.6
(NA)	3.8

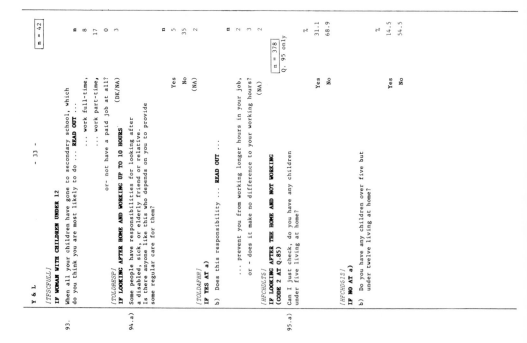

- 35 -

Y & L

IF LOOKING AFTER HOME AND WITH CHILDREN UNDER 12

CARD K [HFCHDPR1, HFCHDPR2]

98. Suppose you decided to take a job outside the home, and you could choose from any of the types of child-care on the card. Which would be your first choice for child-care while you were at work, and which would be your second choice? Please read through the whole list before deciding.

CODE ONE UNDER 'FIRST CHOICE'
AND ONE UNDER 'SECOND CHOICE'

n = 173

	First choice %	Second choice %
I would work only while they are at school	39.1	12.1
They would look after themselves until I got home	0.6	0.6
I would work from home	13.8	11.5
A mother's help or nanny would look after them at home	2.3	4.6
They would go to a workplace nursery	6.3	6.9
They would go to a council-funded day nursery	1.7	3.4
They would go to a private day nursery	1.7	5.7
They would go to a child-minder	5.2	4.6
A relative would look after them	15.5	15.5
A friend or neighbour would look after them	1.7	15.5
(NONE OF THESE)	6.9	13.8
(NA)	5.2	5.7

99. [HFPWCHOIC] And if you did have the child-care arrangement of your choice, would you prefer to ... READ OUT ...

	%
... work part-time,	51.9
work full-time,	12.6
or - would you choose not to work outside the home?	27.0
(Either full-time or part-time)	0.6
(Don't know)	3.4
(NA)	4.6

100. [HFSCFULL] When all your children have gone to secondary school, which do you think you are most likely to do ... READ OUT ...

	%
... work full-time,	37.4
work part-time,	43.1
or - not have a paid job at all?	13.8
(DK/NA)	5.8

101.a) [HOLDRESP] Some people have responsibilities for looking after a disabled, sick, or elderly friend or relative. Is there anyone like this who depends on you to provide some regular care for them?

n = 382 Q.101 only

	%
Yes	2.8
No	40.8
(NA)	56.4

[HOLDAFHR]
IF YES AT a)
b) Does this responsibility ... READ OUT ...

	%
... prevent you from getting a paid job,	1.3
or - would you not want a paid job anyway?	1.2
(NA)	56.7

- 36 -

Y & L
[HCHDLT12]
ALL LOOKING AFTER HOME
INTERVIEWER CHECK:

Respondent has children aged under 12
(CODE 1 AT Q.88a OR Q.88b OR Q.95a OR Q.95b)

n = 420 Q. 102a) only

	%
	47.7
All others	52.3

102a)

IF CODE 1 AT Q.102a)
CARD N [MUMWRK1 - MUMWRK8]
b) I am going to read out some reasons mothers of young children give for not working, or not working many hours. Please use this card to say how important each of these reasons is for you personally.

READ i)- viii) AND CODE
ONE FOR EACH

n = 200 Q. 102b) only

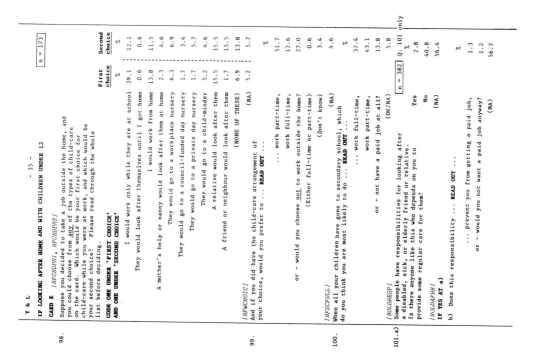

	Very important	Fairly important	Not very important	Not at all important	Does not apply to me	(DK/NA)
i) ... I enjoy spending time with my children more than working. %	73.0	17.6	3.9	0.5	1.7	3.2
ii) ... It's better for the children if I am home to look after them. %	75.7	18.3	2.6	0.0	0.7	2.7
iii) ... It would cost too much to find suitable child-care. %	35.3	21.8	11.0	8.1	20.5	3.7
iv) ... I cannot find the kind of childcare I would like. %	24.5	20.1	11.0	6.7	34.0	3.7
v) ... My life would be too difficult if I had to combine child-care and paid work. %	28.0	23.2	14.0	10.9	20.2	3.7
vi) ... My husband or partner would not want me to work. %	22.9	13.7	14.4	19.4	26.5	3.2
vii) ... I cannot find the kind of work I want with suitable hours. %	36.2	15.5	9.0	6.7	29.8	2.7
viii) ... I cannot find the kind of work I want near my home. %	27.1	20.5	9.3	9.4	29.8	3.7

103. [2WORK10] ALL DOING SOMETHING ELSE (CODE 11 AT Q.23) And in the seven days ending last Sunday, did you have any paid work of less than 10 hours a week?

n = 4 Q.103 only

	n
Yes	0
No	4

SECTION THREE (page - 37 -)

Y & L

n = 2698
Qs. 104-112

[SPEND1, SPEND2]
ASK ALL
CARD O

104. Here are some items of government spending. Which of them, if any, would be your highest priority for extra spending? And which next? Please read through the whole list before deciding.

ONE CODE ONLY IN EACH COLUMN

	1st Priority	2nd Priority
	%	%
Education	24.0	35.8
Defence	0.7	1.2
Health	55.5	25.0
Housing	6.5	13.1
Public transport	1.8	3.7
Roads	1.1	3.2
Police and prisons	1.9	4.6
Social security benefits	4.8	7.7
Help for industry	2.5	3.5
Overseas aid	0.0	0.7
(NONE OF THESE)	0.1	0.2
(Don't know)	0.3	0.5
(NA)	0.7	0.7

[SOCBEN1, SOCBEN2]
CARD P

105. Thinking now only of the government's spending on social benefits like those on the card. Which, if any, of these would be your highest priority for extra spending? And which next?

ONE CODE ONLY IN EACH COLUMN

	1st Priority	2nd Priority
	%	%
Retirement pensions	42.3	23.0
Child benefits	17.0	15.0
Benefits for the unemployed	8.3	13.1
Benefits for disabled people	23.9	35.1
Benefits for single parents	6.7	11.0
(NONE OF THESE)	0.6	1.0
(Don't know)	0.5	1.1
(NA)	0.7	0.7

(page - 38 -)

Y & L

n = 2698

106. I will read two statements. For each one please say whether you agree or disagree. Strongly or slightly?

[FALSECLM]
a) Large numbers of people these days falsely claim benefits. **RECORD IN COLUMN a)**

[FAILCLM]
b) Large numbers of people who are eligible for benefits these days fail to claim them. **RECORD IN COLUMN b)**

	(a) Falsely claim	(b) Fail to claim
	%	%
Agree strongly	44.3	49.3
Agree slightly	25.0	34.4
Disagree slightly	11.5	6.9
Disagree strongly	11.5	2.9
(Don't know)	7.5	6.2
(NA)	0.2	0.4

[DOLE]

107. Opinions differ about the level of benefits for the unemployed. Which of these two statements comes closest to your own ... **READ OUT** ...

	%
... benefits for the unemployed are too low and cause hardship	50.0
OR - benefits for the unemployed are too high and discourage people from finding jobs?	28.8
(Neither)	8.0
Other (**WRITE IN:**)	1.3
(Don't know)	7.2
(NA)	0.5
(Both)	3.5
(About right)	0.6

[TAXSPEND]
CARD Q

108. Suppose the government had to choose between the three options on this card. Which do you think it should choose?

	%
Reduce taxes and spend _less_ on health, education and social benefits	3.2
Keep taxes and spending on these services at the _same_ level as now	37.3
Increase taxes and spend _more_ on health, education and social benefits	54.3
(None)	2.9
(Don't know)	2.0
(NA)	0.2

[NHSSAT]
CARD R

109. All in all, how satisfied or dissatisfied would you say you are with the way in which the National Health Service runs nowadays? Choose a phrase from this card.

	%
Very satisfied	6.6
Quite satisfied	30.4
Neither satisfied nor dissatisfied	15.1
Quite dissatisfied	27.1
Very dissatisfied	20.3
(DK)	0.3
(NA)	0.2

Y & L   - 39 -   n = 2698

CARD R AGAIN

110. From your own experience, or from what you have heard, please say how satisfied or dissatisfied you are with the way in which each of these parts of the National Health Service runs nowadays.

READ OUT i-vi BELOW AND RING ONE CODE FOR EACH

	Very satisfied	Quite satisfied	Neither satisfied nor dissatisfied	Quite dissatisfied	Very dissatisfied	(DK/NA)
[GPSAT] i) First, local doctors/GPs? %	31.3	48.8	7.9	8.6	2.8	0.5
[DENTSAT] ii) National Health Service dentists? %	20.0	48.5	17.4	7.7	3.0	3.3
[HVSAT] iii) Health visitors? %	11.7	31.1	34.9	5.2	2.6	14.4
[DNSAT] iv) District nurses? %	17.5	33.4	31.8	2.7	1.0	13.5
[INPATSAT] v) Being in hospital as an inpatient? %	23.8	39.0	18.8	10.7	4.4	3.2
[OUTPATSAT] vi) Attending hospital as an outpatient? %	14.4	36.6	17.9	18.3	10.0	2.9

[PRIVMED]

111.a) Are you covered by a private health insurance scheme, that is an insurance scheme that allows you to get private medical treatment? For example: BUPA and PPP.

	%
Yes	16.9
No	82.6
(DK/NA)	0.5

[PRIVPAID]

IF YES AT a)

b) Does your employer *(or your husband's/wife's employer)* pay the majority of the cost of membership of this scheme?

	%
Yes	8.9
No	7.6
(Don't know)	0.3
(NA)	0.6

[NHSLIMIT]

ASK ALL

112. It has been suggested that the National Health Service should be available only to those with lower incomes. This would mean that contributions and taxes could be lower and most people would then take out medical insurance or pay for health care. Do you support or oppose this idea?

	%
Support	22.1
Oppose	73.0
(Don't know)	4.3
(NA)	0.6

<u>Note</u>: Question L113-L115 were asked as Y118-Y120 in Section 5 in the Y version of the questionnaire.

Y & L   - 40L -
                    - 42Y -

SECTION FOUR

[RELIGION]

ASK ALL

(113.a) Do you regard yourself as belonging to any particular religion? IF YES: Which?

CODE ONE ONLY - DO NOT PROMPT

n = 2698
Qs. L113-L115 (Y118-Y120)

	%
No religion	36.3
Christian - no denomination	2.4
Roman Catholic	8.9
Church of England/Anglican	37.5
Baptist	1.1
Methodist	3.5
Presbyterian/Church of Scotland	4.3
Free Presbyterian	0.1
Brethren	0.0
United Reform Church (URC)/Congregational	0.6
Other Protestant (**WRITE IN:**)	1.5
Other Christian (**WRITE IN:**)	0.4
Hindu	0.5
Jewish	0.9
Islam/Muslim	0.9
Sikh	0.3
Buddhist	0.1
Other non-Christian (**WRITE IN:**)	0.3
Refused/unwilling to say	0.0
(NA)	0.5

[RELIGFAM]

IF NO RELIGION (CODE 01 AT a)

b) In what religion were you brought up? **PROBE IF NECESSARY:** What was your family's religion?

	%
No religion	4.4
Christian - no denomination	1.2
Roman Catholic	3.8
Church of England/Anglican	21.2
Baptist	0.5
Methodist	1.9
Presbyterian/Church of Scotland	2.1
Free Presbyterian	0.1
Brethren	-
United Reform Church (URC)/Congregational	0.2
Other Protestant (**WRITE IN:**)	0.5
Other Christian (**WRITE IN:**)	0.0
Hindu	0.0
Jewish	0.1
Islam/Muslim	0.1
Sikh	-
Buddhist	0.1
Other non-Christian (**WRITE IN:**)	-
Refused/unwilling to say	0.0

Y & L
- 41L -
- 43Y -

n = 1353

[ATTENDCH]
IF ANY RELIGION AT a) OR b)

114. Apart from such special occasions as weddings, funerals and baptisms, how often nowadays do you attend services or meetings connected with your religion?

	%
PROBE AS NECESSARY　Once a week or more	11.7
Less often but at least once in two weeks	3.0
Less often but at least once a month	6.3
Less often but at least twice a year	12.9
Less often but at least once a year	6.9
Less often	5.9
Never or practically never	47.2
Varies too much to say	0.6
Refused/unwilling to answer	0.1
(NA)	1.0

ASK ALL

CARD S　[RACEORIG]

115. To which of these groups do you consider you belong?

CODE ONE ONLY

	%
Black:　of African or Caribbean or other origin	1.2
Asian:　of Indian origin	1.1
of Pakistani origin	0.7
of Bangladeshi origin	-
of Chinese origin	0.1
of other origin　(WRITE IN)	0.2
White:　of British origin	92.5
of Irish origin	2.1
of other origin　(WRITE IN)	1.8
Refused	0.0
(NA)	0.3

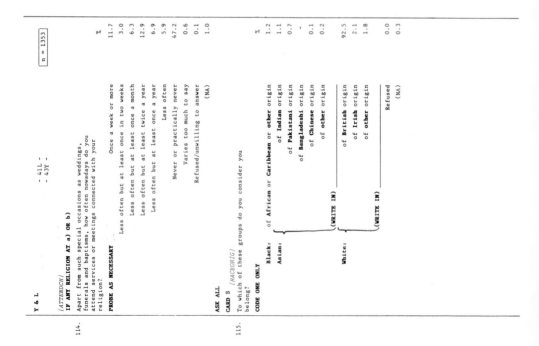

L
- 42L -

n = 1353
Qs. L116-L151

Now I would like to ask you some questions about racial prejudice in Britain.　[PREJAS]

116 a) First, thinking of Asians - that is, people whose families were originally from India and Pakistan - who now live in Britain. Do you think there is a lot of prejudice against them in Britain nowadays, a little, or hardly any?

	%
A lot	56.5
A little	32.8
Hardly any	7.1
(Don't know)	3.2
(NA)	0.4

[PREJBLK]

b) And black people - that is people whose families were originally from the West Indies or Africa - who now live in Britain. Do you think there is a lot of prejudice against them in Britain nowadays, a little, or hardly any?

	%
A lot	47.9
A little	39.1
Hardly any	9.0
(Don't know)	3.5
(NA)	0.5

[PREJNOW]

c) Do you think there is generally more racial prejudice in Britain now than there was 5 years ago, less, or about the same amount?

	%
More now	31.9
Less now	19.8
About the same	45.3
Other answer (WRITE IN:)	0.1
(DK/NA)	2.9

[PREJFUT]

d) Do you think there will be more, less or about the same amount of racial prejudice in Britain in 5 years time compared with now?

	%
More in 5 years	36.6
Less	19.9
About the same	38.8
Other answer (WRITE IN:)	0.3
(DK/NA)	4.5

[SRPREJ]

e) How would you describe yourself: ... READ OUT ...

	%
... as very prejudiced against people of other races,	3.7
a little prejudiced,	31.7
or - not prejudiced at all?	63.5
Other answer (WRITE IN:)	0.2
(DK/NA)	1.0

L   - 43L -

n = 1353

%

117a) [ASJOB]
On the whole, do you think people of Asian origin in Britain are not given jobs these days because of their race ... **READ OUT** ...

... a lot, 14.3
a little, 40.9
or - hardly at all? 35.4
(Don't know) 8.9
(NA) 0.6

b) [WIJOB]
And on the whole, do you think people of West Indian origin in Britain are not given jobs these days because of their race ... **READ OUT** ...

%

... a lot, 20.1
a little, 41.6
or - hardly at all? 30.0
(Don't know) 7.8
(NA) 0.6

118a) [RACELAW]
There is a law in Britain against racial discrimination, that is against giving unfair preference to a particular race in housing, jobs and so on. Do you generally support or oppose the idea of a law for this purpose?

%

Support 68.4
Oppose 28.5
(DK) 2.5
(NA) 0.6

b) [IMMHELP]
Do you think, on the whole, that Britain gives too little or too much help to Asians and West Indians who have settled in this country, or are present arrangements about right?

%

Too little 9.5
Present arrangements right 51.4
Too much 32.1
Other answer (**WRITE IN.**) 0.2
(DK) 6.4
(NA) 0.5

L   - 44L -

n = 1353

119. IF INTERVIEWING IN ENGLAND OR WALES, ASK ABOUT **"BRITAIN"**
IF INTERVIEWING IN SCOTLAND, ASK ABOUT **"SCOTLAND"**

[DIVORCE]
Do you think that divorce in (Britain/Scotland) should be ... **READ OUT** ...

%

... easier to obtain than it is now, 10.9
more difficult, 32.5
or - should things remain as they are? 51.4
(Don't know) 5.0
(NA) 0.2

120. [SEXLAW]
There is a law in Britain against sex discrimination, that is against giving unfair preference to men - or to women - in employment, pay and so on. Do you generally support or oppose the idea of a law for this purpose?

%

Support 80.0
Oppose 16.7
(DK) 2.8
(NA) 0.5

121. CARD T
Now I would like to ask you some questions about sexual relationships.

a) [PMS]
If a man and a woman have sexual relations before marriage, what would your general opinion be? Please choose a phrase from this card. **RECORD IN COL a)**

b) [EXMS]
What about a married person having sexual relations with someone other than his or her partner? Please choose a phrase from this card. **RECORD IN COL b)**

c) [HOMOSEX]
What about sexual relations between two adults of the same sex? Please choose a phrase from this card. **RECORD IN COL c)**

	(a) BEFORE MARRIAGE	(b) EXTRA MARITAL	(c) SAME SEX
	%	%	%
Always wrong	12.5	56.3	57.5
Mostly wrong	9.6	28.5	11.0
Sometimes wrong	20.3	9.8	8.2
Rarely wrong	8.7	1.0	4.3
Not wrong at all	45.2	1.5	14.6
(Depends/varies)	2.9	1.7	3.2
(DK)	0.1	0.3	0.6
(NA)	0.7	0.9	0.7

L   - 45L -

n = 1353

122. Now I would like you to tell me whether, in your opinion, it is acceptable for a homosexual person ... ... READ OUT a)-c) AND CODE ONE FOR EACH ...

%

a) [GAYTEASC]
... to be a teacher in a school?
Yes 44.2
No 49.0
(Depends on person) 1.1
(DK/NA) 3.6

Other answer (WRITE IN:) 2.4

%

b) [GAYTEAHE]
... to be a teacher in a college or university?
Yes 53.1
No 41.7
(Depends on person) 0.4
(DK/NA) 2.5

Other answer (WRITE IN:) 2.2

%

c) [GAYPUB]
... to hold a responsible position in public life?
Yes 56.7
No 38.3
(Depends on person) 0.9
(DK/NA) 1.7

Other answer (WRITE IN:) 2.4

[HOMOMEAN]
What did you understand the word "homosexual" to mean at this question: ... READ OUT ...

%

... men only - that is, gays, 24.0
women only - that is, lesbians, 0.3
or - either? 74.9
(DK/NA) 0.7

123-a) [FGAYADPT]
Do you think female homosexual couples - that is, lesbians - should be allowed to adopt a baby under the same conditions as other couples?

%

Yes 17.4
No 79.5
(Depends on person) 0.1
(DK) 0.7
(NA) 2.0

Other answer (WRITE IN:) 0.2

b) [MGAYADPT]
And do you think male homosexual couples - that is, gays - should be allowed to adopt a baby under the same conditions as other couples?

%

Yes 9.9
No 87.5
(Depends on person) 0.1
(DK) 0.3
(NA) 2.0

Other answer (WRITE IN:) 0.2

L   - 46L -

n = 1353

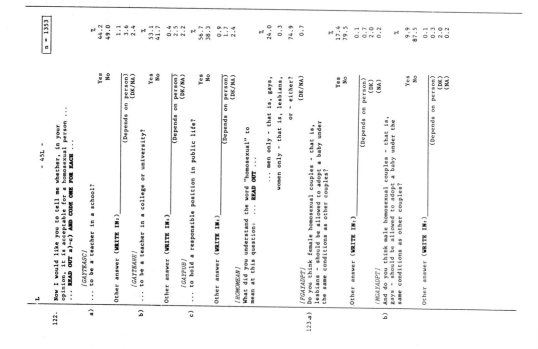

SECTION FIVE

124 a) [VICTIM]
Now some questions about crime. Do you ever worry about the possibility that you or anyone else who lives with you might be the victim of crime?

%

Yes 75.6
No 24.3
(NA) 0.1

[VMWORRY]
IF YES AT a)
b) Is this ... READ OUT ...

%

... a big worry, 17.1
a bit of a worry, 35.2
or - an occasional doubt? 23.2
(NA) 0.2

125 [SAFEDARK]
ASK ALL
How safe do you feel walking alone in this area after dark ... READ OUT ...

%

... very safe, 21.5
fairly safe, 37.6
a bit unsafe, 23.5
or - very unsafe? 15.9
(DK/NA) 1.4

126 a) [BURGLARY]
How common is it for people's homes to be burgled in this area ... READ OUT ...

%

... very common, 12.3
fairly common, 32.5
not very common, 41.2
or - not at all common? 9.5
(Don't know) 4.3
(NA) 0.2

b) [VANDAL]
How common is deliberate damage done by vandals in this area ... READ OUT ...

%

... very common, 14.3
fairly common, 26.9
not very common, 43.8
or - not at all common? 12.5
(Don't know) 2.4
(NA) 0.1

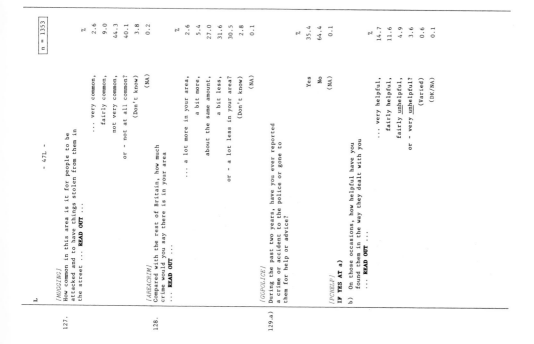

L   - 47L -   n = 1353

%

127. [MUGGING]
How common in this area is it for people to be attacked and to have things stolen from them in the street ... **READ OUT** ...

... very common,	2.6
fairly common,	9.0
not very common,	44.3
or - not at all common?	40.1
(Don't know)	3.8
(NA)	0.2

%

128. [AREACRIM]
Compared with the rest of Britain, how much crime would you say there is in your area ... **READ OUT** ...

... a lot more in your area,	2.6
a bit more,	5.4
about the same amount,	27.0
a bit less,	31.6
or - a lot less in your area?	30.5
(Don't know)	2.8
(NA)	0.1

%

129.a) [GOPOLICE]
During the past two years, have you ever reported a crime or accident to the police or gone to them for help or advice?

Yes	35.4
No	64.4
(NA)	0.1

[PCHELP]
IF YES AT a)
b) On those occasions, how helpful have you found them in the way they dealt with you ... **READ OUT** ...

%

... very helpful,	14.7
fairly helpful,	11.6
fairly unhelpful,	4.9
or - very unhelpful?	3.6
(Varied)	0.6
(DK/NA)	0.1

L   - 48L -   n = 1353

[PCSTOP]
ASK ALL
130.a) During the past two years, have you ever been stopped or asked questions by the police about an offence which they thought had been committed?

%

Yes	15.9
No	84.0
(NA)	0.1

[PCPOLITE]
IF YES AT a)
b) On those occasions, how polite have you found them when they approached you ... **READ OUT** ...

%

... very polite,	8.5
fairly polite,	4.1
fairly _impolite_,	1.3
or - very _impolite_?	1.5
(Varied)	0.3
(NA)	0.1

[PCANNOY]
ASK ALL
131. During the past two years, have you been really annoyed about the way a police officer behaved towards you, or someone you know, or about the way the police handled a matter in which you were involved?

%

Yes	16.7
No	83.1
(NA)	0.2

[PCPLEASE]
132. During the last two years, have you been really pleased about the way a police officer behaved towards you, or someone you know, or about the way the police handled a matter in which you were involved?

%

Yes	30.2
No	68.8
(DK/NA)	0.9

[PCSAT]
CARD V
133. In general, how satisfied or dissatisfied are you with the way the police in Britain do their job? Choose a phrase from the card.

%

Very satisfied	19.4
Quite satisfied	51.9
Neither satisfied nor dissatisfied	14.6
Not very satisfied	12.2
Not at all satisfied	1.7
(DK/NA)	0.2

[PCCONTCT]
134. May I just check, have you, or someone you know, had any contact at all with the police in the past _two years_?

%

Yes	54.5
No	45.0
(NA)	0.6

L   - 50L -

n = 1353

CARD Y

137. All governments keep certain things secret. For each of the following, use this card to say whether you think British governments should or should not be allowed to keep it secret.

READ OUT a)-c) AND CODE ONE FOR EACH

[NUCTELL]
a) ... Suppose there was a minor leak of radiation from a nuclear power station which was unlikely to have harmed anyone. Should the government be allowed to keep it secret or not?

	%
Definitely allowed to keep it secret	9.6
Probably allowed	15.9
Probably not allowed	16.4
Definitely not allowed to keep it secret	56.9
(Don't know)	0.7
(NA)	0.5

[WEAPTELL]
CARD Y AGAIN
b) ... Suppose the government decided to start developing a new weapons system. Should the government be allowed to keep it secret or not?

	%
Definitely allowed to keep it secret	26.0
Probably allowed	22.0
Probably not allowed	15.1
Definitely not allowed to keep it secret	34.3
(Don't know)	2.2
(NA)	0.5

[CABMTELL]
CARD Y AGAIN
c) ... Suppose a cabinet minister was asked to resign for having used his position to make a lot of money. Should the government be allowed to keep the reason secret or not?

	%
Definitely allowed to keep it secret	3.3
Probably allowed	3.9
Probably not allowed	15.9
Definitely not allowed to keep it secret	74.9
(Don't know)	1.5
(NA)	0.5

L   - 49L -

SECTION SIX

n = 1353

CARD W

135. Some countries are called 'free societies' because their citizens' basic rights are protected. Please use this card to say how well-protected you think citizens' basic rights are in each of the following countries. Just say what you think.

READ NAME OF EACH COUNTRY AND CODE ONE FOR EACH

Citizens' basic rights are:

		Very well protected	Fairly well protected	Not very well protected	Not at all well protected	(Don't know/ Can't say)	(NA)
a)	[USAFREE] ... the USA?	26.2	46.6	10.8	0.9	15.2	0.3
b)	[WGFREE] ... West Germany?	25.8	44.0	7.3	0.7	21.8	0.4
c)	[USSRFREE] ... the Soviet Union?	2.3	7.7	47.7	23.3	18.4	0.5
d)	[BRITFREE] ... Britain?	19.5	65.2	9.3	1.8	3.8	0.4
e)	[CHINAFREE] ... China?	1.3	7.7	29.8	37.3	23.4	0.4
f)	[CANFREE] ... Canada?	27.1	50.5	1.7	0.1	20.4	0.3

CARD X

136. Some countries are called 'open societies' because their citizens have a right to know what decisions the government is making and why. Please use this card to say how 'open' you think each of the following countries is. Again, just say what you think.

READ NAME OF EACH COUNTRY AND CODE ONE FOR EACH

Government is:

		Very open	Fairly open	Not very open	Not at all open	(Don't know/ Can't say)	(NA)
a)	[USACPEN] ... the USA?	27.8	48.0	11.5	1.1	11.2	0.3
b)	[WGOPEN] ... West Germany?	9.8	51.2	17.5	1.8	19.3	0.3
c)	[USSROPEN] ... the Soviet Union?	0.8	6.7	43.3	35.2	13.6	0.4
d)	[BRITOPEN] ... Britain?	13.0	57.6	21.7	3.1	4.1	0.5
e)	[CHINAOPEN] ... China?	0.6	6.4	28.5	44.2	19.7	0.6
f)	[CANOPEN] ... Canada?	16.3	56.0	5.7	0.3	21.3	0.3

L   - 51L -   [n = 1353]

[PAPRGOVT]
CARD Z

138 a) Suppose a person leaked secret defence plans to a newspaper, and the government wanted to find out who it was. Using the card, tell me whether you think the paper should have the legal right to keep the person's name secret, or not?

	%
Definitely should have the legal right	16.2
Probably should	17.1
Probably should <u>not</u> have the legal right	20.5
Definitely should <u>not</u> have the legal right	43.0
(Don't know/Can't say)	2.7
(NA)	0.4

[PAPRFIRM]
CARD Z AGAIN

b) Now suppose a person leaked secret plans about a new commercial invention, and the firm wanted to find out who it was. Do you think the paper <u>should</u> have the legal right to keep the person's name secret, or not?

	%
Definitely should have the legal right	15.3
Probably should	21.4
Probably should <u>not</u> have the legal right	24.9
Definitely should <u>not</u> have the legal right	34.4
(Don't know/Can't say)	3.5
(NA)	0.5

[BANBOOK]
CARD AA

139 a) Some books or films offend people in Britain who have strong religious beliefs. Do you think there should or should not be a law to ban such books or films?

	%
Definitely should be a law to ban them	14.0
Probably should be a law to ban them	20.2
Probably should <u>not</u> be a law to ban them	27.1
Definitely should <u>not</u> be a law to ban them	35.7
(Don't know)	2.5
(NA)	0.5

[BLASFEMY]

b) There is a blasphemy law in Britain to punish people who offend against Christian beliefs. Should the law ... **READ OUT** ...

	%
... apply just to Christianity,	9.2
apply to other religions as well,	33.5
or - should the law be abolished altogether?	48.0
(Don't know)	8.9
(NA)	0.5

L   - 52L -   [n = 1353]

CARD BB

140. Some people say that video cameras ought to be installed in public places to detect criminals. Others say that this will cut down on everyone's privacy. Do you think video cameras should or should not be allowed in the following places?

READ OUT a)-d) AND CODE ONE FOR EACH

	Video cameras should:					
	Definitely be allowed	Probably be allowed	Probably not be allowed	Definitely not be allowed	(It depends/ Don't know)	(NA)
a) *[VCROADS]* ... installed on roads to detect speeding drivers?	% 54.6	27.6	6.6	9.2	1.7	0.2
b) *[VCFOOTBL]* ... installed at football grounds to detect troublemakers?	%88.1	9.5	0.5	1.0	0.7	0.2
c) *[VCVANDAL]* ... installed on housing estates to detect vandals?	% 52.6	29.6	10.4	5.7	1.4	0.3
d) *[VCDEMOS]* ... at political demonstrations to identify people taking part?	% 39.6	23.6	16.6	16.8	3.2	0.2

[RACEGLTY]

141.a) Suppose two people - one white, one black - each appear in court charged with a crime they did <u>not</u> commit. What do you think their chances are of being found guilty ... **READ OUT** ...

	%
... the white person is more likely to be found guilty,	2.8
they have the same chance,	49.3
or - the black person is more likely to be found guilty?	41.8
(Don't know)	5.8
(NA)	0.3

[RICHGLTY]

b) Now suppose another two people from different backgrounds - one rich, one poor - each appear in court charged with a crime they did <u>not</u> commit. What do you think their chances are of being found guilty ... **READ OUT** ...

	%
... the rich person is more likely to be found guilty,	2.0
they have the same chance,	37.7
or - the poor person is more likely to be found guilty?	55.9
(Don't know)	4.1
(NA)	0.3

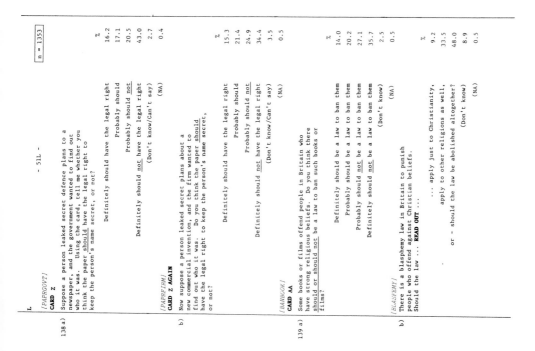

L   - 53L -

142. [REMAND]
CARD CC
Some prisoners in Britain are 'remand prisoners', that is they are waiting, often for long periods, for their cases to come up in court.
Which of the statements on this card comes closest to your views about remand prisoners?
ONE CODE ONLY

n = 1353

%

All those accused of a crime for which they might get a prison sentence should be remanded in prison   20.0

OR Only those who the courts believe might commit another offence or go missing should be remanded in prison   74.5

(Don't know)   5.0

(NA)   0.5

SECTION SEVEN

143. Now I would like to ask some questions about politics.
[POLITICS]
How much interest do you generally have in what is going on in politics ... READ OUT ...

%

... a great deal,   7.0

quite a lot,   22.2

some,   33.0

not very much,   26.3

or - not at all?   11.0

(Don't know)   0.2

(NA)   0.2

144. [VOTESYST]
Some people say that we should change the voting system to allow smaller political parties to get a fairer share of MPs. Others say that we should keep the voting system as it is, to produce more effective government. Which view comes closest to your own ... READ OUT ...
IF ASKED, REFERS TO 'PROPORTIONAL REPRESENTATION'

%

... that we should change the voting system,   34.4

or - keep it as it is?   58.9

(Don't know)   6.4

(NA)   0.2

L   CARD DD   - 54L -   n = 1353

145. Please choose a phrase from this card to say how you feel about ... READ OUT ...

	Very strong-ly in favour	Strong-ly in favour	In favour	Neither in favour nor against	Against	Strong-ly against	Very strong-ly against	Don't know/ Can't say	(NA)
a) [CONFEEL] ... the Conserva-tive Party? %	3.8	5.6	23.6	19.4	17.0	11.6	16.4	1.9	0.6
b) [LABFEEL] ... the Labour Party? %	6.3	8.1	22.5	27.4	21.6	7.2	4.2	2.0	0.8
c) [SLDFEEL] ... the Liberal Democrats? %	0.6	1.9	13.3	55.5	16.2	4.5	1.8	5.1	1.2
d) [SDPFEEL] ... the Social Democrat Party? %	0.4	1.1	6.9	54.5	21.0	5.4	2.7	6.8	1.3

IF NECESSARY, PROMPT. SDP/Owen

IN SCOTLAND ASK: n = 118

	Very strong-ly in favour	Strong-ly in favour	In favour	Neither in favour nor against	Against	Strong-ly against	Very strong-ly against	Don't know/ Can't say	(NA)
e) [SNPFEEL] ... the Scottish Nationalist Party? %	8.5	11.0	20.3	28.0	21.2	4.2	3.4	1.7	3.4

IN WALES ASK: n = 83

	Very strong-ly in favour	Strong-ly in favour	In favour	Neither in favour nor against	Against	Strong-ly against	Very strong-ly against	Don't know/ Can't say	(NA)
f) [PCFEEL] ... Plaid Cymru? %	4.8	4.8	12.0	34.9	22.9	3.6	9.6	6.0	1.2

ASK ALL

	Very strong-ly in favour	Strong-ly in favour	In favour	Neither in favour nor against	Against	Strong-ly against	Very strong-ly against	Don't know/ Can't say	(NA)
g) [GRNFEEL] ... the Green Party? %	3.0	3.8	30.4	38.1	10.6	2.1	1.7	5.7	4.6

146a) [CONXTHMG]
On the whole, would you describe the Conservative Party nowadays as extreme or moderate?
[CONXTHM]
b) And the Labour Party nowadays, is it extreme or moderate?
RECORD IN APPROPRIATE COLUMN

	(a) Conservative	(b) Labour
	%	%
Extreme	57.0	26.1
Moderate	33.3	60.4
(Neither or both)	2.6	4.6
(Don't know)	6.5	8.4
(NA)	0.6	0.5

c) [CONCLASS]
On the whole, would you describe the Conservative Party as good for one class, or good for all classes?
[LABCLASS]
d) And the Labour Party, is it good for one class or good for all classes?
RECORD IN APPROPRIATE COLUMN

	(c) Conservative	(d) Labour
	%	%
Good for one class	66.7	43.9
Good for all classes	25.6	40.1
(Neither or both)	3.5	7.4
(Don't know)	3.6	7.7
(NA)	0.7	1.0

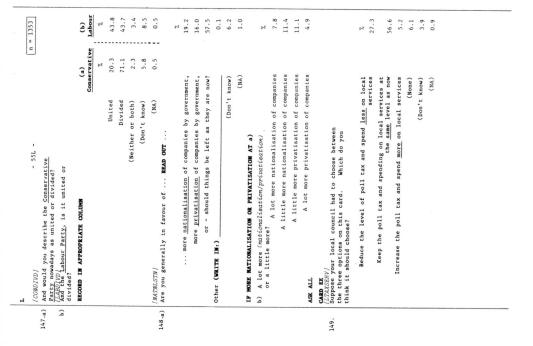

L   - 55L -   n = 1353

147.-a) *[CONTIVD]*
And would you describe the Conservative Party nowadays as united or divided?

b) *[LABTLVD]*
And the Labour Party, is it united or divided?

RECORD IN APPROPRIATE COLUMN

	(a) Conservative	(b) Labour
	%	%
United	20.3	43.8
Divided	71.1	43.7
(Neither or both)	2.3	3.4
(Don't know)	5.8	8.5
(NA)	0.5	0.5

148.-a) *[NATNLSTN]*
Are you generally in favour of ... **READ OUT** ...

	%
... more nationalisation of companies by government,	19.2
more privatisation of companies by government,	16.0
or - should things be left as they are now?	57.5
(Don't know)	0.1
Other (**WRITE IN:**)	6.2
(NA)	1.0

IF MORE NATIONALISATION OR PRIVATISATION AT a)

b) A lot more *(nationalisation/privatisation)* or a little more?

	%
A lot more nationalisation of companies	7.8
A little more nationalisation of companies	11.4
A little more privatisation of companies	11.1
A lot more privatisation of companies	4.9

ASK ALL
CARD EE
[LTAXSERV]

149. Suppose your local council had to choose between the three options on this card. Which do you think it should choose?

	%
Reduce the level of poll tax and spend <u>less</u> on local services	27.3
Keep the poll tax and spending on local services at the <u>same</u> level as now	56.6
Increase the poll tax and spend <u>more</u> on local services	5.2
(None)	6.1
(Don't know)	3.9
(NA)	0.9

L   - 56L -   n = 1353

150. *[LTAXSAME]*
Do you think that local taxes - whether poll tax or rates - should ... **READ OUT** ...

	%
... be at the <u>same</u> level for everyone, except the very poor,	16.2
or - be at different levels, according to people's ability to pay?	81.1
(Don't know)	2.1
(NA)	0.5

151.-a) *[ECLNKINF]*
Do you think that closer links with the European Community would give Britain ... **READ OUT** ...

	%
... <u>more</u> influence in the world,	35.4
<u>less</u> influence in the world,	9.1
or - would it make no difference?	47.2
(Don't know)	8.1
(NA)	0.3

b) *[ECLNKSTR]*
And would closer links with the European Community make Britain ... **READ OUT** ...

	%
... <u>stronger</u> economically,	43.3
<u>weaker</u> economically,	8.3
or - would it make no difference?	36.5
(Don't know)	11.6
(NA)	0.3

c) *[EEJOINEC]*
Should Eastern European countries - the former communist countries - ... **READ OUT** ...

	%
... be encouraged to join the European Community,	58.6
or not?	25.8
(Don't know)	15.3
(NA)	0.3

L   - 57 -   n = 2698   Qs. L152–L157 (Y144–Y146, Y158–Y160)

SECTION EIGHT

ASK ALL
CARD FF
[HOUSESAT]
Now a few questions on housing.

152. First, in general how satisfied or dissatisfied are you with your own (house/flat)? Choose a phrase from the card.

	%
Very satisfied	44.0
Quite satisfied	43.8
Neither satisfied nor dissatisfied	4.5
Quite dissatisfied	4.8
Very dissatisfied	2.7
(NA)	0.1

153.a) [AREACHNG]
How about the area you live in? Taking everything into account, would you say this area has got better, worse or remained about the same as a place to live during the last two years?

	%
Better	11.6
Worse	20.3
About the same	65.1
(Don't know)	2.7
(NA)	0.3

b) [AREAFUT]
And what do you think will happen during the next two years: will this area get better, worse or remain about the same as a place to live?

	%
Better	11.6
Worse	18.4
About the same	66.5
(Don't know)	3.2
(NA)	0.3

154. [TENURE1]
Does your household own or rent this accommodation?
PROBE AS NECESSARY
IF OWN: Outright or on a mortgage?
IF RENTS: From whom?

		%
Owns:	Own (leasehold/freehold) outright	31.0
	Buying (leasehold/freehold) on mortgage	41.3
Rents:	Local authority	18.5
	New Town Development Corporation	0.4
	Housing Association	1.7
	Property company	0.8
	Employer	0.7
	Other organisation	1.0
	Relative	0.4
	Other individual	3.4
Rent free:	Rent free, squatting, etc.	0.5
	(NA)	0.2

Note: Qs. L155–L157 were also asked on the Y version of the questionnaire as Qe. Y158–Y160.

Y & L   - 58L -   - 62Y -   n = 2698

155. INTERVIEWER CODE FROM OBSERVATION AND CHECK WITH RESPONDENT
[HOMETYPE]
Would it be right in describing this accommodation as a ... READ OUT ONE THAT YOU THINK APPLIES

	%
... detached house or bungalow	21.2
... semi-detached house or bungalow	37.8
... terraced house	26.9
... self-contained, purpose-built flat/maisonette (inc. in tenement block)	9.8
... self-contained converted flat/maisonette	2.8
... room(s) - not self-contained	0.4
Other (WRITE IN:)	0.4
(NA)	0.6

156.a) [HOME1YR]
How long have you lived in your present home ... READ OUT ...

	%
... less than a year,	7.0
or ... one year or more?	92.9
(NA)	0.2

[HOME1YR]
b) IF 'ONE YEAR OR MORE' AT a)
How many years?
PROBE FOR BEST ESTIMATE   MEDIAN NUMBER OF YEARS   [0] [7]

157. CARD GG
Please use this card to say how common or uncommon each of the following things is in your area.
READ OUT a)–g) AND CODE
ONE FOR EACH

	In my area, it is...					
	Very common	Fairly common	Not very common	Not at all common	(Don't know/Can't say)	(NA)
a) [NOISYNCB] ... Noisy neighbours or loud parties?	% 4.2	8.3	36.2	50.9	-	0.3
b) [GRAFFITI] ... Graffiti on walls or buildings?	% 3.4	10.6	35.5	50.2	0.1	0.3
c) [TEENONST] ... Teenagers hanging around on the streets?	% 11.1	24.4	30.9	33.1	0.3	0.3
d) [DRUNKS] ... Drunks or tramps on the streets?	% 2.2	6.2	30.7	60.2	0.3	0.3
e) [RUBBISH] ... Rubbish and litter lying about?	% 14.2	26.0	34.3	25.2	-	0.3
f) [HMUNBAD] ... Homes and gardens in bad condition?	% 4.6	11.9	46.5	36.1	0.7	0.3
g) [VANDALS] ... Vandalism and deliberate damage to property?	% 5.6	13.6	43.0	37.0	0.5	0.3

Y & L

- 59L -
- 63Y -

SECTION NINE

n = 2698
Qs. 900-903b

900.a) [MARSTAT]
Can I just check your own marital status?
At present are you ... READ OUT ...
CODE FIRST TO APPLY

	%
... married,	65.8
living as married,	4.0
separated or divorced,	5.3
widowed,	7.6
or - not married?	17.3

b) [HOUSEHLD]
Finally, a few questions about you and your household.
Including yourself, how many people live here regularly as members of this household?
CHECK INTERVIEWER MANUAL FOR DEFINITION OF HOUSEHOLD IF NECESSARY.

MEDIAN: | 0 | 3 |

901. Now I'd like to ask for a few details about each person in your household. Starting with yourself, what was your age last birthday?

WORK DOWN COLUMNS OF GRID FOR EACH HOUSEHOLD MEMBER

	Respondent	2	3	4	5	6	7	8	9	10

a) [RSEX]
Sex:

	%									
Male	45.4									
Female	54.6									

b) Age last birthday:

c) Relationship to respondent:
Spouse/partner
Son/daughter
Parent/parent-in-law
Other relative
Not related

d) [RRESP]
HOUSEHOLD MEMBER WITH LEGAL RESPONSIBILITY FOR ACCOMMODATION (INC. JOINT AND SHARED)

	%									
Yes	81.7									
No	15.6									
(NA)	2.7									

* CHECK THAT NUMBER OF PEOPLE IN GRID EQUALS NUMBER GIVEN AT Q-900b)

Y & L

- 60L -
- 64Y -

[OTHCHILD]
ASK ALL.

n = 2698
Qs. 902-903b

902. Apart from people you've just mentioned who live in your household, have you had any (other) children, including stepchildren, who grew up in your household?
NB: INCLUDES CHILDREN NO LONGER LIVING

		%
	Yes	37.4
	No	62.4
	(NA)	0.2

[RSEX4]
INTERVIEWER TO COMPLETE:
RESPONDENT IS:

	%
Man	45.4
Woman	54.6

903.a) [RFCHILDN]
IF WOMAN:

b) RESPONDENT:

	%
Has children (SEE H/H GRID Q-901) OR Has had children (CODE 1 AT Q-902)	40.1
Has not	14.5

n = 1082
Q. 903a only

IF WOMAN WITH CHILDREN (CODE 1 AT Q.903b)
CARD XI [MARWOWK1 - MARWOWK4]
c) Please use this card to say whether you worked full-time, part-time or not at all ...

READ i)-iv) BELOW AND CODE ONE FOR EACH

	Worked full-time	Worked part-time	Stayed at home	Does not apply	(NA)
i) ... after marrying and before you had children? %	69.4	9.4	16.0	3.3	1.6
ii) ... and what about when a child was under school age? %	10.3	25.8	60.5	1.9	1.6
iii) ... after the youngest child started school? %	15.2	37.3	28.4	17.4	1.8
iv) ... and how about after the children left home? %	19.8	16.3	14.1	48.2	1.7

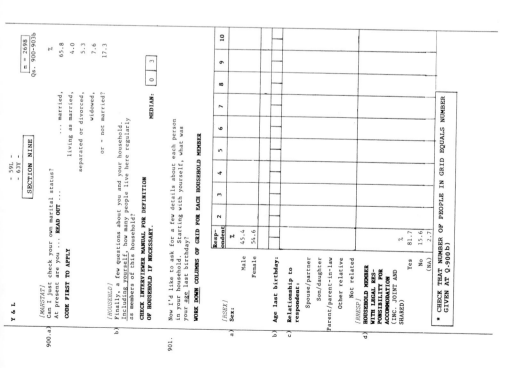

Y & L   - 61L -
       - 65Y -

[RPRIVED]
ASK ALL

		n = 2698 Qs. 904-924

904.a) Have you ever attended a private primary or secondary school in the United Kingdom?

NB: 'PRIVATE' INCLUDES PUBLIC AND DIRECT GRANT SCHOOLS, BUT EXCLUDES NURSERY SCHOOLS AND VOLUNTARY-AIDED SCHOOLS

	%
Yes	14.2
No	85.4
(Don't know/Couldn't establish)	0.1
(NA)	0.3

[MARSTAT2]
INTERVIEWER:
b) RESPONDENT IS:

	%
Married or living as married (CODES 1 OR 2 AT Q.900)	69.8
Not married	30.2

[SPRIVED]
IF MARRIED OR LIVING AS MARRIED
c) And has your (husband/wife/partner) ever attended a private primary or secondary school in the United Kingdom?

	%
Yes	8.9
No	60.2
(Don't know/Couldn't establish)	0.3
(NA)	0.3

[RCHILDS]
INTERVIEWER:
d) RESPONDENT:

	%
Has son or daughter over 5 years old (SEE H/H GRID Q.901) OR Has had children (CODE 1 AT Q.902)	62.2
Has not	37.7
(NA)	0.1

[CHPRIVED]
e) And (have any of your children/has your child) ever attended a private primary or secondary school in the United Kingdom?

	%
Yes	9.3
No	49.0
(Don't know/Couldn't establish)	-
(NA)	4.0

Y & L   - 62L -
       - 66Y -

[SNGPERHH]
ASK ALL

		n = 2698

905.a) INTERVIEWER: IS THIS A SINGLE PERSON HOUSEHOLD - RESPONDENT ONLY PERSON AT Q.901 (p.59)

	%
YES	11.1
NO	88.9

[DUTYRESP]
IF NO AT a)
b) Who is the person mainly responsible for general domestic duties in this household?

	%
Respondent mainly	36.7
Someone else mainly (WRITE IN RELATIONSHIP TO RESP.)	35.7
Duties shared equally (WRITE IN BY WHOM)	15.3
(NA)	1.2

[CHLDINHH]
ASK ALL
906.a) INTERVIEWER: IS THERE A CHILD UNDER 16 YEARS IN HOUSEHOLD? SEE H.H. GRID, Q.901 (p.59).

	%
YES	33.1
NO	66.9

[CHLDRESP]
IF YES AT a)
b) Who is the person mainly responsible for the general care of the child(ren) here?

	%
Respondent mainly	15.8
Someone else mainly (WRITE IN RELATIONSHIP TO RESP.)	12.4
Care shared equally (WRITE IN BY WHOM)	4.6
(NA)	0.3

[TEA]
ASK ALL
907. How old were you when you completed your continuous full-time education?
PROBE AS NECESSARY

	%
15 or under	43.2
16	25.2
17	9.0
18	7.5
19 or over	12.3
Still at school	0.1
Still at college, polytechnic, or university	2.3
Other answer (WRITE IN:)	-
(NA)	0.4

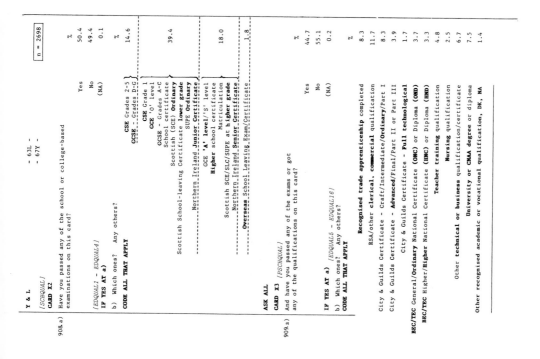

Y & L
- 63L -
- 67Y -

n = 2698

[SCHQUAL]
CARD X2

908.a) Have you passed any of the school or college-based examinations on this card?

	%
Yes	50.4
No	49.4
(NA)	0.1

[EDQUAL1 - EDQUAL4]
IF YES AT a)
b) Which ones? Any others?
CODE ALL THAT APPLY

	%
CSE Grades 2-5	14.6
GCSE - Grades D-G	
CSE Grade 1	
GCE 'O' level	
GCSE - Grades A-C	39.4
School certificate	
Scottish School-leaving Certificate **lower grade**	
Scottish (SCE) **Ordinary**	
SUPE **Ordinary**	
Northern Ireland **Junior Certificate**	
GCE 'A' level/'S' level	
Higher school certificate	18.0
Matriculation	
Scottish SCE/SLC/SUPE at **higher grade**	
Northern Ireland **Senior Certificate**	
Overseas School Leaving Exam/Certificate	1.8

ASK ALL
CARD X3

909.a) And have you passed any of the exams or got any of the qualifications on this card?

	%
Yes	44.7
No	55.1
(NA)	0.2

[EQUALS - EDQUAL6]
IF YES AT a)
b) Which ones? Any others?
CODE ALL THAT APPLY

	%
Recognised trade apprenticeship completed	8.3
RSA/other clerical, commercial qualification	11.7
City & Guilds Certificate - **Craft/Intermediate/Ordinary/Part I**	8.3
City & Guilds Certificate - **Advanced/Final/Part II or Part III**	3.9
City & Guilds Certificate - **Full technological**	1.7
BEC/TEC General/Ordinary National Certificate (ONC) or Diploma (OND)	3.7
BEC/TEC Higher/Higher National Certificate (HNC) or Diploma (HND)	3.3
Teacher training qualification	4.8
Nursing qualification	2.5
Other **technical or business** qualification/certificate	6.7
University or CNAA degree or diploma	7.5
Other recognised academic or vocational qualification, DK, NA	1.4

Y & L
- 64L -
- 68Y -

n = 2698

[RECONAC5]

910. INTERVIEWER: **REFER TO ECONOMIC POSITION OF RESPONDENT** (Q.23, PAGE 9)

	%
RESPONDENT IS IN PAID WORK	54.9
RESPONDENT IS WAITING TO TAKE UP PAID WORK	0.8
ALL OTHERS	44.4

a) [IF EVER HAD A JOB]   [Never had a job 3.5]
Now I want to ask you about your (present/future/last) job.
CHANGE TENSES FOR (BRACKETED) WORDS AS APPROPRIATE.

What (is) your job?
PROBE AS NECESSARY: What (is) the name or title of the job?
IF 'NEVER HAD JOB', WRITE IN AND GO TO Q.911

b) What kind of work (do) you do most of the time?
IF RELEVANT: What materials/machinery (do) you use?

c) What training or qualifications (are) needed for that job?

d) [RSUPER]
(Do) you directly supervise or (are) you directly responsible for the work of any other people?
IF YES: How many?   MEDIAN: 0 0 0 5

	%
Yes	38.1
No	60.9
(DK)	0.3
(NA)	0.7

e) [HEMPLYEE]
Can I just check: (are) you ... READ OUT ...

	%
... an employee,	85.0
or - self-employed?	11.0
(NA)	0.5

Y & L
- 65L -
- 69Y -

n = 2698

[RSECTOR]
IF EMPLOYEE (CODE 1 AT e)

CARD X4

f) Which of the types of organisation on this card (do) you work for?

CODE FIRST TO APPLY

	%
Private firm or company	56.1
Nationalised industry/public corp.	4.6
Local Authority/Local Education Authority	12.6
Health Authority/hospital	4.4
Central Government/Civil Service	4.6
Charity or Trust	0.9
Other (WRITE IN:)	1.5
(NA)	0.2

ASK ALL WHO HAVE EVER WORKED

g) What (does) your employer (IF SELF-EMPLOYED: you) make or do at the place where you usually (work)?

IF FARM, GIVE NO. OF ACRES

[REMPWORK]

h) Including yourself, how many people (are) employed at the place you usually (work) from?

IF SELF-EMPLOYED: (Do) you have any employees?

	%
(No employees)	5.6
Under 10	20.1
10-24	13.4
25-99	20.8
100-499	19.8
500 or more	14.6
(DK)	1.0
(NA)	1.2

[UNION]
ASK ALL

91La) Are you now a member of a trade union or staff association?

CODE FIRST TO APPLY

	%
Yes: trade union	20.8
Yes: staff association	3.0
No	75.9
(NA)	0.3

[UNIONEVR]
IF NO AT a)

b) Have you ever been a member of a trade union or staff association?

CODE FIRST TO APPLY

	%
Yes: trade union	27.7
Yes: staff association	2.1
No	46.0
(NA)	0.4

Y & L
- 66L -
- 70Y -

n = 2698

912. [UNION1 - UNION6]
IF NOW OR EVER A MEMBER (CODES 1 OR 2 AT Q.911)

Have you ever ... READ OUT i)-vi) AND RING ONE CODE FOR EACH

	Yes	No	(NA)
	%	%	%
i) ... attended a union or staff association meeting?	35.5	18.0	0.6
ii) ... voted in a union or staff association election or meeting?	34.5	18.7	0.9
iii) ... put forward a proposal or motion at a union or staff association meeting?	11.4	41.8	0.9
iv) ... gone on strike?	19.4	33.9	0.8
v) ... stood on a picket line?	8.4	44.9	0.8
vi) ... served as a lay representative such as a shop steward or branch committee member?	7.7	45.6	0.8

913.a) INTERVIEWER: [MARSTAT3]
RESPONDENT IS:

	%
Married or living as married (CODES 1 OR 2 AT Q.900)	69.8
All others	30.2

CARD X5 [SECONACT]
b) Which of these descriptions applied to what your [husband/wife/partner] was doing last week, that is the seven days ending last Sunday? PROBE: Any others? CODE ALL THAT APPLY IN COL. I

IF ONLY ONE CODE AT I, TRANSFER IT TO COL. II
IF MORE THAN ONE AT I, TRANSFER HIGHEST ON LIST TO II

	COL. I	COL. II ECONOMIC POSITION
		%
In full-time education (not paid for by employer, including on vacation)	A	0.3
On government training/employment scheme (e.g. Employment Training, Youth Training Scheme etc.)	B	0.2
In paid work (or away temporarily) for at least 10 hours in the week	C	43.4
Waiting to take up paid work already accepted	D	0.1
Unemployed and registered at a benefit office	E	1.2
Unemployed, not registered, but actively looking for a job	F	0.2
Unemployed, wanting a job (of at least 10 hrs per week), but not actively looking for a job	G	0.3
Permanently sick or disabled	H	1.8
Wholly retired from work	J	9.9
Looking after the home	K	12.3
Doing something else (WRITE IN)	L	0.1

IF CODES 01-02, OR 05-11 AT b) [SLASTJOB]
c) How long ago did your [husband/wife/partner] last have a paid job (other than the government scheme you mentioned) of at least 10 hours a week?

	%
Within past 12 months	2.3
Over 1-5 years ago	6.3
Over 5-10 years ago	6.5
Over 10-20 years ago	5.4
Over 20 years ago	3.3
Never had a paid job of 10+ hours a week	1.7
(NA)	0.7

Y & L   - 67L -
                                   - 71Y -   n = 2698

[SECONAC3]
914. INTERVIEWER: REFER TO ECONOMIC POSITION OF SPOUSE/PARTNER (Q.913)

	%
SPOUSE/PARTNER IS IN PAID WORK	43.4
SPOUSE/PARTNER IS WAITING TO TAKE UP PAID WORK	0.1
ALL OTHERS	24.4
(NA)	0.2

915.a) Now I want to ask you about your (husband's/wife's/partner's) job. CHANGE TENSES FOR (BRACKETED) WORDS AS APPROPRIATE
What (is) the name or title of that job?

b) What kind of work (does) he/she do most of the time?
   IF RELEVANT: What materials/machinery (does) he/she use?

c) What training or qualifications (are) needed for that job?

d) [SSUPER]
(Does) he/she directly supervise or (is) he/she directly responsible for the work of any other people?

IF YES: How many?

	%	
Yes	56.6	MEDIAN: 0 0 0 6
No	40.7	
(DK)	2.1	
(NA)	0.7	

e) [SEMPLOYEE]
(Is) he/she ... READ OUT ...

	%
... an employee,	59.4
or - self-employed?	8.2
(DK)	0.1
(NA)	0.4

Y & L   - 68L -
                                   - 72Y -   n = 2698

IF EMPLOYEE (CODE 1 AT e)
CARD X6 [SSECTOR]
f) Which of the types of organisation on this card (does) he/she work for?

	%
Private firm or company	40.3
Nationalised industry/public corporation	3.7
Local Authority/Local Education Authority	7.9
Health Authority/hospital	2.8
Central Government/Civil Service	2.9
Charity or Trust	0.9
Other (WRITE IN) (DK/NA)	0.8
	-

ASK ALL WHO HAVE EVER WORKED
g) What (does) the employer (IF SELF-EMPLOYED: he/she) make or do at the place where he/she usually (works) (from)?
   IF FARM, GIVE NO. OF ACRES

h) [SEMPWORK]
Including him/herself, roughly how many people (are) employed at the place where he/she (works) (from)?

IF SELF-EMPLOYED: (Does) he/she have any employees?

	%
(No employees)	3.5
Under 10	13.2
10-24	9.5
25-99	13.6
100-499	13.1
500 or more	11.6
(DK/NA)	3.6

i) [SPARTFULL]
(Is) the job ... READ OUT ...

	%
... full-time (30 HOURS+)	52.9
or - part-time (10-29 HOURS)?	14.2
(DK)	0.1
(NA)	0.9

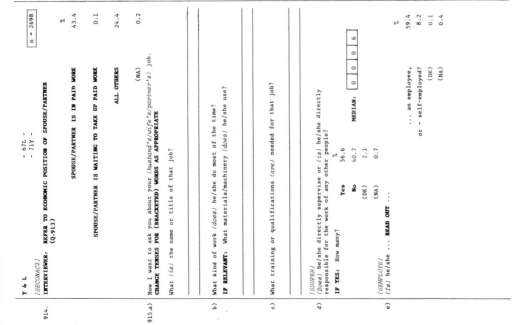

Y & L   - 69L -
          - 73Y -

[CAROWN]
ASK ALL

916. Do you, or does anyone else in your household,
own or have the regular use of a car or a van?

		n = 2698
		%
Yes		76.2
No		23.7
(NA)		0.1

[BENEFT1 - BENEFT14]
CARD X7

917. Have you or anyone in this household received
any of the benefits on this card during the
last *five years?*

IF YES: Which ones? Any others?

CODE ALL THAT APPLY

	%
YES: Child benefit (family allowance)	43.1
Maternity benefit or allowance	9.5
One-parent benefit	4.3
Family credit (family income supplement)	3.4
State retirement or widow's pension	24.6
State supplementary pension	1.8
Invalidity or disabled pension or benefit	7.0
Attendance/Invalid care/Mobility allowance	3.5
State Sickness or injury benefit	7.9
Unemployment benefit	15.5
Income support (supplementary benefit)	11.6
Housing benefit (Community Charge, rate or rent rebate)	15.4
Other state benefit(s) volunteered **(WRITE IN)**	0.2

IF NO: CODE →	**NONE**	18.7
	(DK)	0.1
	(NA)	0.5

Y & L   - 70L -
          - 74Y -

ASK ALL

CARD X8 *[HHINCOME]*

918.a) Which of the letters on this card represents the
total income of your household from all sources
before tax? Please just tell me the letter.
NB: INCLUDES INCOME FROM BENEFITS, SAVINGS, ETC.
[RECOMAC9]
ONE CODE IN COLUMN a)

		n = 2698
INTERVIEWER: CHECK Q.23, PAGE 9:		%
RESPONDENT IS IN PAID WORK		54.9
ALL OTHERS		45.1

b) *[REARN]*
c) Which of the letters on this card represents
your own gross or total earnings, before
deduction of income tax and national insurance?

ONE CODE IN COLUMN c)

		(a) House-hold income	(c) Own earn-ings
		%	%
Less than £3000 p.a.	P =	4.3	3.8
£3000 - £3999 p.a.	Q =	4.7	3.0
£4000 - £4999 p.a.	R =	4.3	2.6
£5000 - £5999 p.a.	T =	4.1	3.2
£6000 - £6999 p.a.	S =	3.3	3.1
£7000 - £7999 p.a.	O =	2.7	2.9
£8000 - £9999 p.a.	K =	4.7	6.2
£10,000 - £11,999 p.a.	L =	6.6	6.1
£12,000 - £14,999 p.a.	B =	8.0	6.2
£15,000 - £17,999 p.a.	Z =	8.5	4.7
£18,000 - £19,999 p.a.	M =	5.1	2.4
£20,000 - £22,999 p.a.	F =	5.4	1.8
£23,000 - £25,999 p.a.	J =	5.1	1.3
£26,000 - £28,999 p.a.	D =	3.7	0.8
£29,000 - £31,999 p.a.	B =	2.6	0.3
£32,000 p.a. or more	C =	6.9	1.2
	(DK)	10.1	1.4
	(NA)	10.0	3.8

ASK ALL
[OWNSHARE]

919. Do you *(or your husband/wife/partner)* own any
shares quoted on the Stock Exchange, including
unit trusts?

		%
	Yes	30.2
	No	68.6
	(DK/NA)	1.3

[PHONE]

920. Is there a telephone in *(your part of)* this
accommodation?

		%
	Yes	89.7
	No	10.1
	(NA)	0.3

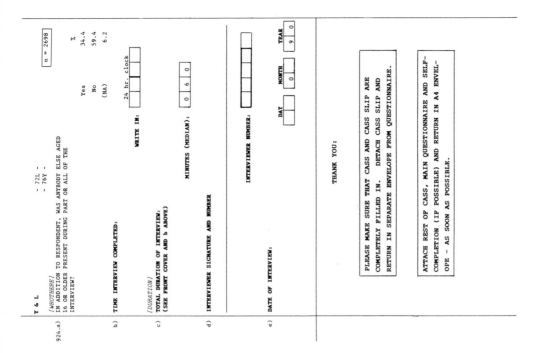

Y & L
- 72L -
- 76Y -
n = 2698

924.a) [WHOTHERE] IN ADDITION TO RESPONDENT, WAS ANYBODY ELSE AGED 16 OR OLDER PRESENT DURING PART OR ALL OF THE INTERVIEW?

	%
Yes	34.4
No	59.4
(NA)	6.2

b) TIME INTERVIEW COMPLETED:
WRITE IN: [ ][ ][ ] 24 hr. clock

c) [DURATION] TOTAL DURATION OF INTERVIEW: (SEE FRONT COVER AND b ABOVE)
MINUTES (MEDIAN): 0 6 0

d) INTERVIEWER SIGNATURE AND NUMBER:
INTERVIEWER NUMBER:

e) DATE OF INTERVIEW:

DAY	MONTH	YEAR
[ ] 0	[ ]	9 0

THANK YOU:

PLEASE MAKE SURE THAT CASS AND CASS SLIP ARE COMPLETELY FILLED IN. DETACH CASS SLIP AND RETURN IN SEPARATE ENVELOPE FROM QUESTIONNAIRE.

ATTACH REST OF CASS, MAIN QUESTIONNAIRE AND SELF-COMPLETION (IF POSSIBLE) AND RETURN IN A4 ENVELOPE - AS SOON AS POSSIBLE.

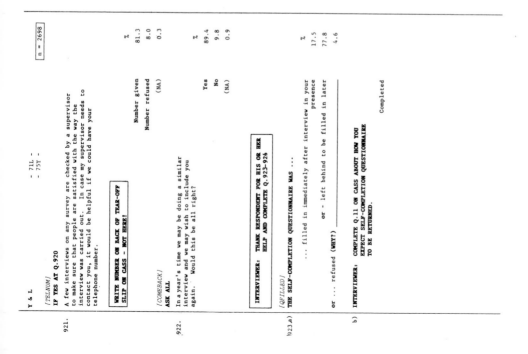

Y & L
- 71L -
- 75Y -
n = 2698

921. [TELNUM] IF YES AT Q.920
A few interviews on any survey are checked by a supervisor to make sure that people are satisfied with the way the interview was carried out. In case my supervisor needs to contact you, it would be helpful if we could have your telephone number.

	%
Number given	81.3
Number refused	8.0
(NA)	0.3

WRITE NUMBER ON BACK OF TEAR-OFF SLIP ON CASS - NOT HERE!

922. [COMEBACK] ASK ALL
In a year's time we may be doing a similar interview and we may wish to include you again. Would this be all right?

	%
Yes	89.4
No	9.8
(NA)	0.9

INTERVIEWER: THANK RESPONDENT FOR HIS OR HER HELP AND COMPLETE Q.923-926

923.a) [QFILLED] THE SELF-COMPLETION QUESTIONNAIRE WAS ...

	%
... filled in immediately after interview in your presence	17.5
or - left behind to be filled in later	77.8
or ... refused (WHY?)	4.6

b) INTERVIEWER: COMPLETE Q.11 ON CASS ABOUT HOW YOU EXPECT SELF-COMPLETION QUESTIONNAIRE TO BE RETURNED.
Completed

Y

SCPR

Head Office: 35 NORTHAMPTON SQUARE,
LONDON EC1V 0AX Telephone 01-250 1866

Field and DP Office: BRENTWOOD, ESSEX.
Northern Field Office: DARLINGTON, CO. DURHAM

Spring 1990

P.1090/Britain

BRITISH SOCIAL ATTITUDES:
1990 SURVEY

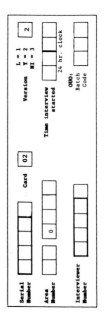

Serial Number

Card 02

Area Number 0

Version
L = 1
Y = 2
NI = 3

2

Time interview started

24 hr. clock

Interviewer Number

000:
Batch
Code

- 40Y -

n = 1345
Qs. Y113-Y117

SECTION FOUR

ASK ALL

Now a few questions on education.

113. CARD S [EDSPEND1, EDSPEND2]

First, which of the groups on this card, if any, would be your highest priority for extra government spending on education, and which next?
ONE CODE ONLY IN EACH COLUMN

	1st Priority %	2nd Priority %
Nursery/pre-school children	16.0	12.2
Primary school children	15.4	17.8
Secondary school children	27.3	21.9
Less able children with special needs	28.9	27.1
Students at colleges, universities or polytechnics	8.7	15.9
(NONE OF THESE)	1.0	1.3
(Don't know)	2.2	3.0
(NA)	0.6	0.7

114. CARD T

Here are a number of factors that some people think would improve education in our schools. [PRIMED]

a) Which do you think is the **most** important one for children in **primary** schools - aged 5-11 years? Please look at the whole list before deciding. **ONE CODE ONLY IN COLUMN a)** [SECED]

b) and which do you think is the **most** important one for children in **secondary** schools - aged 11-18 years? **ONE CODE ONLY IN COLUMN b)**

	(a) PRIMARY %	(b) SECONDARY %
More resources for books and equipment	18.6	13.2
Better buildings	2.5	0.8
Better pay for teachers	7.1	7.3
More involvement of parents in governing bodies	3.1	1.4
More discussion between parents and teachers	5.2	2.7
Smaller classes	28.1	9.5
More emphasis on preparation for exams	1.4	8.0
More emphasis on developing the child's skills and interests	18.0	10.4
More training and preparation for jobs	1.1	21.4
More emphasis on arts subjects	-	0.2
More emphasis on mathematics	1.0	2.3
More emphasis on English	2.2	2.0
Stricter discipline	8.8	17.5
(NONE OF THESE)	0.2	0.1
(Don't know)	2.0	2.4
(NA)	0.5	0.5

- 41Y -

n = 1345

115. [EDCURRIC]

Do you think that what is taught in schools should be up to ... **READ OUT** ...

	%
... the local education authority to decide,	45.8
or - should central government have the final say?	48.1
(Don't know) ...	4.9
(NA)	1.2

116. [SELECTED]

Some people think it is best for secondary schoolchildren to be separated into grammar and secondary modern schools according to how well they have done when they leave primary school. Others think it is best for secondary school-children not to be separated in this way, and to attend comprehensive schools.

On balance, which system do you think provides the best all-round education for secondary schoolchildren ... **READ OUT** ...

	%
... a system of grammar and secondary modern schools,	48.2
or - a system of comprehensive schools?	44.5
Other (**WRITE IN:**)	0.8
(Don't know)	5.6
(NA)	1.0

117a) [HEDOPP]

Do you feel that opportunities for young people in Britain to go on to higher education - to a university, college or polytechnic - should be increased or reduced, or are they at about the right level now?

IF INCREASED OR REDUCED: A lot or a little?

	%
Increased a lot	31.6
Increased a little	19.5
About right	42.6
Reduced a little	1.2
Reduced a lot	0.5
(Don't know)	3.8
(NA)	0.8

b) [HEGRANT]

When British students go to university or college they generally get grants from the local authority. Do you think they should get grants as now, or loans which would have to be paid back when they start working?

	%
Grants	71.4
Loans	24.0
(Don't know)	3.5
(NA)	0.8

SECTION FIVE

pp. 42Y and 43Y: same as pp.40L and 41L

- 44Y -

SECTION SIX

n = 1345

Qs. Y121-Y133

Now I'd like to ask you a few questions about the countryside and the environment.

CARD W
(INTERVIEWER: PRINTED BELOW) [LEISURE]

121 a) On this card are some activities people do in their leisure time. Have you taken part in any of these leisure activities in the last four weeks?

	%
Yes	68.4
No	31.4
(NA)	0.2

IF NO AT a) [LEISURE6]

b) Can you remember when you last did any of these activities in the countryside?
IF YES: How long ago was that?
PROBE FOR CORRECT CODE

	%
Within past month	0.6
1-3 months ago	5.6
4-6 months ago	3.8
7-12 months ago	7.8
More than one year ago	8.6
No, can't remember	4.9
(NA)	0.3

ASK ALL [CTRYSAME]

122 a) Do you think the countryside generally is much the same as it was twenty years ago, or do you think it has changed? IF CHANGED: Has it changed a bit or a lot?

	%
Much the same	14.6
Changed a bit	21.0
Changed a lot	60.5
(Don't know)	3.8
(NA)	0.1

IF CHANGED A BIT OR A LOT (CODES 2 OR 3 AT a)
[CTRYBETR]
b) Do you think the countryside generally has changed for the better or worse?

	%
Better	8.0
Worse	66.0
(Better in some ways/worse in others)	7.2
(DK,NA)	4.1

(INTERVIEWER REFERENCE ONLY)
CARD W

In the last four weeks have you ...

... been for a drive, outing or picnic in the countryside

... been for a long walk, ramble or hike (of more than 2 miles) in the country-side

... visited any historic or stately homes, gardens, zoos or wildlife parks in the countryside

... gone fishing, horse riding, shooting or hunting in the countryside

... visited seacoast or cliffs

- 45Y -

n = 1345

ASK ALL [CTRYCONC]

123. Are you personally concerned about things that may happen to the countryside, or does it not concern you particularly?

IF CONCERNED: Are you very concerned, or just a bit concerned?

	%
Very concerned	49.3
A bit concerned	32.7
Does not concern me particularly	17.9
(NA)	0.1

CARD X [CTHREAT1]

124-a) Which, if any, of the things on this card do you think is the greatest threat to the countryside: if you think none of them is a threat, please say so.
CODE ONE ONLY IN COL a) BELOW
[CTHREAT2]
b) And which do you think is the next greatest threat?
CODE ONE ONLY IN COL b)

	(a) Greatest threat	(b) Next greatest
	%	%
Motorways and road building	13.2	11.4
Industrial pollution	35.6	21.7
Removal by farmers of traditional landscape, such as hedgerows, woodlands	8.2	10.7
Tourism and visitors	1.2	1.5
Litter	8.8	12.4
Urban growth and housing development	15.3	13.7
Use of chemicals and pesticides in farming	16.1	26.2
NONE OF THESE	0.9	1.3
(Don't know)	0.8	0.9
(NA)	0.1	0.1

- 47Y -

n = 1345

127.a) Do you do any of the following <u>regularly</u>, sometimes or not at all nowadays?

READ OUT i)-x) AND CODE ONE FOR EACH AT a)

DOES NOT APPLY MEANS PHYSICALLY IMPOSSIBLE (EG. NO CAR)

FOR EACH ITEM CODED 3 (NOT AT ALL) AT a)

b) Do you intend to ... **READ ITEM** ... in the next year or so, or not?

CODE AT b)

	(a) Does:						(b) Intend to:			
	Regularly	Sometimes	Not at all	Does not apply	(DK)	(NA)	Yes	No	(DK)	(NA)
i) [RECYCLDO, RECYCLFT] return bottles, tins, newspapers and so on for recycling?	% 34.9	24.9	39.1	0.9	0.1	1.9	%15.3	15.6	6.4	
ii) [UNLEADDO, UNLEADFT] use unleaded petrol?	% 28.5	2.7	38.8	29.7	0.2	1.4	%18.8	13.5	5.3	
iii) [ORGANCDO, ORGANCFT] buy organically-grown fruit and vegetables?	% 7.6	31.2	56.1	4.6	0.4	2.6	%12.2	32.7	8.9	
iv) [NOTESTDO, NOTESTFT] buy toiletries or cosmetics not tested on animals?	% 29.5	28.7	31.7	8.5	1.5	1.9	% 8.5	16.8	4.8	
v) [GRWASHDO, GRWASHFT] buy environment-friendly washing powders or detergents?	% 26.5	22.8	41.4	8.4	1.0	2.4	%11.5	21.1	6.5	
vi) [LSMEATDO, LSMEATFT] choose to eat less meat?	% 25.7	20.4	51.7	1.5	0.8	3.5	% 3.2	43.6	2.1	
vii) [RECPRDDO, RECPRDFT] choose products made out of recycled materials?	% 17.8	39.3	40.1	1.8	0.9	3.2	% 9.1	22.5	6.0	
viii) [SVELECDO, SVELECFT] make a conscious effort to save electricity?	% 48.4	23.0	27.8	0.5	0.2	1.8	% 7.4	16.6	2.2	
ix) [DRIVLSDO, DRIVLSFT] cut back on driving your car?	%10.9	13.3	45.4	30.3	0.2	3.3	% 3.2	37.9	1.3	
x) [AEROSLDO, AEROSLFT] buy environment-friendly aerosols?	%57.7	19.4	16.2	6.1	0.5	1.8	% 2.9	9.6	2.1	

- 46Y -

n = 1345

CARD Y

125. How concerned are you about each of these environmental issues? Please choose a phrase from the card.

READ OUT a)-i) AND CODE ONE FOR EACH

	Very concerned	A bit concerned	Not very concerned	Not at all concerned	Don't know/ Can't say	(NA)
a) [INSECTCD] insecticides, fertilisers and chemical sprays?	% 57.0	34.2	5.9	2.0	0.9	0.1
b) [SEWAGE] disposal of sewage?	% 69.2	24.5	3.4	1.8	0.9	0.1
c) [OZLAYER] thinning of the ozone layer?	% 56.5	30.1	8.0	2.2	3.1	0.2
d) [NUCPRISK] risks from nuclear power stations?	% 53.4	27.6	12.9	4.6	1.3	0.3
e) [POPGROW] the growth in the world's population?	% 29.6	39.1	24.3	5.1	1.6	0.2
f) [GRNHSEEF] the 'greenhouse effect' - a rise in the world's temperature?	% 45.5	36.3	11.5	3.7	2.8	0.2
g) [FOSLFUEL] using up the earth's remaining coal, oil and gas?	% 36.7	37.9	18.9	4.1	1.9	0.5
h) [WATNQUAL] the quality of drinking water?	% 50.7	31.4	13.2	3.6	0.9	0.2
i) [SPECLOSS] the loss of plant and animal species?	% 57.2	30.5	8.4	2.5	1.3	0.2

CARD Z

126. Do you personally belong to any of the groups listed on this card?

CODE ALL THAT APPLY

	Yes %	No %
YES: MEMBER OF:		
[CLUB1] The National Trust	8.8	91.2
[CLUB2] Royal Society for the Protection of Birds	4.6	95.4
[CLUB6] Friends of the Earth	1.0	99.0
[CLUB7] World Wildlife Fund/Worldwide Fund for Nature	3.2	96.8
[CLUB8] Greenpeace	2.8	97.2
[CLUB9] Council for the Protection of Rural (England/Scotland/Wales)	0.3	99.7
[CLUB3] Other wildlife or countryside protection group	1.6	98.4
[CLUB10] Ramblers Association	1.2	98.8
[CLUB4] Other countryside sport or recreation group	3.1	96.9
[CLUB11] Urban conservation group	0.4	99.6
[CLUB12] Campaign for Nuclear Disarmament	0.8	99.2
NO: [CLUB5] **NONE OF THESE**	81.3	

- 48Y -

n = 1345

128. ASK ALL [ENVIRPTY]
Which political party's views on the environment would you say come closest to your own views?

DO NOT PROMPT
ONE CODE ONLY

	%
Conservative	14.5
Labour	15.9
(Social and) Liberal Democrat/Liberal/SLD	3.3
SDF/Social Democrat	1.0
(Alliance) - **AFTER PROBE**	0.1
Green Party/(Ecology Party)	25.3
Other (**WRITE IN:**) _____	0.7
(Don't know)	33.3
None	5.2
(NA)	0.7

129. [AREALIVE]
INTERVIEWER: CODE FROM OBSERVATION AND THEN CHECK WITH RESPONDENT:
Can I just check, would you describe the place where you live as being ... **READ OUT SELECTED CODE** ...

	%
... in a big city,	9.3
in the suburbs or outskirts of a city,	29.2
in a small city or town,	30.6
in a country village or town,	27.5
or - in the countryside?	3.2
(NA)	0.2

- 49Y -

n = 1345

SECTION SEVEN

[IMPHLTH1 - IMPHLTH3]
CARD AA

130. Suppose you were advising a young person on how best to improve his or her health generally.

Please tell me, using this card, which you would say are the three most important things he or she should do to improve his or her health generally.

a) First, tell me the **most** important thing.
RECORD IN COLUMN (a) **BELOW.**

b) Now, tell me the **second** most important thing.
RECORD IN COLUMN (b) **BELOW.**

c) And now, the **third** most important thing.
RECORD IN COLUMN (c) **BELOW.**

	(a) Most important %	(b) Second most important %	(c) Third most important %
Eat less fatty food	10.9	17.6	18.4
Eat more fresh fruit and vegetables	10.7	14.2	19.3
Not to smoke	61.3	17.5	7.9
Take more exercise	8.8	21.6	21.9
Drink less alcohol	3.4	21.2	14.7
Take less sugar	0.3	1.5	3.3
Try to reduce stress	4.1	5.8	13.7
(NONE OF THESE)	0.1	0.3	0.1
(Don't know)	0.1	0.1	0.4
(NA)	0.3	0.3	0.2

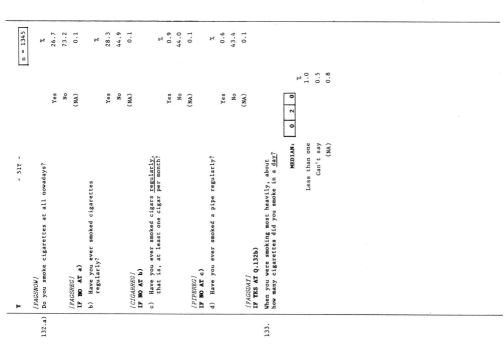

Y — 51Y — | n = 1345

[FAGSNOW]
132.a) Do you smoke cigarettes at all nowadays?

	%
Yes	26.7
No	73.2
(NA)	0.1

[FAGSREG]
IF NO AT a)
b) Have you ever smoked cigarettes regularly?

	%
Yes	28.3
No	44.9
(NA)	0.1

[CIGARREG]
IF NO AT b)
c) Have you ever smoked cigars regularly, that is, at least one cigar per month?

	%
Yes	0.9
No	44.0
(NA)	0.1

[PIPEREG]
IF NO AT c)
d) Have you ever smoked a pipe regularly?

	%
Yes	0.6
No	43.4
(NA)	0.1

[FAGSDAY]
IF YES AT Q.132b)
133. When you were smoking most heavily, about how many cigarettes did you smoke in a day?

MEDIAN: | 0 | 2 | 0 |

	%
Less than one	1.0
Can't say	0.5
(NA)	0.8

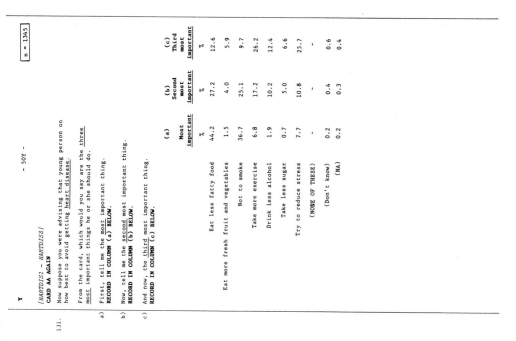

Y — 50Y — | n = 1345

[HARTDIS1 - HARTDIS3]
CARD AA AGAIN
131. Now suppose you were advising that young person on how best to avoid getting heart disease.

From the card, which would you say are the <u>three</u> <u>most</u> important things he or she should do.

a) First, tell me the <u>most</u> important thing. **RECORD IN COLUMN (a) BELOW.**
b) Now, tell me the second most important thing. **RECORD IN COLUMN (b) BELOW.**
c) And now, the third most important thing. **RECORD IN COLUMN (c) BELOW.**

	(a) Most important	(b) Second most important	(c) Third most important
	%	%	%
Eat less fatty food	44.2	27.2	12.6
Eat more fresh fruit and vegetables	1.5	4.0	5.9
Not to smoke	36.7	25.1	9.7
Take more exercise	6.8	17.2	26.2
Drink less alcohol	1.9	10.2	12.4
Take less sugar	0.7	5.0	6.6
Try to reduce stress	7.7	10.8	25.7
(NONE OF THESE)	-	-	-
(Don't know)	0.2	0.4	0.6
(NA)	0.2	0.3	0.4

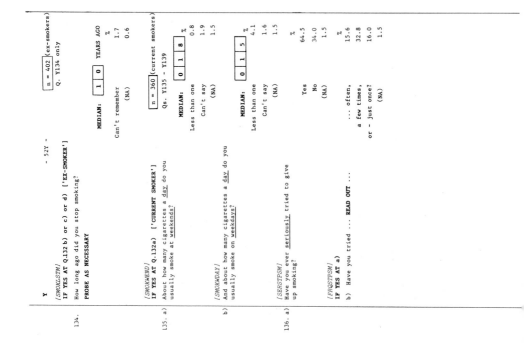

Y   - 52Y -

[SMOKLSTM]
IF YES AT Q.132 b) or c) or d) ['EX-SMOKER']

134. How long ago did you stop smoking?
     PROBE AS NECESSARY

n = 402 (ex-smokers)
Q. Y134 only

MEDIAN: [1][0] YEARS AGO

	%
Can't remember	1.7
(NA)	0.6

[SMOKWEND]
IF YES AT Q.132a) ['CURRENT SMOKER']

135.a) About how many cigarettes a __day__ do you
     usually smoke at __weekends__?

n = 360 (current smokers)
Qs. Y135 - Y139

MEDIAN: [0][1][8]

	%
Less than one	0.8
Can't say	1.9
(NA)	1.5

[SMOKWDAY]
b) And about how many cigarettes a __day__ do you
   usually smoke on __weekdays__?

MEDIAN: [0][1][5]

	%
Less than one	4.1
Can't say	1.6
(NA)	1.5

[SERSTPSM]
136.a) Have you ever __seriously__ tried to give
     up smoking?

	%
Yes	64.5
No	34.0
(NA)	1.5

[FRQSTPSM]
IF YES AT a)
b) Have you tried ... READ OUT ...

	%
... often,	15.6
a few times,	32.8
or - just once?	16.0
(NA)	1.5

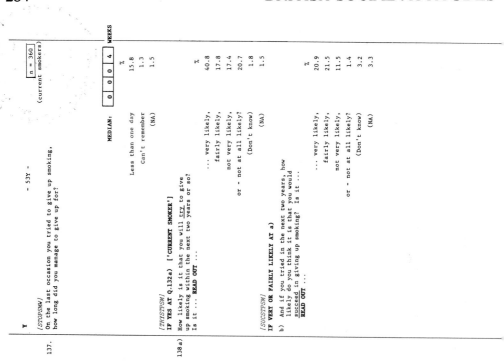

n = 360 (current smokers)

Y   - 53Y -

[STOPPSM]
137. On the last occasion you tried to give up smoking,
     how long did you manage to give up for?

WEEKS
MEDIAN: [0][0][0][4]

	%
Less than one day	15.8
Can't remember	1.3
(NA)	1.5

[TRYSTPSM]
IF YES AT Q.132a) ['CURRENT SMOKER']

138.a) How likely is it that you will __try__ to give
     up smoking within the next two years or so?
     Is it ... READ OUT ...

	%
... very likely,	40.8
fairly likely,	17.8
not very likely,	17.4
or - not at all likely?	20.7
(Don't know)	1.8
(NA)	1.5

[SUCSTPSM]
IF VERY OR FAIRLY LIKELY AT a)
b) And if you tried in the next two years, how
   likely do you think it is that you would
   __succeed__ in giving up smoking? Is it ...
   __READ OUT__ ...

	%
... very likely,	20.9
fairly likely,	21.5
not very likely,	11.5
or - not at all likely?	1.4
(Don't know)	3.2
(NA)	3.3

- 54Y -

Y

IF YES AT Q.132a) ['CURRENT SMOKER']

CARD BB [WNTSTPSM]

n = 360 (current smokers)
Q. 139

139. How much, if at all, do you want to give up smoking? Please choose a phrase from this card.

	%
Very much	29.5
Quite a lot	27.4
Not very much	25.0
Not at all	16.2
(Don't know)	0.5
(NA)	1.5

IF YES AT Q.132b) OR c) OR d) ('EX-SMOKER') OR WANTS TO GIVE UP SMOKING AT ALL (CODES 1-3 AT Q.139)

INTERVIEWER: USE SECOND PHRASE IN BRACKETS FOR EX-SMOKERS

CARD CC [YSTOPSM1 -YSTOPSM7]

n = 761 (ex- and current smokers)
Qs. Y140 - Y141

140. Please use this card to say how important to you each of the following reasons (is/was) for wanting to give up smoking?

READ OUT a)-g) AND CODE ONE FOR EACH

	Very important reason	Fairly important reason	Not a very important reason	Not a reason at all	(NA)
a) ...because it cost(s) too much to continue smoking?	% 21.9	25.5	24.2	19.0	1.7
b) ...for health reasons?	% 66.8	13.3	5.6	4.8	1.7
c) ...because there (are/were) more and more places where I (can't/couldn't) smoke?	% 4.5	10.6	28.0	47.3	1.9
d) ...because my family (wants/wanted) me to give up?	% 19.4	20.1	16.7	34.2	1.9
e) ...because smoking (is/was) getting less and less fashionable?	% 4.0	12.1	21.0	53.4	1.9
f) ...because more and more of the people I mix(ed) with (are/were) non-smokers?	% 7.6	15.1	23.4	44.5	1.7
g) ...because I (do/did) not want tobacco smoke on my clothes and hair?	% 12.6	21.1	21.3	35.6	1.7

- 55Y -

Y

IF YES AT Q.132b) OR c) OR d) ('EX-SMOKERS') OR YES AT Q.132a) ('CURRENT SMOKER')

INTERVIEWER: USE SECOND PHRASE IN BRACKETS FOR EX-SMOKERS

CARD CC AGAIN [YSMOKE1 -YSMOKE9]

n = 761 (ex- and current smokers)
Q. 141 only

141. People smoke for different reasons. Using this card, please say how important each of the following reasons (is/was) for you?

READ OUT a)-i) AND CODE ONE FOR EACH

	Very important reason	Fairly important reason	Not a very important reason	Not a reason at all	(DK/NA)
a) ...smoking (helps/helped) me relax?	% 25.3	44.1	16.8	12.4	1.3
b) ...smoking (is/was) just a very hard habit to give up?	% 42.1	24.6	16.0	15.7	1.5
c) ...smoking (helps/helped) me feel more confident with other people?	% 6.0	16.3	29.3	46.9	1.4
d) ...smoking (helps/helped) me keep my weight down?	% 10.4	16.5	22.2	49.4	1.5
e) ...smoking (is/was) the normal thing to do among people I (mix/mixed) with?	% 9.5	24.9	22.1	42.1	1.4
f) ...smoking (helps/helped) me cope with everyday life?	% 11.8	25.1	24.3	37.3	1.4
g) ...smoking (helps/helped) me concentrate?	% 8.5	26.4	24.4	39.2	1.4
h) ...I just (don't/didn't) have the willpower to give up?	% 23.1	25.0	18.0	32.1	1.8
i) ...smoking (is/was) simply something I (enjoy/enjoyed)?	% 40.1	43.3	9.4	5.7	1.5

Y   - 56Y -

[BOTHERSM]

ASK ALL

142a) Are you bothered by other people's cigarette smoke ... **READ OUT** ...

	n = 1345 Qs. 142-143
	%
... often,	32.7
sometimes,	29.9
hardly ever	10.7
or - never?	26.6
(Don't know)	
(NA)	0.1

[AVOIDSM]

IF OFTEN, SOMETIMES OR HARDLY EVER AT a)

b) Do you regularly avoid places or events because you would be bothered by cigarette smoke ... **READ OUT** ...

	%
... often,	14.2
sometimes,	21.5
hardly ever,	12.1
or - never?	25.0
(Don't know)	0.4
(NA)	0.1

[SPRTSPON]

ASK ALL

143a) Tobacco companies give money to **sport** in return for publicity. On the whole, are you ... **READ OUT** ...

	%
... strongly in favour,	2.6
in favour,	13.2
neither in favour nor against,	39.4
against,	24.4
or - strongly against this?	18.3
(Don't know)	2.0
(NA)	0.1

[ARTSSPON]

b) Tobacco companies also give money to **the arts** - for concerts, plays and so on - in return for publicity. On the whole, are you ... **READ OUT** ...

	%
... strongly in favour,	3.7
in favour,	17.9
neither in favour nor against,	41.3
against,	21.6
or - strongly against this?	13.3
(Don't know)	2.1
(NA)	0.1

- 57Y - = - 57L -

Note: Y144 - Y146 were also asked as Qs. L152 - L154 on the L version of the questionnaire, and the responses are recorded there.

Y   - 58Y -

[CNCLBUY]

IF LOCAL AUTHORITY OR NEW TOWN DEVELOPMENT CORPORATION TENANT (CODES 03 OR 04 AT Q.146)

147. Is it likely or unlikely that you - or the person responsible for paying the rent - will buy this accommodation at some time in the future?

	n = 257 Q. Y147 only
IF LIKELY OR UNLIKELY: Very or quite?	%
Very likely	10.5
Quite likely	12.5
Quite unlikely	9.7
Very unlikely	58.4
Not allowed to buy	4.3
(Don't know)	3.9
(NA)	0.4

[RENTLEVL]

ASK ALL RENTERS (CODES 03-10 AT Q.146)

148. How would you describe the rent - not including rates - for this accommodation? Would you say it was ... **READ OUT** ...

	n = 376 Q. Y148 only
	%
... on the high side,	29.7
reasonable,	60.6
or - on the low side?	6.8
(DK/NA)	2.9

[BUYFRMLA]

IF CURRENTLY OWNS ACCOMMODATION (CODES 01 OR 02 AT Q.146)

149.a) Did you, or the person responsible for the mortgage, buy your present home from the local authority as a tenant?

'LOCAL AUTHORITY' INCLUDES GLC, London Residuary Body and New Town Development Corp.

	n = 962 Q. Y149 only
	%
Yes	9.9
No	90.0
(NA)	0.1

[EVERRENT]

IF NO AT a)

b) Have you <u>ever</u> lived in rented accommodation?

	%
Yes	45.4
No	44.6
(NA)	0.1

[WHENRENT]

IF YES AT a) OR b)

c) How long ago was it that you last lived in rented accommodation? **INCLUDES PRESENT HOUSE/FLAT**

MEDIAN **NO. OF YEARS AGO:**   1 4

(DK,NA) 1.0

[WHOMRENT]

d) Were you renting then from a local authority or from someone else?

'LOCAL AUTHORITY' INCLUDES GLC, London Residuary Body and New Town Development Corp.

	%
Local authority	43.2
Someone else (WRITE IN:)	53.9
(Don't know)	0.1
(NA)	2.7

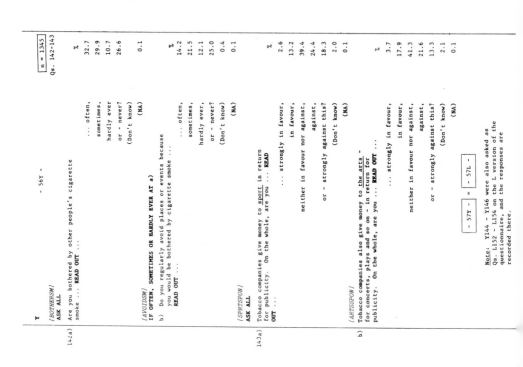

Y   - 59Y -

n = 1345
Qs. Y150-Y152

150. [HOMEMOVE]
ASK ALL
a) If you had a free choice, would you choose to stay in your present home, or would you choose to move out?

		%
Would choose to stay		61.5
Would choose to move out		36.5
(Don't know)		1.8
(NA)		0.3

[HOMEKEEN]
IF MOVE OUT AT a)
b) How keen are you to move out? Are you ... **READ OUT** ...

	%
... very keen,	11.3
fairly keen,	15.6
or - not that keen?	9.5
(DK)	0.1
(NA)	2.0

151. [HOMEEXPT]
ASK ALL
a) And apart from what you would like, where do you expect to be living in two years time - do you expect to ... **READ OUT** ...

	%
... stay in this house/flat,	73.8
or - move elsewhere?	22.1
(Don't know)	3.8
(NA)	0.3

[TENREXPT]
IF MOVE ELSEWHERE AT a)
b) Which do you think is most likely - that you will **buy** or **rent** your next home?
IF RENT: **PROBE FOR LOCAL AUTHORITY/ COUNCIL OR OTHER LANDLORD**

	%
Buy	15.8
Rent: from local authority/council	2.2
Rent: from other landlord	3.2
(Don't know)	0.9
(NA)	4.2

152. **INTERVIEWER CHECK:**
RESPONDENT:

	%
Lives in rented accommodation (**CODES 03-10 AT Q.146**)	28.0
Others	72.0

Y   - 60Y -

n = 376
Qs. Y153-Y156

[RENTPREF]
IF RENTS AT Q. 152
153. If you had a free **choice** would you choose to rent accommodation, or would you choose to buy?

	%
Would choose to rent	28.9
Would choose to buy	67.5
(Don't know)	3.1
(NA)	0.5

[RENTEXPT]
154. And apart from what you would **like**, do you expect to buy a house or a flat in the next two years, or not?
INCLUDES BUYING PRESENT HOUSE/FLAT

	%
Yes - expect to buy	18.9
No - do not expect to buy	74.9
(Don't know)	5.6
(NA)	0.5

[EVEROWND]
155.a) Have you ever owned your own accommodation? That is, lived in a house or flat, which was in your sole or joint name?

	%
Yes	19.4
No	79.4
(NA)	1.2

[OWNEDYRS]
IF YES AT a)
b) How long ago was it that you last owned your own accommodation?
PROBE FOR BEST ESTIMATE

MEDIAN NO. OF YEARS AGO: | 0 | 5 |

Y
[NOTBUY1 - NOTBUY10]   - 61Y -   n = 376

ASK ALL RENTERS

156. Here are some reasons people might give for **not** wanting to buy a home. As I read out each one, please tell me whether or not it applies to you, **at present**. ... **READ OUT** ...

	Applies	Does not apply	(Don't know)	(NA)
a) ... I could not afford the deposit	% 70.4	27.7	1.2	0.7
b) ... I would not be able to get a mortgage	% 58.9	33.8	6.4	0.9
c) ... It might be difficult to keep up the repayments	% 73.4	23.5	2.4	0.7
d) ... I can't afford any of the properties I'd want to buy	% 70.9	26.0	2.4	0.7
e) ... I do not have a secure enough job	% 49.4	48.2	1.7	0.7
f) ... I would not want to be in debt	% 62.0	35.8	1.4	0.7
g) ... It would cost too much to repair and maintain	% 50.8	44.0	4.5	0.7
h) ... I might not be able to resell the property when I wanted to	% 35.7	55.3	8.3	0.7
i) ... It is just too much of a responsibility	% 50.7	46.1	2.5	0.7
j) ... At my age, I would not want to change	% 40.7	54.4	4.1	0.7

ASK ALL [PTENURE]

n = 1345
Q. Y157 only

157. When you were a child, did your parents own their home, rent it from a local authority, or rent it from someone else?

IF DIFFERENT TYPES OF TENURE,
PROBE FOR ONE RESPONDENT LIVED
IN LONGEST

	%
Owned it	42.2
Rented from local authority	33.4
Rented from someone else	20.9
Other (**WRITE IN:**)	1.7
(DK/NA)	1.8

INTERVIEWER CODE FROM OBSERVATION AND CHECK WITH RESPONDENT

n = 2698
Qs. Y158 - Y160

158. Would I be right in describing this accommodation as a ... **READ OUT ONE THAT YOU THINK APPLIES** ...

Note: Qs. Y158-Y160 were also asked as Qs. L155-L157 on the L version of the questionnaire and the responses are recorded there.

... detached house or bungalow

... semi-detached house or bungalow

... terraced house

... self-contained, purpose-built flat/maisonette (inc. in tenement block)

... self-contained converted flat/maisonette

... room(s) - not self-contained

Other (**WRITE IN:**)

(NA)

L

SCPR
SOCIAL & COMMUNITY PLANNING RESEARCH

Head Office: 35 NORTHAMPTON SQUARE,
LONDON EC1V 0AX Telephone 01-250 1866

Field and DP Office: BRENTWOOD, ESSEX
Northern Field Office: DARLINGTON, CO. DURHAM

P.1090/GB

BRITISH SOCIAL ATTITUDES 1990

SELF-COMPLETION QUESTIONNAIRE

Spring 1990

OFFICE USE ONLY:	Area No.
Interviewer	0
to enter:	Serial No.
Rec.	Interviewer No.

To the selected respondent:

Thank you very much for agreeing to take part in this important study— the seventh in this annual series. The study consists of this self-completion questionnaire, and the interview you have already completed. The results of the survey are published in a book each autumn; some of the questions are also being asked in ten other countries, as part of an international survey.

Completing the questionnaire:

The questions inside cover a wide range of subjects, but each one can be answered simply by placing a tick (✓) or a number in one or more of the boxes. No special knowledge is required: we are confident that everyone will be able to take part, not just those with strong views or particular viewpoints. The questionnaire should not take very long to complete, and we hope you will find it interesting and enjoyable. It should be filled in only by the person actually interviewed at your address. The answers you give will be treated as confidential and anonymous.

Returning the questionnaire:

Your interviewer will arrange with you the most convenient way of returning the questionnaire. If the interviewer has arranged to call back for it, please complete it and keep it safely until then. If not, please complete it and post it back in the pre-paid, addressed envelope, AS SOON AS YOU POSSIBLY CAN.

THANK YOU AGAIN FOR YOUR HELP.

Social and Community Planning Research is an independent social research institute registered as a charitable trust. Its projects are funded by government departments, local authorities, universities and foundations to provide information on social issues in Britain. The British Social Attitudes Survey series has been funded mainly by the Sainsbury Family Charitable Trusts, with contributions also from government departments, the Nuffield Foundation, universities and industry. Please contact us if you would like further information.

- 1 -

n = 1163 Qs.2.01-2.10

L.

2.01 *[SCOBEYLW]*
In general, would you say that people should obey the law without exception, or are there exceptional occasions on which people should follow their consciences even if it means breaking the law?

PLEASE TICK ONE BOX

	%
Obey the law without exception	41.3
Follow conscience on occasions	51.8
Can't choose	4.9
(NA)	2.0

2.02 *[PROTEST1 - PROTEST6]*
There are many ways people or organisations can protest against a government action they strongly oppose.

Please show which you think should be allowed and which should not be allowed by ticking a box on each line.

PLEASE TICK ONE LINE
ON EACH LINE

		Should it be allowed?				
	Defin-itely	Prob-ably	Probably not	Definitely not	Can't choose	(NA)
Organising public meetings to protest against the government	% 62.1	25.7	4.8	3.8	2.8	0.9
Publishing pamphlets to protest against the government	% 53.2	30.8	7.0	4.7	2.3	2.1
Organising protest marches and demonstrations	% 39.1	30.9	13.8	11.9	2.5	1.7
Occupying a government office and stopping work there for several days	% 3.1	7.3	26.9	58.1	2.5	2.1
Seriously damaging government buildings	% 0.8	0.5	4.3	90.5	1.7	2.2
Organising a nationwide strike of all workers against the government	% 12.0	19.1	20.0	43.3	3.4	2.2

Please continue ......

- 2 -

L.

2.03 There are some people whose views are considered extreme by the majority.

First, consider people who want to overthrow the government by revolution. Do you think such people should be allowed to ...

PLEASE TICK ONE LINE
ON EACH LINE

	Defin-itely	Prob-ably	Probably not	Definitely not	Can't choose	(NA)
i) *[REVMEET]* ... hold public meetings to express their views?	% 21.5	27.0	17.8	29.6	3.2	0.9
ii) *[REVPUB]* ... publish books expressing their views?	% 21.4	37.0	16.3	20.2	3.5	1.7

2.04 Second, consider people who believe that whites are racially superior to all other races. Do you think such people should be allowed to ...

PLEASE TICK ONE LINE
ON EACH LINE

	Defin-itely	Prob-ably	Probably not	Definitely not	Can't choose	(NA)
i) *[PRJMEET]* ... hold public meetings to express their views?	% 9.0	17.5	22.1	47.2	3.6	0.8
ii) *[PRJPUB]* ... publish books expressing their views?	% 10.8	23.3	21.7	39.2	3.8	1.1

2.05 *[CRIMIN1 - CRIMIN4]*
Suppose the police get an anonymous tip that a man with a long criminal record is planning to break into a warehouse.

PLEASE TICK ONE BOX ON EACH LINE

Do you think the police should be allowed, without a Court Order ...

	Defin-itely	Prob-ably	Probably not	Definitely not	Can't choose	(NA)
i) ... to keep the man under surveillance?	% 61.8	28.5	3.1	4.7	1.2	0.7
ii) ... to tap his telephone?	% 13.8	22.8	25.9	32.3	2.5	2.7
iii) ... to open his mail?	% 8.6	14.7	27.9	43.8	2.3	2.7
iv) ... to detain the man overnight for questioning?	27.6	36.7	17.7	14.4	1.5	2.1

L.

- 3 -

2.06 [JUSTICE]
All systems of justice make mistakes, but
which do you think is worse:

PLEASE TICK ONE BOX

	%
to convict an innocent person,	61.5
OR	
to let a guilty person go free?	18.8
Can't choose	19.1
(NA)	0.5

2.07 What are your personal feelings about...

A. [DEMOFEEL]
People who organise protests against a
government action they strongly oppose?

PLEASE TICK ONE BOX

	%
Extremely favourable	11.5
Favourable	34.2
Neither favourable or unfavourable	35.8
Unfavourable	11.1
Extremely unfavourable	2.7
Can't choose	4.4
(NA)	0.3

B. [REVFEEL]
People who want to overthrow the government
by revolution?

PLEASE TICK ONE BOX

	%
Extremely favourable	0.9
Favourable	2.9
Neither favourable or unfavourable	14.7
Unfavourable	31.4
Extremely unfavourable	46.0
Can't choose	3.9
(NA)	0.3

C. [RACFEEL]
People who believe whites are racially superior
to all other races?

PLEASE TICK ONE BOX

	%
Extremely favourable	0.9
Favourable	3.2
Neither favourable or unfavourable	15.5
Unfavourable	32.0
Extremely unfavourable	45.2
Can't choose	2.9
(NA)	0.3

Please continue ......

L.

- 4 -

2.08 [HIGHINC]
Some people think those with high incomes should
pay a larger proportion (percentage) of their
earnings in taxes than those who earn low incomes.
Other people think that those with high incomes
and those with low incomes should pay the same
proportion (percentage) of their earnings in taxes.

Do you think those with **high** incomes should ...

PLEASE TICK ONE BOX.

	%
... pay a **much larger** proportion,	21.0
pay a **larger** proportion,	61.4
pay the **same** proportion as those who earn low incomes,	13.8
pay a **smaller** proportion,	0.4
or - pay a **much smaller** proportion?	0.3
Can't choose	2.2
(NA)	1.0

2.09 [INCDIFF]
What is your opinion of the following statement:
It is the responsibility of the government to
reduce the differences in income between people
with high incomes and those with low incomes.

PLEASE TICK ONE BOX

	%
Agree strongly	18.5
Agree	37.6
Neither agree nor disagree	18.3
Disagree	20.0
Disagree strongly	4.6
(DK)	0.2
(NA)	0.8

L.   - 6 -

n = 1163
Qs. 2.12-2.19

2.12 [UNEMINF2]
If the government had to choose between keeping down inflation or keeping down unemployment, to which do you think it should give highest priority?
PLEASE TICK ONE BOX

	%
Keeping down inflation	52.1
Keeping down unemployment	39.3
Can't choose	8.2
(NA)	0.4

2.13 [TUPOWER]
Do you think that trade unions in this country have too much power or too little power?
PLEASE TICK ONE BOX

	%
Far too much power	9.6
Too much power	25.5
About the right amount of power	44.9
Too little power	11.4
Far too little power	1.6
Can't choose	6.6
(NA)	0.3

2.14 [BUSPOWER]
How about business and industry? Do they have too much power or too little power?
PLEASE TICK ONE BOX

	%
Far too much power	4.8
Too much power	23.6
About the right amount of power	50.3
Too little power	8.2
Far too little power	0.3
Can't choose	12.3
(NA)	0.6

L.   - 5 -

2.10 [GOVECON1 - GOVECON8]
Here are some things the government might do for the economy. Please show which actions you are in favour of and which you are against.
PLEASE TICK ONE BOX ON EACH LINE

	Strongly in favour of	In favour of	Neither in favour of nor against	Against	Strongly against	(DK/NA)
A. Control of wages by law	% 6.7	18.8	15.8	44.2	12.1	2.5
B. Control of prices by law	% 15.2	39.3	13.7	24.0	6.1	1.7
C. Cuts in government spending	% 10.9	29.8	25.8	25.9	5.1	2.5
D. Government financing of projects to create new jobs	% 26.4	55.2	11.1	4.8	0.9	1.6
E. Less government regulation of business	% 7.8	34.3	41.4	12.0	1.8	2.8
F. Support for industry to develop new products and technology	% 34.0	54.3	8.7	1.3	0.3	1.4
G. Support for declining industries to protect jobs	% 18.2	40.9	19.2	18.2	2.2	1.3
H. Reducing the working week to create more jobs	% 10.3	30.4	28.6	25.8	3.7	1.2

2.11 Listed below are various areas of government spending. Please show whether you would like to see more or less government spending in each area.
Remember that if you say "much more", it might require a tax increase to pay for it.
PLEASE TICK ONE BOX ON EACH LINE
[GVSPEND1 - GVSPEND8]

n = 2349
Also asked on Version Y (Q.209)

	Spend much more	Spend more	Spend the same as now	Spend less	Spend much less	Can't choose	(NA)
A. The environment	% 14.3	46.6	31.0	2.1	0.4	2.4	3.1
B. Health	% 38.4	50.5	9.2	0.3	0.1	0.6	0.9
C. The police and law enforcement	% 12.0	38.1	42.9	3.0	0.8	1.6	1.6
D. Education	% 27.9	50.2	17.9	1.1	0.4	1.0	1.5
E. The military and defence	% 2.1	6.3	39.3	32.1	16.1	2.3	1.8
F. Old age pensions	% 29.7	50.8	17.0	0.6	0.2	0.9	1.0
G. Unemployment benefits	% 7.7	28.2	43.1	13.1	4.1	2.2	1.5
H. Culture and the arts	% 2.0	10.4	41.5	26.5	13.5	4.7	1.3

Please continue ......

- 7 -

L.

2.15 [GOVPOWER]
And what about the government, does it have too much power or too little power?
PLEASE TICK ONE BOX

	%
Far too much power	15.2
Too much power	32.0
About the right amount of power	43.4
Too little power	2.6
Far too little power	0.2
Can't choose	6.0
(NA)	0.5

2.16 [TUCUNTRY]
In general, how good would you say trade unions are for the country as a whole?
PLEASE TICK ONE BOX

	%
Excellent	2.1
Very good	15.2
Fairly good	51.3
Not very good	19.5
Not good at all	5.7
Can't choose	5.7
(NA)	0.5

2.17 What do you think the government's role in each of these industries and services should be?

PLEASE TICK ONE BOX ON EACH LINE

	Own it	Control prices and profits but not own it	Neither own it nor control its prices & profits	Can't choose	(NA)
A. [GOVRULE1] Electricity	28.2	45.7	18.9	6.7	0.5
B. [GOVRULE8] The steel industry	12.6	37.9	37.2	11.2	1.2
C. [GOVRULE4] Banking and insurance	5.8	39.6	42.5	10.8	1.3

Please continue ......

- 8 -

L.

2.18 [GOVRESP1 - GOVRESP9]
On the whole, do you think it should or should not be the government's responsibility to ...
PLEASE TICK ONE BOX ON EACH LINE

	Definitely should be	Probably should be	Probably should not be	Definitely should not be	Can't choose	(NA)
A. ... provide a job for everyone who wants one	22.5	37.7	21.0	13.6	3.5	1.6
B. ... keep prices under control	47.4	39.1	6.8	3.5	2.0	1.1
C. ... provide health care for the sick	83.6	13.9	0.6	0.3	0.9	0.7
D. ... provide a decent standard of living for the old	77.2	20.1	0.9	0.3	0.9	0.5
E. ... provide industry with the help it needs to grow	41.0	49.6	4.9	1.1	2.5	1.0
F. ... provide a decent standard of living for the unemployed	30.3	46.4	14.2	4.3	4.2	0.7
G. ... reduce income differences between the rich and poor	40.2	30.4	15.2	9.4	4.5	0.3
H. ... give financial help to university students from low-income families	47.6	42.8	4.9	2.2	1.9	0.6
I. ... provide decent housing for those who can't afford it	45.0	44.9	5.4	1.4	3.0	0.3

2.19 [POLITIC2]
How interested would you say you personally are in politics?
PLEASE TICK ONE BOX

	%
Very interested	9.1
Fairly interested	30.2
Somewhat interested	25.9
Not very interested	24.3
Not at all interested	7.9
Can't choose	1.0
(NA)	1.5

- 9 -

2.20 Now for some questions on different subjects

From what you know or have heard, please tick a box for each of the items below to show whether you think the National Health Service in your area is, on the whole, satisfactory or in need of improvement.

PLEASE TICK ONE BOX ON EACH LINE

[HSAREA1 - HSAREA15]

n = 2349
Also asked on Version Y (Q.2.01)

	In need of a lot of improvement	In need of some improvement	Satis-factory	Very good	(DK/NA)
a. GPs' appointment systems	% 11.3	29.4	45.2	13.2	0.9
b. Amount of time GP gives to each patient	% 9.4	21.5	52.9	15.0	1.2
c. Being able to choose which GP to see	% 9.0	18.5	53.3	17.2	2.0
d. Quality of medical treatment by GPs	% 6.4	18.1	50.8	22.1	2.6
e. Hospital waiting lists for non-emergency operations	% 42.2	40.6	13.5	1.4	2.3
f. Waiting time before getting appointments with hospital consultants	% 42.5	39.8	13.4	1.6	2.8
g. General condition of hospital buildings	% 17.5	36.3	34.2	9.7	2.3
h. Hospital casualty departments	% 17.1	34.9	36.8	8.8	2.3
i. Staffing level of nurses in hospitals	% 31.1	40.7	22.5	3.0	2.7
j. Staffing level of doctors in hospitals	% 29.1	38.8	24.7	3.3	4.1
k. Quality of medical treatment in hospitals	% 7.2	23.7	48.6	18.1	2.3
l. Quality of nursing care in hospitals	% 4.8	19.1	43.8	29.7	2.6
m. Waiting areas in casualty departments in hospitals	% 18.8	38.4	35.5	5.2	2.0
n. Waiting areas for out-patients in hospitals	% 16.9	35.6	39.8	5.4	2.3
o. Waiting areas at GPs' surgeries	% 7.6	20.4	56.2	14.3	1.4

Please continue ...

- 10 -

2.21 In the last two years, have you or a close family member ...

PLEASE TICK ONE BOX ON EACH LINE

[NHSDOC]

n = 2349
Also asked on Version Y (Q.2.02)

		Yes	No	(DK/NA)
	... visited an NHS GP?	% 95.3	4.0	0.7
[NHSOUTP]	... been an out-patient in an NHS hospital?	% 65.9	32.1	2.0
[NHSINP]	... been an in-patient in an NHS hospital?	% 46.1	51.2	2.7
[NHSVISIT]	... visited a patient in an NHS hospital?	% 75.4	22.8	1.8
[PRIVPAT]	... had any medical treatment as a private patient?	% 14.2	83.7	2.1

2.22 [ABORT1 - ABORT7]
Here are a number of circumstances in which a woman might consider an abortion. Please say whether or not you think the law should allow an abortion in each case.

PLEASE TICK ONE BOX ON EACH LINE

n = 1163
Qs.2.22 - 2.25

	Should abortion be allowed by law?		
	Yes	No	(DK/NA)
The woman decides on her own she does not wish to have the child	% 56.3	41.2	2.3
The couple agree they do not wish to have the child	% 62.3	35.3	2.3
The woman is not married and does not wish to marry the man	% 56.1	41.3	2.6
The couple cannot afford any more children	% 62.2	35.3	2.4
There is a strong chance of a defect in the baby	% 88.2	10.1	1.6
The woman's health is seriously endangered by the pregnancy	% 93.3	5.6	1.0
The woman became pregnant as a result of rape	% 92.0	6.7	1.3

L.

- 12 -

2.26 Do you agree or disagree ... ?
PLEASE TICK ONE BOX ON EACH LINE

n = 2349
Also asked on Version Y (Q.2.06)

	Strongly agree	Agree	Neither agree nor disagree	Disagree	Strongly disagree	Can't choose	(NA)
a. [WWRELCHD] A working mother can establish just as warm and secure a relationship with her children as a mother who does not work. %	13.7	34.9	13.6	25.7	8.6	2.4	1.0
b. [WWCHDSUF] A pre-school child is likely to suffer if his or her mother works. %	9.9	36.6	18.0	24.8	6.4	3.2	1.1
c. [WWFAMSUF] All in all, family life suffers when the woman has a full-time job. %	10.0	35.1	16.4	27.1	7.7	2.5	1.1
d. [WWHAPPIR] A woman and her family will all be happier if she goes out to work. %	2.5	14.1	39.7	32.5	5.5	4.7	0.9
e. [WANTHOME] A job is all right, but what most women really want is a home and children. %	4.4	25.1	23.8	29.7	12.4	3.7	1.0
f. [JOBBEST] Having a job is the best way for a woman to be an independent person. %	8.4	45.2	22.1	18.6	2.1	2.7	0.9
g. [HJOBEARN] A husband's job is to earn money; a wife's job is to look after the home and family. %	6.4	18.7	18.5	33.2	20.3	2.1	0.9
h. [WWXPTEMP] Mothers of young children should not expect employers to make special arrangements to help them combine jobs and child-care. %	5.2	27.0	15.0	34.7	14.3	2.9	1.0
i. [GOVCARE] The government should provide money for child-care, so that mothers of young children can work if they want to. %	15.6	35.3	13.5	25.8	6.4	2.5	0.8

L.

- 11 -

2.23 [PORNO] Which of these statements comes closest to your views on the availability of pornographic magazines and films?
PLEASE TICK ONE BOX

	%
They should be banned altogether	39.4
They should be available in special adult shops but not displayed to the public	40.2
They should be available in special adult shops with public display permitted	9.4
They should be available in any shop for sale to adults only	9.0
They should be available in any shop for sale to anyone	0.3
(DK/NA)	1.7

2.24a) Britain controls the numbers of people from abroad that are allowed to settle in this country. Please say, for each of the groups below, whether you think Britain should allow more settlement, less settlement, or about the same amount as now.
PLEASE TICK ONE BOX ON EACH LINE

	More settlement	Less settlement	About the same as now	(DK/NA)
[AUSIEIMM] Australians and New Zealanders %	8.7	31.4	58.7	1.2
[ASIANIMM] Indians and Pakistanis %	2.2	61.8	34.7	1.4
[EECIMM] People from European Community countries %	6.5	40.9	50.9	1.7
[WIIMM] West Indians %	2.3	57.9	38.5	1.3

b) Now thinking about the families (husbands, wives, children, parents) of people who have already settled in Britain, would you say in general that Britain should ...
PLEASE TICK ONE BOX

	%
... be stricter in controlling the settlement of close relatives	55.7
or - be less strict in controlling the settlement of close relatives	9.9
or - keep the controls about the same as now	33.1
(DK/NA)	1.4

2.25 [CAPPUN1 - CAPPUN3] Are you in favour of or against the death penalty for ...
PLEASE TICK ONE BOX ON EACH LINE

	In favour	Against	(DK/NA)
... murder in the course of a terrorist act? %	70.3	26.3	3.4
... murder of a police officer? %	66.8	29.1	4.0
... other murders? %	61.0	35.8	3.2

Please continue ...

- 13 -

2.27 [WWCHLD1 - WWCHLD4]
Do you think that women should work outside the home full-time, part-time or not at all under these circumstances?

PLEASE TICK ONE BOX ON EACH LINE

n = 2349
Also asked on Version Y (Q.2.07)

	Work full-time	Work part-time	Stay at home	Can't choose	(NA)
	%				
a. After marrying and before there are children?	80.5	10.0	1.6	7.1	0.8
b. When there is a child under school age?	4.0	28.4	58.3	8.1	1.1
c. After the youngest child starts school?	15.6	66.9	8.5	7.9	1.1
d. After the children leave home?	68.9	17.4	1.7	10.7	1.3

2.28 [CHDCARE1 - CHDCARE6]
Think of a child under 3 years old whose parents both have full-time jobs.
How suitable do you think each of these child-care arrangements would be for the child?

PLEASE TICK ONE BOX ON EACH LINE

n = 2349
Also asked on Version Y (Q.2.08)

	Very suitable	Somewhat suitable	Not very suitable	Not at all suitable	Can't choose	(NA)
	%					
a. A state or local authority nursery?	26.7	40.5	16.3	6.8	7.7	2.0
b. A private creche or nursery?	30.8	43.2	11.3	5.0	8.0	1.8
c. A child-minder or baby-sitter?	15.9	41.6	25.9	7.7	6.8	2.1
d. A neighbour or friend?	9.8	34.8	34.2	13.1	5.8	2.2
e. A relative?	35.6	41.5	12.6	4.3	4.4	1.5
f. A workplace nursery or creche?	44.3	33.9	9.5	4.6	6.3	1.4

2.29 [TERPTVBAN]
Should the law allow television to show interviews with people who support acts of terrorism in the UK?

PLEASE TICK ONE BOX

n = 1163
Qs.2.29 -2.38

%
The law definitely should allow it, 12.3
probably should allow it, 16.8
probably should not allow it, 25.9
or - the law definitely should not allow it? 40.3
Can't choose 3.7
(NA) 0.9

Please continue ...

- 14 -

2.30a) [TERNPBAN]
And should the law allow newspapers to publish interviews with people who support acts of terrorism in the UK?

PLEASE TICK ONE BOX

%
The law definitely should allow it, 11.2
probably should allow it, 21.0
probably should not allow it, 27.1
or - the law definitely should not allow it? 35.6
Can't choose 4.4
(NA) 0.7

b) [TERBKBAN]
And should the law allow people who support acts of terrorism in the UK to publish books expressing their views?

PLEASE TICK ONE BOX

%
The law definitely should allow it, 9.2
probably should allow it, 20.0
probably should not allow it, 29.8
or - the law definitely should not allow it? 36.2
Can't choose 4.4
(NA) 0.4

2.31 [JURYRGHT]
Which of these two statements comes closest to your views?

PLEASE TICK ONE BOX

%
People charged with serious crimes should **always** have the right to a jury trial 48.6

OR

There should **not always** be a right to a jury trial - for instance when the jury might be in danger 37.8

Can't choose 12.9
(NA) 0.7

L.

- 15 -

[FINEPANA]
2.32 Suppose a 16-year old is fined by a court, but does not pay the fine. Should the parents be required by law to pay the fine, or not?

PLEASE TICK ONE BOX

	%
Definitely should be required to pay	34.9
Probably should be required to pay	27.6
Probably should not be required to pay	16.6
Definitely should not be required to pay	17.2
Can't choose	3.3
(NA)	0.4

2.33 As long as there is no threat to security, should prisoners be allowed to ...

PLEASE TICK ONE BOX
ON EACH LINE

	Yes	No	(DK/NA)
[PRISBKS] a) ... have as many books as they wish to read?	% 88.9	9.6	1.4
[PRISLTRS] b) ... write and receive as many letters as they wish?	% 81.5	16.0	2.5

2.34 Do you think that people in each of these sorts of jobs should or should not be allowed the right to go on strike?

PLEASE TICK ONE BOX
ON EACH LINE

	Definitely should be allowed to strike	Probably should be allowed to strike	Probably should not be allowed to strike	Definitely should not be allowed to strike	(DK/NA)
[PCSTRK] a) ... police officers?	% 14.9	17.3	27.3	39.7	0.9
[NURSTRK] b) ... nurses?	% 19.2	30.3	28.0	21.4	1.0
[CARWSTRK] c) ... car workers?	% 28.0	47.2	15.2	8.4	1.2
[COUNSTRK] d) ... council workers?	% 23.8	42.1	22.0	10.9	1.3
[ELECSTRK] e) ... electricity supply workers?	% 18.8	28.8	28.2	23.2	1.1
[HDOCSTRK] f) ... hospital doctors?	% 16.3	22.0	26.9	33.9	0.9

Please continue ...

L.

- 16 -

[CSSILENT]
2.35 Suppose a cabinet minister gives false information to parliament about an important national issue.

PLEASE TICK ONE BOX

	%
Should the law allow civil servants in the minister's department to reveal the correct facts,	83.3
OR Should civil servants be required by law to keep silent?	6.9
Can't choose	8.9
(NA)	0.9

[BILRITES]
2.36 Some people support a Bill of Rights for Britain which would give the courts rather than parliament the final say on any laws or government actions which threaten basic freedoms. Others say it is better to leave things as they are. What do you think?

PLEASE TICK ONE BOX

	%
Definitely should be a Bill of Rights	27.3
Probably should be a Bill of Rights	30.4
Probably should not be a Bill of Rights	13.2
Definitely should not be a Bill of Rights	5.6
Can't choose	22.5
(NA)	1.1

2.37 Please tick one box for each statement below to show how much you agree or disagree with it.

PLEASE TICK ONE BOX
ON EACH LINE

	Agree strongly	Agree	Neither agree nor disagree	Disagree	Disagree strongly	(DK/NA)
[ESCORTAG] a) People on probation or parole should be fitted with a transmitter - that is, an electronic tag - so the police can check where they are.	% 19.1	38.8	22.2	15.0	3.7	1.3
[PCGUNS] b) On-duty police officers should always carry guns	% 3.4	10.3	17.6	43.3	24.0	1.4
[LITSENT] c) Too many convicted criminals are let off lightly by the courts.	% 35.6	43.0	14.6	4.7	1.0	1.1
[CONFESSN] d) A confession made during police questioning and later withdrawn should not on its own be enough to convict someone.	% 18.4	55.1	17.3	7.0	1.0	1.2

- 17 -

2.38 And please tick one box for each statement below to show how much you agree or disagree with it.

PLEASE TICK ONE BOX ON EACH LINE

	Agree strongly	Agree	Neither agree nor disagree	Disagree	Disagree strongly	(DK/NA)
[PCONSOLC] a) The police should be allowed to question suspects for up to a week without letting them see a solicitor.	% 2.3	6.8	9.2	53.8	26.7	1.2
[REFUGEES] b) Refugees who are in danger because of their political beliefs should always be welcome in Britain.	% 5.2	17.0	29.0	38.0	9.7	1.2
[PCCOMPLN] c) Serious complaints against the police should be investigated by an independent body, not by the police themselves.	% 37.5	54.9	3.9	1.8	0.7	1.1
[IDCARDS] d) Every adult in Britain should have to carry an identity card.	% 10.4	26.4	21.9	28.7	11.2	1.4
[CRIMSLNT] e) If someone remains silent under police questioning, it should count against them in court.	% 5.1	25.6	25.4	34.2	8.3	1.5
[NIMPRISN] f) The prisons contain too many people who ought to be given a lighter punishment.	% 8.7	39.5	27.3	19.8	3.3	1.4
[NOWARRNT] g) The police should not need a warrant to search the homes of suspects.	% 3.9	12.4	9.1	50.6	22.8	1.2

2.39 [TECHSYR]
New kinds of technology are being introduced more and more in Britain: computers and word processors, robots in factories and so on. Please tick one box to show what effect you think this technology will have over the next five years?

PLEASE TICK ONE BOX

n = 2349
Also asked on Version Y(Q.2.26)

	%
It will increase the number of jobs available	8.8
It will reduce the number of jobs available	63.9
It will make no difference to the number of jobs available	25.8
(DK/NA)	3.2

Please continue ...

- 18 -

n = 2349
Also asked on Version Y (Q.2.27)

2.40a) [TECHBORE]
Do you think that the introduction of new technology in Britain over the next five years will ...

PLEASE TICK ONE BOX

	%
... make work more interesting,	38.1
make work more boring,	36.4
or - will it make no difference to work?	23.7
(DK/NA)	1.8

b) [TECHEASE]
And will it ...

PLEASE TICK ONE BOX

	%
... make life more difficult,	10.3
make life easier,	62.9
or - will it make no difference?	24.6
(DK/NA)	2.1

c) [NEWTECH]
Please tick one box to show whether you agree or disagree with the following statement: the government should do more to encourage the spread of new technology in Britain.

PLEASE TICK ONE BOX

	%
Agree strongly	21.9
Agree	45.0
Neither agree nor disagree	27.7
Disagree	4.0
Disagree strongly	0.3
(DK/NA)	1.1

2.41 Please tick one box for each statement below to show how much you agree or disagree with it.

PLEASE TICK ONE BOX ON EACH LINE

n = 2349
Also asked on Version Y (Q.2.28)

	Agree strongly	Agree	Neither agree nor disagree	Disagree	Disagree strongly	(DK/NA)
[REDISTRB] a) Government should redistribute income from the better-off to those who are less well off.	% 17.4	32.1	19.5	24.4	5.5	1.2
[BIGBUSNN] b) Big business benefits owners at the expense of workers.	% 13.4	39.0	23.6	19.5	3.1	1.5
[WEALTH] c) Ordinary working people do not get their fair share of the nation's wealth.	% 18.8	46.3	18.6	13.7	1.6	1.0
[RICHLAW] d) There is one law for the rich and one for the poor.	% 27.6	39.6	13.6	15.3	2.9	0.9
[INDUST4] * e) Management will always try to get the better of employees if it gets the chance.	% 18.8	42.5	18.7	16.4	2.6	1.1

* The third character of the variable is an 'o', not a 'd'.

L.

- 19 -

n = 2349
Also asked on Version Y (Q.2.28f-n)

2.42 And please tick one box for each statement below to show how much you agree or disagree with it.

PLEASE TICK ONE BOX ON EACH LINE

		Agree strongly	Agree	Neither agree nor disagree	Disagree	Disagree strongly	(DK/NA)
a)	*[TRADVALS]* Young people today don't have enough respect for traditional British values.	% 18.8	48.4	20.4	10.6	0.9	1.0
b)	*[STIFSENT]* People who break the law should be given stiffer sentences.	% 26.5	43.7	20.9	7.3	0.7	1.0
c)	*[PROTMEET]* People should be allowed to organise public meetings to protest against the government.	% 15.3	54.4	20.1	8.2	1.0	1.0
d)	*[DEATHAPP]* For some crimes, the death penalty is the most appropriate sentence.	% 32.0	37.0	7.9	12.7	9.6	0.9
e)	*[PROTLEAF]* People should be allowed to publish leaflets to protest against the government.	% 15.1	54.7	19.0	8.5	1.3	1.4
f)	*[OBEY]* Schools should teach children to obey authority.	% 27.1	51.5	13.4	5.9	0.9	1.1
g)	*[PROTDEMO]* People should be allowed to organise protest marches and demonstrations.	% 13.0	50.4	21.8	11.6	2.0	1.1
h)	*[WRONGLAW]* The law should always be obeyed, even if a particular law is wrong.	% 9.6	35.8	24.7	25.8	3.1	1.1
i)	*[CENSOR]* Censorship of films and magazines is necessary to uphold moral standards.	% 19.1	47.7	14.8	14.1	3.6	0.7

2.43 *[BRITPOWR]*
Please tick one box to show how much you agree or disagree with this statement: "the days when Britain was an important world power are over".

PLEASE TICK ONE BOX

n = 1163

	%
Strongly agree	20.9
Just agree	40.1
Neither agree nor disagree	17.9
Just disagree	15.3
Disagree strongly	4.7
(DK/NA)	1.1

Please continue .....

L.

- 20 -

n = 2349
Also asked on Version Y (Q.2.29)

2.43a) *[QTIME]* To help us plan better in future, please tell us about **how long** it took you to complete this questionnaire?

PLEASE TICK ONE BOX

	%
Less than 15 minutes	6.9
Between 15 and 20 minutes	27.4
Between 20 and 30 minutes	31.4
Between 30 and 45 minutes	21.3
Between 45 and 60 minutes	7.7
Over one hour	3.9
(NA)	1.4

b) *[SQDATE2]* And on what **date** did you fill in the questionnaire?

PLEASE WRITE IN

DATE   MONTH   9 0 YEAR

THANK YOU VERY MUCH FOR YOUR HELP!

Please keep the completed questionnaire for the inter-viewer if he or she has arranged to call for it. Other-wise, please post it as soon as possible in the pre-paid addressed envelope provided.

Y

Head Office: 35 NORTHAMPTON SQUARE,
LONDON EC1V 0AX Telephone: 01-250 1866

Field and OP Office: BRENTWOOD, ESSEX
Northern Field Office: DARLINGTON, CO. DURHAM

P.1090/GB

BRITISH SOCIAL ATTITUDES 1990
SELF-COMPLETION QUESTIONNAIRE

Spring 1990

OFFICE USE ONLY: Area No.
Interviewer   0
to enter: Serial No.

Rec.   Interviewer No.

To the selected respondent:

Thank you very much for agreeing to take part in this important study— the seventh
in this annual series. The study consists of this self-completion questionnaire, and
the interview you have already completed. The results of the survey are published in
a book each autumn; some of the questions are also being asked in ten other countries,
as part of an international survey.

Completing the questionnaire:

The questions inside cover a wide range of subjects, but each one can be answered
simply by placing a tick (✓) or a number in one or more of the boxes. No special
knowledge is required; we are confident that everyone will be able to take part, not
just those with strong views or particular viewpoints. The questionnaire should not
take very long to complete, and we hope you will find it interesting and enjoyable.
It should be filled in only by the person actually interviewed at your address. The
answers you give will be treated as confidential and anonymous.

Returning the questionnaire:

Your interviewer will arrange with you the most convenient way of returning the
questionnaire. If the interviewer has arranged to call back for it, please complete
it and keep it safely until then. If not, please complete it and post it back in the
pre-paid, addressed envelope, AS SOON AS YOU POSSIBLY CAN.

THANK YOU AGAIN FOR YOUR HELP.

*Social and Community Planning Research is an independent social research institute
registered as a charitable trust. Its projects are funded by government departments,
local authorities, universities and foundations to provide information on social
issues in Britain. The British Social Attitudes Survey series has been funded mainly
by the Sainsbury Family Charitable Trusts, with contributions also from government
departments, the Nuffield Foundation, universities and industry. Please contact us if
you would like further information.*

2.01 (p. 1) Same as Q. 2.20 in L version

- 2 -

n = 2349

2.02 In the last two years, have you or a close family member ...
PLEASE TICK ONE BOX ON EACH LINE

Also asked on version LQ.2.21)

	Yes	No	(DK/NA)
[NHSDOC] ... visited an NHS GP?	%95.3	4.0	0.7
[NHSOUTP] ... been an out-patient in an NHS hospital?	%65.9	32.1	2.0
[NHSINP] ... been an in-patient in an NHS hospital?	%46.1	51.2	2.6
[NHSVISIT] ... visited a patient in an NHS hospital?	%75.4	22.8	1.8
[PRIVPAT] ... had any medical treatment as a private patient?	%14.2	83.7	2.1

2.03 n = 1186   Qs.2.03-2.05

Please tick one box to show how much you agree or disagree with each of these statements about secondary schooling.
PLEASE TICK ONE BOX ON EACH LINE

[SECSCHL1 - SECSCHL4]

	Agree strongly	Agree	Neither agree nor disagree	Dis-agree	Disagree strongly	(DK/NA)
a) Formal exams are the best way of judging the ability of pupils.	% 8.2	39.3	18.3	26.8	5.9	1.6
b) On the whole, pupils are too young when they have to decide which subjects to specialise in.	% 14.8	51.0	16.5	15.4	0.5	1.8
c) The present law allows pupils to leave school when they are too young.	% 4.4	21.6	25.4	42.9	3.9	1.7
d) So much attention is given to exam results in Britain that a pupil's everyday classroom work counts for too little.	% 17.4	44.5	17.3	16.7	1.9	2.2

2.04 From what you know or have heard, please tick one box on each line to show how well you think state secondary schools nowadays ...
PLEASE TICK ONE BOX ON EACH LINE

[STATSEC1 - STATSEC3]

	Very well	Quite well	Not very well	Not at all well	(DK/NA)
a) ... prepare young people for work?	% 2.4	34.6	50.4	10.7	2.0
b) ... teach young people basic skills such as reading, writing and maths?	% 8.7	47.9	33.3	8.2	1.9
c) ... bring out young people's natural abilities?	% 3.8	32.3	50.0	11.6	2.2

- 3 -

2.05 From what you know or have heard, please tick one box for each statement about state secondary schools now compared with 10 years ago.
PLEASE TICK ONE BOX ON EACH LINE

	Much better now than 10 years ago	A little better	About the same	A little worse	Much worse now than 10 years ago	(DK/NA)
a) [SCHLLEAV] On the whole, do you think school-leavers are better qualified or worse qualified nowadays than they were 10 years ago?	% 10.6	26.4	26.1	22.2	12.5	2.2
b) [TEACHPAY] Do you think teachers are better paid or worse paid nowadays than they were 10 years ago?	% 18.9	23.9	20.3	22.0	12.5	2.4
c) [CLASSBEH] And do you think classroom behaviour is better or worse nowadays than it was 10 years ago?	% 0.9	2.0	12.3	26.1	57.0	1.7

	Much more now than 10 years ago	A little more	About the same	A little less	Much less now than 10 years ago	(DK/NA)
d) [PARTEACH] Do you think parents have more respect or less respect for teachers nowadays than they did 10 years ago?	% 2.4	4.6	25.6	36.2	29.2	2.0
e) [PUPTEACH] And do you think pupils have more respect or less respect for teachers nowadays than they did 10 years ago?	% 0.9	1.9	12.1	30.0	53.3	1.8
f) [TEACHDED] Do you think teachers are more dedicated to their jobs or less dedicated nowadays than they were 10 years ago?	% 3.6	5.7	36.2	34.3	18.7	1.5
g) [TEACHDIF] And, on the whole, do you think the job of a state secondary school-teacher is more difficult or less difficult nowadays than it was 10 years ago?	% 40.8	29.6	13.0	5.3	9.7	1.5

Please continue ...

Y.

2.06-2.08 (pp. 4-5) Same as Qs. 2.26-2.28 in L version

- 6 -

2.09 [GVSPEND1 - GVSPEND8]

Listed below are various areas of government spending. Please show whether you would like to see more or less government spending in each area.

Remember that if you say "much more", it might require a tax increase to pay for it.

Also asked on version L.(Q.2.11)

n = 2349

PLEASE TICK ONE BOX ON EACH LINE

	Spend much more	Spend more	Spend the same as now	Spend less	Spend much less	Can't choose	(NA)
A. The environment	14.3	46.6	31.0	2.1	0.4	2.4	3.1
B. Health	38.4	50.5	9.2	0.3	0.1	0.6	0.9
C. The police and law enforcement	12.0	38.1	42.9	3.0	0.8	1.6	1.6
D. Education	27.9	50.2	17.9	1.1	0.4	1.0	1.5
E. The military and defence	2.1	6.3	39.3	32.1	16.1	2.3	1.8
F. Old age pensions	29.7	50.8	17.0	0.6	0.2	0.9	1.0
G. Unemployment benefits	7.7	28.2	43.1	13.1	4.1	2.2	1.5
H. Culture and the arts	2.0	10.4	41.5	26.5	13.5	4.7	1.3

(values are %)

2.10 [ENVIR1 - ENVIR9]

How serious an effect on our environment do you think each of these things has?

PLEASE TICK ONE BOX ON EACH LINE

n = 1186
Qs.2.10-2.25

	Very serious	Quite serious	Not very serious	Not at all serious	(DK/NA)
Noise from aircraft	6.6	25.3	56.6	10.1	1.3
Lead from petrol	37.6	51.4	9.3	0.7	1.0
Industrial waste in the rivers and sea	74.9	22.5	1.5	0.3	0.7
Waste from nuclear electricity stations	64.0	26.1	7.9	1.2	0.7
Industrial fumes in the air	57.6	36.3	4.7	0.6	0.8
Noise and dirt from traffic	28.2	52.8	17.0	1.1	0.9
Acid rain	53.4	36.3	7.8	1.1	1.4
Certain aerosol chemicals in the atmosphere	51.4	37.1	9.2	1.1	1.1
Cutting down tropical rainforests	67.9	24.8	5.6	0.8	0.9

(values are %)

- 7 -

Y.

2. 11a) [POWER]

Which one of these three possible solutions to Britain's electricity needs would you favour most? (Q.2.11)

PLEASE TICK ONE BOX

	%
We should make do with the power stations we have already	55.4
We should build more coal-fuelled power stations	28.1
We should build more nuclear power stations	13.5
(DK/NA)	3.0

b) [NUCPOWER]

As far as nuclear power stations are concerned, which of these statements comes closest to your own feelings?

PLEASE TICK ONE BOX

	%
They create very serious risks for the future	42.5
They create quite serious risks for the future	31.9
They create only slight risks for the future	18.9
They create hardly any risks for the future	5.3
(DK/NA)	1.3

2. 12a) [DAMAGE]

Which one of these two statements comes closest to your own views?

PLEASE TICK ONE BOX

	%
Industry should be prevented from causing damage to the countryside, even if this sometimes leads to higher prices	88.6
OR	
Industry should keep prices down, even if this sometimes causes damage to the countryside	9.1
(DK/NA)	2.3

b) [CTRYJOBS]

And which of these two statements comes closest to your own views?

PLEASE TICK ONE BOX

	%
The countryside should be protected from development, even if this sometimes leads to fewer new jobs	72.6
OR	
New jobs should be created, even if this sometimes causes damage to the countryside	24.8
(DK/NA)	2.6

Y.

- 8 -

2. 13 Please tick one box on each line to show how you feel about ...

PLEASE TICK ONE BOX ON EACH LINE

	It should be stopped altogether	It should be discouraged	Don't mind one way or the other	It should be encouraged	(DK/NA)
a) [CTRYFARM] ... Increasing the amount of countryside being farmed	% 5.9	31.3	38.9	22.1	1.8
b) [CTRYHSNG] ... Building new housing in country areas	% 13.4	56.9	21.3	7.5	0.9
c) [WILDLIFE] ... Putting the needs of farmers before protection of wildlife	% 16.4	58.7	17.2	6.1	1.6
d) [CTRYROAD] ... Providing more roads in country areas	% 13.4	52.3	23.5	9.8	1.1
e) [PICNIC] ... Increasing the number of picnic areas and camping sites in the countryside	% 3.2	16.5	32.2	46.8	1.3

2. 14 Here is a list of predictions. For each one, please say how likely or unlikely you think it is to come true within the next ten years?

PLEASE TICK ONE BOX FOR EACH PREDICTION

[PREDICT1 - PREDICT7]

	Very likely	Quite likely	Not very likely	Not at all likely	(DK/NA)
a) Acts of political terrorism in Britain will be common events	% 16.1	48.6	30.9	3.0	1.4
b) Riots and civil disturbance in our cities will be common events	% 18.4	48.5	28.5	3.5	1.2
c) There will be a world war involving Britain and Europe	% 2.2	8.4	52.1	35.6	1.7
d) There will be a serious accident at a British nuclear power station	% 12.9	46.0	35.0	5.2	1.0
e) The police in our cities will find it impossible to protect our personal safety on the streets	% 18.3	41.7	33.3	5.8	0.8
f) The government in Britain will be over-thrown by revolution	% 3.5	8.2	42.6	44.4	1.3
g) A nuclear bomb will be dropped somewhere in the world	% 6.3	22.8	43.4	26.3	1.2

Y.

- 9 -

2. 15 Please tick one box for each statement below to show how much you agree or disagree with it.

PLEASE TICK ONE BOX ON EACH LINE

	Agree strongly	Agree	Neither agree nor disagree	Disagree	Disagree strongly	(DK/NA)
a) [GOVENVIR] The government should do more to protect the environment, even if it leads to higher taxes.	% 17.9	48.4	23.2	8.7	0.8	1.0
b) [INDENVIR] Industry should do more to protect the environment, even if it leads to lower profits and fewer jobs.	% 21.3	53.7	16.6	6.6	0.5	1.3
d) [PPLENVIR] Ordinary people should do more to protect the environment, even if it means paying higher prices.	% 21.3	53.2	15.4	7.8	1.1	1.1

2. 16a) Please tick one box to show which is closest to your views about the following statement:

"Within twenty years, life on earth will be seriously damaged by a rise in the world's temperature."

PLEASE TICK ONE BOX

[WRLDTEMP]

	%
It is highly exaggerated	11.3
It is slightly exaggerated	37.9
It is more, or less true	49.4
(DK/NA)	1.4

b) [ENVIRDAM] And please tick one box to show which is closest to your views about this statement:

"Within twenty years, damage to the environment will be the biggest single problem facing Europe."

PLEASE TICK ONE BOX

	%
It is highly exaggerated	9.5
It is slightly exaggerated	38.4
It is more or less true	50.8
(DK/NA)	1.3

Please continue .....

r.

- 10 -

2.17 Please tick one box for each statement below to show how much you agree or disagree with it.

PLEASE TICK ONE BOX ON EACH LINE

		Agree strongly	Agree	Neither agree nor disagree	Disagree	Disagree strongly	(DK/NA)
a)	[RARPLANT] Too much money is spent trying to protect rare plants and animals %	1.8	12.3	31.1	44.5	9.3	1.1
b)	[SCNCSOLV] Science can solve environmental problems without any need for people to change their behaviour %	1.4	12.1	17.6	51.8	15.7	1.3
c)	[COSMTEST] It is acceptable to use animals for testing and improving cosmetics %	1.2	4.2	8.2	35.1	50.3	1.0
d)	[MEDITEST] It is acceptable to use animals for testing medicines if it could save human lives %	10.1	47.8	15.2	16.3	9.2	1.5
e)	[FOXHUNT] Fox hunting should be banned by law %	36.9	30.8	15.7	9.0	6.8	0.8
f)	[CARTAXHI] For the sake of the environment, car users should pay higher taxes %	5.3	18.4	21.3	41.4	12.3	1.2
g)	[POLUTAID] Richer countries ought to give financial help to poorer countries, to help them cut back on their pollution %	12.9	46.9	22.1	13.1	4.0	1.0
h)	[IMPROAD] If the government had to choose, it should improve roads rather than public transport %	6.6	29.8	19.5	30.7	12.5	1.0

2.18 Please tick one box on each line to show what you think about allowing people to smoke in each of the following places.

PLEASE TICK ONE BOX ON EACH LINE

		Smoking should be...				
		...freely allowed	...restricted to certain areas	...banned altogether	Can't choose	(NA)
a)	[SMKPLANE] ... on airline flights? %	2.4	44.1	51.7	1.3	0.5
b)	[SMKTRAIN] ... on trains? %	2.6	57.9	36.0	1.1	0.4
c)	[SMKHOSPL] ... in hospitals? %	0.4	25.7	72.4	0.9	0.6
d)	[SMKWORK] ... at people's places of work? %	4.7	59.7	33.2	1.5	0.8
e)	[SMKCINMA] ... in cinemas? %	2.9	34.6	60.8	1.1	0.5
f)	[SMKRSTWT] ... in restaurants? %	4.4	36.8	57.3	1.0	0.5
g)	[SMKPUBS] ... in pubs? %	25.0	45.3	25.8	3.3	0.6

r.

- 11 -

2.19 [NONSMRSK] Suppose a non-smoker lives, or works closely, with a heavy smoker. How risky is it for the **non-smoker**?

PLEASE TICK ONE BOX

	%
... a very serious health risk,	22.8
a fairly serious health risk,	51.1
not much of a health risk,	22.0
or - not a health risk at all?	2.1
(Can't choose)	1.5
(NA)	0.5

2.20 Please tick one box for each statement below to show what you think about it.

PLEASE TICK ONE BOX ON EACH LINE

		Definitely should	Probably should	Probably should not	Definitely should not	Can't choose	(NA)
a)	[EMPBANSM] Employers should ban smoking altogether at workplaces %	31.6	29.0	20.1	13.8	5.3	0.3
b)	[SMINSURE] Insurance companies should charge smokers much more than non-smokers for their life insurance %	39.1	33.6	10.0	13.2	3.7	0.3
c)	[SMLOWOP] NHS hospitals should give smokers low priority for heart or lung operations %	8.9	16.7	21.1	45.7	7.2	0.3

2.21 [SMWKFREE] Suppose an employer **had** to choose between the rights of smokers and non-smokers. Which of these comes closest to your view?

PLEASE TICK ONE BOX

	%
Smokers should have the right to smoke freely at work	10.6
OR	
Non-smokers should have the right to work in smoke-free surroundings	77.1
Can't choose	11.8
(NA)	0.5

Please continue ......

- 12 -

Y.

2.22 Please tick one box for each statement below to show how much you agree or disagree with it.

PLEASE TICK ONE BOX ON EACH LINE

		Agree strongly	Agree	Neither agree nor disagree	Disagree	Disagree strongly	(DK/NA)
a)	[SMKRESTR] There are already enough restrictions on where people can smoke.	% 4.2	22.1	17.1	42.6	13.0	0.9
b)	[TAXCIGHI] The government should tax cigarettes much more heavily to encourage people to stop smoking.	% 26.6	33.3	13.4	21.3	4.8	0.6
c)	[SMOWNCH] If people choose to smoke, nobody should try to persuade them to stop.	% 7.2	27.0	18.1	36.8	10.2	0.8
d)	[AGEBUYSM] The age at which young people are allowed to buy cigarettes should be reduced from 16 to 14.	% 4.1	1.4	1.9	26.4	65.6	0.6
e)	[DESPISSM] Nowadays most people look down on smokers.	% 7.3	45.9	25.4	19.1	1.6	0.8
f)	[STOPIMPH] Even if people have smoked for a long time, giving up will still improve their health.	% 23.6	60.0	10.4	4.7	0.7	0.7
g)	[HLTHLUCK] Good health is just a matter of luck.	% 2.8	12.4	14.2	46.6	23.1	0.9
h)	[HEARTDIS] If heart disease is in your family, there is little you can do to reduce your chances of getting it.	% 1.3	11.1	12.3	53.7	20.9	0.8
i)	[BANSMAD] All cigarette advertising should be banned.	% 30.9	33.2	19.2	13.6	2.4	0.7

- 13 -

Y.

2.23 a) [HSEVALUE] Central government provides financial support to housing in two main ways.
Second, by means of tax relief to people with mortgages.
First, by means of allowances to low income tenants.

On the whole, which of these three types of family would you say benefits **most** from central government support for housing?

PLEASE TICK **ONE** BOX

	%
Families with **high** incomes	37.3
Families with **middle** incomes	21.5
Families with **low** incomes	37.8
(DK/NA)	3.4

b) [CNCLSALE] Which of these three views comes closest to your own on the sale of council houses and flats to tenants?

PLEASE TICK **ONE** BOX

	%
Council tenants **should not** be allowed to buy their houses or flats	11.9
Council tenants **should** be allowed to buy but **only** in areas with no housing shortage	33.3
Council tenants **should generally** be allowed to buy their houses or flats	53.4
(DK/NA)	1.3

2.24 Which of the following statments do you think are generally true and which false?

PLEASE TICK ONE BOX ON EACH LINE
[COUNCIL1 - COUNCIL3]

	True	False	(DK/NA)
Council tenants pay low rents	%34.4	59.2	6.3
Councils give a poor standard of repairs and maintenance	%60.2	34.6	5.2
Council estates are generally pleasant places to live	%31.5	63.0	5.5

Please continue .....

Y.

- 14 -

2.25a) *[RENTBUY]*
Suppose a newly-married young couple, both with steady jobs, asked your advice about whether to buy or rent a home. If they had the choice, what would you advise them to do?

PLEASE TICK *ONE* BOX

	%
To buy a home as soon as possible	69.9
To wait a bit, then try to buy a home	23.5
Not to plan to buy a home at all	1.0
Can't choose	5.0
(NA)	0.6

b) Still thinking of what you might say to this young couple, please tick one box for **each** statement below to show how much you agree or disagree with it.

PLEASE TICK ONE BOX ON EACH LINE

	Agree strongly	Just agree	Neither agree nor dis-agree	Just dis-agree	Disagree strongly	(DK/NA)
i) *[HOMERISK]* Owning your home can be a risky investment	6.4	27.3	15.5	29.1	20.8	1.0
ii) *[BUYCHEAP]* Over time, buying a home works out less expensive than paying rent	33.1	44.1	11.7	8.1	2.2	0.8
iii) *[MOVEHOME]* Owning your home makes it easier to move when you want to	18.8	36.4	24.0	16.2	3.7	0.9
iv) *[MONEYTIE]* Owning a home ties up money you may need urgently for other things	6.9	30.2	23.9	30.8	7.1	1.1
v) *[FREEDOM]* Owning a home gives you the freedom to do what you want to it	30.7	48.9	10.3	7.4	1.9	0.9
vi) *[FINBURDN]* Owning a home is a big financial burden to repair and maintain	13.7	41.0	22.9	17.2	4.3	0.9
vii) *[LEAVEFAM]* Your own home will be something to leave your family	33.8	50.3	10.9	2.6	1.1	1.2
viii) *[HOMERESP]* Owning a home is just too much of a responsibility	2.6	7.8	20.5	40.2	27.9	1.1
ix) *[RISKJOB]* Owning a home is too much of a risk for couples without secure jobs	26.1	37.7	15.4	15.6	4.5	0.8
x) *[WAITFAM]* Couples who buy their own homes would be wise to wait before starting a family	18.0	42.7	21.8	12.7	4.1	0.8

2.26-2.27   (p. 15) Same as Qs. 2.36-2.37 in L version

2.28-2.29   (pp. 16-17) Same as Qs. 2.21-2.43 in L version

Social & Community Planning Research

SCPR

Head Office: 35 NORTHAMPTON SQUARE,
LONDON EC1V 0AX Telephone 01-250 1866

Field and DP Office: BRENTWOOD, ESSEX
Northern Field Office: DARLINGTON, CO. DURHAM

Spring 1990

P.1090/Northern Ireland

NORTHERN IRELAND SOCIAL ATTITUDES:

1990 SURVEY

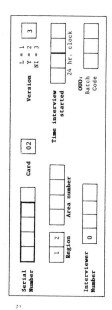

Serial
Number

Card   02

Version   L = 1
           Y = 2   3
           NI = 3

Region
1   2

Area number

Time interview
started   24 hr. clock

Interviewer
Number   0

OUO:
Batch
Code

- 1 -

N.I. | SECTION ONE | n = 896
                                                            Qs. 1-21

1.a) [READPAP]
Do you normally read any daily morning newspaper at least 3 times a week?

	%
Yes	56.4
No	43.6

IF YES
b) [WHPAPER]
Which one do you normally read?
IF MORE THAN ONE ASK: Which one do you read most frequently?
ONE CODE ONLY

	%
(Scottish) Daily Express	2.6
Daily Mail	3.9
Daily Mirror/Record	10.7
Daily Star	2.2
The Sun	11.8
Today	1.2
Daily Telegraph	1.5
Financial Times	0.2
The Guardian	0.7
The Independent	0.9
The Times	0.2
Morning Star	-
The News Letter	10.2
The Irish News	7.8
The Irish Times	0.5
Other Irish/Northern Irish/Scottish regional or local daily morning paper **(WRITE IN:)**	0.3

Other **(WRITE IN:)** _____

ASK ALL
2.a) Now a few questions about the UK's relationships with other countries. [EEC]
Do you think the UK should continue to be a member of the EC - the Common Market - or should it withdraw?

		%
EC:	Continue	77.5
	Withdraw	12.7
	(DK)	9.8

b) [NATO]
And do you think the UK should continue to be a member of NATO - the North Atlantic Treaty Organisation - or should it withdraw?

		%
NATO:	Continue	70.4
	Withdraw	9.8
	(DK)	19.8

- 2 -

N.I.

3. [NATION]
On the whole, do you think that the UK's interests are better served by ... **READ OUT** ...

	%
... closer links with Western Europe,	43.8
or - closer links with America?	16.8
(Both equally)	25.2
(Neither)	2.3
(Don't know)	12.0

4.a) [USANUKE]
Do you think that the siting of <u>American</u> nuclear missiles in Britain makes Britain a safer or a less safe place to live?

	%
Safer	27.1
Less safe	59.9
(Don't know)	12.4

b) [OWNNUKE]
And do you think that having its <u>own</u> independent nuclear missiles makes Britain a safer or a less safe place to live?

	%
Safer	43.8
Less safe	43.4
(No difference)	0.6
(Don't know)	12.0
(NA)	0.2

5. CARD A [UKNUCPOL]
Which, if either, of these two statements comes closest to your own opinion on UK nuclear policy?

	%
The UK should <u>rid</u> itself of nuclear weapons while persuading others to do the same	36.1
The UK should <u>keep</u> its nuclear weapons until it can persuade others to reduce theirs	59.5
(Neither of these)	2.6
(DK)	1.8

6. [DEFPARTY]
Which political party's views on defence would you say comes <u>closest</u> to your own views?
ONLY CODE ALLIANCE AFTER PROBE:
CODE ONE ONLY

	%
Conservative	35.3
Labour	22.6
Social and Liberal Democrats or SDP (Owen)? (Social and) Liberal Democrat/Liberal/SLD	1.5
Mainland or Northern Ireland? SDP/Social Democrat	0.9
(Mainland - Alliance)	0.3
(Green Party)	1.0
Other **(WRITE IN:)**	1.1
(Don't know)	29.7
None	7.6

- 3 -

N.I.

CARD B [PEACE]

7. Which of the phrases on this card is closest to your opinion about threats to world peace?

	%
America is a greater threat to world peace than Russia	9.9
Russia is a greater threat to world peace than America	23.0
Russia and America are equally great threats to world peace	40.3
Neither is a threat to world peace	20.9
(Don't know)	5.6
(NA)	0.3

8.a) [NIRELAND]
Do you think the long term policy for Northern Ireland should be for it ... READ OUT ...

	%
... to remain part of the United Kingdom,	67.6
or - to reunify with the rest of Ireland?	25.0
(DK)	3.2
Other answer (WRITE IN:)	3.5
(NA)	0.7

b) [TROOPOUT]
Some people think that government policy towards Northern Ireland should include a complete withdrawal of British troops. Would you personally support or oppose such a policy? PROBE: Strongly or a little?

	%
Support strongly	17.3
Support a little	13.0
Oppose strongly	50.1
Oppose a little	13.9
(DK)	1.1
Other answer (WRITE IN:)	4.1
(NA)	0.5

9.a) [TROOPSHT]
If British troops were withdrawn from Northern Ireland, do you think there would be more or less bloodshed in the short-term, or would it make no difference? IF MORE/LESS: A lot (more/less) bloodshed or a little (more/less)?

	%
A lot more bloodshed	51.8
A little more bloodshed	18.6
A little less bloodshed	4.0
A lot less bloodshed	3.6
No difference	18.8
(DK)	3.0
(NA)	0.1

b) [TROOPLNG]
And in the long-term, if British troops were withdrawn, do you think there would be more or less bloodshed or would it make no difference? IF MORE/LESS: A lot (more/less) bloodshed or a little (more/less)?

	%
A lot more bloodshed	29.9
A little more bloodshed	13.6
A little less bloodshed	12.8
A lot less bloodshed	15.5
No difference	23.9
(DK)	4.3

- 4 -

N.I.

SECTION TWO

10. Now I would like to ask you about two economic problems - inflation and unemployment.
[PRICES]
First, inflation: in a year from now, do you expect prices generally to have gone up, to have stayed the same, or to have gone down?

IF COME UP OR COME DOWN:
By a lot or a little?

	%
To have gone up by a lot	45.5
To have gone up by a little	42.8
To have stayed the same	5.9
To have gone down by a little	4.4
To have gone down by a lot	0.6
(Don't know)	0.7
(NA)	0.1

11. [UNEMP]
Second, unemployment: in a year from now, do you expect unemployment to have gone up, to have stayed the same, or to have gone down?

IF COME UP OR COME DOWN:
By a lot or a little?

	%
To have gone up by a lot	19.5
To have gone up by a little	27.6
To have stayed the same	33.2
To have gone down by a little	15.2
To have gone down by a lot	1.6
(Don't know)	2.7
(NA)	0.1

12.a) [UNEMPINF]
If the government had to choose between keeping down inflation or keeping down unemployment, to which do you think it should give highest priority?

	%
Keeping down inflation	40.4
Keeping down unemployment	56.2
(Both equally)	1.2
Other answer (WRITE IN:) (DK)	1.0
(NA)	1.2

b) [CONCERN]
Which do you think is of most concern to you and your family ... READ OUT ...

	%
... inflation,	64.1
or - unemployment?	33.9
(Both equally/Neither)	1.0
Other answer (WRITE IN:) (DK)	0.8
(NA)	

- 5 -

N.I.

13. *[INDUSTRY]*
Looking ahead over the next year, do you think the UK's general industrial performance will improve, stay much the same, or decline?

IF IMPROVE OR DECLINE:
By a lot or a little?

	%
Improve a lot	2.8
Improve a little	15.6
Stay much the same	50.7
Decline a little	18.1
Decline a lot	4.0
(Don't know)	8.7

14. Here are a number of policies which might help the UK's economic problems. As I read them out, will you tell me whether you would support such a policy or oppose it?

READ OUT ITEMS i)-x) AND CODE FOR EACH

		Support	Oppose	(DK/NA)
i)	*[ECOHELP1]* Control of wages by law	% 33.9	62.4	3.6
ii)	*[ECOHELP2]* Control of prices by law	% 63.6	34.0	2.4
iii)	*[ECOHELP3]* Reducing the level of government spending on health and education	% 9.1	89.9	1.0
iv)	*[ECOHELP4]* Government controls to cut down goods from abroad	% 71.1	25.6	3.2
v)	*[ECOHELP5]* Increasing government subsidies for private industry	% 63.7	30.4	5.8
vi)	*[ECOHELP7]* Reducing government spending on defence	% 64.7	31.5	3.8
vii)	*[ECOHELP8]* Government schemes to encourage job sharing	% 74.7	20.9	4.5
viii)	*[ECOHELP9]* Government to set up construction projects to create more jobs	% 89.8	9.1	1.1
ix)	*[ECOHELPA]* Government action to cut interest rates	% 91.4	6.2	2.4
x)	*[ECOHELPB]* Government controls on hire purchase and credit	% 81.8	14.8	3.4

15. *[STATEOWN]*
On the whole, would you like to see **more** or **less** state ownership of industry, or about the **same** amount as now?

	%
More	20.2
Less	16.4
About the same amount	57.3
(Don't know)	6.1

16. *[INCOMGAP]*
Thinking of income levels generally in the UK today, would you say that the **gap** between those with high incomes and those with low incomes is ... **READ OUT** ...

	%
... too large,	82.8
about right,	11.3
or - too small?	4.0
(DK)	1.8
(NA)	0.1

- 6 -

N.I.

CARD C

17. Generally, how would you describe levels of taxation?

a) *[TAXHI]*
Firstly for those with **high** incomes? Please choose a phrase from this card. **RECORD ANSWER IN COL. a) BELOW**

b) *[TAXMID]*
Next for those with **middle** incomes? Please choose a phrase from this card. **RECORD ANSWER IN COL. b) BELOW**

c) *[TAXLOW]*
And lastly for those with **low** incomes? Please choose a phrase from this card. **RECORD ANSWER IN COL. c) BELOW**

	(a) High incomes	(b) Middle incomes	(c) Low incomes
	%	%	%
Taxes are: Much too high	5.1	5.4	42.4
Too high	13.0	32.4	38.5
About right	27.1	55.1	15.3
Too low	36.1	4.4	1.2
Much too low	16.5	0.2	0.2
(DK/NA)	2.3	2.5	2.5

18.a) *[SRINC]*
Among which group would you place yourself ... **READ OUT** ...

	%
... high income,	2.9
middle income,	46.3
or - low income?	50.7
(NA)	0.1

CARD D

b) *[HINCDIFF]*
Which of the phrases on this card would you say comes closest to your feelings about your household's income these days?

	%
Living comfortably on present income	21.2
Coping on present income	49.3
Finding it difficult on present income	21.5
Finding it very difficult on present income	8.0
Other **(WRITE IN:)**	-

19. *[HINCPAST]*
Looking back over the last year or so, would you say your household's income has ... **READ OUT** ...

	%
... fallen behind prices,	51.1
kept up with prices,	40.9
or - gone up by more than prices?	5.9
(Don't know)	2.2

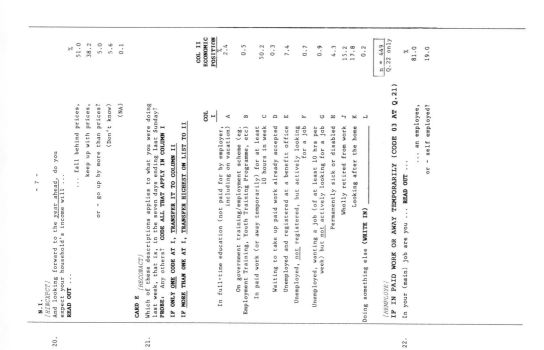

- 8 -

n = 364
Qs.23-33

%

N.I.
[ESHRJBTIM]
ALL EMPLOYEES (CODE 1 AT Q.22)

23. In your present job, are you working ... **READ OUT** ...

RESPONDENT'S OWN DEFINITION

	%
... full-time,	84.9
or - part-time?	15.1

24. *[EJBHOURS]*
How many hours a week do you normally work in your (main) job?
(IF RESPONDENT CANNOT ANSWER, ASK ABOUT LAST WEEK)

ROUND TO NEAREST HOUR
MEDIAN: 3 8

[EJBHRCAT]   **AND CODE:**

	%
10-15 hours a week	3.8
16-23 hours a week	6.3
24-29 hours a week	2.4
30 or more hours a week	87.3
(NA)	0.3

25a) *[WAGENOW]*
How would you describe the wages or salary you are paid for the job you do - on the low side, reasonable, or on the high side? **IF LOW:** Very low or a bit low?

	%
Very low	9.8
A bit low	24.9
Reasonable	61.3
On the high side	3.6
(NA)	0.1
Other answer **(WRITE IN)**	0.3

b) **CARD F** *[PAYGAP]*
Thinking of the highest and the lowest paid people at your place of work, how would you describe the gap between their pay, as far as you know? Please choose a phrase from this card.

	%
Much too big a gap	18.5
Too big	24.2
About right	45.0
Too small	2.8
Much too small a gap	0.6
(Don't know)	8.3
(NA)	0.7

- 7 -

20. **N.I.**
[HINCXPCT]
And looking forward to the year ahead, do you expect your household's income will ...
READ OUT ...

	%
... fall behind prices,	51.0
keep up with prices,	38.2
or - go up by more than prices?	5.0
(Don't know)	5.0
(NA)	0.1

21. **CARD E** *[RECONACT]*
Which of these descriptions applies to what you were doing last week, that is, in the seven days ending last Sunday?
PROBE: Any others? **CODE ALL THAT APPLY IN COLUMN I**
IF ONLY ONE CODE AT I, TRANSFER IT TO COLUMN II
IF MORE THAN ONE AT I, TRANSFER HIGHEST ON LIST TO II

	COL I	COL II ECONOMIC POSITION %
In full-time education (not paid for by employer, including on vacation)	A	2.4
On government training/employment scheme (eg. Employment Training, Youth Training Programme, etc)	B	0.5
In paid work (or away temporarily) for at least 10 hours in week	C	50.2
Waiting to take up paid work already accepted	D	0.3
Unemployed and registered at a benefit office	E	7.4
Unemployed, not registered, but actively looking for a job	F	0.7
Unemployed, wanting a job (of at least 10 hrs per week) but not actively looking for a job	G	0.9
Permanently sick or disabled	H	4.3
Wholly retired from work	J	15.2
Looking after the home	K	17.8
Doing something else **(WRITE IN)**	L	0.2

22. *[REMPLOYE]*
IF IN PAID WORK OR AWAY TEMPORARILY (CODE 03 AT Q.21)
In your (main) job are you ... **READ OUT** ...

n = 449
Q.22 only

	%
... an employee,	81.0
or - self employed?	19.0

- 9 -

N.I.

[WAGEXPCT]

26 If you stay in this job, would you expect your wages or salary over the coming year to ... **READ OUT** ...

	%
... rise by <u>more</u> than the cost of living,	14.3
rise by the <u>same</u> as the cost of living,	46.7
rise by <u>less</u> than the cost of living,	25.5
or - <u>not</u> to rise at all?	9.4
(Will not stay in job)	2.8
(Don't know)	1.4

[NUMEMP]

27 Over the coming year do you expect your workplace will be ... **READ OUT** ...

	%
... increasing its number of employees,	24.1
reducing its number of employees,	22.4
or - will the number of employees stay about the same?	52.7
Other answer (**WRITE IN**)	0.8

[LEAVEJOB]

28a) Thinking now about your own job. How likely or unlikely is it that you will leave this employer over the next year for any reason? Is it ... **READ OUT** ...

	%
... very likely,	11.0
quite likely,	7.8
not very likely,	27.7
or - not at all likely?	53.4

IF VERY OR QUITE LIKELY AT a)

CARD G

b) Why do you think you will leave? Please choose a phrase from this card or tell me what other reason there is.

MORE THAN ONE CODE MAY BE RINGED

	%
[WHYGO1] Firms will close down	0.3
[WHYGO2] I will be declared redundant	2.5
[WHYGO3] I will reach normal retirement age	0.4
[WHYGO4] My contract of employment will expire	3.4
[WHYGO5] I will take early retirement	1.1
[WHYGO6] I will decide to leave and work for another employer	9.5
[WHYGO7] I will decide to leave and work for myself, as self-employed	1.1
[WHYGO10] I will leave to look after home/children/relative	1.1
[WHYGO8] Other answer (**WRITE IN**)	0.1

- 10 -

N.I.

[EUNEMP]

ASK ALL EMPLOYEES

29.a) During the last <u>five years</u> - that is since March 1985 - have you been unemployed and seeking work for any period?

	%
Yes	21.8
No	78.2

[EUNEMPT]

IF YES AT a)

b) For how many months in total during the last five years?

MEDIAN: | MONTHS |
|---|
| 1 | 2 |

[ESELFEM]

ASK ALL EMPLOYEES

30.a) For any period during the last <u>five years</u> have you worked as a self-employed person as your main job?

	%
Yes	2.5
No	97.5

[ESELFSER]

IF NO AT a)

b) How seriously in the last five years have you considered working as a self-employed person ... **READ OUT** ...

	%
... very seriously,	4.2
quite seriously,	5.7
not very seriously,	12.7
or - not at all seriously?	74.3
(NA)	0.6

[WPUNIONS]

ASK ALL EMPLOYEES

31.a) At your place of work are there unions, staff associations, or groups of unions recognised by the management for negotiating pay and conditions of employment?

	%
Yes	69.9
No	30.1

[WPUNIOWN]

IF YES AT a)

b) On the whole, do you think these unions or staff associations do their job well or not?

	%
Yes	40.1
No	28.3
(DK)	1.1
(NA)	0.4

N.I.   - 11 -

[INDREL]

ASK ALL EMPLOYEES

32. In general how would you describe relations between management and other employees at your workplace ... **READ OUT** ...

	%
... very good,	39.3
quite good,	48.4
not very good,	7.0
or - not at all good?	4.9
(NA)	0.4

[WORKRUN]

33. And in general, would you say your workplace was ... **READ OUT** ...

	%
... very well managed,	30.9
quite well managed,	55.8
or - not well managed?	13.8

ALL SELF-EMPLOYED (CODE 2 AT Q.22) [SSRJBTIM]

n = 86
Qs.34-41

34. In your present job, are you working ... **READ OUT** ...

RESPONDENT'S OWN DEFINITION

	%
... full-time,	91.7
or - part-time?	8.3

[SJBHOURS]

35. How many hours a week do you normally work in your (main) job?

(IF RESPONDENT CANNOT ANSWER, ASK ABOUT 'LAST WEEK')

MEDIAN: | 5 | 5 | HOURS

[SJBHRCAT]

AND CODE:

	%
10-15 hours a week	6.5
16-23 hours a week	0.6
24-29 hours a week	-
30 or more hours a week	92.9

[SUNEMP]

36. During the last 5 years - that is since March 1985 - have you been unemployed and seeking work for any period?

	%
Yes	19.6
No	80.4

N.I.   - 12 -

[SEMPLEE]

37. Have you, for any period in the last five years, worked as an employee as your main job rather than as self-employed?

	%
Yes	16.7
No	83.3

[BUSIOK]

38. Compared with a year ago, would you say your business is doing ... **READ OUT** ...

	%
... very well,	12.5
quite well,	20.8
about the same,	45.2
not very well,	15.5
or - not at all well?	1.8
(Business not in existence then)	4.2

[BUSIFUT]

39. And over the coming year, do you think your business will do ... **READ OUT** ...

	%
... better,	22.0
about the same,	55.4
or - worse than this year?	14.3
Other (WRITE IN) _____	6.5
(Don't know) (NA)	1.8

[SPARTNRS]

40. In your work or business, do you have any partners or other self-employed colleagues?

NOTE: DOES NOT INCLUDE EMPLOYEES

	%
Yes, have partner(s)	37.5
No	62.5

[SNUMEMP]

41. And in your work or business do you have any employees, or not?

N.B. FAMILY MEMBERS MAY BE EMPLOYEES ONLY IF THEY RECEIVE A REGULAR WAGE OR SALARY.

	%
Yes, has employee(s)	28.0
No	72.0

N.I.

- 13 -

[EDWORK10]
ALL IN FULL-TIME EDUCATION (CODE 01 AT Q.21)

42. And in the seven days ending last Sunday, did you have paid work of less than ten hours a week?

n = 21
Q.42 only

	n
Yes	2
No	20

[GUNEMP]
43. **ALL ON GOVERNMENT SCHEMES (CODE 02 AT Q.21)**

During the last five years - that is since March 1985 - have you been unemployed and seeking work for any period?

n = 5
Q.43 only

	n
Yes	2
No	3

[WWWORK10]
ALL THOSE WAITING TO TAKE UP PAID WORK (CODE 04 AT Q.21)

44a) And in the seven days ending last Sunday, did you have paid work of less than ten hours a week?

n = 3
Q.44 only

	n
Yes	-
No	3

[WWUNEMP]
b) During the last five years - that is since March 1985 - have you been unemployed and seeking work for any period?

	n
Yes	2
No	1

[UINEMPT]
45a) **ALL UNEMPLOYED (CODES 05, 06, 07 AT Q.21)**

In total how many months in the last five years - that is, since March 1985 - have you been unemployed and seeking work?

n = 81
Qs.45-48

MONTHS
MEDIAN: 3 6

[CURUNEMP]
c) How long has this present period of unemployment and seeking work lasted so far?

MONTHS
MEDIAN: 2 4

N.I.

- 14 -

[UWORK10]
46. And in the seven days ending last Sunday, did you have any paid work of less than ten hours a week?

	%
Yes	1.3
No	98.7

[JOBQUAL]
47. How confident are you that you will find a job to match your qualifications ... **READ OUT** ...

	%
... very confident,	4.4
quite confident,	25.8
not very confident,	39.0
or - not at all confident?	30.8

[UFINDJOB]
48.a) Although it may be difficult to judge, how long from now do you think it will be before you find an acceptable job?

MONTHS
MEDIAN: 0 6

		%
OR CODE:	Never	13.2
	Don't know	44.0

[WJOBCHNC]
b) Do you think that there is a real chance nowadays that you will get a job in this area, or is there no real chance nowadays?

	%
Real chance	29.6
No real chance	69.2
(DK)	1.3

[DWORK10]
49. **ALL PERMANENTLY SICK OR DISABLED (CODE 08 AT Q.21)**

And in the seven days ending last Sunday, did you have any paid work of less than ten hours a week?

n = 39
Q.49 only

	n
Yes	-
No	39

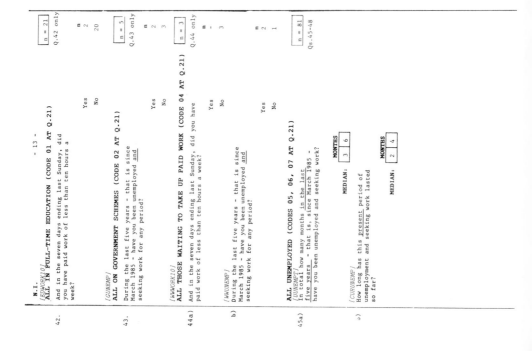

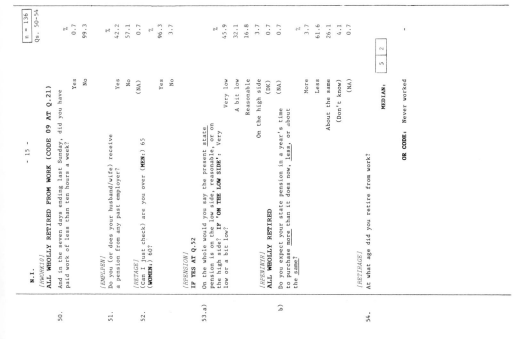

- 15 -

N.I.

[RWORK10]
ALL WHOLLY RETIRED FROM WORK (CODE 09 AT Q.21)

		n = 136 Qs. 50-54

50. And in the seven days ending last Sunday, did you have paid work of less than ten hours a week?

		%
	Yes	0.7
	No	99.3

[EMPLPEN]
51. Do you (or does your husband/wife) receive a pension from any past employer?

	%
Yes	42.2
No	57.1
(NA)	0.7

[RETAGE]
52. (Can I just check) are you over **(MEN:)** 65 **(WOMEN:)** 60?

	%
Yes	96.3
No	3.7

[RPENSION]
IF YES AT Q.52

53.a) On the whole would you say the present state pension is on the low side, reasonable, or on the high side? **IF 'ON THE LOW SIDE':** Very low or a bit low?

	%
Very low	45.9
A bit low	32.1
Reasonable	16.8
On the high side	3.7
(DK)	0.7
(NA)	0.7

[RPENINYR]
ALL WHOLLY RETIRED

b) Do you expect your state pension in a year's time to purchase **more** than it does now, **less**, or about **the same**?

	%
More	3.7
Less	61.6
About the same	26.1
(Don't know)	4.1
(NA)	0.7

[RETIRAGE]
54. At what age did you retire from work?

MEDIAN: | 5 | 2 |

OR CODE: Never worked —

- 16 -

N.I.

[HWORK10]
ALL LOOKING AFTER HOME (CODE 10 AT Q.21)

		n = 160 Qs. 55-59

55. And in the seven days ending last Sunday, did you have paid work of less than ten hours a week?
INCLUDE THOSE TEMPORARILY AWAY FROM A PAID JOB OF LESS THAN 10 HOURS A WEEK

		%
	Yes	13.1
	No	86.6
	(NA)	0.3

[NGJOB1] - [NGJOB3]
56. What are the main reasons you do not have a paid job (of more than 10 hours a week) outside the home?
PROBE FULLY FOR MAIN REASONS AND RECORD VERBATIM.

	%
Raising children	41.3
'Poverty trap'	3.1
Retired/too old	19.4
Already works (less than 10 hours a week)	1.9
Prefer looking after home/family	17.5
Childcare costs	3.8
No jobs available	6.3
Unpaid work/family business	0.6
Unsuited for available jobs	4.4
(Other answer)	0.6
Pregnancy/ill health	11.3
(NA)	6.3
Dependent relative	10.0
Husband against working	1.3

[EVERJOB]
57.a) Have you, during the last five years, ever had a full- or part-time job of 10 hours per week or more?

		%
	Yes	20.4
	No	79.3
	(NA)	0.3

[EVERJOBT]
IF YES AT a)

b) How long ago was it that you left that job?

NO. OF MONTHS AGO

| 2 | 0 |

MEDIAN:

N.I.

— 18 —

SECTION THREE

n = 896
Qs. 61-124

ASK ALL

CARD H [SPEND1] [SPEND2]

61. Here are some items of government spending. Which of them, if any, would be your highest priority for *extra* spending? And which next? Please read through the whole list before deciding.

ONE CODE ONLY IN EACH COLUMN

	1st Priority	2nd Priority
	%	%
Education	16.3	28.4
Defence	0.5	1.4
Health	54.7	23.7
Housing	6.5	14.0
Public transport	0.6	1.6
Roads	2.4	3.1
Police and prisons	1.0	1.8
Social security benefits	11.9	16.4
Help for industry	5.4	7.4
Overseas aid	0.2	0.4
(NONE OF THESE)	-	1.0
(Don't know)	0.6	0.9

CARD J [SOCBEN1] [SOCBEN2]

62. Thinking now only of the government's spending on social benefits like those on the card. Which, if any, of these would be your highest priority for extra spending? And which next?

ONE CODE ONLY IN EACH COLUMN

	1st Priority	2nd Priority
	%	%
Retirement pensions	39.4	22.2
Child benefits	19.1	18.2
Benefits for the unemployed	12.7	17.8
Benefits for disabled people	21.5	31.8
Benefits for single parents	6.5	8.2
(NONE OF THESE)	-	0.6
(Don't know)	0.7	1.1

N.I.

— 17 —

IF NO AT Q.57a) [FT/JOBSER]

58a) How seriously in the past five years have you considered getting a full-time job?
... READ OUT ...

PROMPT, IF NECESSARY: FULL TIME IS 30 HRS+ PER WEEK

	%
... very seriously,	2.5
quite seriously,	3.2
not very seriously,	7.6
or - not at all seriously?	65.0
(NA)	1.3

[PT/JOBSER]
IF NOT VERY OR NOT AT ALL SERIOUSLY

b) How seriously, in the past five years, have you considered getting a part-time job?
... READ OUT ...

	%
... very seriously,	4.5
quite seriously,	9.6
not very seriously,	8.6
or - not at all seriously?	50.0
(NA)	1.3

[HLOOKJOB]
ASK ALL LOOKING AFTER THE HOME

59. Do you think you are likely to look for a paid job in the next 5 years?

IF YES: Full-time or part-time?

	%
Yes - full-time	6.7
Yes - part-time	31.2
No	58.0
Other (WRITE IN)	-
(Don't know)	3.8
(NA)	0.3

n = 2
Q. 60 only

[2WORK10]
ALL DOING SOMETHING ELSE (CODE 11 AT Q.21)

60. And in the seven days ending last Sunday, did you have paid work of less than 10 hours a week?

	n
Yes	-
No	2

N.I.

- 19 -

63. I will read two statements. For each one please say whether you agree or disagree? Strongly or slightly?
[FALSECLM]

a) Large numbers of people these days *falsely* claim benefits.
[FALCLM]

b) Large numbers of people who are eligible for benefits these days *fail* to claim them.
[FAILCLM]

	(a) Falsely claim	(b) Fail to claim
	%	%
Agree strongly	43.1	41.7
Agree slightly	23.2	40.0
Disagree slightly	13.8	9.2
Disagree strongly	12.0	3.6
(Don't know)	8.0	5.5

64. Opinions differ about the level of benefits for the unemployed. Which of these two statements comes closest to your own ... **READ OUT** ..
[DOLE]

	%
... benefits for the unemployed are too *low* and cause hardship	56.0
OR - benefits for the unemployed are too *high* and discourage people from finding jobs?	29.9
(Neither)	5.0
Other (**WRITE IN:**) ___	3.5
(Don't know)	5.3
(NA)	0.3

65. Suppose the government had to choose between the three options on this card. Which do you think it should choose?
[TAXSPEND] CARD K

	%
Reduce taxes and spend *less* on health, education and social benefits	6.1
Keep taxes and spending on these services at the *same* level as now	42.0
Increase taxes and spend *more* on health, education and social benefits	46.4
(None)	2.9
(Don't know)	2.4
(NA)	0.1

66. All in all, how satisfied or dissatisfied would you say you are with the way in which the National Health Service runs nowadays? Choose a phrase from this card.
[NHSSAT] CARD L

	%
Very satisfied	6.9
Quite satisfied	34.8
Neither satisfied nor dissatisfied	17.0
Quite dissatisfied	24.1
Very dissatisfied	16.6
(DK,NA)	2.6

N.I.

- 20 -

67. CARD L AGAIN

From your own experience, or from what you have heard, please say how satisfied or dissatisfied you are with the way in which each of these parts of the National Health Service runs nowadays?

READ OUT i-vi BELOW AND RING ONE CODE FOR EACH

		Very satisfied	Quite satisfied	Neither satisfied nor dissatisfied	Quite dis-satisfied	Very dis-satisfied	(DK/NA)
i)	First, local doctors/GPs? *[GPSAT]*	% 30.6	51.0	7.8	7.5	2.9	0.3
ii)	National Health Service dentists? *[DENTSAT]*	% 21.1	52.1	11.6	8.9	3.1	3.3
iii)	Health visitors? *[HVSAT]*	% 15.3	36.2	21.9	4.2	2.2	20.0
iv)	District nurses? *[DNSAT]*	% 22.7	36.6	20.6	2.0	0.9	17.3
v)	Being in hospital as an inpatient? *[INPATSAT]*	% 32.6	40.3	11.8	6.6	3.0	5.6
vi)	Attending hospital as an outpatient? *[OUTPASAT]*	% 20.5	41.1	10.6	15.5	6.5	6.0

68. a) Are you covered by a private health insurance scheme, that is an insurance scheme that allows you to get private medical *treatment?*
FOR EXAMPLE: BUPA and PPP
[PRIVMED]

		%
	Yes	8.4
	No	91.5
	(NA)	0.1

b) Does your employer *(or your husband's/wife's employer)* pay the majority of the cost of membership of this scheme?
[PRIVPAID] IF YES AT a)

		%
	Yes	4.0
	No	4.0
	(Don't know)	0.1
	(NA)	0.3

69. It has been suggested that the National Health Service should be available *only* to those with *lower incomes.* This would mean that contributions and taxes could be lower and most people would then take out medical insurance or pay for health care. Do you support or oppose this idea?
[NHSLIMIT] ASK ALL

		%
	Support	24.9
	Oppose	70.9
	(Don't know)	4.1
	(NA)	0.1

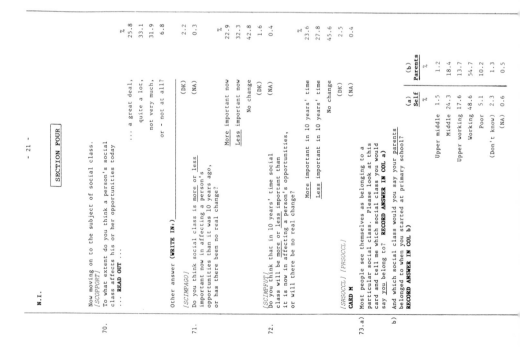

- 21 -

N.I.

| SECTION FOUR |

Now moving on to the subject of social class.
[SCCPPORT]

70. To what extent do you think a person's social class affects his or her opportunities today
... **READ OUT** ...

	%
... a great deal,	25.8
quite a lot,	33.1
not very much,	31.9
or - not at all?	6.8

Other answer **(WRITE IN:)**

| (DK) | 2.2 |
| (NA) | 0.3 |

[SCIMPAGO]
71. Do you think social class is <u>more</u> or <u>less</u> important now in affecting a person's opportunities than it was 10 years ago, or has there been no real change?

	%
More important now	22.9
Less important now	32.3
No change	42.8
(DK)	1.6
(NA)	0.4

[SCIMPFUT]
72. Do you think that in 10 years' time social class will be <u>more</u> or <u>less</u> important than it is now in affecting a person's opportunities, or will there be no real change?

	%
More important in 10 years' time	23.6
Less important in 10 years' time	27.8
No change	45.6
(DK)	2.5
(NA)	0.4

[SRSOCCL] [PRSOCCL]
CARD M
73.a) Most people see themselves as belonging to a particular social class. Please look at this card and tell me which social class you would say <u>you</u> belong to? **RECORD ANSWER IN COL. a)**

b) And which social class would you say your parents belonged to when you started at primary school?
RECORD ANSWER IN COL b)

	(a) Self %	(b) Parents %
Upper middle	1.5	1.2
Middle	24.3	18.4
Upper working	17.6	13.7
Working	48.6	54.7
Poor	5.1	10.2
(Don't know)	2.3	1.3
(NA)	0.6	0.5

N.I.

- 22 -

[RELIGION]
ASK ALL
74.a) Do you regard yourself as belonging to any particular religion?
IF YES: Which?

CODE ONE ONLY - DO NOT PROMPT

	%
No religion	12.6
Christian - no denomination	1.3
Roman Catholic	36.2
Church of Ireland/Anglican	16.8
Baptist	0.9
Methodist	4.4
Presbyterian	23.4
Free Presbyterian	0.4
Brethren	0.9

Other Protestant **(WRITE IN:)** | 2.0
Other Christian **(WRITE IN:)** | 0.3

	%
Hindu	-
Jewish	-
Muslim	0.1
Sikh	-
Buddhist	-

Other non-Christian **(WRITE IN:)**

| Refused/unwilling to say | 0.1 |
| (NA) | 0.6 |

[RELIGFAM]
IF NO RELIGION (CODE 01 AT a)

| | % |
| | 0.1 |

b) In what religion were you brought up? **PROBE IF NECESSARY:** What was your family's religion?

	%
No religion	1.0
Christian - no denomination	0.1
Roman Catholic	2.2
Church of Ireland/Anglican	4.1
Baptist	0.2
Methodist	0.5
Presbyterian	4.0
Free Presbyterian	0.2
Brethren	0.2

Other Protestant **(WRITE IN:)** | 0.2
Other Christian **(WRITE IN:)**

	%
Hindu	-
Jewish	-
Muslim	-
Sikh	-
Buddhist	-

Other non-Christian **(WRITE IN:)**

Refused/unwilling to say | -

N.I. - 23 -

[ATTENDCH]
IF ANY RELIGION AT a) OR b) ASK c) - OTHERS SKIP TO Q.75

c) Apart from such special occasions as weddings, funerals and baptisms, how often nowadays do you attend services or meetings connected with your religion?

PROBE AS NECESSARY

	%
Once a week or more	50.9
Less often but at least once in two weeks	7.6
Less often but at least once a month	8.5
Less often but at least twice a year	6.7
Less often but at least once a year	3.5
Less often	3.4
Never or practically never	16.8
Varies too much to say	0.3
Refused/unwilling to answer	0.5
(NA)	0.9

[DIVORCE]
ASK ALL
75. Do you think that divorce in Northern Ireland should be ... READ OUT ...

	%
... easier to obtain than it is now,	15.0
more difficult,	29.4
or - should things remain as they are?	47.3
(Don't know)	7.7
(NA)	0.6

[SEXLAW]
76. There is a law in the U.K. against sex discrimination, that is against giving unfair preference to men - or to women - in employment, pay and so on. Do you generally support or oppose the idea of a law for this purpose?

	%
Support	86.6
Oppose	10.9
(DK)	1.5
(NA)	1.0

CARD N
77. Now I would like to ask you some questions about sexual relationships.
[PMS]
a) If a man and a woman have sexual relations before marriage, what would your general opinion be? Please choose a phrase from this card. RECORD IN COL a)
[EXMS]
b) What about a married person having sexual relations with someone other than his or her partner? Please choose a phrase from this card. RECORD IN COL b)
[HOMOSEX]
c) What about sexual relations between two adults of the same sex? Please choose a phrase from this card. RECORD IN COL c)

	(a) BEFORE MARRIAGE	(b) EXTRA MARITAL	(c) SAME SEX
	%	%	%
Always wrong	30.2	74.8	78.9
Mostly wrong	12.4	14.6	5.5
Sometimes wrong	16.4	4.7	3.9
Rarely wrong	5.9	1.2	1.8
Not wrong at all	27.3	1.3	6.1
(Depends/varies)	7.2	2.8	2.9
(DK/NA)	0.8	0.5	1.0

N.I. - 24 -

SECTION FIVE

I am now going to ask some questions about crime and the police. I will ask about sectarian crime - that is, crime directly to do with the Troubles - in a moment.

[VICTIM]
78.a) But first, thinking about crime in general - do you ever worry about the possibility that you or anyone else who lives with you might be the victim of crime?

	%
Yes	62.8
No	37.1
(NA)	0.1

[VMWORRY]
IF YES AT a)
b) Is this ... READ OUT ...

	%
... a big worry,	11.5
a bit of a worry,	29.1
or - an occasional doubt?	22.0
(DK/NA)	0.2

[SAFEDARK]
ASK ALL
79. How safe do you feel walking alone in this area after dark ... READ OUT ...

	%
... very safe,	35.1
fairly safe,	40.2
a bit unsafe,	15.6
or - very unsafe?	8.5
(DK/NA)	0.5

[BURGLARY]
80.a) How common is it for people's homes to be burgled in this area ... READ OUT ...

	%
... very common,	9.3
fairly common,	21.5
not very common,	43.6
or - not at all common?	23.8
(Don't know)	1.8
(NA)	0.1

[VANDAL]
b) How common is deliberate damage done by vandals in this area ... READ OUT ...

	%
... very common,	9.9
fairly common,	18.6
not very common,	40.6
or - not at all common?	29.9
(Don't know)	0.9
(NA)	0.1

N.I.

- 25 -

[MUGGING]

81. How common in this area is it for people to be attacked and to have things stolen from them in the street ... **READ OUT** ...

	%
... very common,	1.1
fairly common,	3.6
not very common,	30.6
or - not at all common?	63.1
(Don't know)	1.5
(NA)	0.1

[AREACRIM]

82. Now thinking only about non-sectarian crime - crime not related to the Troubles. Compared with the rest of Northern Ireland, how much non-sectarian crime would you say there is in your area ... **READ OUT** ...

	%
... a lot more in your area,	1.5
a bit more,	4.7
about the same amount,	19.1
a bit less,	27.3
or - a lot less in your area?	45.6
(Don't know)	1.7
(NA)	0.1

[NIARCRIM]

83. And what about non-sectarian crime in Northern Ireland compared with Great Britain? Would you say there is ... **READ OUT** ...

	%
... a lot more crime in Northern Ireland,	4.0
a bit more crime,	6.3
about the same amount,	17.4
a bit less crime,	35.9
or - a lot less crime in Northern Ireland?	34.7
(Don't know)	1.7
(NA)	0.1

[CRMNITVGB]

CARD O

84. If you happened to see a house being burgled, which of the things on this card would you be most likely to do?

ONE CODE ONLY

	%
Not report it at all	2.9
Report it by: Using the confidential telephone, without giving my name	9.8
Telephoning the police directly	77.3
Asking someone else to report it	4.1
Going to the police myself	3.4
(Refused/unwilling)	0.2
(Don't know)	1.5
(NA)	0.7

N.I.

- 26 -

[BURGLECT]

85. And if you had witnessed that burglary, how likely would you be to come forward to give evidence in court? Would you ... **READ OUT** ...

	%
... definitely come forward,	35.7
probably come forward,	35.1
probably not come forward,	14.7
definitely not come forward?	11.3
(Refused/unwilling)	0.2
(Don't know)	2.6
(NA)	0.5

[HIJACKDO]

CARD O AGAIN

86. Now suppose you saw a car being hijacked, which of the things on this card would you be most likely to do?

ONE CODE ONLY

	%
Not report it at all	8.2
Report it by: Using the confidential telephone, without giving my name	18.7
Telephoning the police directly	61.9
Asking someone else to report it	3.5
Going to the police myself	3.4
(Refused/unwilling)	0.2
(Don't know)	3.5
(NA)	0.6

[HIJACKCT]

87. And if you had witnessed that hijacking, how likely would you be to come forward to give evidence in court? Would you ... **READ OUT** ...

	%
... definitely come forward,	25.2
probably come forward,	28.8
probably not come forward,	17.7
definitely not come forward?	22.2
(Refused/unwilling)	0.4
(Don't know)	4.8
(NA)	0.9

- 27 -

N.I.

[GOPOLICE]

88.a) During the past two years have you ever reported a crime or accident to the police or gone to them for help or advice?

	%
Yes	29.3
No	70.4
(NA)	0.3

[PCHELP]

IF YES AT a)

b) On those occasions, how helpful have you found them in the way they dealt with you ... **READ OUT** ...

	%
... very helpful,	14.1
fairly helpful,	10.9
fairly unhelpful,	1.9
or - very unhelpful?	1.6
(Varied)	0.8
(DK)	0.1
(NA)	0.3

[PCSTOP]

ASK ALL

89.a) During the past two years, have you ever been stopped or asked questions by the police about an offence which they thought had been committed?

DOES NOT INCLUDE RANDOM CHECKS; 'POLICE' MEANS RUC

	%
Yes	10.9
No	88.9
(NA)	0.2

[PCPOLITE]

IF YES AT a)

b) On those occasions, how polite have you found them when they approached you ... **READ OUT** ...

	%
... very polite,	4.1
fairly polite,	3.0
fairly impolite,	1.6
or - very impolite?	1.8
(Varied)	0.3
(NA)	0.2

[PCANNOY]

ASK ALL

90. During the past two years, have you ever been really annoyed about the way a police officer behaved towards you (or someone you know) or about the way the police handled a matter in which you were involved?

	%
Yes	20.2
No	79.4
(NA)	0.3

[PCPLEASE]

91. During the last two years, have you ever been really pleased about the way a police officer behaved towards you (or someone you know) or about the way the police handled a matter in which you were involved?

	%
Yes	29.8
No	69.7
(DK/NA)	0.5

- 28 -

N.I.

[PCSAT]

CARD P

92. In general, how satisfied or dissatisfied are you with the way the police in Northern Ireland do their job? Choose a phrase from the card.

	%
Very satisfied	25.1
Quite satisfied	45.3
Neither satisfied nor dissatisfied	15.1
Not very satisfied	9.8
Not at all satisfied	4.4
(DK/NA)	0.3

[PCCONTCT]

93. May I just check, have you (or someone you know) had any contact at all with the police in the past two years?

	%
Yes	51.9
No	47.8
(NA)	0.3

CARD Q

94. For each of the next questions, please use this card to say whether you think Catholics are treated better than Protestants in Northern Ireland, or whether Protestants are treated better than Catholics, or whether both are treated equally.

READ OUT EACH ITEM AND CODE ONE FOR EACH

	Catholics treated much better	Catholics treated a bit better	Both treated equally	Protestants treated a bit better	Protestants treated much better	(it depends/Don't know/Can't say)	(NA)
a) *[RUCHLGPJ]* First, the RUC - how do they treat Catholic and Protestant members of the public? %	1.0	1.3	58.7	20.8	10.1	8.0	0.2
b) *[ARMHLGPJ]* What about the army - how do they treat Catholic and Protestant members of the public? %	0.4	0.3	59.5	19.8	8.5	11.2	0.2
c) *[UDRHLGPJ]* And the Ulster Defence Regiment - how do they treat Catholic and Protestant members of the public? %	0.2	0.2	45.3	19.9	22.0	12.1	0.2
d) *[NTRHLGPJ]* And the courts - how do they treat Catholics and Protestants accused of committing non-terrorist offences? %	0.7	2.4	83.3	2.8	2.1	8.4	0.2
e) *[TERHLGPJ]* And how do the courts treat Catholics and Protestants accused of committing terrorist offences? %	1.4	8.5	67.6	9.0	5.0	8.4	0.2

N.I.   - 29 -

[RUCNTRCR]

95. From what you know or have heard, would you say the RUC do a good job or a bad job in controlling non-sectarian crime - crime not to do with the Troubles?
IF GOOD OR BAD: Very (good/bad) or fairly (good/bad)?

	%
Very good	27.7
Fairly good	57.4
Fairly bad	9.0
Very bad	2.9
(Don't know)	2.8
(NA)	0.2

[RUCTERCR]

96. And from what you know or have heard, would you say the RUC do a good job or a bad job in controlling sectarian crime?
IF GOOD OR BAD: Very (good/bad) or fairly (good/bad)?

	%
Very good	20.1
Fairly good	51.1
Fairly bad	15.2
Very bad	8.5
(Don't know)	4.8
(NA)	0.3

[NISECFR1]

97.a) Which of the security forces in Northern Ireland do you think is most effective in controlling sectarian crime ... READ OUT AND CODE AT a) BELOW

[NISECFR2]

b) And which do you think is next most effective in controlling sectarian crime ... READ OUT TWO NOT CODED AT a) AND CODE AT b)

	(a) Most effective	(b) Next most
	%	%
... the RUC,	61.2	16.2
the army,	18.1	42.0
or - the Ulster Defence Regiment?	3.9	17.2
(None of them)	7.6	11.7
(Don't know)	8.7	12.1
(NA)	0.5	0.7

N.I.   - 30 -

ASK ALL

98. There are a number of different security operations in use as a result of the Troubles. I would like to ask your views about a few of them.

[VEHCHECK]

a) First, vehicle check points, where cars are stopped for random or routine search. Do you think they are used ... READ OUT ...

	%
... too much,	21.0
about the right amount,	48.9
or - too little?	25.2
(Don't know)	4.8
(NA)	0.2

[PEDSERCH]

b) And what about random searches of pedestrians - are they used ... READ OUT ...

	%
... too much,	18.4
about the right amount,	38.0
or - too little?	22.7
-(Don't know)	20.5
(NA)	0.3

[HSESERCH]

c) And what about house searches - are they used ... READ OUT ...

	%
... too much,	15.2
about the right amount,	36.8
or - too little?	17.4
(Don't know)	30.4
(NA)	0.2

[RCMARCH]

d) And what about controls on Catholic protest marches and demonstrations - are they used ... READ OUT ...

	%
... too much,	20.0
about the right amount,	48.6
or - too little?	17.4
(Don't know)	13.7
(NA)	0.3

[PRTMARCH]

e) And what about controls on Protestant protest marches and demonstrations - are they used ... READ OUT ...

	%
... too much,	10.4
about the right amount,	53.2
or - too little?	22.5
(Don't know)	13.5
(NA)	0.3

N.I.

- 31 -

[RUCJOIN1] [RUCJOIN2]

CARD R

99. There are many reasons why Catholics are put off from joining the RUC. On this card are some possible reasons. Please read through the whole list and then tell me which you think is the most important reason and which is the next most important.

CODE ONE UNDER 'MOST IMPORTANT' AND ONE UNDER 'NEXT MOST'

	Most important %	Next most important %
They try to join but are not chosen because they are Catholic	4.7	8.9
They do not want to join because they feel they will be treated badly by the RUC	12.8	32.6
Other Catholics put pressure on them not to join the RUC	68.7	11.1
They are not as well-qualified as Protestants to join the RUC	0.2	3.2
(None of these)	5.5	24.1
(Don't know)	7.6	18.0
(NA)	0.5	2.0

[RUCCMNOW] [RUCCONSHD]

CARD S

100.a) If there is a complaint against the police in Northern Ireland, which of these bodies do you think is responsible for looking into it?
RECORD IN COLUMN (a) BELOW

b) And who do you think should be responsible?
RECORD IN COLUMN (b) BELOW

	(a) Who is responsible %	(b) Who should be %
The Home Office	6.5	11.3
The Northern Ireland office	15.1	15.5
The Police Authority of Northern Ireland	43.7	28.2
The Chief Constable of the RUC	18.2	16.6
The British army	0.1	0.5
The courts	3.6	10.8
District or local councils	0.6	3.1
(None of these)	1.5	4.7
(Don't know)	10.2	8.5
(NA)	0.5	0.8

N.I.

- 32 -

[NISUPPTY]

101.a) Generally speaking, do you think of yourself as a supporter of any one political party?

Yes — 35.7
No — 63.7
(NA) — 0.6

IF NO AT a) [NICLSPTY]
b) Do you think of yourself as a little closer to one political party than to the others?

Yes — 20.9
No — 42.7
(NA) — 0.7

IF NO AT b)
c) If there were a general election tomorrow, which political party do you think you would be most likely to support?
CODE ONE ONLY UNDER c & d)
IF MAINLAND ALLIANCE, PROBE: Liberal Democrat or SDP (Owen)?

IF YES AT a) OR b)
d) Which one? **CODE ONE ONLY UNDER c & d).**
IF MAINLAND ALLIANCE, PROBE: Liberal Democrat or SDP (Owen)?

IF MAINLAND PARTY NAMED AT c) OR d)
e) If there were a general election in which only Northern Ireland parties were standing, which one do you think you would be most likely to support?
CODE ONE ONLY UNDER e)

	[NIPPTYID1] c & d) %	[NIPPTYID2] e) %
Conservative	11.7	
Labour	8.8	
(Social and) Liberal Democrat/Liberal/SLD	0.5	
SDP/Social Democrat	0.3	
(Mainland) Alliance (AFTER PROBE)	0.3	
Alliance (NI)	5.3	9.0
DUP/Democratic Unionist Party	7.4	9.3
OUP/Official Unionist Party/Ulster Unionist Party	23.8	30.2
Other Unionist	0.2	0.7
Sinn Fein	2.4	2.8
SDLP	13.2	15.9
Workers Party	1.3	2.3
Campaign for Equal Citizenship	0.1	0.1
Green Party/Ecology Party	1.1	1.2
Other party (WRITE IN)	0.5	1.1
Other answer (WRITE IN)	0.3	0.3
None	16.2	18.8
Refused/unwilling to say	4.8	5.5
(DK/NA)	1.6	2.9

[NITDSTRN]

IF ANY NORTHERN IRELAND PARTY CODED AT c) & d) or e)
f) Would you call yourself very strong ... (QUOTE PARTY NAMED) ... fairly strong, or not very strong?

Very strong — 7.0
Fairly strong — 27.0
Not very strong — 38.1
(Don't know) — 0.2
(NA) — 3.5

N.I.

- 33 -

SECTION SIX

CARD T

102. Some countries are called 'free societies' because their citizens' basic rights are protected. Please use this card to say how well-protected you think citizens' basic rights are in each of the following countries. Just say what you think.

READ NAME OF EACH COUNTRY AND CODE ONE FOR EACH

		Citizens' basic rights are:					
		Very well protected	Fairly well protected	Not very well protected	Not at all well protected	(Don't know/ Can't say)	(NA)
a)	[USAFREE] ... the USA?	% 33.3	45.2	7.6	0.2	13.3	0.5
b)	[WGFREE] ... West Germany?	% 19.5	39.9	15.6	2.0	22.6	0.5
c)	[USSRFREE] ... the Soviet Union?	% 2.7	7.8	42.7	29.4	16.9	0.5
d)	[BRITFREE] ... Britain?	% 18.5	61.8	10.9	1.8	6.7	0.5
e)	[CHINAFREE] ... China?	% 1.8	10.2	26.1	35.6	25.8	0.5
f)	[CANFREE] ... Canada?	% 31.0	48.9	1.6	0.2	17.8	0.5

CARD U

103. Some countries are called 'open societies' because their citizens have a right to know what decisions the government is making and why. Please use this card to say how 'open' you think each of the following countries is. Again, just say what you think.

READ NAME OF EACH COUNTRY AND CODE ONE FOR EACH

		Government is:					
		Very open	Fairly open	Not very open	Not at all open	(Don't know/ Can't say)	(NA)
a)	[USAOPEN] ... the USA?	% 33.4	42.9	10.1	1.9	11.3	0.5
b)	[WGOPEN] ... West Germany?	% 11.7	45.6	19.1	3.4	19.7	0.5
c)	[USSROPEN] ... the Soviet Union?	% 1.3	7.0	39.4	36.2	15.6	0.5
d)	[BRITOPEN] ... Britain?	% 13.2	56.6	18.0	4.3	7.3	0.6
e)	[CHINAOPEN] ... China?	% 1.6	9.1	25.5	41.0	22.2	0.6
f)	[CANOPEN] ... Canada?	% 20.2	56.5	4.3	1.0	17.4	0.6

N.I.

- 34 -

.04.

CARD W

All governments keep certain things secret. For each of the following, use this card to say whether you think British governments should or should not be allowed to keep it secret.

READ OUT a)-c) AND CODE ONE FOR EACH

a) [NUCTELL]
... Suppose there was a minor leak of radiation from a nuclear power station which was unlikely to have harmed anyone. Should the government be allowed to keep it secret or not?

	%
Definitely allowed to keep it secret	9.8
Probably allowed	13.1
Probably not allowed	13.9
Definitely not allowed to keep it secret	61.2
(Don't know)	1.2
(NA)	0.6

b) **CARD W AGAIN**
[WEAPTELL]
... Suppose the government decided to start developing a new weapons system. Should the government be allowed to keep it secret or not?

	%
Definitely allowed to keep it secret	20.9
Probably allowed	18.9
Probably not allowed	17.0
Definitely not allowed to keep it secret	40.4
(Don't know)	2.2
(NA)	0.6

c) **CARD W AGAIN**
[CABMTELL]
... Suppose a cabinet minister was asked to resign for having used his position to make a lot of money. Should the government be allowed to keep the reason secret or not?

	%
Definitely allowed to keep it secret	3.2
Probably allowed	4.5
Probably not allowed	17.2
Definitely not allowed to keep it secret	72.4
(Don't know)	2.0
(NA)	0.6

N.I.
[PAPRGOVT]
CARD X

105.-a) Suppose a person leaked secret defence plans to a newspaper, and the government wanted to find out who it was. Using the card, tell me whether you think the paper should have the legal right to keep the person's name a secret, or not?

	%
Definitely should have the legal right	16.6
Probably should	17.3
Probably should not	21.2
Definitely should not have the legal right	38.4
(Don't know/Can't say)	5.9
(NA)	0.6

[PAPRFIRM]
CARD X AGAIN

b) Now suppose a person leaked secret plans about a new commercial invention, and the firm wanted to find out who it was. Do you think the paper should have the legal right to keep the person's name secret, or not?

	%
Definitely should have the legal right	15.8
Probably should	19.8
Probably should not	24.0
Definitely should not have the legal right	32.6
(Don't know/Can't say)	7.2
(NA)	0.6

[BABBOOK]
CARD Y

106.-a) Some books or films offend people in the U.K. who have strong religious beliefs. Do you think there should or should not be a law to ban such books or films?

	%
Definitely should be a law to ban them	26.9
Probably should be a law to ban them	22.3
Probably should not be a law to ban them	20.9
Definitely should not be a law to ban them	25.9
(Don't know)	3.4
(NA)	0.6

[BLASFEMY]

b) There is a blasphemy law in the U.K. to punish people who offend against Christian beliefs. Should the law ... READ OUT ...

	%
... apply just to Christianity,	9.8
apply to other religions as well,	45.6
or - should the law be abolished altogether?	33.7
(Don't know)	10.2
(NA)	0.6

N.I.
[VCROADS][VCFOOTBL][VCVANDAL][VCDEMOS]   - 36 -
CARD Z

107. Some people say that video cameras ought to be installed in public places to detect criminals. Others say that this will cut down on everyone's privacy. Do you think video cameras should or should not be allowed in the following places?

READ OUT a)-d) AND CODE ONE FOR EACH

	Video cameras should:					
	Definitely be allowed	Probably be allowed	Probably not be allowed	Definitely not be allowed	(It depends/Don't know)	(NA)
a) ... installed on roads to detect speeding drivers?	% 49.0	29.6	8.9	10.1	1.8	0.6
b) ... installed at football grounds to detect troublemakers?	% 82.3	14.4	0.9	0.8	1.0	0.6
c) ... installed on housing estates to detect vandals?	% 49.3	27.9	11.9	7.3	3.0	0.6
d) ... at political demonstrations to identify people taking part?	% 35.0	24.1	16.4	21.0	2.9	0.6

[RACEGLTY]

108.a) Suppose two people - one white, one black - each appear in court charged with a crime they did not commit. What do you think their chances are of being found guilty ... READ OUT ...

	%
... the white person is more likely to be found guilty,	1.2
they have the same chance,	48.2
or - the black person is more likely to be found guilty?	45.2
(Don't know)	4.8
(NA)	0.6

[RICHGLTY]

b) Now suppose another two people from different backgrounds - one rich, one poor - each appear in court charged with a crime they did not commit. What do you think their chances are of being found guilty ... READ OUT ...

	%
... the rich person is more likely to be found guilty,	1.8
they have the same chance,	36.5
or - the poor person is more likely to be found guilty?	57.3
(Don't know)	3.8
(NA)	0.6

[RELIGLTY]

c) Now suppose another two people of different religions - one Protestant, one Catholic - each appear in court charged with a crime they did not commit. What do you think their chances are of being found guilty ... READ OUT ...

	%
... the Protestant is more likely to be found guilty,	3.7
they have the same chance,	75.3
or - the Catholic is more likely to be found guilty?	14.5
(Don't know)	5.8
(NA)	0.6

N.I.   - 37 -

[REMAND]
CARD AA

109. Some prisoners in Britain are 'remand prisoners', that is they are waiting, often for long periods, for their cases to come up in court.

Which of the statements on this card comes closest to your views about remand prisoners?

ONE CODE ONLY

	%
All those accused of a crime for which they might get a prison sentence should be remanded in prison	27.2
OR Only those who the courts believe might commit another offence or go missing should be remanded in prison	64.5
(Don't know)	7.7
(NA)	0.6

SECTION SEVEN

Now I'd like to ask you a few questions about the countryside and the environment.

CARD BB
(INTERVIEWER: SEE BELOW)
[LEISURE]

110.a) On this card are some activities people do in their leisure time. Have you taken part in any of these leisure activities in the last four weeks?

	%
Yes	60.9
No	38.7
(NA)	0.5

IF NO AT a) *[LEISURE6]*

b) Can you remember when you last did any of these activities in the countryside?
IF YES: How long ago was that?
PROBE FOR CORRECT CODE

	%
Within past month	0.8
1-3 months ago	4.2
4-6 months ago	8.6
7-12 months ago	14.2
More than one year ago	6.6
No, can't remember	4.2
(NA)	0.5

(INTERVIEWER REFERENCE ONLY)

CARD BB

In the last four weeks have you ...

... been for a drive, outing or picnic in the countryside

... been for a long walk, ramble or hike of more than 2 miles) in the countryside

... visited any historic or stately homes, gardens, zoos or wildlife parks in the countryside

... gone fishing, horse riding, shooting or hunting in the countryside

... visited seacoast or cliffs

N.I.   - 38 -

[CTRYSAME]
ASK ALL

111.a) Do you think the countryside generally is much the same as it was twenty years ago, or do you think it has changed? **IF CHANGED:** Has it changed a bit or a lot?

	%
Much the same	18.1
Changed a bit	28.2
Changed a lot	51.9
(Don't know)	1.4
(NA)	0.5

[CTRYBETR]
IF CHANGED A BIT OR A LOT (CODES 2 OR 3 AT a)

b) Do you think the countryside generally has changed for the better or worse?

	%
Better	25.9
Worse	45.3
(Better in some ways/worse in others)	8.7
(DK)	0.1
(NA)	1.9

[CTRYCONC]
ASK ALL

112. Are you personally concerned about things that may happen to the countryside, or does it not concern you particularly?

IF CONCERNED: Are you very concerned, or just a bit concerned?

	%
Very concerned	32.3
A bit concerned	34.3
Does not concern me particularly	32.9
(NA)	0.5

CARD CC

113.a) Which, if any, of the things on this card do you think is the greatest threat to the countryside; if you think none of them is a threat, please say so.
CODE ONE ONLY IN COL a) BELOW

b) And which do you think is the next greatest threat?
CODE ONE ONLY IN COL b)

	[CTHREAT1] (a) Greatest threat	*[CTHREAT2]* (b) Next greatest
	%	%
Motorways and road building	7.5	7.7
Industrial pollution	35.1	19.9
Removal by farmers of traditional landscape, such as hedgerows, woodlands	8.4	7.7
Tourism and visitors	0.2	1.5
Litter	16.2	17.3
Urban growth and housing development	12.1	10.3
Use of chemicals and pesticides in farming	16.9	30.5
NONE OF THESE	2.2	2.2
(Don't know)	1.0	2.4
(NA)	0.5	0.5

N.I. - 39 -

114.

CARD DD

How concerned are you about each of these environmental issues? Please choose a phrase from the card.

READ OUT a)-i) AND CODE ONE FOR EACH

		Very concerned	A bit concerned	Not very concerned	Not at all concerned	Don't know/Can't say	(NA)
a)	[INSECTCD] ... insecticides, fertilisers and chemical sprays?	% 46.5	33.9	13.9	4.2	1.1	0.5
b)	[SEWAGE] ... disposal of sewage?	% 56.3	30.5	9.0	2.7	1.0	0.5
c)	[OZLAYER] ... thinning of the ozone layer?	% 47.7	31.4	10.5	4.1	5.8	0.5
d)	[NUCPRISK] ... risks from nuclear power stations?	% 56.4	26.4	11.2	4.0	1.6	0.5
e)	[POPGROW] ... the growth in the world's population?	% 16.0	38.4	33.4	9.5	2.0	0.7
f)	[GRNHSEF] ... the 'greenhouse effect' - a rise in the world's temperature?	% 37.6	37.3	14.7	6.4	3.5	0.5
g)	[FOSLFUEL] ... using up earth's remaining coal, oil and gas?	% 24.9	41.3	22.9	7.8	2.3	0.9
h)	[WATRQUAL] ... the quality of drinking water?	% 43.2	33.0	17.5	5.3	0.4	0.6
i)	[SPECLOSS] ... the loss of plant and animal species?	% 41.3	37.4	14.4	4.9	1.3	0.6

115.

CARD EE

Do you personally belong to any of the groups listed on this card?

CODE ALL THAT APPLY

%

YES: MEMBER OF:

		%
[CLUB1]	The National Trust	2.1
[CLUB2]	Royal Society for the Protection of Birds	1.6
[CLUB6]	Friends of the Earth	0.6
[CLUB7]	World Wildlife Fund/Worldwide Fund for Nature	1.8
[CLUB8]	Greenpeace	1.0
[CLUB9]	Ulster Wildlife Trust/CPRE (England/Scotland/Wales)	0.3
[CLUB3]	Other wildlife or countryside protection group	0.2
[CLUB10]	Ramblers Association	0.5
[CLUB11]	Other countryside sport or recreation group	2.5
[CLUB11]	Urban conservation group	0.2
[CLUB12]	Campaign for Nuclear Disarmament	0.3

NO: [CLUB5] NONE OF THESE   90.2

N.I. - 40 -

116.a)

Do you do any of the following regularly, sometimes or not at all nowadays?

READ OUT i)-x) AND CODE ONE FOR EACH AT a)

FOR EACH ITEM CODED 3 (NOT AT ALL) AT a)

b) Do you intend to ... READ ITEM ... in the next year or so, or not?

CODE AT b)

		(a) Does:					(b) Intend to:			(NA)
		Regularly	Sometimes	Not at all	Does not apply	(DK/NA)	Yes	No	(DK)	
i)	[RECYCLDO]/[RECYCLPT] ... return bottles, tins, newspapers and so on for recycling?	% 21.0	20.5	56.9	1.0	0.7	22.0	23.7	8.8	2.8
ii)	[UNLEADDO]/[UNLEADPT] ... use unleaded petrol?	% 22.3	3.1	42.4	31.3	0.9	18.0	17.4	4.9	2.8
iii)	[ORGANCDO]/[ORGANCPT] ... buy organically-grown fruit and vegetables?	% 7.8	23.0	66.4	2.0	0.8	16.9	36.1	10.3	3.6
iv)	[NOTESTDO]/[NOTESTPT] ... buy toiletries or cosmetics not tested on animals?	% 18.7	26.6	49.3	3.3	2.1	10.7	25.5	10.7	2.9
v)	[GRWASHDO]/[GRWASHPT] ... buy environment-friendly washing powders or detergents?	% 18.8	18.7	53.6	6.2	2.5	13.6	26.8	10.3	4.1
vi)	[LSMEATDO]/[LSMEATPT] ... choose to eat less meat?	% 21.0	23.7	53.1	1.3	0.9	3.1	42.2	4.4	4.0
vii)	[RECPRDDO]/[RECPRDPT] ... choose products made out of recycled materials?	% 11.7	26.6	59.7	0.9	1.2	13.4	31.9	11.1	3.8
viii)	[SVELECDO]/[SVELECPT] ... make a conscious effort to save electricity?	% 40.1	27.8	31.3	0.1	0.7	7.8	18.5	2.8	2.7
ix)	[DRIVLSDO]/[DRIVLSPT] ... cut back on driving your car?	% 6.9	11.5	49.5	31.2	0.9	2.8	39.7	4.1	3.5
x)	[AEROSLDO]/[AEROSLPT] ... buy environment-friendly aerosols?	% 48.8	20.5	25.4	4.1	1.1	3.8	14.8	4.9	2.4

N.I.

- 41 -

[ENVIRPTY]
ASK ALL

117. Which political party's views on the environment would you say come closest to your own views?

DO NOT PROMPT
ONE CODE ONLY

	%
Conservative	15.3
Labour	9.9
(Social and) Liberal Democrat/Liberal/SLD	1.9
SDP/Social Democrat	0.1
(Alliance) - AFTER PROBE	0.8
Green Party/(Ecology Party)	22.9
Other (WRITE IN)	0.7
Don't know	40.9
None	6.9
(NA)	0.5

[AREALIVE]
118. INTERVIEWER: CODE FROM OBSERVATION AND THEN CHECK WITH RESPONDENT:
Can I just check, would you describe the place where you live as being ... READ OUT SELECTED CODE ...

	%
... in a big city,	10.6
in the suburbs or outskirts of a city,	19.4
in a small city or town,	21.4
in a country village or town,	21.7
or - in the countryside?	26.4
(NA)	0.5

N.I.

- 42 -

SECTION EIGHT

ASK ALL
CARD FF [HOUSESAT]

Now a few questions on housing.

119. First, in general how satisfied or dissatisfied are you with your own (house/flat)? Choose a phrase from the card.

	%
Very satisfied	44.5
Quite satisfied	40.3
Neither satisfied nor dissatisfied	5.2
Quite dissatisfied	5.2
Very dissatisfied	4.3
(NA)	0.3

[AREACHNG]
120.a) How about the area you live in? Taking everything into account, would you say this area has got better, worse or remained about the same as a place to live during the last two years?

	%
Better	16.4
Worse	11.7
About the same	70.3
(Don't know)	1.1
(NA)	0.5

[AREAFUT]
b) And what do you think will happen during the next two years: will this area get better, worse or remain about the same as a place to live?

	%
Better	14.4
Worse	11.6
About the same	70.7
(Don't know)	2.8
(NA)	0.5

[TENURE1]
121. Does your household own or rent this accommodation?
PROBE AS NECESSARY
IF OWN: Outright or on a mortgage?
IF RENTS: From whom?

		%
Owns:	Own (leasehold/freehold) outright	33.7
	Buying (leasehold/freehold) on mortgage	34.5
Rents:	Housing Executive	25.6
	Housing Association	0.9
	Property company	0.7
	Employer	0.3
	Other organisation	0.4
	Relative	0.1
	Other individual	2.8
Rent free:	Rent free, squatting, etc.	0.7
	(NA)	0.3

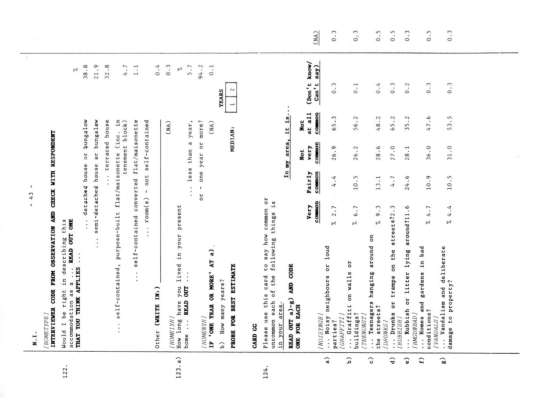

N.I. - 43 -

[HOMETYPE]
INTERVIEWER CODE FROM OBSERVATION AND CHECK WITH RESPONDENT

122. Would I be right in describing this accommodation as a ... **READ OUT ONE THAT YOU THINK APPLIES** ...

	%
... detached house or bungalow	38.8
... semi-detached house or bungalow	21.9
... terraced house	32.8
... self-contained, purpose-built flat/maisonette (inc. in tenement block)	4.7
... self-contained converted flat/maisonette	1.1
... room(s) - not self-contained	0.4
Other (WRITE IN:)	0.3
(NA)	

[HOMEIYR]
123.a) How long have you lived in your present home ... **READ OUT** ...

	%
... less than a year,	5.7
or - one year or more?	94.2
(NA)	0.1

[HOMENYR]
IF 'ONE YEAR OR MORE' AT a).

b) How many years?   **YEARS** [1] [2]

PROBE FOR BEST ESTIMATE   MEDIAN: [1] [2]

CARD GG

124. Please use this card to say how common or uncommon each of the following things is in your area.

READ OUT a)-g) AND CODE ONE FOR EACH

	Very common	Fairly common	Not very common	Not at all common	(Don't know/Can't say)	(NA)
a) *[NOISYNGB]* ... Noisy neighbours or loud parties?	% 2.7	4.4	26.9	65.3	0.3	0.3
b) *[GRAFFITI]* ... Graffiti on walls or buildings?	% 6.7	10.5	26.2	56.2	0.1	0.3
c) *[TEENONST]* ... Teenagers hanging around on the streets?	% 9.3	13.1	28.6	48.2	0.4	0.5
d) *[DRUNKS]* ... Drunks or tramps on the streets?	% 22.3	4.7	27.0	65.2	0.3	0.5
e) *[RUBBISH]* ... Rubbish or litter lying around?	% 11.6	24.6	28.1	35.2	0.2	0.3
f) *[HMGDNBAD]* ... Homes and gardens in bad conditions?	% 4.7	10.9	36.0	47.6	0.3	0.5
g) *[VANDALS]* ... Vandalism and deliberate damage to property?	% 4.4	10.5	31.0	53.5	0.3	0.3

In my area, it is...

N.I. - 44 -   n = 896

Qs. 900-923

SECTION NINE

[MARSTAT]
900a) Can I just check your own marital status? At present are you ... **READ OUT** ...

CODE FIRST TO APPLY

	%
... married,	61.4
living as married,	1.6
separated or divorced,	4.1
widowed,	10.2
or - not married?	22.7

[HOUSEHOLD]
b) Finally, a few questions about you and your household. Including yourself, how many people live here regularly as members of this household?

CHECK INTERVIEWER MANUAL FOR DEFINITION OF HOUSEHOLD IF NECESSARY

MEDIAN: [0] [3]

901. Now I'd like to ask for a few details about each person in your household. Starting with yourself, what was your age last birthday?

WORK DOWN COLUMNS OF GRID FOR EACH HOUSEHOLD MEMBER

	Respondent	2	3	4	5	6	7	8	9	10
a) *[RSEX]* *[P2SEX - P10SEX]* Sex:	%									
Male	48.9									
Female	51.1									
b) *[RAGE]* *[P2AGE - P10AGE]* Age last birthday:										
c) *[P2REL - P10REL]* Relationship to respondent: (NA)										
Spouse/partner										
Son/daughter										
Parent/parent-in-law										
Other relative										
Not related										
d) *[RRESP]* *[P2RESP - P10RESP]* HOUSEHOLD MEMBER WITH LEGAL RESPONSIBILITY FOR ACCOMMODATION (INC. JOINT AND SHARED)	%									
Yes	76.9									
No	23.0									
(NA)	0.1									

* **CHECK THAT NUMBER OF PEOPLE IN GRID EQUALS NUMBER GIVEN AT Q.900b)**

N.I. - 45 -

[SLFMXSCH]
902a) Did you ever attend a mixed or integrated school, that is, a school with fairly large numbers of both Catholic and Protestant children?

IF YES: In Northern Ireland or somewhere else?

	%
Yes - in Northern Ireland	16.1
Yes, somewhere else	2.9
No, did not	80.7
(Don't know)	0.3

[NIRCHILD]
b) INTERVIEWER CHECK:

RESPONDENT HAS CHILD(REN) AGED 5 OR OLDER IN HOUSEHOLD - SEE GRID AT Q.901

	%
	43.3
DOES NOT	56.7

[CHDMXSCH]
IF CODE 1 AT b)
c) And have any of your children ever attended a mixed or integrated school, with fairly large numbers of both Catholics and Protestants attending?

IF YES: In Northern Ireland or somewhere else?

	%
Yes - in Northern Ireland	5.7
Yes, somewhere else	0.7
No, have not	29.7
(Don't know)	0.5
(NA)	6.6

[SNGPERHH]
ASK ALL
903a) INTERVIEWER: IS THIS A SINGLE PERSON HOUSEHOLD - RESPONDENT ONLY PERSON AT Q.901 (p.44)

	%
YES	13.5
NO	86.5

[DUTYRESP]
IF NO AT a)
b) Who is the person mainly responsible for general domestic duties in this household?

	%
Respondent mainly	34.9
Someone else mainly (WRITE IN RELATIONSHIP TO RESP.)	41.1
Duties shared equally (WRITE IN BY WHOM)	9.5
(NA)	1.0

N.I. - 46 -

ASK ALL
[CHLDINHH]
904a) INTERVIEWER: IS THERE A CHILD UNDER 16 YEARS IN HOUSEHOLD? SEE H.H. GRID, Q.901 (p.44).

	%
YES	38.2
NO	61.8

[CHLDRESP]
IF YES AT a)
b) Who is the person mainly responsible for the general care of the child(ren) here?

	%
Respondent mainly	15.8
Someone else mainly (WRITE IN RELATIONSHIP TO RESP.)	16.5
Care shared equally (WRITE IN BY WHOM)	5.9

[TEA]
ASK ALL
905. How old were you when you completed your continuous full-time education?
PROBE AS NECESSARY

	%
15 or under	42.9
16	25.2
17	11.5
18	7.2
19 or over	11.0
Still at school	0.7
Still at college, polytechnic, or university	1.5
Other answer (WRITE IN)	-

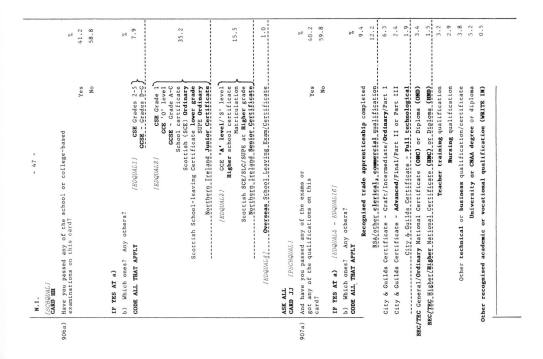

- 48 -

N.I.
[RECONAC5]
INTERVIEWER: REFER TO ECONOMIC POSITION OF RESPONDENT (Q.21, PAGE 7)

908.

	%
RESPONDENT IS IN PAID WORK	50.2
	0.3
RESPONDENT IS WAITING TO TAKE UP PAID WORK	49.5
ALL OTHERS	7.3]

[Never had a job]

a) [IF EVER HAD A JOB]
Now I want to ask you about your (present/future/last) job.
CHANGE TENSES FOR (BRACKETED) WORDS AS APPROPRIATE.

What (is) your job?
PROBE AS NECESSARY: What (is) the name or title of the job?
IF 'NEVER HAD JOB', WRITE IN AND GO TO Q.909

b) What kind of work (do) you do most of the time?
IF RELEVANT: What materials/machinery (do) you use?

c) What training or qualifications (are) needed for that job?

d) [RSUPER]
(Do) you directly supervise or (are) you directly responsible for the work of any other people?

		%
IF YES: How many?	Yes	29.8
	No	62.3
	(DK)	0.1
	(NA)	0.6

MEDIAN: | 0 | 0 | 0 | 5 |

e) [REMPLYEE]
Can I just check: (are) you ... READ OUT ...

	%
... an employee,	79.8
or - self-employed?	12.4
(NA)	0.5

- 47 -

N.I.
[PSCHQUAL]
CARD HH
906a) Have you passed any of the school or college-based examinations on this card?

	%
Yes	41.2
No	58.8

IF YES AT a)
b) Which ones? Any others?
CODE ALL THAT APPLY

	%
[EDQUAL1] CSE Grades 2-5 / GCSE - Grades D-G	7.9
[EDQUAL2] CSE Grade 1 / GCE 'O' level / GCSE - Grade A-C / School certificate / Scottish (SCE) Ordinary / Scottish School-leaving Certificate lower grade / SUPE Ordinary / Northern Ireland Junior Certificate	35.2
[EDQUAL3] GCE 'A' level/'S' level / Higher school certificate / Matriculation / Scottish SCE/SLC/SUPE at Higher grade / Northern Ireland Senior Certificate	15.5
[EDQUAL4] Overseas School-leaving Exam/Certificate	1.0

ASK ALL
CARD JJ [PSCHQUAL]
907a) And have you passed any of the exams or got any of the qualifications on this card?

	%
Yes	40.2
No	59.8

IF YES AT a)
b) Which ones? Any others?   [EDQUAL5 - EDQUAL16]
CODE ALL THAT APPLY

	%
Recognised trade apprenticeship completed	9.4
RSA/other clerical, commercial qualification	12.2
City & Guilds Certificate - Craft/Intermediate/Ordinary/Part I	6.3
City & Guilds Certificate - Advanced/Final/Part II or Part III	2.4
City & Guilds Certificate - Full technological	1.9
BEC/TEC General/Ordinary National Certificate (ONC) or Diploma (OND)	3.4
BEC/TEC Higher/Higher National Certificate (HNC) or Diploma (HND)	1.5
Teacher training qualification	3.2
Nursing qualification	2.9
Other technical or business qualification/certificate	3.8
University or CNAA degree or diploma	5.2
Other recognised academic or vocational qualification (WRITE IN)	0.5

- 49 -

N.I.
[RSECTOR]
IF EMPLOYEE (CODE 1 AT e)
CARD KK

f) Which of the types of organisation on this card (do) you work for?

CODE FIRST TO APPLY

	%
Private firm or company	46.4
Nationalised industry/public corp.	5.9
District Authority/Education and Library Board	7.4
Health Board/NHS hospital	8.8
Central Government/Civil Service	8.0
Charity or Trust	1.4
Other (WRITE IN)	1.9
(NA)	0.1

ASK EMPLOYEES AND SELF-EMPLOYED

g) What (does) your employer (IF SELF-EMPLOYED: you) make or do at the place where you usually (work)?

IF FARM, GIVE NO. OF ACRES

[REMPWORK]
h) Including yourself, how many people (are) employed at the place you usually (work) from?

IF YES: How many?

	%
(No employees)	7.8
Under 10	19.6
10-24	11.4
25-99	18.6
100-499	22.4
500 or more	11.5
(DK)	0.5
(NA)	0.9

IF SELF-EMPLOYED: (Do) you have any employees?

	%
Yes: trade union	24.1
staff association	3.2
No	72.4
(NA)	0.3

[UNION]
ASK ALL
909a) Are you now a member of a trade union or staff association?

CODE FIRST TO APPLY

Yes: trade union
Yes: staff association
No
(NA)

[UNIONEVH]
IF NO AT a)
b) Have you ever been a member of a trade union or staff association?

CODE FIRST TO APPLY

	%
Yes: trade union	24.3
Yes: staff association	2.2
No	45.7
(NA)	0.4

- 50 -

N.I.
IF NOW OR EVER A MEMBER (CODES 1 OR 2 AT Q.909)
[UNION1 - UNION6] READ OUT i)-vi) AND RING ONE CODE FOR EACH
910. Have you ever ...

		Yes	No	(NA)
i)	... attended a union or staff association meeting?	% 35.5	18.4	0.4
ii)	... voted in a union or staff association election or meeting?	% 32.0	21.8	0.4
iii)	... put forward a proposal or motion at a union or staff association meeting?	% 13.5	40.3	0.5
iv)	... gone on strike?	% 21.5	32.3	0.4
v)	... stood in a picket line?	% 11.8	42.1	0.4
vi)	... served as a lay representative such as a shop steward or branch committee member?	% 9.7	44.1	0.5

911a) INTERVIEWER: CHECK RESPONDENT'S MARITAL STATUS AT Q.900:
[MARSTAT3]

	%
RESPONDENT IS MARRIED OR LIVING AS MARRIED (CODES 1 OR 2 AT Q.900)	63.0
ALL OTHERS	37.0

CARD LL [SECONACT]
b) Which of these descriptions applied to what your (husband/wife/partner) was doing last week, that is the seven days ending last Sunday? PROBE: Any others? CODE ALL THAT APPLY IN COL. I

IF ONLY ONE CODE AT I, TRANSFER IT TO COL. II
IF MORE THAN ONE AT I, TRANSFER HIGHEST ON LIST TO II

	COL. I	COL. II ECONOMIC POSITION
		%
In full-time education (not paid for by employer, including on vacation)	A	0.2
On government training/employment scheme (e.g. Employment Training, Youth Training Programme etc.)	B	0.3
In paid work (or away temporarily) for at least 10 hours in the week	C	36.0
Waiting to take up paid work already accepted	D	0.1
Unemployed and registered at a benefit office	E	2.2
Unemployed, not registered, but actively looking for a job	F	0.5
Unemployed, wanting a job (of at least 10 hrs per week), but not actively looking for a job	G	0.1
Permanently sick or disabled	H	2.2
Wholly retired from work	J	7.8
Looking after the home	K	13.5
Doing something else (WRITE IN)	L	0.2

IF CODES 01-02, OR 05-11 AT b) [SLASTJOB]
c) How long ago did your (husband/wife/partner) last have a paid job (other than the government scheme you mentioned) of at least 10 hours a week?

	%
Within past 12 months	2.7
Over 1-5 years ago	7.1
Over 5-10 years ago	6.5
Over 10-20 years ago	4.5
Over 20 years ago	3.4
Never had a paid job of 10+ hours a week	2.4
(DK/NA)	0.2

N.I. - 51 -

[SECONAC3]

INTERVIEWER: REFER TO ECONOMIC POSITION OF SPOUSE/PARTNER (Q.911)

	%
SPOUSE/PARTNER IS IN PAID WORK	36.0
SPOUSE/PARTNER IS WAITING TO TAKE UP PAID WORK	0.1
ALL OTHERS	24.3
(NA)	0.1

912. a) Now I want to ask you about your (husband's/wife's/partner's) job. CHANGE TENSES FOR (BRACKETED) WORDS AS APPROPRIATE

What (is) the name or title of that job?

b) What kind of work (does) he/she do most of the time?

IF RELEVANT: What materials/machinery (does) he/she use?

c) What training or qualifications (are) needed for that job?

d) [SSUPER]
(Does) he/she directly supervise or (is) he/she directly responsible for the work of any other people?

IF YES: How many?

	%
Yes	18.8
No	40.1
(DK)	1.1
(NA)	0.6

MEDIAN: | 0 | 0 | 0 | 6 |

e) [SEMPLOYE]
(Is) he/she ... **READ OUT** ...

	%
... an employee,	51.1
or - self-employed?	9.0
(NA)	0.4

N.I. - 52 -

[SSECTOR]
IF EMPLOYEE (CODE 1 AT e)

CARD MM

f) Which of the types of organisation on this card (does) he/she work for?

	%
Private firm or company	29.3
Nationalised industry/public corporation	3.6
District Authority/Education and Library Board	5.2
Health Board/NHS hospital	6.5
Central Government/Civil Service	4.9
Charity or Trust	0.9
Other (WRITE IN)	0.7

ASK ALL WHO HAVE EVER WORKED

g) What (does) the employer (IF SELF-EMPLOYED: he/she) make or do at the place where he/she usually (works)?

IF FARM, GIVE NO. OF ACRES

h) [SEMPWORK]
Including him/herself, roughly how many people (are) employed at the place where he/she usually (works) (from)?

IF SELF-EMPLOYED: (Does) he/she have any employees?

IF YES: How many?

	%
(No employees)	5.7
Under 10	11.5
10-24	9.9
25-99	13.1
100-499	12.3
500 or more	6.5
(DK)	0.9
(NA)	0.7

i) [SPARTFUL]
(Is) the job ... **READ OUT** ...

	%
... full-time (30 HOURS+)	49.5
or - part time (10-29 HOURS)?	10.2
(NA)	0.9

N.I.   - 53 -

[RELIGSAM]

IF MARRIED OR LIVING AS MARRIED

913. And is your (husband/wife/partner) the same religion as you?

	%
PROBE AS NECESSARY Yes - same religion	58.4
No - not same religion	3.2
No religion at all	1.0
(Refused)	0.1
(NA)	0.3

[CAROWN]

ASK ALL

914. Do you, or does anyone else in your household, own or have the regular use of a car or a van?

	%
Yes	72.2
No	27.4
(NA)	0.4

[BENEFT1 - BENEFT14]

CARD NN

915. Have you or anyone in this household received any of the benefits on this card during the last five years?

IF YES: Which ones? Any others?

CODE ALL THAT APPLY

YES:	%
Child benefit (family allowance)	50.3
Maternity benefit or allowance	9.8
One-parent benefit	3.2
Family credit (family income supplement)	4.5
State retirement or widow's pension	27.3
State supplementary pension	1.4
Invalidity or disabled pension or benefit	9.2
Attendance/Invalid care/Mobility allowance	4.2
State Sickness or injury benefit	9.4
Unemployment benefit	20.0
Income support (supplementary benefit)	20.7
Housing benefit (Community Charge, rate or rent rebate)	13.4
Other state benefit(s) volunteered **(WRITE IN)**	0.5

IF NO: CODE → **NONE**	11.9
(NA)	0.2

N.I   - 54 -

[EVRLIVGB]

916a) Have you ever lived in mainland Britain for more than one year?

	%
Yes	16.4
No	83.6
(NA)	0.1

[EVRLIVER]

b) And have you ever lived in the Republic of Ireland for more than one year?

	%
Yes	5.1
No	94.9
(NA)	0.1

[UNINATID]

917a) Generally speaking, do you think of yourself as a unionist, a nationalist or neither?

	%
Unionist	41.2
Nationalist	17.6
Neither	41.0
(NA)	0.1

[UNINATST]

IF UNIONIST OR NATIONALIST AT a)

b) Would you call yourself a very strong ... **(QUOTE ANSWER AT a)** ... fairly strong, or not very strong?

	%
Very strong	8.9
Fairly strong	25.6
Not very strong	24.3
(Don't know)	0.1
(NA)	0.1

N.I.

- 55 -

ASK ALL [HHINCOME]

CARD OO

918a) Which of the letters on this card represents the total income of your household from all sources before tax? Please just tell me the letter.

NB: INCLUDES INCOME FROM BENEFITS, SAVINGS, ETC.

ONE CODE IN COLUMN a)

b) INTERVIEWER: CHECK Q. 21, PAGE 7

	%
RESPONDENT IS IN PAID WORK	50.2
ALL OTHERS	49.8

[REARN]

c) Which of the letters on this card represents your own gross or total earnings, before deduction of income tax and national insurance?

ONE CODE IN COLUMN c)

		(a) Household income %	(c) Own earnings %
Less than £3000 p.a.	P =	9.1	4.0
£3000 - £3999 p.a.	Q =	5.0	2.7
£4000 - £4999 p.a.	R =	5.7	3.5
£5000 - £5999 p.a.	T =	5.3	3.0
£6000 - £6999 p.a.	S =	4.3	5.6
£7000 - £7999 p.a.	O =	5.7	3.6
£8000 - £9999 p.a.	K =	7.7	4.8
£10,000 - £11,999 p.a.	L =	7.3	4.9
£12,000 - £14,999 p.a.	B =	7.4	4.9
£15,000 - £17,999 p.a.	Z =	7.9	4.2
£18,000 - £19,999 p.a.	M =	2.3	1.0
£20,000 - £22,999 p.a.	F =	5.1	1.2
£23,000 - £25,999 p.a.	J =	3.9	0.5
£26,000 - £28,999 p.a.	D =	1.9	0.6
£29,000 - £31,999 p.a.	H =	1.3	0.5
£32,000 p.a. or more	C =	5.6	1.3
(DK/NA)		14.5	3.8

ASK ALL [OWNSHARES]

919. Do you (or your husband/wife/partner) own any shares quoted on the Stock Exchange, including unit trusts?

	%
Yes	16.2
No	83.6
(DK)	0.2

[PHONE]

920. Is there a telephone in (your part of) this accommodation?

	%
Yes	80.1
No	19.9

N.I.

- 56 -

921a) INTERVIEWER: CHECK RESPONDENT'S SERIAL NUMBER:

EVEN NUMBER (0, 2, 4, 6, 8)

ODD NUMBER (1, 3, 5, 7, 9)

[LETTERRM]

IF EVEN SERIAL NUMBER AT a)

SHOW ADVANCE LETTER

b) In February we sent your household a letter, giving advance notice that an interviewer would be calling to ask for an interview. The letter looked like this (SHOW).

Do you remember receiving this letter?

	%
Yes, remembers letter	33.8
No, does not	14.0
Other (WRITE IN) _____	1.0
(NA)	1.1

ASK ALL [LETTERPR]

c) If you were given a choice, would you have preferred ... READ OUT ...

	%
... to have a letter in advance saying an interviewer would call,	40.6
or - to have an interviewer simply call round,	4.9
or - wouldn't it really matter?	53.0
(Don't know)	0.9
(NA)	0.6

> INTERVIEWER: **THANK RESPONDENT FOR HIS OR HER HELP AND COMPLETE Q. 922-923**

[QFILLED]

922a) THE SELF-COMPLETION QUESTIONNAIRE WAS ...

	%
... filled in immediately after interview in your presence	36.9
or - left behind to be filled in later	58.8
or ... refused (WHY?)	4.4

b) INTERVIEWER: **COMPLETE Q.11 ON CASS ABOUT HOW YOU EXPECT SELF-COMPLETION QUESTIONNAIRE TO BE RETURNED.**

Completed

- 57 -

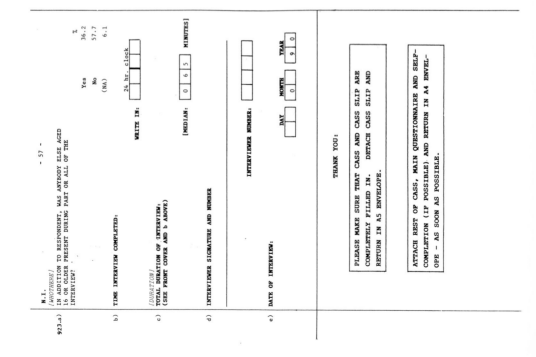

N.I.
[WHOTHERE]
923.a) IN ADDITION TO RESPONDENT, WAS ANYBODY ELSE AGED 16 OR OLDER PRESENT DURING PART OR ALL OF THE INTERVIEW?

		%
Yes		36.2
No		57.7
(NA)		6.1

b) TIME INTERVIEW COMPLETED: WRITE IN: 24 hr. clock [ ]

c) [DURATION]
TOTAL DURATION OF INTERVIEW:
(SEE FRONT COVER AND b ABOVE)   [MEDIAN: 0 6 5 MINUTES]

d) INTERVIEWER SIGNATURE AND NUMBER   INTERVIEWER NUMBER: [ ][ ][ ]

e) DATE OF INTERVIEW: DAY MONTH YEAR   [ ] [0] [9 0]

THANK YOU:

PLEASE MAKE SURE THAT CASS AND CASS SLIP ARE COMPLETELY FILLED IN.   DETACH CASS SLIP AND RETURN IN A5 ENVELOPE.

ATTACH REST OF CASS, MAIN QUESTIONNAIRE AND SELF-COMPLETION (IF POSSIBLE) AND RETURN IN A4 ENVELOPE - AS SOON AS POSSIBLE.

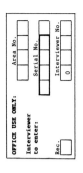

Head Office: 35 NORTHAMPTON SQUARE, LONDON EC1V 0AX Telephone 01-250 1866

Field and DP Office: BRENTWOOD, ESSEX
Northern Field Office: DARLINGTON, CO. DURHAM

P.1090/NI

NORTHERN IRELAND SOCIAL ATTITUDES: 1990

SELF-COMPLETION QUESTIONNAIRE

Feb/March 1990

OFFICE USE ONLY:	Area No.
Interviewer to enter:	Serial No.
	Interviewer No.
Rec	0

To the selected respondent.

We hope very much that you will agree to participate in this important study - the seventh in this annual series. The results are published in a book each autumn. The study consists of this self-completion questionnaire and an interview. Some of the questions are also being asked in ten other countries, as part of an international survey.

Completing the questionnaire:

The questions inside cover a wide range of subjects, but each one can be answered simply by placing a tick (✓) or a number in one or more of the boxes. No special knowledge is required. we are confident that everyone will be able to offer an opinion on all questions. And we want everyone to take part, not just those with strong views or particular viewpoints. The questionnaire should not take very long to complete, and we hope you will find it interesting and enjoyable. It should be filled in by the person selected by the interviewer at your address. The answers you give will be treated as confidential and anonymous.

Returning the questionnaire:

Your interviewer will arrange with you the most convenient way of returning the questionnaire. If the interviewer has arranged to call back for it, please complete it and keep it safely until then. If not, please complete it and post it back in the pre-paid, addressed envelope as soon as you possibly can.

Thank you for your help.

Social and Community Planning Research is an independent social research institute registered as a charitable trust. Its projects are funded by government departments, local authorities, universities and foundations to provide information on social issues in the UK. This survey series has been funded mainly by the Sainsbury Family Charitable Trusts, with contributions also from government departments. The Nuffield Foundation, universities and industry. Please contact us if you require further information.

- 1 -

N.I.

2.01 [SCOBEY1W]
In general, would you say that people should obey the law without exception, or are there exceptional occasions on which people should follow their consciences even if it means breaking the law?

PLEASE TICK ONE BOX

	%
Obey the law without exception	48.0
Follow conscience on occasions	45.4
Can't choose	4.4
(NA)	2.2

2.02 [PROTEST1 - PROTEST6]
There are many ways people or organisations can protest against a government action they strongly oppose.

Please show which you think should be allowed and which should not be allowed by ticking a box on each line.

PLEASE TICK ONE BOX ON EACH LINE

	Should it be allowed?					
	Defin- itely	Prob- ably	Probably not	Definitely not	Can't choose	(NA)
A. Organising public meetings to protest against the government	% 49.5	29.9	9.0	5.9	4.7	1.0
B. Publishing pamphlets to protest against the government	% 41.4	33.7	10.9	8.6	3.2	2.1
C. Organising protest marches and demonstrations	% 29.8	33.9	14.2	17.3	2.5	2.2
D. Occupying a government office and stopping work there for several days	% 2.9	6.9	29.3	54.9	3.1	2.9
E. Seriously damaging government buildings	% 1.0	0.4	6.0	88.2	1.4	3.0
F. Organising a nationwide strike of all workers against the government	% 12.0	20.1	21.5	39.8	3.8	2.9

n = 783

Please continue ......

- 2 -

N.I.

2.03 There are some people whose views are considered extreme by the majority.

First, consider people who want to overthrow the government by revolution. Do you think such people should be allowed to ...

PLEASE TICK ONE BOX ON EACH LINE

	Defin- itely	Prob- ably	Probably not	Definitely not	Can't choose	(NA)
[REVMEET] i) ... hold public meetings to express their views?	% 15.1	24.8	19.0	34.3	4.2	2.6
[REVPUB] ii) ... publish books expressing their views?	% 16.9	35.0	18.5	20.2	5.3	4.1

2.04 Second, consider people who believe that whites are racially superior to all other races. Do you think such people should be allowed to ...

PLEASE TICK ONE BOX ON EACH LINE

	Defin- itely	Prob- ably	Probably not	Definitely not	Can't choose	(NA)
[PRIMEET] i) ... hold public meetings to express their views?	% 7.2	20.1	18.1	47.3	4.2	3.1
[PRPUB] ii) ... publish books expressing their views?	% 9.6	24.2	20.0	37.6	4.2	4.4

2.05 [CRIMIN1 - CRIMIN4]
Suppose the police get an anonymous tip that a man with a long criminal record is planning to break into a warehouse.

PLEASE TICK ONE BOX ON EACH LINE

Do you think the police should be allowed, without a Court Order ...

	Defin- ately	Prob- ably	Probably not	Definitely not	Can't choose	(NA)
i) ... to keep the man under surveillance?	% 57.5	27.1	3.7	6.8	1.3	3.5
ii) ... to tap his telephone?	% 18.5	21.3	22.3	30.6	1.8	5.5
iii)... to open his mail?	% 10.1	13.7	26.5	42.1	2.1	5.5
iv) ... to detain the man overnight for questioning?	% 31.7	34.1	11.6	16.3	1.9	4.6

N.I.

- 3 -

2.06 [JUSTICE]
All systems of justice make mistakes, but which do you think is worse:

PLEASE TICK ONE BOX

	%
to convict an innocent person,	67.1
OR	
to let a guilty person go free?	19.2
Can't choose	10.3
(NA)	3.4

2.07 What are your personal feelings about ...

[DEMOFEEL]
A. People who organise protests against a government action they strongly oppose?

PLEASE TICK ONE BOX

	%
Extremely favourable	11.1
Favourable	32.6
Neither favourable or unfavourable	34.5
Unfavourable	9.2
Extremely unfavourable	2.7
Can't choose	7.3
(NA)	2.5

[REVFEEL]
B. People who want to overthrow the government by revolution?

PLEASE TICK ONE BOX

	%
Extremely favourable	1.7
Favourable	2.7
Neither favourable or unfavourable	19.7
Unfavourable	32.1
Extremely unfavourable	35.0
Can't choose	6.2
(NA)	2.6

[RACFEEL]
C. People who believe whites are racially superior to all other races?

PLEASE TICK ONE BOX

	%
Extremely favourable	0.8
Favourable	3.3
Neither favourable or unfavourable	15.7
Unfavourable	29.3
Extremely unfavourable	42.9
Can't choose	5.1
(NA)	3.0

Please continue .....

N.I.

- 4 -

2.08 [HIGHINC]
Some people think those with high incomes should pay a larger proportion (percentage) of their earnings in taxes than those who earn low incomes. Other people think that those with high incomes and those with low incomes should pay the same proportion (percentage) of their earnings in taxes.

Do you think those with **high** incomes should ...

PLEASE TICK ONE BOX

	%
... pay a **much larger** proportion,	32.6
pay a **larger** proportion,	50.3
pay the **same** proportion as those who earn low incomes,	12.6
pay a **smaller** proportion,	0.5
or - pay a **much smaller** proportion?	0.5
Can't choose	2.3
(NA)	1.1

2.09 [INCDIFF]
What is your opinion of the following statement:
It is the responsibility of the government to reduce the differences in income between people with high incomes and those with low incomes.

PLEASE TICK ONE BOX

	%
Agree strongly	22.6
Agree	39.5
Neither agree nor disagree	18.0
Disagree	15.9
Disagree strongly	2.7
(DK/NA)	1.3

- 5 -

N.I.

2.10 [GOVECON1 - GOVECON6]
Here are some things the government might do for the economy. Please show which actions you are in favour of and which you are against.

PLEASE TICK ONE BOX ON EACH LINE

	Strongly in favour of	In favour of	Neither in favour nor against	Against	Strongly against	(DK/NA)
A. Control of wages by law	% 9.0	23.9	13.5	39.8	9.7	4.1
B. Control of prices by law	% 18.4	39.2	12.9	22.1	4.7	2.8
C. Cuts in government spending	% 10.4	30.0	19.4	26.5	8.6	5.1
D. Government financing of projects to create new jobs	% 29.4	54.7	7.8	4.0	0.8	3.3
E. Less government regulation of business	% 7.0	35.2	38.8	12.4	2.1	4.5
F. Support for industry to develop new products and technology	% 30.5	53.7	11.2	1.2	0.6	2.8
G. Support for declining industries to protect jobs	% 21.3	41.2	20.4	12.6	1.4	3.1
H. Reducing the working week to create more jobs	% 12.1	30.0	26.5	23.4	5.5	2.5

2.11 Listed below are various areas of government spending. Please show whether you would like to see more or less government spending in each area.

Remember that if you say "much more", it might require a tax increase to pay for it.

PLEASE TICK ONE BOX ON EACH LINE

[GVSPEND1 - GVSPEND8]

	Spend much more	Spend more	Spend the same as now	Spend less	Spend much less	Can't choose	(NA)
A. The environment	% 12.8	41.2	34.0	3.5	0.5	4.2	3.8
B. Health	% 39.3	48.5	8.9	0.8	-	0.8	1.7
C. The police and law enforcement	% 8.3	25.8	50.1	8.3	2.4	2.2	2.9
D. Education	% 23.3	47.8	22.8	2.2	-	1.0	2.8
E. The military and defence	% 3.8	10.1	39.4	27.4	13.8	2.6	2.9
F. Old age pensions	% 39.5	48.8	8.6	0.2	-	0.8	2.1
G. Unemployment benefits	% 17.0	34.4	32.8	8.8	2.1	1.9	3.0
H. Culture and the arts	% 1.1	11.5	40.5	24.9	11.6	7.3	3.1

Please continue ....

- 6 -

N.I.

2.12 [UNEMINF2]
If the government had to choose between keeping down inflation or keeping down unemployment, to which do you think it should give highest priority?

PLEASE TICK ONE BOX

	%
Keeping down inflation	48.2
Keeping down unemployment	45.6
Can't choose	5.0
(NA)	1.2

2.13 [TUPOWER]
Do you think that trade unions in this country have too much power or too little power?

PLEASE TICK ONE BOX

	%
Far too much power	8.6
Too much power	23.1
About the right amount of power	41.8
Too little power	13.3
Far too little power	2.9
Can't choose	9.3
(NA)	1.0

2.14 [BUSPOWER]
How about business and industry? Do they have too much power or too little power?

PLEASE TICK ONE BOX

	%
Far too much power	5.3
Too much power	17.8
About the right amount of power	53.6
Too little power	9.0
Far too little power	0.7
Can't choose	12.5
(NA)	1.2

- 8 -

N.I.

2.18 [GOVRESP1 - GOVRESP9]
On the whole, do you think it should or should not be the government's responsibility to ...

PLEASE TICK ONE BOX ON EACH LINE

	Definitely should be	Probably should be	Probably should not be	Definitely should not be	Can't choose	(NA)
A. ... provide a job for everyone who wants one	%30.9	39.5	15.9	8.5	2.3	2.9
B. ... keep prices under control	%48.5	38.8	6.9	1.8	0.7	3.3
C. ... provide health care for the sick	%79.9	16.1	0.7	0.3	0.2	2.9
D. ... provide a decent standard of living for the old	%78.9	17.5	0.9	0.3	0.3	2.1
E. ... provide industry with the help it needs to grow	%41.4	47.5	5.1	1.0	2.2	2.7
F. ... provide a decent standard of living for the unemployed	%42.4	42.4	8.9	2.6	1.2	2.5
G. ... reduce income differences between the rich and poor	%42.8	32.8	13.8	4.9	2.5	3.3
H. ... give financial help to university students from low-income families	%52.9	36.6	4.7	2.0	1.4	2.4
I. ... provide decent housing for those who can't afford it	%52.1	36.7	5.7	1.4	1.7	2.4

2.19 [POLITIC2]
How interested would you say you personally are in politics?

PLEASE TICK ONE BOX

	%
Very interested	6.2
Fairly interested	23.3
Somewhat interested	20.7
Not very interested	29.2
Not at all interested	17.4
Can't choose	1.0
(NA)	2.2

- 7 -

N.I.

2.15 [GOVPOWER]
And what about the government, does it have too much power or too little power?

PLEASE TICK ONE BOX

	%
Far too much power	17.9
Too much power	27.6
About the right amount of power	44.1
Too little power	3.1
Far too little power	0.7
Can't choose	5.5
(NA)	1.0

2.16 [TUCUNTRY]
In general, how good would you say trade unions are for the country as a whole?

PLEASE TICK ONE BOX

	%
Excellent	1.9
Very good	15.0
Fairly good	54.9
Not very good	14.2
Not good at all	4.0
Can't choose	9.2
(NA)	0.8

2.17 What do you think the government's role in each of these industries and services should be?

PLEASE TICK ONE BOX ON EACH LINE

The government should:

	Own it	Control prices and profits but not own it	Neither own it nor control its prices & profits	Can't choose	(NA)
A. [GOVROLE1] Electricity	% 25.6	47.0	16.3	9.8	1.4
B. [GOVROLE8] The steel industry	% 13.7	38.9	28.5	16.6	2.3
C. [GOVROLE4] Banking and insurance	% 7.1	41.4	34.3	15.1	2.1

Please continue ......

N.I.

- 9 -

Now for some questions on different subjects.

[ABORP1 - ABORP7]
2.20 Here are a number of circumstances in which a woman might consider an abortion. Please say whether or not you think the law should allow an abortion in each case.

PLEASE TICK ONE BOX ON EACH LINE

	Should abortion be allowed by law?		
	Yes	No	(DK/NA)
The woman decides on her own she does not wish to have the child	% 32.3	62.8	4.9
The couple agree they do not wish to have the child	% 34.8	59.8	5.4
The woman is not married and does not wish to marry the man	% 32.5	61.9	5.6
The couple cannot afford any more children	% 29.5	64.8	5.8
There is a strong chance of a defect in the baby	% 59.4	35.1	5.5
The woman's health is seriously endangered by the pregnancy	% 75.9	19.2	4.8
The woman became pregnant as a result of rape	% 70.6	24.8	4.5

[PORNO]
2.21 Which of these statements comes **closest** to your views on the availability of pornographic magazines and films?

PLEASE TICK ONE BOX

	%
They should be banned altogether	50.7
They should be available in special adult shops but not displayed to the public	33.3
They should be available in special adult shops with public display permitted	5.6
They should be available in any shop for sale to adults only	7.1
They should be available in any shop for sale to anyone	1.2
(DK/NA)	2.2

N.I.

- 10 -

2.22a) The UK controls the numbers of people from abroad that are allowed to settle in this country. Please say, for **each** of the groups below, whether you think the UK should allow more settlement, less settlement, or about the same amount as now.

PLEASE TICK ONE BOX ON EACH LINE

	More settlement	Less settlement	About the same as now	(DK/NA)
[AUSIEIMM] Australians and New Zealanders	% 8.5	25.7	62.8	3.0
[ASIANIMM] Indians and Pakistanis	% 2.7	55.6	38.9	2.8
[ECIMM] People from common market countries	% 8.8	35.6	52.5	3.1
[WIIMM] West Indians	% 2.8	54.1	40.2	3.0

b) *[RELCONT1]* Now thinking about the families (husbands, wives, children, parents) of people who have **already** settled in the UK, would you say in general that the UK should ...

PLEASE TICK ONE BOX

	%
... be **stricter** in controlling the settlement of close relatives	35.9
... be **less strict** in controlling the settlement of close relatives	17.0
or - keep the controls about the **same** as now	44.3
(DK/NA)	2.8

[CAPPUN1 - CAPPUN3]
2.23 Are you in favour of or against the death penalty for ...

PLEASE TICK ONE BOX ON EACH LINE

	In favour	Against	(DK/NA)
... murder in the course of a terrorist act?	% 53.6	42.4	4.1
... murder of a police officer?	% 53.5	41.2	5.3
... other murders?	% 46.9	47.3	5.7

2.24 Please tick one box for each statement below to show how much you agree or disagree with it.

PLEASE TICK ONE BOX ON EACH LINE

	Agree strongly	Agree	Neither agree nor disagree	Disagree	Disagree strongly	(DK/NA)
[CRIME1] a. Except for the Troubles, there is generally little crime in Northern Ireland	% 14.0	55.4	13.0	13.7	2.5	1.5
[SFTSNTN1] b. Sentences for crimes connected with the Troubles are generally much too soft	% 29.8	34.2	15.6	15.2	3.1	2.2
[AFRCRIM] c. People are generally more afraid of crime than they need to be	% 6.1	33.9	26.5	28.2	2.8	2.6

N.I.

- 11 -

2.25 And please tick one box for each statement below to show how much you agree or disagree with it.

PLEASE TICK ONE BOX ON EACH LINE

	Agree strongly	Agree	Neither agree nor disagree	Dis-agree	Disagree strongly	(DK/NA)
a. [PEACELNI] Northern Ireland is a much more peaceful place then people living in Britain think	%39.0	50.7	4.4	4.1	0.6	1.3
b. [PCARMYOF] When the police or the army commit an offence in Northern Ireland, they usually get away with it	%13.8	21.1	21.5	32.8	8.9	1.9
c. [RCINRUC] It would be better for Northern Ireland if there were more Catholics in the RUC	%20.1	38.4	28.0	7.5	4.4	1.7

2.26 [DSBNDUDR]
Some people say that the Ulster Defence Regiment - the UDR - should be disbanded. Others say it is necessary.

Which comes closest to your views?

PLEASE TICK ONE BOX

	%
The UDR definitely should be disbanded	21.3
The UDR probably should be disbanded	11.3
The UDR probably should not be disbanded	18.5
The UDR definitely should not be disbanded	37.5
OR It doesn't matter either way	9.2
(DK/NA)	2.2

N.I.

- 12 -

2.27a) [TERTVBAN]
Should the law allow television to show interviews with people who support acts of terrorism in the UK?

PLEASE TICK ONE BOX

	%
The law definitely should allow it,	11.8
probably should allow it,	14.8
probably should not allow it,	18.7
or - the law definitely should not allow it?	46.8
Can't choose	6.2
(NA)	1.7

b) [TERNPBAN]
And should the law allow newspapers to publish interviews with people who support acts of terrorism in the UK?

PLEASE TICK ONE BOX

	%
The law definitely should allow it	12.0
probably should allow it,	18.5
probably should not allow it,	21.0
or - the law definitely should not allow it?	40.7
Can't choose	6.0
(NA)	1.8

c) [TERBKBAN]
And should the law allow people who support acts of terrorism in the UK to publish books expressing their views?

PLEASE TICK ONE BOX

	%
The law definitely should allow it,	10.5
probably should allow it,	21.1
probably should not allow it,	24.2
or - the law definitely should not allow it?	36.3
Can't choose	6.4
(NA)	1.6

N.I.

- 13 -

2.28 [JURYRIGHT]
Which of these two statements comes closest to your views?

PLEASE TICK ONE BOX

%

People charged with serious crimes should <u>always</u> have the right to a jury trial 42.1

OR

There should not always be a right to a jury trial - for instance when the jury might be in danger 45.7

Can't choose 10.2

(NA) 2.0

2.29 [FINEPANA]
Suppose a 16-year old is fined by a court, but does not pay the fine. Should the parents be required by law to pay the fine, or not?

PLEASE TICK ONE BOX

%

Definitely should be required to pay 35.2

Probably should be required to pay 28.7

Probably should <u>not</u> be required to pay 18.7

Definitely should <u>not</u> be required to pay 11.6

Can't choose 4.3

(NA) 1.4

2.30 As long as there is no threat to security, should prisoners be allowed to ...

PLEASE TICK ONE BOX FOR EACH ITEM

	Yes	No	(DK/NA)
a) [PRISBKS] ... have as many books to read as they wish?	% 89.3	7.5	3.2
b) [PRISLTRS] ... write and receive as many letters as they wish?	% 81.7	14.6	3.7

Please continue .....

N.I.

- 14 -

2.31 Do you think that people in each of these sorts of jobs <u>should</u> or <u>should not</u> be allowed the right to go on strike?

PLEASE TICK ONE LINE

	Definitely should be allowed to strike	Probably should be allowed to strike	Probably should not be allowed to strike	Definitely should not be allowed to strike	(DK/NA)
a) [PCSTRK] ... police officers?	% 14.0	24.3	30.6	28.9	2.2
b) [NURSSTRK] ... nurses?	% 23.9	35.8	22.7	15.5	2.2
c) [CARWSTRK] ... car workers?	% 24.6	54.0	12.5	5.7	3.2
d) [COUNSTRK] ... council workers?	% 21.8	48.4	18.7	8.0	3.1
e) [ELECTRK] ... electricity supply workers?	% 17.8	32.7	26.3	20.4	2.8
f) [HDOCSTRK] ... hospital doctors?	% 19.3	27.2	23.3	28.1	2.1

2.32 [CSSILENT]
Suppose a cabinet minister gives false information to parliament about an important national issue.

Should the law allow civil servants in the minister's department to reveal the correct facts, % 79.3

OR

Should civil servants be required by law to keep silent? 8.3

Can't choose 10.9

(NA) 1.5

2.33 [BILRITES]
Some people support a Bill of Rights for the UK which would give the <u>courts</u> rather than parliament the final say on any laws or government actions which threaten basic freedoms. Others say it is better to leave things as they are. What do you think?

PLEASE TICK ONE BOX

%

Definitely should be a Bill of Rights 22.7

Probably should be a Bill of Rights 35.9

Probably should <u>not</u> be a Bill of Rights 12.1

Definitely should <u>not</u> be a Bill of Rights 3.3

Can't choose 24.8

(NA) 1.3

N.I. - 15 -

2. 34 Please tick one box for each statement below to show how much you agree or disagree with it.

PLEASE TICK ONE BOX ON EACH LINE

	Agree strongly	Agree	Neither agree nor disagree	Disagree	Disagree strongly	(DK/NA)
[ELECHTAG] a) People on probation or parole should be fitted with a transmitter - that is, an electronic tag - so the police can check where they are.	% 20.8	35.9	18.5	17.3	5.8	1.7
[PCGUNS] b) On-duty police officers should always carry guns.	% 29.6	37.2	14.2	14.7	3.1	1.2
[LITESENT] c) Too many convicted criminals are let off lightly by the courts.	% 33.6	40.4	14.4	8.6	1.9	1.1
[CONFESSN] d) A confession made during police questioning and later withdrawn should not be enough to convict someone.	% 17.9	47.3	18.7	11.2	2.6	2.3
[PCNOSOLC] e) The police should be allowed to question suspects for up to a week without letting them see a solicitor.	% 5.4	12.0	11.6	42.5	27.0	1.6
[REFUGEES] f) Refugees who are in danger because of their political beliefs should always be welcome in the UK.	% 6.9	29.2	30.5	24.8	7.0	1.7
[PCCOMPLN] g) Serious complaints against the police should be investigated by an independent body, not by the police themselves.	% 36.0	42.5	10.0	7.9	1.7	1.9
[IDCARDS] h) Every adult in the UK should have to carry an identity card.	% 9.4	28.0	22.2	26.5	12.2	1.8
[CRIMSLNT] i) If someone remains silent under police questioning, it should count against them in court.	% 13.4	30.1	17.9	27.0	10.1	1.5
[NINPRISN] j) The prisons contain too many people who ought to be given a lighter punishment.	% 8.3	28.2	32.6	24.8	4.2	1.8
[NOWARRNT] k) The police should not need a warrant to search the homes of suspects.	% 9.0	15.5	9.5	41.7	22.9	1.4

N.I. - 16 -

[ENVIR1 - ENVIR7]

2. 35 How serious an effect on our environment do you think each of these things has?

PLEASE TICK ONE BOX ON EACH LINE

	Very serious	Quite serious	Not very serious	Not at all serious	(DK/NA)
Noise from aircraft	%14.0	58.7	18.4	5.5	3.4
Lead from petrol	% 3.3	15.3	50.0	28.5	2.9
Industrial waste in the rivers and sea	% 1.2	5.3	30.0	61.4	2.1
Waste from nuclear electricity stations	% 2.4	8.5	23.2	62.8	3.1
Industrial fumes in the air	% 2.1	7.5	36.8	50.9	2.7
Noise and dirt from traffic	% 2.6	22.1	48.4	23.9	2.9
Acid rain	%3.0	14.3	37.0	42.0	3.7

2. 36a) *[POWER]* Which one of these three possible solutions to the UK's electricity needs would you favour most?

PLEASE TICK ONE BOX

	%
We should make do with the power stations we have already	58.9
We should build more coal-fuelled power stations	30.7
We should build more nuclear power stations	6.6
(DK/NA)	3.8

b) *[NUCPOWER]* As far as nuclear power stations are concerned, which of these statements comes closest to your own feelings?

PLEASE TICK ONE BOX

	%
They create very serious risks for the future	47.3
They create quite serious risks for the future	31.1
They create only slight risks for the future	13.7
They create hardly any risks for the future	3.5
(DK/NA)	4.3

2. 37a) *[DAMAGE]* Which one of these two statements comes <u>closest</u> to your own views?

PLEASE TICK ONE BOX

	%
Industry should be prevented from causing damage to the countryside, even if this sometimes leads to higher prices	82.2
OR	
Industry should keep prices down, even if this sometimes causes damage to the countryside	14.8
(DK/NA)	3.0

b) *[CTRYJOBS]* And which of these two statements comes <u>closest</u> to your own views?

PLEASE TICK ONE BOX

	%
The countryside should be protected from development, even if this sometimes leads to fewer new jobs	67.2
OR	
New jobs should be created, even if this sometimes causes damage to the countryside	28.4
(DK/NA)	4.4

N.I.   - 18 -

2.40 Please tick one box for each statement below to show how much you agree or disagree with it.
PLEASE TICK ONE BOX ON EACH LINE

	Agree strongly	Agree	Neither agree nor disagree	Disagree	Disagree strongly	(DK/NA)
a) [GOVENVIR] The government should do more to protect the environment, even if it leads to higher taxes.	% 15.0	42.5	24.1	13.0	1.6	3.8
b) [INDENVIR] Industry should do more to protect the environment, even if it leads to lower profits and fewer jobs.	% 15.9	42.5	23.7	12.8	1.2	3.9
c) [PPLENVIR] Ordinary people should do more to protect the environment, even if it means paying higher prices.	% 16.3	47.3	21.7	10.1	1.6	3.0

2.41a) [WRLDTEMP] Please tick one box to show which is closest to your views about the following statement:

"Within twenty years, life on earth will be seriously damaged by a rise in the world's temperature."

PLEASE TICK ONE BOX

%

It is highly exaggerated 12.8

It is slightly exaggerated 34.6

It is more or less true 49.2

(DK/NA) 3.4

b) [ENVIRDAM] And please tick one box to show which is closest to your views about this statement:

"Within twenty years, damage to the environment will be the biggest single problem facing Europe."

PLEASE TICK ONE BOX

%

It is highly exaggerated 12.4

It is slightly exaggerated 34.5

It is more or less true 49.7

(DK/NA) 3.4

N.I.   - 17 -

2.38 Please tick one box on each line to show you you feel about ...
PLEASE TICK ONE BOX ON EACH LINE

	It should be stopped altogether	It should be discouraged	Don't mind one way or the other	It should be encouraged	(DK/NA)
[CTRYFARM] ... Increasing the amount of countryside being farmed	% 3.4	24.9	46.0	23.5	2.2
[CTRYHSNG] ... Building new housing in country areas	% 9.2	44.1	29.8	15.3	1.5
[WILDLIFE] ... Putting the needs of farmers before protection of wildlife	% 10.7	46.9	27.6	12.4	2.4
[CTRYROAD] ... Providing more roads in country areas	% 7.3	37.8	32.3	20.5	2.1
[PICNIC] ... Increasing the number of picnic areas and camping sites in the countryside	% 2.7	12.8	36.2	46.9	1.4

2.39 [PREDICT1 - PREDICT7] Here is a list of predictions. For each one, please say how likely or unlikely you think it is to come true within the next ten years?
PLEASE TICK ONE BOX FOR EACH PREDICTION

	Very likely	Quite likely	Not very likely	Not at all likely	(DK/NA)
Acts of political terrorism in the UK will be common events	% 19.8	51.0	24.3	2.1	2.8
Riots and civil disturbance in our cities will be common events	% 15.1	48.4	30.9	2.7	2.9
There will be a world war involving the UK and Europe	% 2.0	10.6	57.2	26.8	3.4
There will be a serious accident at a UK nuclear power station	% 15.2	46.6	31.3	3.6	3.4
The police in our cities will find it impossible to protect our personal safety on the streets	% 10.5	37.9	43.8	5.1	2.8
The government in the UK will be overthrown by revolution	% 2.3	7.9	52.0	34.7	3.1
A nuclear bomb will be dropped somewhere in the world	% 5.0	18.7	44.1	29.1	3.1

Please continue .....

N.I.   - 19 -

2.42 Please tick **one** box for **each** statement below to show how much you agree or disagree with it.

PLEASE TICK ONE BOX ON EACH LINE

	Agree strongly	Agree	Neither agree nor disagree	Disagree	Disagree strongly	(DK/NA)
[RAREPLANT] a) Too much money is spent trying to protect rare plants and animals.	% 4.9	18.3	32.8	35.2	5.8	3.0
[SCNSOLV] b) Science can solve environmental problems without any need for people to change their behaviour.	% 1.1	17.0	22.6	43.9	11.8	3.7
[COSMTEST] c) It is acceptable to use animals for testing and improving cosmetics.	% 1.4	5.5	11.4	45.5	33.6	2.6
[MEDITEST] d) It is acceptable to use animals for testing medicines it could save human lives.	% 9.2	50.5	16.2	14.8	6.3	3.0
[FOXHUNT] e) Fox hunting should be banned by law.	% 24.4	32.6	19.9	13.1	6.4	3.6
[CARTAXHI] f) For the sake of the environment, car users should pay higher taxes.	% 3.4	13.3	21.7	45.4	13.3	2.9
[POORPAID] g) Richer countries ought to give financial help to poorer countries, to help them cut back on their pollution.	% 18.7	53.6	16.4	7.2	1.2	2.8
[IMPRROAD] h) If the government had to choose, it should improve roads rather than public transport.	% 10.0	34.5	24.6	23.5	4.7	2.7

2.43 Please tick **one** box for **each** statement below to show how much you agree or disagree with it.

PLEASE TICK ONE BOX ON EACH LINE

	Agree strongly	Agree	Neither agree nor disagree	Disagree	Disagree strongly	(DK/NA)
[REDISTRB] a) Government should redistribute income from the better-off to those who are less well off.	% 16.6	39.3	19.2	19.2	2.8	2.9
[BIGBUSNN] b) Big business benefits owners at the expense of workers.	% 14.6	42.7	18.7	18.0	2.3	3.8
[WEALTH] c) Ordinary working people do not get their fair share of the nation's wealth.	% 20.5	50.8	15.7	9.6	0.7	2.8
[RICHLAW] d) There is one law for the rich and one for the poor.	% 25.4	39.8	15.0	14.9	1.8	3.1
[INDUST4]/* e) Management will always try to get the better of employees if it gets the chance.	% 21.1	45.0	14.8	15.6	1.0	2.6

* The third character of the variable is an 'o', not a 'd'.

N.I.   - 20 -

2.44 And please tick **one** box for **each** statement below to show how much you agree or disagree with it.

PLEASE TICK ONE BOX ON EACH LINE

	Agree strongly	Agree	Neither agree nor disagree	Disagree	Disagree strongly	(DK/NA)
[TRADVALS] a) Young people today don't have enough respect for traditional values.	% 24.1	49.2	16.1	9.1	0.6	1.0
[STIFSENT] b) People who break the law should be given stiffer sentences.	% 22.0	48.3	19.3	9.1	0.3	1.1
[PROTMEET] c) People should be allowed to organise public meetings to protest against the government.	% 13.6	53.4	19.1	11.8	0.8	1.3
[DEATHAPP] d) For some crimes, the death penalty is the most appropriate sentence.	% 22.1	31.1	6.9	23.4	14.6	1.8
[PROTLEAF] e) People should be allowed to publish leaflets to protest against the government.	% 12.7	51.1	20.8	12.5	1.2	1.7
[OBEY] f) Schools should teach children to obey authority.	% 29.8	54.4	8.3	5.7	0.9	0.9
[PROTDEMO] g) People should be allowed to organise protest marches and demonstrations.	% 11.4	45.8	22.3	17.0	2.1	1.3
[WRONGLAW] h) The law should always be obeyed, even if a particular law is wrong.	% 7.6	32.6	22.2	31.0	5.3	1.3
[CENSOR] i) Censorship of films and magazines is necessary to uphold moral standards.	% 23.7	45.3	14.9	11.8	3.3	1.0

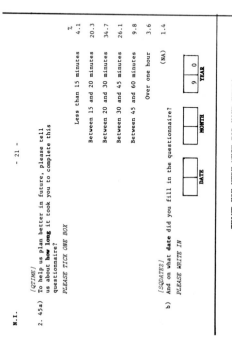

N.I.

- 21 -

[QTIME]

2. 45a) To help us plan better in future, please tell us about **how long** it took you to complete this questionnaire?

PLEASE TICK ONE BOX

		%
Less than 15 minutes		4.1
Between 15 and 20 minutes		20.3
Between 20 and 30 minutes		34.7
Between 30 and 45 minutes		26.1
Between 45 and 60 minutes		9.8
Over one hour		3.6
(NA)		1.4

[SQDATE2]

b) And on what **date** did you fill in the questionnaire?

PLEASE WRITE IN

DATE	MONTH	YEAR
		9 0

THANK YOU VERY MUCH FOR YOUR HELP!

Please keep the completed questionnaire for the interviewer if he or she has arranged to call for it. Otherwise, please post it as soon as possible in the pre-paid
addressed envelope provided.

Subject Index

Population, growth in world 114
Pornography, censorship of 6-7
Postmaterialism 109, 112, 124
Poverty,
    explanations for 189
    extent of 189
Pre-marital sex 6-7
Prices, higher to protect environment
    118-119
Primary schools,
    as priority for extra spending 45-47
    priorities for improvements in 27,
        47-48, 57
    also see Secondary schools
Prison service, confidence in 175, 193
Private education, growth of 49
Private health care, support for NHS
    by those with access to 39-41
Private nurseries and creches,
    government funding for 133,
        151-152
    use of 139-140, 149-150
Private renters,
    mobility of 91
    tenure profiles 90-93
Privatisation, support for 213
Public Order Act 1986, 178
Public places, smoking in 164-168
Public transport, road improvement
    versus 119-120

Q

The questionnaires 237-348

R

Race Relations Act 1976, 189
Racial discrimination,
    in employment 189
    law against 189
Racists,
    approval and disapproval of 188
    freedom of to express views 9-10,
        73-75, 86, 186-187, 188
Rainforest depletion 114-115
Redistribution, role of government in
    3-4, 7, 10-14, 18, 24, 29, 34
Refugees,
    welcome for 71-73, 85, 191-192
    also see Immigration
Region, analysis definition of 225
Religion, in Northern Ireland 60-61, 79

'Residualisation' of council housing
    89-97, 103
Respondents,
    selection of addresses 223, 232
    selection of individuals 223-224,
        232-233
Response rates,
    on British Social Attitudes 224-225
    on Northern Ireland Social Attitudes
        233-234
Reunification of Ireland 61, 79
Revolutionaries,
    approval and disapproval of 188
    freedom of to express views 9-10,
        11, 73-75, 86, 186-187, 188
Right to buy,
    and accommodation type 93-94
    likelihood of exercising 98
    support for 96, 103
    whether exercised 87, 93
Rights,
    protection of citizens' 176-177
    also see Minority rights; and 175-
        202 passim
Roads, versus public transport 119-120
Royal Ulster Constabulary (RUC)
    accountability of 70, 78-79, 81
    efficiency of 67
    participation of Catholics in 77-78,
        80-81
    perceived evenhandedness of 68
    role of 66
    satisfaction with 67-68
    also see Police

S

Sampling points,
    selection of parliamentary
        constituencies 222
    selection of polling districts 223
Sampling errors,
    on British Social Attitudes 227-230
    on Northern Ireland Social Attitudes
        234
Sample design,
    for British Social Attitudes 221-224
    for Northern Ireland Social Attitudes
        232-233
School leavers,
    and age of leaving 53-54
    qualifications of compared to past
        54
Scientific findings, knowledge of 123